PEACE PACT

AMERICAN POLITICAL THOUGHT
EDITED BY
WILSON CAREY MCWILLIAMS AND LANCE BANNING

PEACE PACT

The Lost World of the American Founding

David C. Hendrickson

University Press of Kansas

Published by the University Press of Kansas (Lawrence, Kansas 66049), which was organized by the Kansas Board of Regents and is operated and funded by Emporia State University, Fort Hays State University, Kansas State University, Pittsburg State University, the University of Kansas, and Wichita State University

Library of Congress Cataloging-in-Publication Data

Hendrickson, David C.

Peace pact: the lost world of the American founding /

David C. Hendrickson.

p. cm. — (American political thought)

Includes bibliographical references and index.

ISBN 0-7006-1237-8 (alk. paper)

1. United States—Politics and government—18th century. 2. United States—Foreign relations—18th century. 3. Federal government—United States—History—18th century. 4. Political science—United States—History—18th century. I. Title. II. Series.

JK116 H45 2003   320.973'09'033—dc21   2002154345

British Library Cataloguing in Publication Data is available.

Printed in the United States of America

10 9 8 7 6 5 4 3 2 1

The paper used in this publication meets the minimum requirements of the American National Standard for Permanence of Paper for Printed Library Materials Z39.48-1984.

THIS BOOK IS DEDICATED TO

TIGER

KOOKIE

BEANSTERS

KAPPY

L.Q.

&

ROSALITA ISABELLA

People will not look forward to posterity, who never look
backward to their ancestors. . . .
By adhering in this manner and on those principles to
our forefathers,
we are guided not by the superstition of antiquarians,
but by the spirit of philosophic analogy.
EDMUND BURKE
Reflections on the Revolution in France

CONTENTS

PREFACE AND ACKNOWLEDGMENTS

THIS STUDY examines American political thought and experience during the twenty to thirty years in which Americans first enjoyed a common existence. Little contact had existed between the American colonies before the great war, begun in 1754, that expelled the French empire from North America. The consequences of that war, however, brought them together, and it is at this point that a common history—as opposed to a number of separate histories—may be said to begin.

The point of departure for this work is an assumption at odds with conventional understandings of early American history. Habitually, historians and political scientists think of the United States as a national unit and have seen the development of the nation's institutions in a context essentially domestic. I am impressed, by contrast, with what the Continental Congress called in 1777 "the difficulty of combining in one general system . . . a continent divided into so many sovereign and independent communities."[1] That difficulty was made manifest both in the decade-long conflict that had disrupted the British Empire and in the trying decade that followed the Declaration of Independence in 1776. Indeed, from the Albany Congress of 1754 to the debates over the ratification of the Constitution in 1788—a period marked by two great wars and continuing constitutional upheaval— the problem of securing a basis of cooperation among the colonies and states in North America was at the center of political and constitutional thought in the Atlantic world.

While the idea of American nationhood was registered in 1776 and in the years to follow, it is easy and commonplace to confuse the acorn with the oak and to exaggerate the significance of the national idea in the era of revolution and constitution-building. My own view, developed at some length in the pages to follow, is that the sense of common nationality was more a consequence of mutual entanglement and exiguous necessity than of a sense of common peoplehood. At the beginning, in 1776, Americans constituted not a body politic but an association of bodies politic, readily recognizable to eighteenth-century taxonomists of political forms as a "league of firm friendship," a *"république fédérative,"* or a "system of states."

Today, a state system is normally defined as simply a grouping of independent sovereignties who have regular interactions with one another and

whose relations are ultimately regulated by the threat of war. Earlier understandings were different. In his classic study of the political system of
Europe, the German historian Arnold H. L. Heeren employed the term
"system of states" to designate "the union of several contiguous states,
resembling each other in their manners, religion, and degree of social
improvement, and cemented together by a reciprocity of interests."[2] That
way of thinking of the relations among the powers and principalities of
Europe is itself somewhat jarring to modern sensibilities, accustomed as we
are to viewing the European system as a cauldron of rival animosities and
self-regarding *raison d'état*. Heeren's depiction reminds us that the
European system of his day had elements of sociality or cooperation as well
as egotism and conflict. In the eighteenth and nineteenth centuries, it could
be and was seen at various moments as a working "federative system." In
1806, Friedrich Gentz, later to rise to fame as "Secretary of Europe,"
denounced "THE NEW FEDERAL SYSTEM" advocated by Napoleon and
praised "THE TRUE FEDERAL SYSTEM" that Napoleon had smashed. The
characteristic object of "the old magnificent constitution of Europe" was
"the preservation and reciprocal guarantee of the rights of all its members." According to Gentz, it had "for centuries protected the liberty of
Europe, with all its ornaments and excellencies, its constitutions and laws,
its territorial limitations, and its adjudication of rights."[3]

Whereas the customary understanding of the European state system min-
imizes the elements of sociality and felt allegiance to common norms, the
reverse error has been made in the American case, and conventional understandings have stressed the element of common nationality and shared
aspirations to the exclusion of the elements of conflict and fractured identities that existed in continental politics from the beginning. Contrary to
the common mythology—that America enjoyed an epoch of "free security"
until the cataclysmic upheavals of the twentieth century—the denizens of
the thirteen states faced a very serious security problem, to which the federal constitution proved to be a lasting though not altogether permanent
remedy. America, indeed, formed a system of states not only in the sense
identified by Heeren but also in the more familiar and existential sense: a
system in which the danger of war lurked in the background as a potential
way in which state and sectional differences would get resolved. Like the
European system at various points in its history, the American system had
varying elements of "sociality" and "anarchy," and the periodic sense that
the states stood on the verge of disunion and war coexisted with elements
of common purpose and cooperative endeavor.[4]

Seen in this light, the American founding appears as a distinctive and most remarkable attempt to turn back the tide of war—that is, as a peace pact. It bears comparison to the great peace settlements of European and world history—Westphalia (1648), Utrecht (1713), Vienna (1815), Paris (1919), and San Francisco (1945)—save that it occurred in the anticipated prelude to rather than the bloody aftermath of a war. It may probably be considered as the most self-conscious "security community" in world history until the eighteenth century—the most innovative attempt yet to overcome the serious obstacles that states had traditionally faced in securing effective cooperation with one another. Certainly it was the first to make the attempt on a continental scale.

A projected second volume, under the title *The Long Peace,* will trace the fortunes of the American system of states from the inauguration of the new government in 1789 to the outbreak of the Civil War. The present volume concerns the foundations of American constitutionalism and diplomacy as these were established in the formative years of American independence. Its structure and argument are based on the premise that these two (normally separated) worlds of thought and practice constantly impinged on one another and need to be considered together if either is to be fully understood. Its principal focus is on the constitutional settlement of 1787–88, and it seeks to provide a satisfactory explanation of why that event transpired. It does so by reconstructing the intellectual world inhabited by the framers, as that was affected by their practical experience and their speculative reasonings. It deals with the world of "high politics," and its most important sources are the speeches, pamphlets, and letters of the principal political personages of the time.

The appendix to this work displays visually the principal arguments of the book and counterpoises them to commonly accepted interpretations that I regard as deficient, misleading, or erroneous. The book is organized primarily as a historical narrative, and interpretive questions are usually considered in a place where their importance is suggested by the story that I have to tell. Readers who wish to obtain straightaway a bird's-eye view of the book's argument should look at the appendix. There is unfolded the following claims:

- that federal union is a distinct species of the genus "federative system," similar in crucial respects to the grand alliances and concerts that dot international history and radically distinct from "international anarchy" or "universal empire." Understanding federal union in this way enables us to think of it as a case within a larger grouping of other such cooperative ventures among states;

- that the constellation of imperial and continental organizations existing from 1763 to 1787 were all considered (by many, though not by all, observers) to be various forms of federal union. All these associations raised common problems (e.g., the appropriate bases of representation and burden-sharing, the location of sovereignty), and the claims of legitimacy or illegitimacy associated with each particular union strongly affected succeeding versions as they rose or fell over time;

- that the conventional ways of describing the American political inheritance, focusing on its "liberal" or "republican" character, need to be supplemented by recognition of a third paradigm of thought ("the unionist paradigm")—one centered on the problem of cooperation among "the several states in the union of the empire";

- that the most potent factors in explaining the trajectory of American politics were the multiplicity of loyalties to and identities with particular colonies and states; the bipolar rivalry that split continental politics on a geographic or sectional line; and the exigencies of the union (reflecting the impulse to cooperate in a milieu where the first two factors made that quest seem eminently problematic). The consensus, Progressive, and pluralist schools, to which these interpretations are counterpoised, neglect those factors in their depiction of the "motive forces" of American politics;

- that American reflection on the world of states was "internationalist" or "Grotian" in character. It recognized the binding character of the "law of nature and of nations" and displayed certain tendencies that set it apart from realist (or Machiavellian) and revolutionist (or Kantian) perspectives. These proclivities, in turn, are registered in both the successive manifestations of federal union and the emergence of a distinct diplomatic outlook toward the Atlantic and European political system;

- that the key objectives, doctrines, and principles of American foreign policy were profoundly shaped by the imperatives of "union and independence"—here characterized as the *Staatsräson* of the American states-union;

- that these various interpretations, relevant to a variety of distinct academic specialties, are mutually reinforcing and constitute a distinct (and hitherto much-neglected) way of understanding the formative years of American constitutionalism and diplomacy.

There are two scholarly communities to which this book is particularly directed, though in the normal course of disciplinary business they have lit-

tle contact with one another. One is the community of intellectual, diplomatic, and constitutional historians who have made the study of the early
American republic their speciality; the other is those workers in the discipline of international relations, with its intensive preoccupation with the
historical development of the state system, the causes of war and peace, the
nature and character of international institutions, and rival theoretical
approaches to conflict and cooperation among states. I have taught these
subjects in a department of political science for the last two decades, but in
my years of graduate training at Johns Hopkins I developed a consuming
interest in the epoch that forms the subject of this book. Indeed, at one time
I had contemplated a doctoral dissertation broaching many of the themes
that appear herein. That project, however, was abandoned at the time, and
when I left graduate school I turned my attention to other things. It has
been a long and circuitous route back to the eighteenth century, but a journey I am glad to have made.

For a work written at the junction point of the worlds of constitutionalism and diplomacy, it is appropriate that its author should himself be something of a divided soul, one who considers himself both a historian and a
political scientist. At darker moments, I fear that I have taken up a subject
in which historians are no longer interested and treated it in a fashion that
will be found insufficiently scientific by political scientists. If I have taken a
wrong turn, however, it has been of my own volition, and I am gratified for
the freedom I have had at Colorado College to make my own way. To
Timothy Fuller and Richard Storey, who have given me support and encouragement, and to the many students and colleagues who have joined me in
friendship and in devotion to liberal learning, I extend my profound thanks.

A half-year fellowship from the National Endowment for the
Humanities in the fall of 1995, in conjunction with a half-year sabbatical
from Colorado College in the fall of 1996, were of critical importance in
the research and writing of *Peace Pact* and the successor volume, the first
draft of which was completed in 1998. The present work was greatly
expanded and entirely rewritten from 1999 to 2001. In 1998, Joel
Rosenthal of the Carnegie Council on Ethics and International Affairs
sponsored a seminar where I presented selections from my work in
progress, and my old friend and collaborator, Robert W. Tucker, read and
commented on many drafts. Andy O'Riley devoted long hours to ensuring
that the notes were in acceptable form and to supervising the transition
from Wordperfect to Word, not a task for the faint of heart. Three scholars whose work I greatly admire—Lance Banning, Peter Onuf, and Karl
Walling—gave me numerous helpful suggestions in their reviews of the

manuscript. Lance and Karl gave me the opportunity to participate in numerous Liberty Fund seminars in early American constitutionalism and diplomacy, from which I derived great profit. Peter has been very gracious in his reception of my work, affording me both needed encouragement and perceptive recommendations. Hearty thanks to all of them, but especially to Peter.

This book enjoins the reader to consider the founders in the eighteenth-century world that they inhabited. It seeks to view their work as diplomatists and constitution-builders "as it really was," shorn of the encrusted precedents that have grown about their accomplishment over time. It is thus the meaning this experience had for its progenitors, and not the relevance this tradition might have for the contemporary world, that is the subject of the history I propose to tell, but perhaps the reader may find a speck of the useful in this survey of the historical and the contingent. The lesson I draw is a relatively simple one: that as between the rival specters of international anarchy and universal empire, America must find in the federal tradition the desirable middle path that entails the simultaneous rejection of both extremes. Such, in my view, is the line of policy most compatible with a milieu in which free government and international peace may be best secured, and it is one, I think, that is inescapably suggested by the domain of thought I have sought to explicate. The history of American foreign policy in the twentieth century has often been written as a kind of careening back and forth between the rival temptations of the Lone Republic and the World Empire. As a commentator on that history, and as a citizen, I have regarded those alternatives as deceitful sirens and believe that the path of safety and justice consists of the fruitful application of federal values to the world of states. As for the specific institutional form and geographic reach such federative systems should have, Clio, alas, forbids that we should penetrate the veil: "The fathers are dead; the prophets are silent. The questions are new, and have no answer but in time."

PART ONE
Introduction

I

To Philadelphia

As DELEGATES FROM the American states gathered at Philadelphia in the late spring of 1787, the preponderant number believed that they faced a critical and perilous state of affairs. The league of states loosely joined together by the Articles of Confederation had lost the cohesion that had sustained it through the initial stages of the war against Great Britain. Its debts were unpaid and its credit was nonexistent. It was destitute of revenue. Nearly all the sister states that had formed this league nursed the grievance that they had unfairly shouldered the burdens of the war for independence and would never get the compensation they deserved. They had therefore resolved to send no more funds to the general treasury until a settlement of accounts was fairly made. The congress had, in turn, shown itself incapable, as then constituted, of agreeing on the terms of such a settlement.

The Treaty of Peace the United States had made with Great Britain in 1783 had not been executed on either side. Congress lacked the means to ensure the observance by the American states that was a necessary preliminary to getting execution from Great Britain. That still powerful state, nursing its wounded pride, was in turn led after 1784 by men who believed that the peace settlement—made by Lord Shelburne, who had opposed the American war—had been far too generous to the Americans; the new ministry, led by William Pitt the younger, was populated largely by those who had supported the war, and it was pursuing a policy toward the former colonies that scorned the sentiments of reconciliation and restored harmony that Shelburne had hoped to revive through generous terms.

The commerce of the American states was slowly returning to life, but in channels—auguring a new dependence on Great Britain—that betrayed the expectations of many southerners and that frustrated as well the commercial objectives of the "Eastern" states, which were shut out of the markets and shipping routes they had enjoyed as members of the British Empire. The commercial weakness of the union was such that in 1786 John Jay, the secretary of foreign affairs, had sought to open Spanish markets by surrendering the American claim to navigate the Mississippi River for a period of twenty-five to thirty years. That proposal had in turn aroused powerful suspicions on sectional lines—a development that seemed to augur the prospective division of the continent into rival confederacies based on the sections.

3

The "imbecility" of the confederation was not pretty, and it inspired the search for metaphors that adequately conveyed the pathetic excuse for a government that, to its critics, it had become: it reminded one observer of a man "attempting to walk with both legs cut off." "No money," Madison wrote on the eve of the Philadelphia convention, "is paid into the public Treasury; no respect is paid to the federal authority. Not a single State complies with the requisitions, several pass them over in silence, and some positively reject them. The payments ever since the peace have been decreasing, and of late fall short even of the pittance necessary for the Civil list of the Confederacy." The larger question, therefore, was not whether it might continue to exist in its present crippled state but whether agreement on any form of union might be reached. "In general," Madison said, "I find men of reflection much less sanguine as to a new than despondent as to the present System."[1]

That the union would not survive these exiguous circumstances was considered highly probable by the diplomatic agents of Britain, France, and Spain. Their respective courts were warned not to harbor illusions: dissolution was forthcoming; separate confederacies were the foreordained conclusion; it was only a matter of time. Josiah Tucker established the tone of such prophecies when he wrote, in 1781, that the prospect of a "rising Empire" in America was "one of the idlest, and most visionary Notions, that ever was conceived even by Writers of Romance." The diversity of climates and manners comprehended within the American confederation, together with their "mutual Antipathies, and clashing Interests," ensured that Americans could never "be united into one compact Empire, under any Species of Government whatever. Their Fate seems to be—A DISUNITED PEOPLE, till the End of Time."[2] It was no exaggeration to say, as Benjamin Franklin did in his speech at the conclusion of the convention, that the Constitution, though imperfect, would "astonish our enemies, who are waiting with confidence to hear, that our councils are confounded like those of the builders of Babel, and that our States are on the point of separation, only to meet hereafter for the purpose of cutting one another's throats."[3]

Franklin's speech was the capstone of proceedings that had begun on May 25, 1787, and had lasted throughout the long, hot summer. There were indeed various moments during the summer when "the difficulty of reconciling the interests of the several states was so near to *insuperable*" that the convention was "upon the very point" of a breakdown, its members "dispersing in the utmost disorder, jealousy and resentment."[4] Usually the primary conflict within the convention is understood as one between "nationalists" and "federalists," or as one between those who sought to establish a national government that was supreme and those who insisted that sovereignty must continue to reside in the states. That conflict existed, but the more important and vital question—the knot of the most Gordian character—concerned the bases of representation in the new government.[5] It was the inability to reach agreement on this question that led some delegates to threaten to go home. The conflict was partially resolved by the so-called Great Compromise of July 16, a package that gave to the states an equal vote in the upper chamber and confirmed a rule of population for the lower house that counted African slaves as three-fifths of a person. Though usually seen as a compromise between the large and the small states, the July 16 vote was also crucially important as a compromise between the southern and the eastern states. A sectional bargain also underlay the second great compromise of the convention in late August, when South Carolina and Georgia gained the right to import slaves until 1808 and the southern states surrendered their demand requiring regulations of commerce to pass with a two-thirds vote in congress. Of equal importance to these two compromises was the Northwest Ordinance, the third great compromise of the summer of 1787. Passed by the Continental Congress on July 13, it carved out sectional spheres of influence in the western territory and was a vital though informal part of the constitutional settlement reached in Philadelphia. As James Madison, Rufus King, and others emphasized, the fundamental problem of the convention was that of ensuring a balance of power among the great sections of the union. These compromises did that, giving to the North a temporary majority in the House of Representatives and a more durable bastion in the Senate, and giving to the South the prospect that with the growth of population it would one day achieve the weight within the union that was its due.

By contrast with the heated disputes over representation, the division over the extent of the national powers was less contentious. Since "who would rule?" was a question that had to be answered before "with what powers?" could be addressed, the convention made little progress in defining the spheres of power that would belong to the local and general governments until the first great compromise was made. On this point, however, the positions among the delegates were not terribly far apart. Most saw that they must find a middle ground between the "two extremes" that, in Madison's words, lay before them: "a perfect separation & a perfect incorporation, of the 13 States. In the first case they would be independent nations subject to no law, but the law of nations. In the last, they would be mere counties of one entire republic, subject to one common law."[6] Neither alternative found significant support within the convention.

As James Wilson noted in his important explication of the new Constitution, "consolidation" would demand "a system of the most unqualified and unremitted despotism," whereas separation into "a number of separate states, continuous in situation, unconnected and disunited in government," would make the states "at one time, the prey of foreign force, foreign influence, and foreign intrigue; at another, the victims of mutual rage, rancor, and revenge."[7]

Those opposing and widely shared specters pushed the delegates onto a middle ground that none of them anticipated when the convention began. Conscious that the states would have to give up some of their sovereignty if the purposes of "the subsisting federal government" were to be realized, and conscious, too, of the impossibility of legislating for communities as opposed to individuals, the framers brought forth a new political edifice fashioned on the norms and institutions of constitutional government existing within the American states. The federal government, like most of the state governments, would now enjoy a bicameral regime of separated powers, with a regular executive and judicial establishment capable of bringing individuals under the cognizance of its laws. The federal government created by the Constitution, however, fell short of a "full-fledged state," or what was called at the time a "consolidated" government.[8] Unlike the state governments, which generally claimed a plenary authority over the lives and liberties of their citizens, the federal government was one of enumerated and limited powers. Supremacy was accorded neither to the federal government nor to the state governments but to the Constitution itself, though the more perfect union was justified by Federalists as being an indispensable means to the preservation of both states and nation. "The state government," observed Fisher Ames in the Massachusetts ratifying convention, "is a beautiful structure. It is situated, however, upon the naked beach. The Union is the dyke to fence out the flood." Securing the union was equally instrumental to the preservation—or creation—of the nation. The union "is essential to our being as a nation," Ames argued. It was "the vital sap that nourishes the tree"; without it, "we girdle the tree, its leaves will wither, its branches drop off, and the mouldering trunk will be torn down by the tempest."[9]

Both at the time and subsequently, there would be much disagreement over the powers that the Constitution did give; it was birthed and subsequently lived under the shadow of a multitude of uncertainties. Despite those uncertainties, no one could doubt that it represented a unique and unprecedented solution to the question of continental governance. "Partly national and partly federal," it proposed that America pursue the aims long associated with confederations through the creation of a general government that acted directly upon individuals, avoiding the direct reliance on the states that had proved fatal to the old confederation. The national government, that is to say, was to have the powers traditionally invested in the state to secure objects avowedly federal, with its enumerated powers largely confined to the "federative" or "external" functions of war and peace, diplomacy, and foreign commerce.[10] Advocates said that it would secure "federal liberty" and that the states needed a compact to get them out of the state of nature for the same reason that individuals in a state of nature needed a government.[11]

But the Constitution was a federative act not only in these respects. More fundamentally, its acceptance or rejection was seen by its advocates as posing the fundamental question of peace or war. "Once dissolve the tie by which we are united and alone preserved," James McHenry argued on behalf of ratification, "and the prediction of our Enemies would be compleat in the bloodshed in contending and opposite interests."[12] If the Constitution were rejected, argued Edmund Randolph in the Virginia convention, "the Union will be dissolved, the dogs of war will break loose, and anarchy and discord will complete the ruin of this country."[13] "Among the upright and intelligent," Randolph pleaded, "few can read without emotion the future fate of the states, if severed from each other. Then shall we learn the full weight of foreign intrigue—Then shall we hear of partitions of our country."[14] There is no important statement of the case for the Constitution that does not pose the alternative simply and starkly as being one between peace and war. Washington, Hamilton, Madison, Jay, Wilson, Dickinson, King, Coxe, Pinckney, and the two Websters all said it, as did many lesser lights.[15] Believing that the interests of the states met in more points than they differed, and mortally fearing a dissolution that would ineluctably produce the features of the European state system in North America, the Federalists of 1788 labored hard to secure the ratification of a frame of government that would be adequate to the exigencies of the union, giving to each potential fragment a vital interest in its perpetuation. As they continually counterpoised the state of peace with the state of war, and made a bid for the former against the perceived threat of the latter, it seems fair to denominate the federal Constitution as a peace pact, the most unusual specimen of this kind yet known to history.

2

The Great Debate of 1788

THE ABILITY OF the Philadelphia convention to reach agreement and near unanimity on the new Constitution, given the numerous and heated disputes that had arisen over its features, was itself something of a miracle, as many of the delegates began immediately to call it. Even more remarkable, perhaps, was the wide-reaching debate that took place in America in response to the convention's plan. The uncertainty attached to the secret deliberations of the "plenipotentiary convention" had brought political discussions to a standstill, but when the convention gave birth to its child, there followed an utterly unprecedented flood of pamphlets, letters, and speeches. The whole country, as if spellbound, read, listened, and thought; "industry gave up its fruits, and dissipation forbore its indulgences."[1]

From the Federalists came the plea that a strengthened union was necessary "as our bulwark against foreign danger, as the conservator of peace among ourselves, as the guardian of our commerce and other common interests, as the only substitute for those military establishments which have subverted the liberties of the old world; and as the proper antidote for the diseases of faction, which have proved fatal to other popular governments, and of which alarming symptoms have been betrayed by our own."[2] In the absence of ratification, they warned, the division of the continent was at hand. As a consequence of this division, they speculated, regional confederacies would form that would entertain relations with one another indistinguishable from those prevailing in the European state system. This development—inevitably accompanied by perennial rivalries and by the standing armies and wars bred by these—would jeopardize the fragile growth of republican government on the American continent. "To be more safe," Publius warned, the separate and rival confederacies of North America would "at length become willing to run the risk of being less free." In the absence of union, these confederacies would likely attach themselves to the interests of foreign powers, and the American continent would become, like the petty republics of Greece and Italy, the scene of foreign involvement and perpetual war. With unity, as Publius observed, "[e]xtensive military establishments cannot . . . be necessary to our security. But if we should be disunited, and the integral parts should either remain separated, or, which is most probable, should be thrown together into two or three confederacies, we should be, in a short course of time, in the predicament of the continental powers of Europe—our liberties would be a prey to the means of defending ourselves against the ambition and jealousy of each other." The republican character of America's institutions would not enable them to escape the conflagration that awaited disunion. Nor would geographic distance. Though "the distance of the United States from the powerful nations of the world gave them the same happy security" enjoyed by Great Britain in relation to the continent of Europe, it ought "never for a moment be forgotten that they are indebted for this advantage to their Union alone. The moment of its dissolution will be the date of a new order of things. . . . Instead of deriving from our situation the precious advantage which Great Britain has derived from hers, the face of America will be but a copy of that of the continent of Europe. It will present liberty everywhere crushed between standing armies and perpetual taxes."[3]

The Federalists argued, quite plausibly, that the alternative to union was not a division into thirteen separate sovereignties but the emergence of two to three separate confederacies based on the sections. "The entire separation of the States into thirteen unconnected sovereignties," as Hamilton put it in *Federalist* No. 13, "is a project too extravagant and too replete with danger to have many advocates. The ideas of men who speculate upon the dismemberment of the empire, seem generally turned towards three confederacies; one consisting of the four northern, another of the four middle, and a third of the five southern States. There is little probability that there would be a greater number."[4] The former alternative was obviously unstable; it would leave the states with little power to assert their interests against either the European powers or one another. The demonstration of this point served a practical purpose in that it enabled the Federalists to show that the corporate identity of the individual states would be far less secure under disunion than under the proposed constitution; still, the point was not simply a rhetorical device but a deeply held conviction, identifying dangers that were "real, certain, and formidable."[5] Hamilton himself believed that the likely division would be into two: "New York, situated as she is, would never be unwise enough to oppose a feeble and unsupported flank to the weight of" a New England confederacy, and Pennsylvania's best chance to avoid becoming "the FLANDERS of America" lay in having "her exposed side turned toward the weaker power of the southern, rather than towards the stronger power of the northern confederacy."[6] The difficulty of forecasting the role the middle states would play in this unfolding dynamic—whether, in other words, the initial division would be into two or three—itself pointed to the likelihood of intense competition among these confederacies. That they would inevitably find themselves also in a contest for the control of the territories beyond the Appalachian Mountains—that they would have, "in the wide field of Western territory, . . . an ample theater for hostile pretensions"—added a fertile source of additional conflict.[7] This perception of an unfolding competition among regional confederacies is a vital factor to keep in mind in considering the Federalist outlook: because such a system was the great alternative to union, it also pointed to the demon that union must somehow try to suppress.[8]

Closely related to the fear of separate confederacies based on sections were the dangers posed by the European powers. It was the mutual interaction between the separate confederacies of North America and the pretensions and interests of the European powers that constituted the core of the dynamic Publius sketched out. It was this interaction that drove the sequence at the end of which would be a replication of the European experience. As a result, the distinction between the dangers to which America would be exposed, "in a state of disunion, from all the arms and arts of foreign nations," and "those which will in all probability flow from dissensions between the States themselves," was a thin one. Each phenomenon would feed on and mutually reinforce the other. In the Federalist estimation, that dynamic constituted the core of the American security problem.[9]

Perhaps the most remarkable feature of the case the Federalists put forward for ratification of the Constitution is what might be termed its thoroughgoing "structural realism"—that is, its propensity to explain not only the causes of war but also the internal character of states as being a function of powerful systemic pressures generated by the structure of the "international system."[10] America was without kings or military establishments; it would acquire both in circumstances of disunion. It had no class of white men who, profiting from the "military system" so deeply entrenched in Europe, made the European laborer "go supperless to bed, and to moisten his bed with the sweat of his brows."[11] Disunion would bring that as well. The contrast between Europe and America has always been a fertile source of speculation among observers on both sides of the Atlantic, and we are accustomed to seeing the contrast in the terms made famous by Tocqueville: "The great advantage of the Americans is, that they have arrived at a state of democracy without having to endure a democratic revolution; and that they are born equal, instead of becoming so."[12] The Federalists of 1788 accepted that the contrast existed but denied that it would continue in circumstances of disunion. That state, to which America was fast approaching, meant, in the end, the obliteration of every contrast between the two hemispheres.

If the Federalist fear of a raging state system in the Americas constituted the dominant motif in the American founding, there was also in existence a countermotif sounded by the Anti-Federalists. Despite divisions among the Antis, their complaints did coalesce around one great theme: their fear of "consolidation," or "empire," or "despotic centralization." The Constitution, said one antifederal writer, was "a hasty stride to Universal Empire in this Western World." Anti-Federalists looked upon what Hamilton and Wilson had called "the amazing extent of country" and stood slack-jawed at the idea that it might be governed from a common center. "It is impossible for one code of laws to suit Georgia and Massachusetts," wrote Agrippa, yet it seemed undeniable to him that "the new system" was "a consolidation of all the states into one large mass."[13]

Like the Federalists, the Antis saw "union and independence" as vital, but they differed on the degree of centralization, or the extent of powers, that needed to be lodged in any general authority. They, too, wished to secure common American objectives as against the European powers, but they feared the creation of an empire that would extinguish the liberty and independence of the American states. "If we admit this consolidated government," as Patrick Henry described the "tyranny" that had issued from Philadelphia, "it will be because we like a great, splendid one. Some way or other we must be a great and mighty empire; we must have an army, and a navy, and a number of things. When the American spirit was in its youth, the language of America was different; liberty, sir, was then the primary object." In Henry's estimation, like that of other Antis, union could be acceptable only if it supported unequivocally the independence for which the states had fought. This kind of union, they believed, promised to subvert it.[14]

With other Anti-Federalists, Henry also denied that the situation facing the American states was nearly as critical as the supporters of the new Constitution were maintaining. Dismissing the projections of inevitable war as a "hobgoblin" that had "sprung from the deranged brain of *Publius,* a New-York writer," Centinel thought it absurd that this specter should be used to banish the sober second thought of the people in their consideration of the proposed union.[15] William Grayson of Virginia ridiculed the notion as well:

> We are now told by the honorable gentleman (Governor Randolph) that we shall have wars and rumors of wars, that every calamity is to attend us, and that we shall be ruined and disunited forever, unless we adopt this Constitution. Pennsylvania and Maryland are to fall upon us from the north, like the Goths and Vandals of old; the Algerines, whose flat-sided vessels never came farther than Madeira, are to fill

the Chesapeake with mighty fleets, and to attack us on our front; the Indians are to invade us with numerous armies on our rear, in order to convert our cleared lands into hunting-grounds; and the Carolinians, from the south, (mounted on alligators, I presume,) are to come and destroy our cornfields, and eat up our little children! These, sir, are the mighty dangers which await us if we reject—dangers which are merely imaginary, and ludicrous in the extreme! Are we to be destroyed by Maryland and Pennsylvania? What will democratic states make war for, and how long since have they imbibed a hostile spirit?

James Monroe returned to the same charge as Grayson and presented in the debates over the Constitution the fullest statement of the theory that democracies are inherently pacific, and that "all those terrors which splendid genius and brilliant imagination" had depicted were "imaginary—mere creatures of fancy." "The causes of half the wars that have thinned the ranks of mankind, and depopulated nations, are caprice, folly, and ambition: these belong to the higher orders of governments, where the passions of one, or of a few individuals, direct the fate of the rest of the community. But it is otherwise with democracies, where there is an equality among the citizens."[16] Tied together by the umbilical cords of commerce, and restrained from ambition by their democratic character, the American states had no motive for war and every motive for peace. In effect, the Anti-Federalists presented, in counterpoise to the structural realism of the Federalists, a full-blown theory of the liberal democratic peace.[17]

Federalists did not deny that despotism "would be the consequence of *a single national constitution, in which all the objects of society and government were so compleatly provided for, as to place the several states in the union on the footing of counties of the empire.*"[18] They did most emphatically deny, however, that acceptance of the Constitution would lead to this result. It was a federal union rather than a consolidated government, they insisted. Standing at a middle point between the rival specters of international anarchy and universal empire, it gave powers sufficient to arrest the descent into anarchy while falling entirely short of a consolidated empire. The powers of the general government were separated, but also sometimes mixed, but in either event they were so arranged and balanced as to ensure that it would not pass beyond its authoritative jurisdiction. Its objects were largely external, concerned with war, peace, negotiation, and foreign commerce; everything else was to remain with the states. Authority over such federal objects had been lodged in congress under the Articles of Confederation; what was wanting was appropriate means to carry that authority into effect. Responding to charges that it meant a government of force, Federalists patiently explained that it would be a government of laws, and not of force, substituting reason and deliberation for the sword.[19] Confronted with the accusation that the "We the People" of the Preamble meant the people of a consolidated nation, Federalists explained that the states could not be enumerated without unreasonably presuming they would join; the phrase meant "We the People of the Several States," each a body politic solely accountable for the act of ratification.[20] Confronted with the accusation that ratification meant eternal slavery, binding to the last generation, most Federalists said that its perpetuity could not in all honesty be answered for, but that it was an experiment that had to be run. The Anti-Federalists, they insisted, had it all backward, and the very course the Antis counseled would lead inevitably to the result they most feared. The rejection of the Constitution meant the emergence of separate confederacies and the acceptance, with all its fateful consequences, of the precedents and practices of the European state system, thence onward to war and despotism. That the democratic character of the states, or the ties of commerce among them, would arrest this consequence they considered highly improbable. Those "projectors in politics" who held that the genius of republics is pacific, or who thought that "the spirit of commerce has a tendency to soften the manners of men, and to extinguish those inflammable humors which have so often kindled into wars," were alike mistaken in inferring a state of "perpetual peace between the States, though dismembered and alienated from each other." Republics, being "administered by men," were no less prone to war than monarchies; commerce, unhappily, had done nothing more than "change the objects of war."[21]

3

The Unionist Paradigm

THE COMPLEX OF THOUGHT represented in this great debate is sufficiently rich and complex to justify the appellation of "ideology" or "paradigm." By those terms I mean a structure of ideas with which individuals order and generalize about reality; affirm or reprobate the various norms regulating human conduct; understand causal relationships among phenomena; anticipate and predict future developments; distinguish what is important from what is unimportant; and develop policies to avoid dangers and achieve their goals.[1] Like other such paradigms, it does not reflect simply one idea but many ideas—mutually interrelated, to be sure, yet nevertheless distinct. Both Federalists and Anti-Federalists spoke the language of this paradigm, thought in its categories, affirmed the values that it recognized, and investigated the questions that it prompted. At its core were two competing fears—of the anarchy of states and the despotism of consolidated empire—and two mutually interdependent values: independence and union.[2]

In considering how to overcome these fears and secure these values, American thinkers took up a wide variety of questions. Committed to government resting on the consent of the governed, they wondered whether such little commonwealths would invariably maintain peaceful relations with one another or were subject to the same impulses that led other states to war. They asked whether the entangling ties associated with commerce tended to promote pacific relations among states, or whether commercial interdependence might actually promote conflict. They prized both individual freedom and collective autonomy, the rights of individuals and the liberties of states, and had to discover how those values could be reconciled with one another if they came into conflict. The world being a dangerous place, they saw that a union that would aggregate strength against potential enemies was a necessity, but they wondered whether great size in the union or great power in the general government would introduce into their association forces that made for its disruption, or otherwise corrupted its republican principles. Confronting a multitude of dilemmas of collective action that they needed to resolve to make their union work, they were led to consider how to allocate the division of responsibilities among levels of government, how to arrive at an equitable sharing of the burdens of the association, how to ensure fair representation and thus to obtain the consent on which the system would rest, how to balance power at home and abroad, where to locate sovereignty. The founders are usually credited with making substantial contributions to "the science of politics." Less well appreciated is the fact that they created, in effect, a sophisticated science of international politics, focused on the conditions and possibilities of cooperation among independent republics.

In their encounter with the peace problem, the founders anticipated what has been called "perhaps the most significant split" among twentieth-century thinkers concerned with the reform of the state system: "whether to fashion world order solutions on the basis of transferring norms, procedures, and institutions from domestic life or to work within the state system as now structured to maximize its distinctive ordering capabilities. The outer limit of the former approach is a full-fledged world state; the outer limit of the latter is a humane, prosperous, and balanced international society composed of serene and satisfied sovereign states."[3] Anti-Federalists sought to work within a system of sovereign states to maximize its distinctive ordering capabilities; they were intent on showing that the absence of a central sovereign would not entail continual war; that a much looser form of association could in fact be held together through sentiment rather than the sword; that the American states, because they were democratic and enjoyed ties of commercial interdependence, would have no motive for war with one another if they refused to accept a consolidated government. They imagined a humane, prosperous, and balanced American system composed of serene and satisfied sovereign states. The Federalists, who appropriated as their own the word that had previously signified this ideal, argued that the thirteen states would have to give up some of their sovereignty if the purposes of "the subsisting federal government" were to be realized; that experience had shown the impossibility of legislating for communities as opposed to individuals; and that a new political edifice, fashioned with the norms, procedures, and institutions of constitutional government existing within the American states, had to be erected were the descent into anarchy and war to be avoided.[4] Altogether, the argument this generation conducted on these questions constituted a far richer examination of the possibilities and limits of international cooperation and peace than anything written by Immanuel Kant, usually considered the formative influence on contemporary internationalism.[5]

To insist that there was a body of thought or "structure of ideas" identifiable as "the unionist paradigm" does not mean that there was unanimity of opinion with respect to the problems it posed—indeed, that paradigm was as much a set of questions as a résumé of foreordained conclusions.

While there was a seeming consensus within the United States on certain fundamentals—the need for union to counteract both anarchy and despotism, and the need for union to secure independence, particularly—Americans otherwise had profound differences with one another at all points of the paradigm. Disagreement often centered on the meaning and characteristics of the variety of political associations that inhabited their world: *commonwealth, republic, state,* and *nation,* each of which signified a single body politic, and *system of states, confederation, federal union, alliance,* and *empire,* each of which signified an association of bodies politic. The difficulty of accurate description is underlined by Madison's later observation that the Constitution was "sui generis," "so unexampled in its origin, so complex in its structure, and so peculiar in some of its features, that in describing it the political vocabulary does not furnish terms sufficiently distinctive and appropriate, without a detailed resort to the facts of the case."[6] But what Madison said of the federal constitution was also true of the constitution of the British Empire and the Articles of Confederation. Was the British Empire based on the sovereignty of the king in Parliament, or was it held together simply by the force of royal authority and prerogative, with the colonial assemblies enjoying an equal legislative authority with Parliament? Was the Continental Congress a diplomatic assembly, a national government, or something in between? Whence came its authority? From the sovereign states? The nation? The people?

These associations needed to be precisely understood not only to understand the basis of their authority but also to project their movement over time—a question that could not be seen apart from their legitimacy. Those closely entangled questions of normative and empirical theory produced a kind of historical sociology examining how and why these peculiar associations held together or fell apart; whether they preserved or threatened important values in the law of nations, including peace, neutrality, and the balance of power; and why they rose or fell. The fate of the common cause rested on getting these things right, understanding them truly and without illusion, and that helps account for the intrepidity and zeal with which they were taken up in the late 1780s. At the same time, none of these questions had arisen suddenly at the time of founding. Americans had gotten on this line of thought—jumped headlong, as it were, into the paradigm—at a fairly early stage of the controversy with Great Britain, and they were still in it as they immersed themselves in the debate over the federal constitution.

In thus characterizing the leading elements of the "unionist paradigm," I mean to distinguish it from the "liberal ideology" and "republican paradigm" that historians have alternately identified as being emblematic of early American thought. Both liberal and republican ideas were of great importance at the time of the American founding, and early Americans may without inaccuracy be described as both liberal and republican. Indeed, the antagonism between those two paradigms is often exaggerated: "we are all liberals, we are all republicans" is a better gauge of the early American outlook than the assumption that these ideologies stood in sharp conflict with one another. It was not simply possible, but characteristic, for these early Americans to love the commonwealth because it alone provided a certain foundation for individual liberty, to thrill to sublime examples of virtue, like Washington, while accepting that there were certain things that no state had a right to exact from its citizens. The terms of this dialogue are interesting because they suggest that early American political thought was vitally concerned with balancing the perennially conflicting—though also correlative—claims of civic participation and a private sphere, of community needs and individual rights, of order and liberty. But it is crucially important to realize that the order they wanted to constitute would have to take place over a territory of "imperial" dimensions, and that the liberty they wanted to preserve consisted as much of "the liberty of states" as the freedom of individuals. These facts put the problem on an altogether different basis and ensured that the basic categories of liberal and republican thought would be thrown into a state of great perplexity by the problems that lay at the core of the unionist paradigm.

Both liberal ideas of consent and individual rights, on the one hand, and republican ideas of civic virtue and community, on the other, were thus immensely complicated by the existence in America of different conceptions of the commonwealth—centering on state, section, and nation—to which the idea of consent, the vindication of individual rights, or the sentiment of virtue was appropriate. Americans, in other words, belonged to multiple communities and had multiple identities and loyalties, and it was the relationship among these communities, identities, and loyalties that constituted the essence of their political problem during this period. In understanding the foundations of American political thought, it is crucial to distinguish between what Rufus Choate would call the "long series of influences that trained us for representative and free government" and "that other series of influences which welded us into a united government"; between "the whole train of causes from the Reformation downwards, which prepared us to be Republicans," and "that other train of causes which led us to be Unionists." That is an instructive passage not only because it unites traditions ("liberalism" and "republicanism") that historians have often cast asunder but also because it separates them both from the "series of influences" and "train of causes" that made the union.[7]

The "series of influences" and "train of causes" that made the federal union, culminating in the writing and ratification of the Constitution, is the principal subject of this book. Only part six, however, is directly concerned with the events of 1787 and 1788. As Choate suggested, the inquiry into those influences and causes requires an investigation that looks beyond the immediate events surrounding the making of the Constitution, and I propose to do this through an examination of the ways in which Americans had, over the previous three decades, explored the problems raised by the unionist paradigm. This is in large part the history of an argument, conducted on the assumption that a political culture "achieves identity not so much through the ascendancy of one particular set of convictions as through the emergence of its peculiar and distinctive dialogue." "Intellectual history," in the words of R. W. B. Lewis, "exposes not only the dominant ideas of a period" but also "the dominant clashes of ideas," with the historian looking "not only for the major terms of discourse, but also for major pairs of opposed terms which, by their very opposition, carry discourse forward." At the same time, our subject matter cannot simply be an "intellectual history" or history of ideas. The significance of the ideas that gripped this generation and with which they understood their world cannot be fully grasped unless we set those ideas in the context of the political forces, interests, and developments that swirled about them.[8]

Though their own experience in rejecting the authority of Great Britain and then in fashioning a union among themselves was doubtless of primary significance in understanding the road to Philadelphia, the founding generation had keen historical imaginations, and they ransacked ancient and modern history for lessons. Their uses of the past are examined in part two. From that investigation, it will become apparent that the images they called forth in the debate over the Constitution were not mere abstractions but carried historical resonance. "Universal Empire," "consolidation," "centralization," "despotism" recalled for them a succession of images: the expansion and corruption of Rome; the mad search for universal monarchy by a line of continental European monarchs; the sinister views of a British court that had attempted to foist on the American provinces a condition supposedly akin to absolute slavery. "Anarchy," "chaos," "disintegration" had a comparable, though opposing, significance. The fatal consequences to which anarchy might lead could be seen in the rise and fall of the unions made by the Greek city-states of antiquity to secure their liberty; in the civil wars and foreign interventions of Italy at the birth of the modern age; in the endless internal dissensions and wars of the Holy Roman Empire; and perhaps most of all in the experience of the modern European state system. American thought was heavily imbued with equilibrist notions of all sorts, but in the operation of the old European system they saw nothing but danger. The system of the balance of power, wrote William Vans Murray, "affected to smother the breath of universal monarchy," but it had "in fact organized the system of universal slavery." Armed with these historical analogies, Federalists attempted to show that the failure to ratify would lead America to repeat the experience of Greece, Italy, and the modern European system, with disunion inevitably producing foreign intervention, war, and despotism. Anti-Federalists espied a set of precedents from Britain and Rome that made them condemn the new government as "the tyranny of Philadelphia."[9]

The intellectual antecedents of the federal constitution also require an investigation of the great conflict that tore asunder the British Empire, the subject of part three. Americans' understanding of their rights and duties within the British Empire, which they came to understand as a "foederal" relationship among coequal legislative authorities united by a common king, had a profound influence on their conception of the sort of union they ought to make among themselves. A great many of the questions that preoccupied Americans after 1776 had already been given extensive consideration in the ten years before the outbreak of hostilities, both by themselves and by a host of scintillating thinkers in Great Britain, among them Edmund Burke, Adam Smith, and Josiah Tucker. The location and origin of sovereignty within the empire; the authoritative boundaries between one legislature with "general" or "external" responsibilities, and others with "local" or "internal" responsibilities; the requirements of representation; the benefits and burdens associated with the maintenance of their association; the overriding question of whether thirteen independent sovereignties could cooperate in defense of their liberty or would fall into anarchy and confusion—all these were taken up widely in the years before independence. The transatlantic argument over the American role within the British Empire, in turn, strongly prefigures the debate over the conditions, features, and problematics of the federal union among the American states. The American theory of "the union of the empire" from which they revolted formed a template of legitimacy by which to assess their own union, but also created expectations that were very difficult to satisfy. In the course of making the Articles of Confederation, indeed, it became apparent that the construction of their own union threatened to undermine one or more crucial founts of legitimacy, implicating the union in a violation of the very principles they had taken up arms to oppose.

Part four examines the unions that preceded the federal constitution, and especially the Articles of Confederation. I say "unions" rather than "union" because there was in fact more than one. The collection of independent plenipotentiaries that met in 1774 and 1775 transformed itself into something different with the Declaration of Independence in 1776 ("the fundamental act of union of these States," as Jefferson called it in 1825).[10] The sacred vows then exchanged were predicated on the assumption that congress would soon agree upon formal articles of confederation, but that proved a very difficult task. The first committee report on the confederation was not submitted until July 12, a week after the Declaration, and the heated debates of late summer revealed an absence of consensus on its most vital provisions. It was not submitted to the states until November 1777 and not ratified until 1781. That sequence of events inevitably made for much confusion and uncertainty over the basis of congressional authority, and put the union at risk. The formal ratification of the articles, from which so much was expected during the war, created a yet different situation, mandating different rules of representation and voting from those congress had observed from 1776 to 1781 and creating, in effect, a new union. Each of these associations—1774–76, 1776–81, and 1781–88—was headed by a body called a congress, but they were nevertheless different in signal respects from one another (as they were, of course, from the congress that first sat in 1789).

Despite fundamental uncertainties over their basic character, it is impossible to understand the federal constitution unless the experience with and disputes over the preceding unions are brought into view. In one sense, the new Constitution repudiated the Articles of Confederation and put the federal government on an altogether different basis. The Articles, as Hamilton wrote, were a system "radically vicious and unsound" that required not amendment but "an entire change in its leading features and characters."[11] In another and equally important sense, however, the federal constitution built on the foundation laid by its predecessor. The change that was proposed, as Madison insisted, consisted "much less in the addition of NEW POWERS to the Union, than in the invigoration of its ORIGINAL POWERS." It was based on principles which "may be considered less as absolutely new, than as the expansion of principles which are found in the articles of Confederation."[12] On this view, the innovation of 1787 lay much more in the means than in the end; it was to "perfect" their system of cooperation by making a more perfect union. The class of powers given to the generality remained largely the same, concerning "the interests of the states in relation to each other, and in relation to foreign powers."[13] Put differently, the normative elements of the original union persisted with the construction of a new union, and the great difference lay in the institutional mechanism by which this was to be effected. Whether that was a difference of degree or of kind was one of the great questions surrounding the ratification of the Constitution, on which dispute raged from that day forward. However that constitutional question is resolved, it should not bar recognition of the substantial commonalities that did exist between the two instruments.

Finally, the antecedents of the Constitution need also to be seen in relation to the formation of a common American approach to the external world, the subject of part five. The early American outlook toward Europe and the world of states is not, I think, well understood. It is too often seen in a sort of binary opposition—with realists in one camp and idealists in the other—that does not reveal the context or contours of American thought. Instead, I place them in what has been called the "Whig or constitutional tradition in diplomacy." This tradition of thought—also called the "Grotian" or "internationalist"—placed fundamental importance on the law of nature and of nations, "sacred throughout the civilized world." American thinkers identified closely with the celebrated writers on the law of nations—Grotius, Pufendorf, and Vattel, among others—and went on to elaborate a set of improvements to international society that they hoped the American Revolution would inaugurate. The checking of Britain's thirst for universal monarchy; the beneficial effects, both for Europe and America, of a commerce no longer shackled by the jealousy of a selfish mercantilism; the prospect of a vast emigration from Europe that would force improvement on Europe's rulers; and the advance in knowledge encouraged by the competitive emulation of the American states were among the beneficial results they saw as resulting from the independence of the colonies.[14]

Those optimistic forecasts, however, were from the beginning tempered by recognition of the difficulty of creating a truly independent American system that could maintain its neutrality in the wars of Europe. That "union and independence" would be their motto and their great desideratum of policy was an idea that occurred to most whigs at the outset of independence. Independence meant, above all, their common freedom from British rule and the avoidance of dependence on the wars and politics of Europe; union meant, above all, the reconciliation of difference so as to achieve the classic aims of the federative system—peace among the several states in the union of the empire, preparedness against and immunity from the wiles and threats of foreign powers. From the beginning these imperatives were joined at the hip. They were, at the same time, aspiration and not fact. While union and independence were in one sense mutually supportive, weakness in the one gnawed at the foundations of the other. During the war, the weakness of the union continually threatened the objective of in-dependence, and the practical dependency on foreign assistance threatened to undermine the union. After the war, the inability of the union to secure compliance in the states with the treaty of peace made almost nugatory the achievement of the negotiators and seemed to put it in the power of any state to implicate the others in effective postures that might end in war and break the union.

The mutual dependence of union and independence suggests that the customary separation of constitutional and diplomatic questions in the history of this era needs to be rethought. If the mental image with which we approach the constitutional era is that of a nation struggling to find its way in a hostile world, that customary separation of the constitutional and diplomatic realms makes a certain kind of sense. If, on the other hand, we see an American system of states inside a larger system of states, each of them needing but impatient under the restraints of law, each of them strongly affected by parochialism and the belligerent defense of particular interests, each of them needing checks and balances against overbearing power, it seems apparent that the "foreign" and "domestic" spheres were so closely entangled as to be virtually inseparable in practice. When John Adams said that "[j]ealousies and rivalries have been my theme, and checks and balances as their antidotes, till I am ashamed to repeat the words," he described his diplomatic outlook as much as his constitutionalism.[15] It was not only in their elaboration of the bases of security and in the principles of foreign policy that Americans found themselves considering the rights and duties of states; they did so as well in their consideration of the union. "We are not working on the natural rights of men not yet gathered into society," minuted Edmund Randolph to himself during the federal convention, "but upon those rights, modified by society, and interwoven with what we call the rights of states." Randolph was right: that is exactly what they were "working on."[16]

The emphasis on both constitutionalism and diplomacy makes this work an entry into what may be called the federal interpretation of American history. The word "federal," to be sure, is one that must be used with some caution, since it now carries meanings and connotations distinctly at odds with the understanding of the eighteenth century. In the late twentieth century, the meaning attached to "federalism" is one difficult to disassociate from a strong central government, and the federal idea has almost altogether lost its formerly close association with diplomacy and international order. In its eighteenth-century signification, the case was otherwise. The term "federal" then comprehended constitutionalism and diplomacy alike.

The federative power, as Locke had defined it, concerned those powers of war and peace, of treaty and alliance that commonwealths had need of in their transactions with other states; the formal compacts among equal parties resulting from the exercise of this power—written constitutions, treaties, alliances—were things to which the adjective "federal" might apply. European publicists could speak of the "federal constitution" of Europe as actually existing, and they meant by the term the web of treaties, laws, and restraints that was to govern the relations of civilized states.[17] When Adam Smith called for a "federal union" between Britain and America, he meant a relationship founded on equal respect and mutual interest, and by the explicit renunciation by Britain of her authority over the colonies.[18] In 1776, the word "federal" was poised on the brink of some rather extraordinary perambulations, and what it meant to be a federalist or "federal man" in 1786, 1788, and 1790 varied significantly. The soil from which these changes sprung, however, is not in doubt: it found states bound in compact, treaty, or alliance.

At the root of the federal principle, as then conceived, was the idea of a covenant or *foedus* (its etymological root). This and "synonymous ideas of promise, commitment, undertaking, or obligating, vowing and plighting one's word," as S. Rufus Davis has suggested, were joined together with two other things: "the idea of cooperation, reciprocity, mutuality," and "the need for some measure of predictability, expectation, constancy, and reliability in human relations." As important as these three concepts—of commitment, reciprocity, predictability—are to human relations generally, it was when states and peoples had need of them that the term "federal" was made use of. Today, "internationalism" or "multilateralism" would be used to describe the application of these values to interstate relations. Though those words were unknown to the political vocabulary in the era of the American founding, the phenomenon or aspiration they describe was well known. Statesmen who sought to instantiate such values in the world of states spoke instead of the construction of a "federative system" or a "federal union."[19] That ideal proposed itself as a means of contending with the opposing specters of international anarchy and universal empire, and as offering a solution to the baffling question of how to secure international order in a system of sovereignties prone to collective violence and unilateral action.

4

An Experiment in International Cooperation

JUST AS DELIBERATIONS were getting under way over the terms of confederation in 1776, John Witherspoon of New Jersey placed the American experiment within an internationalist context. He then expressed the hope that "a well planned confederacy among the states of America" might "hand down the blessings of peace and public order to many generations." Though Witherspoon saw this as an immensely difficult undertaking, he affirmed that such progress was indeed possible. "Every body is able to look back to the time in Europe, when the liberal sentiments that now prevail upon the rights of conscience, would have been looked upon as absurd. It is but little above two hundred years"—that is, the time of Machiavelli's Italy—"since that enlarged system called the balance of power, took place; and I maintain, that it is a greater step from the former disunited and hostile situation of kingdoms and states, to their present condition, than it would be from their present condition to a state of more perfect and lasting union."[1] At the conclusion of the federal convention a decade later, the same aspiration was stated by James Wilson. Now at last, claimed Wilson in his celebrated defense of the Constitution, "is accomplished, what the great mind of Henry IV of France had in contemplation, a system of government, for large and respectable dominions, united and bound together in peace, under a superintending head, by which all their differences may be accommodated, without the destruction of the human race!!" The same point was made shortly after the convention by Benjamin Franklin, in a letter to a French friend. "I do not see," wrote Franklin, "why you might not in Europe carry the Project of good Henry the 4th into Execution, by forming a Federal Union and One Grand Republick of all its different States and Kingdoms, by means of a like convention, for we had many different Interests to reconcile."[2]

These comments invite us to view the making of the union as an experiment in international cooperation, as a working out, under the novel conditions and circumstances of North America, of the peace plan tradition in European thought. The paradigm shift that Witherspoon described—from balance of power to federal union—conveys a world of meaning and experience intensely relevant to this generation. It suggests that the American founders saw themselves and their experiment in close relationship—indeed, as essentially coterminous—with that stream of speculation on the great problems of international peace that had preoccupied the makers of Europe's various "peace plans" from Dante to Rousseau, a search that was usually understood, by those who conducted it, as an inquiry into the "federal constitution" of Europe. The founders understood that the space over which their own experiment in federal union might reach was that of a world equal to, if not indeed greater than, the whole European system; and they were as a consequence keenly aware of the powerful forces that might smash it to pieces. That the founders put themselves in that tradition of European internationalism means that we should put them there as well. In fact, however, this way of understanding their purpose and predicament has—with a few outstanding exceptions—been virtually ignored in the last fifty years of writing on the constitutional era. That neglect is reciprocated in the histories of European internationalism—of the law of nations and the peace plans—which give almost no attention to American developments prior to the twentieth century, as if the great current of European internationalism had never touched American shores.[3]

One reason for the neglect of this discourse is that it has seemed unreal to a great many writers. Powerfully entrenched are a set of historical judgments that make the questions raised in the unionist paradigm seem irrelevant or inconsequential:

1. In constitutional interpretation, the orthodoxy of the last fifty years has been that "a national government was in operation before the formation of the states," that the Continental Congress was organized "with the consent of the people acting directly in their primary, sovereign capacity," and that the union was "spontaneously formed by the people of the United States." The states, according to this view, did not create the union; instead, "the separate States, possessing a limited or internal sovereignty," were "a creation of the Continental Congress, which preceded them in time and brought them into being."[4]

2. The drama of the federal constitution is still largely seen as posing the issue of aristocracy or democracy, and widely accepted is Gordon Wood's view that the focus of the Federalists "was not so much on the politics of the Congress as it was on the politics of the states." "More than anything else," Wood writes, "the Federalists' obsession with disorder in American society and politics accounts for the revolutionary nature of the nationalist proposals offered by men like Madison in 1787 and for the resultant Federalist Constitution." "It was certainly not the defects of the Articles of Confederation" that caused Federalists to speak of a "critical period."[5]

3. Twentieth-century historians writing in the consensus, pluralist, and Progressive schools have predominantly questioned the importance of sectional factors in explaining the antagonisms within the Continental Congress or the federal convention, serving to render inexplicable (save as clever propaganda) the Federalist prediction of a split into two or three confederacies in the event the Constitution were rejected.[6]

4. The customary way of writing about the era sees a structure of identities that has made loyalty to "the nation" primary. Whereas nineteenth-century historians were impressed by the fragility of the nation and stressed that America had "drifted, almost unconsciously, into nationality," most historians writing in the twentieth century have treated "the new nation" born in 1776 as a kind of fixed and unchallengeable essence. Progressives and neo-whigs, realists and revisionists, consensus historians and pluralists, liberals and republicans nearly all seem to concur in that point, however much they differ in other respects.[7]

In my view, each of these mutually supporting judgments is "a revision in need of revising," and I shall criticize them in the following chapters. Their prevalence, however, has made and continues to make it difficult to see the Constitution as an experiment in international cooperation or as a peace pact.[8]

American nationalism has existed as a living force since Patrick Henry exclaimed in 1774 that "the distinctions between Virginians, Pennsylvanians, New Yorkers and New Englanders are no more! I am not a Virginian, but an American!"[9] The questions are not whether such sentiments and loyalties were felt but how strong they were; the kind of relationship they had to the other loyalties that also undoubtedly existed; and how this structure of loyalties and identities changed over time. The sense of homogeneity inseparable from our idea of nationalism was not missing at the outset of independence: American whigs had a keen sense that their political principles set them apart from Europe; they spoke (for the most part) a common language, and they knew the safety and independence of each colony were vitally dependent on the union. But if these things held in common were necessary elements in the forging of a national identity, they were not by themselves sufficient. As John Adams noted in 1775, "The Characters of Gentlemen in the four New England colonies, differ as much from those in the others, as that of the Common People differs, that is as much as several distinct Nations almost." Adams dreaded the "Consequences of this Disimilitude of Character" and worried that "without the Utmost Caution on both sides, and the most considerate Forbearance with one another and prudent Condescention on both sides, they will certainly be fatal." States and sections that differed "as much as several distinct Nations almost" is a very exact way of putting the matter, and it made highly problematic the establishment of a secure national identity. "The colonies," as Adams recalled in 1818, "had grown up under constitutions so different, there was so great a variety of religions, they were composed of so many different nations, their customs, manners, and habits had so little resemblance, and their intercourse had been so rare, and their knowledge of each other so imperfect, that to unite them in the same principles in theory and the same system of action, was certainly a very difficult enterprise."[10]

So it proved to be from 1776 to 1787. The war not only created a sense of nationalism but also confirmed the distinctive interests and deep-rooted particularism of the several states. More ominously, it produced on a wide range of continental issues fundamentally different perspectives in the southern and the eastern states. New England and the South were indeed sufficiently different from one another—as different as Russia and Turkey, said one observer—that they constituted the core of alternate confederacies or nations. Neither region wished for a separate national identity, but forming a durable union out of these heterogeneous materials often seemed from 1776 to 1787 to be a virtually hopeless enterprise. If the union was at risk, so too was the nation, for everyone saw that if they were to be a nation they had to have the union. Indeed, in a critical sense the nation *was* the union, and it could neither see nor hear nor act—could, in short, do nothing—without the machinery the union afforded. But the union was as much a question as a fact, an aspiration conjoined to a speculative theorem. It lived and breathed in crisis and demonstrated the adage that for confederacies at war the simplest things are difficult. Like a troubled marriage, it held together at critical moments not from joy of cohabitation but from fear of the grim prospects of a divorce.

It was a sort of axiom in eighteenth-century political science that "the human affections, like solar heat, lose their intensity, as they depart from the center, and become languid, in proportion to the expansion of the circle, on which they act." Alexander Hamilton, who made that observation to the New York ratifying convention, was himself a nationalist, probably more so than any other American of his generation. Birthed in the West Indies and schooled to a continental perspective by his service in the army, Hamilton lacked the intense local attachments of native-born provincials. He espied, as few others did, a vision of national greatness. At the same time, Hamilton was the last man to depreciate the power and weight of state loyalties and sectional interests in the political circumstances he confronted, attachments that persisted well after the making of the federal constitution. Describing the general sentiment of congress in 1792, where he sat as a representative of Massachusetts, Fisher Ames lamented that "instead of feeling as a Nation, a State is our country. We look with indifference, often with hatred, fear, and aversion to the other States." This "habit of thinking," he judged, was far more important than "change in forms. We have paper enough blotted with theories of government."[11]

That habit of thinking and the other considerations I have adduced justify us in considering the making of the union and the Constitution to be an experiment in international cooperation, albeit one that produced, in some senses, a nation. They also enable us to see, in a way that the literature on liberalism and republicanism does not, what was most original in American thought in the era of revolution and constitution-making. The ideas concerning political, civil, and religious liberty associated with the American Revolution were not, for the most part, sudden discoveries of 1776 but an invigoration of principles and ideas long embedded in colonial thought and experience. When the reform program of George Grenville was still but a gleam in his eye, the colonists already believed themselves in possession of the essentials of self-government. Given the parlous condition of the royal governors in most of the colonies, the revolt against the king required no fundamental reorientation in the basics of constitutional thought. Though the struggle over Pennsylvania's 1776 constitution was protracted and bitter, Pennsylvania was not representative: neither its unicameral legislature nor its highly illiberal test oath typified constitutional practice in the other states. Representative government, the rule of law, bicameral legislatures, independent judiciaries, and the role of government as a vindicator of individual rights were already embedded in the tradition of English constitutionalism, and on this score American thought had a fairly straightforward task of adaptation. It required no great leap to substitute republican executives for royally appointed governors or to conceive a regime of separated executive, legislative, and judicial powers, checked and balanced against one another, instead of the mixture of social estates found in the English constitution. A host of republican writers had treated of the subject, and there were lots of useful precedents as a stimulus to thought and action.[12]

Altogether different was the case of the union. Whereas the challenge of establishing constitutional government in the states might find a host of useful precedents, no such fund of practical experience or theoretical speculation existed for creating a stable system of cooperation on a continent "divided into so many sovereign and independent communities." The precedent closest to home was the extended polity of the British Empire, and the drafting of the confederation in 1776 and 1777 had in critical respects flowed directly from the understanding of the imperial constitution the colonists developed in the decade before 1776. Trouble was, that ungainly structure—which transferred a limited monarchical authority to the Continental Congress—had barely worked during the war and by 1787 had clearly broken down. Nor were the philosophers of much help. The long line of ancient and modern thinkers who had probed the foundations of balanced government—Aristotle, Polybius, and Cicero among the ancients, Machiavelli, Harrington, Montesquieu, and Locke among the moderns—had virtually nothing to say on the question of how a multitude of commonwealths might concert their common action. Montesquieu's few observations on the subject, though tantalizing, stated an intelligible goal— a *république fédérative* should somehow combine the force of a monarchy with the freedom and independence of the small republic—but left obscure the means of reaching it. Pufendorf and Althusius grappled with the question in their speculations on what held together the ungainly mass of the Holy Roman Empire, but neither writer was readily translatable—either literally or figuratively—to the new republican environment of North America. No more adaptable were the succession of thinkers—Sully, Crucé, Penn, St. Pierre, and Rousseau—who had examined the peace problem on a continental scale. However laudable their ambition, none of their plans had been reduced to practice. Europe's catechism was instead the balance of power, and on the old continent there were formidable obstacles to the establishment of any system that had perpetual peace as its aim. Practical speculation had long since turned away from political unity and sought progress through a legal order where peace was an obligation and war a frequent occurrence. In framing a united government over distinct and widely separated communities, the founders were left "almost without precedent or guide."

PART TWO
The Lessons of History

5

An Age of Inquiry

THAT THE FOUNDING FATHERS sought conscientiously to digest the lessons of history has always been recognized; that they drew from an extraordinary range of sources is equally apparent. It was "a peculiar moment in history," as Gordon Wood has remarked of the outpouring of speculation that coincided with the onset of the American Revolution, "when all knowledge coincided, when classical antiquity, Christian theology, English empiricism, and European rationalism could all be linked. Thus Josiah Quincy, like other Americans, could without any sense of incongruity cite Rousseau, Plutarch, Blackstone, and a seventeenth-century Puritan all on the same page."[1] The eighteenth century was a great age of inquiry; few doubted that it had brought remarkable advances in every area of human understanding, touching even to all religious verities. Americans of this generation approached this outpouring of speculation with relish, and it was with no dyspeptic air, and no consciousness of fulfilling a dreary task, that they conducted their researches. They felt themselves to be in great need of the understanding it might bring them. The importance of doing so could not be doubted: "The system of Henry IV to unite Europe as a Republic," said Wilson, "had trifling Objects to those we are now engaged in attaining." The "happiness of *the Globe*" was involved in it.[2] Thus driven by a kind of felt necessity, they opened themselves to a stream of speculation remarkable for its depth and breadth; with precious few schools, there was much schooling.

It is a famous saying of William James, apropos the American people, that "[a]ngelic impulses and predatory lusts divide our hearts exactly as they divide the heart of other countries."[3] Chief among these angelic impulses in the founding generation were the diligent researches they conducted into history, law, and philosophy. Their materials were those that John Adams once prescribed for the education of an American foreign minister: he needed "an education in classical learning, and in the knowledge of general history, ancient and modern, and particularly the history of France, England, Holland, and America. He should be well versed in the principles of ethics, of the law of nature and nations, of legislation and government, of the civil Roman law, of the laws of England and the United States, of the public law of Europe, and in the letters, memoirs, and histories of those great men, who have heretofore shone in the diplomatic order, and conducted the affairs of nations, and the world."[4] Adams was describing a corpus of knowledge that he knew well, but there were many others who knew almost as much as he did in that vein of learning. The founders digested and made comprehensible to their countrymen the lessons taught in this body of knowledge, an inheritance that subsequent generations received with gratitude. The debt of those epigones was well conveyed by George Bancroft in a 1866 eulogy of the life and character of Abraham Lincoln. Writing of the America of the founders, Bancroft held that "[f]rom whatever there was of good in the systems of former centuries she drew her nourishment; the wrecks of the past were her warning. The wisdom which had passed from India through Greece, with what Greece had added of her own; the jurisprudence of Rome; the mediæval municipalities; the Teutonic method of representation; the political experience of England; the benignant wisdom of the expositors of the law of nature and of nations in France and Holland, all shed on her their selectest influence. She washed the gold of political wisdom from the sands wherever it was found; she cleft it from the rocks; she gleaned it among ruins."[5] This well conveys, I think, the spirit of the undertaking for an Adams or a Madison. Bancroft's estimate of what those influences were is also notable, for it differs substantially from the enumerations that have become customary in recent historiography. We find in this passage no battle of paradigms between Locke and Harrington, save as that is suggested by "the political experience of England." A broader range of influences is suggested.

In one sense, it seems almost hopeless to raise the question of intellectual influence; to do so is to enter a boundless sea of endless speculation. In the first instance, at least, it would seem more profitable to ask, not "Who constituted the greatest influence on the outlook of these early Americans?" but "What were the historical analogies that seemed most relevant to their situation?" To pose the question this way invites an inquiry rather different from that which intellectual historians are accustomed to make. But it is only to suggest that before there can be influence, there must be analogy; before another writer's voice is registered and made one's own, he must be speaking to circumstances roughly parallel to those with which the historical actor believes himself to be confronted. The founders are unusual in history because they were both thinkers and actors—the closest thing yet on this earth to Plato's fabled vision of philosopher kings. How did they make use of the past?

The preceding description of the "unionist paradigm" suggests a plausible way into this subject. When the framers gathered at Philadelphia in the late spring of 1787, they stood high atop a ridge, on either side of which there lay an imposing and dangerous abyss. On one side was "empire," "consolidation," "despotism," "centralization"; on the other, "anarchy," "dissolution," "chaos," "disintegration." These words were not simply abstractions; they carried historical resonance. In the broadest sense, they were suggestive of an unresolved predicament in Western civilization, one that had arisen in antiquity, had assumed a new shape in the Europe that emerged from the medieval period, and had managed to migrate across the Atlantic and to form a vital part of the controversy that had led to the disruption of the British Empire and the experiment in union that had been launched with the Articles of Confederation. The predicament stemmed from the fact that the experience of neither ancient nor modern European politics, nor indeed the thirty-year experience through which they had themselves just passed, suggested any stable resolution.

Both at the time and subsequently, the purpose of the enterprise was seen as requiring the achievement of something called "ordered liberty." The order they were looking to constitute, however, was an "imperial" order, one that would unfold over an "amazing extent of country," embracing within it an extraordinary variety of interests, peoples, and ways of life; the liberty they wished to preserve was not simply individual liberty, though that was recognized by nearly all as a fundamental political value, but the "liberty of states." They needed to find a via media between "*imperium et libertas,* which Nerva was deified for reconciling,"[6] yet to do so in circumstances where there existed only precedents to be avoided, not examples to be imitated.

6

Greece and Rome

THE EDUCATION OF AMERICANS still began with the classics and would continue to do so for several generations to come. The experience of Greece and Rome had a closeness, a relevance, for early Americans that is difficult to recapture but is everywhere apparent—in their choice of pseudonyms, in the allusions sprinkled lavishly throughout their writings, and in the colonnades, porticoes, domes, and balustrades that came to dot their landscape.[1] If one were to summarize, in the briefest of terms, the political lesson they drew from antiquity, it would be that Greece destroyed itself by falling victim to the forces of disintegration and anarchy, and that Rome corrupted itself through territorial expansion and military conquest. "It is impossible," remarked Hamilton, "to read the history of the petty republics of Greece and Italy without feeling sensations of horror and disgust at the distractions with which they were continually agitated, and at the rapid succession of revolutions by which they were kept in a state of perpetual vibration between the extremes of tyranny and anarchy."[2]

There was much to admire, to be sure, in the thought and experience of these Grecian commonwealths, and one might indeed thrill to "the momentary rays of glory" that broke forth "from the gloom," or be dazzled by the "transient and fleeting brilliance" of the "bright talents and exalted endowments" that were, in Hamilton's age, "justly celebrated." Certainly there was much to admire in the repulse of the bid for universal dominion made by Xerxes, who had wished to "so extend the empire of Persia that its boundaries will be God's own sky" and who thought that "there is not a city or nation in the world which will be able to withstand us, once these are out of the way." The Greeks had performed that valiant service against overbearing power, as Herodotus explained, by the formation of a union in defense of their liberty.[3] Subsequent experience after the repulse of the Persians, however, was not so kind. The great war chronicled by Thucydides showed that unity could not be maintained, and its devastating outcome prepared the ground for subsequent foreign domination. That the division of America would render foreign domination inevitable was an inescapable deduction from the experience of the Greek city-states; Federalists were acutely conscious of "the danger of having the same game played on our confederacy by which Philip managed that of the Grecian state," and of be-

36

coming, like Greece, "an infinity of little, jealous, clashing, tumultuous commonwealths, the wretched nurseries of unceasing discord and the miserable objects of universal pity or contempt." When Americans unfolded the logic between internal division and foreign domination, and saw in "union and independence" the remedy for what ailed them, the experience of Greece was continually recalled. That it had occurred two millennia before was of no matter; the experience, though distant in time, was close in memory and significance.[4]

In important respects, to be sure, the prospects of the American states were better than those of ancient Greece. From the beginning of the Revolution, Americans insisted on the distinction, in Benjamin Constant's later formulation, between the liberty of the ancients and the liberty of the moderns. Richard Henry Lee put the case plainly in his renowned speech on behalf of American independence in 1776: "If so many and distinguished praises have always been lavished upon the generous defenders of Greek and of Roman liberty, what will be said of us who defend a liberty which is founded not upon the capricious will of an unstable multitude, but upon immutable statutes and tutelary laws; not that which was the exclusive privilege of a few patricians, but that which is the property of all; not that which was stained by iniquitous ostracisms, or the horrible decimation of armies, but that which is pure, temperate and gentle, and comformed to the civilization of the present age."[5] In *Federalist* No. 9, Hamilton made a similar distinction, noting the great improvement that had been made since antiquity in "the science of politics." The ancients knew little or nothing about the separation of powers, checks and balances, the principle of representation, or of independent judiciaries; armed with these "wholly new discoveries," the American states enjoyed much better prospects for successful republican government.

Hamilton attributed the cause of the "frequent revolutions and civil broils with which [the Grecians] were distracted" to the unwillingness of the people, having originally been governed by kings, to surrender "out of their own hands a competent authority, to maintain the repose and stability of the commonwealth." This same "JEALOUSY OF POWER" existed in America, he had written in 1781, but there every power was "exercised by representation, not in tumultuary assemblies of the collective body of the people." Notwithstanding their "imperfections," the state constitutions of America might therefore "operate in such a manner, as to answer the purposes of the common defence and the maintenance of order; and they seem to have, in themselves, and in the progress of society among us, the seeds of improvement." But if the "evil" was "perhaps . . . not very great" with respect to the state constitutions, the case was far otherwise with respect to "the FŒDERAL GOVERNMENT." "The ambition and local interests of the respective members, will be constantly undermining and usurping upon its prerogatives, till it comes to a dissolution; if a partial combination of some of the more powerful ones does not bring it to a more SPEEDY and VIOLENT END." In Greece, this "want of a solid fœderal union to restrain the ambition and rivalship of the different cities" had ended, "after a rapid succession of bloody wars, . . . in their total loss of liberty and subjugation to foreign powers." In America it was likely to do the same.[6]

If the history of Greece foretold the awful fate that awaited a divided America, the history of Rome held out the opposite lesson; it was a case study of the perils of conquest and the thirst for imperial and despotic rule over distant provinces. All throughout the Revolution the charge had been rung against Great Britain that its aspirations for the colonies were equivalent to those of the "plundered and spoiled" provinces conquered by the Romans in the "one hundred years before Caesar's dictatorship."[7] Anti-Federalists rang the same charge in the debates over the Constitution. It required no great imagination to trace the connection between great size and despotism, to see why empire meant both the exploitation of subjects and the loss of republican liberty, to espy the fatal sequence by which Caesar had crossed the Rubicon and seized the purple. The Roman experience was evoked continually by the Anti-Federalists, who spoke often of "crossing the Rubicon" as they set out their objections to the new Constitution. "Brutus," one of the most adept of Anti-Federalist pamphleteers, was only replaying the role of his forebear in seeking, as the self-appointed executioner of his country's vengeance, to plunge his sword into the instrument that threatened his country's liberty. "History furnishes no example," he wrote, "of a free republic, any thing like the extent of the United States." When Rome and other ancient republics had become too large, they had become "the most tyrannical that ever existed in the world."[8] That Rome showed the equation between "consolidation," great size, and "despotism" was a lesson that Federalists could not, and did not, deny. They deflected it, however, by pointing to the liberty and independence that the states would retain under the new Constitution, and by showing that there was, after all, more than one route to despotic institutions. The contrasting experiences of Greece and Rome, so often recalled during the debates over the new Constitution, would continue to exercise a powerful influence over the minds of Americans throughout the whole duration of federal union; the perils that they respectively embodied—those of despotic consolidation and anarchic decentralization—remaining as a standing travel guide to the route by which America's republican liberty might be fatally compromised. "Recollect," said Senator Richard M. Johnson of Kentucky during the debates over the Missouri crisis in 1820, that "Greece was destroyed by division, and Rome by consolidation. Then let us be content with our inheritance, and profit by their example; lest, in our zeal to perform what we cannot accomplish, we one day become what Greece and Rome now are."[9]

7

Universal Monarchy and the Balance of Power: The View from the Eighteenth Century

IT WAS NOT ONLY the contrasting experience of Greece and Rome that conveyed important historical lessons for the Americans of 1787. The whole history of the modern European state system did so as well. Not surprisingly, James Madison gave the most trenchant historical analysis among the founders of the forces at work in that system. Defending the "INDEFINITE POWER" of raising standing forces in peace as well as in war, Madison observed that such a grant of power was dispensable only on the absurd supposition that "we could prohibit in like manner the preparations and establishments of every hostile nation." But the whole history of international relations demonstrated that if one nation raised up outsized military forces, its neighbors were obliged to take similar precautions. Such had been the experience of Europe since the early 1400s, when Charles VII of France had introduced standing military forces in time of peace. "All Europe has followed, or been forced to follow, the example. Had the example not been followed by other nations, all Europe must long ago have worn the chains of a universal monarch. Were every nation except France now to disband its peace establishment, the same event might follow." The same dynamic would inevitably play itself out in North America in the event of disunion: "The fears of the weaker, and the ambition of the stronger States, or Confederacies, will set the same example in the new as Charles VII did in the old world." They would arm for their protection. Modern European governments had taken to heart the lesson from antiquity, when "the veteran legions of Rome were an over-match for the undisciplined valor of all other nations, and rendered her mistress of the world." Madison had no intention of denigrating that resistance: "universal monarchy" appeared to him, as it did to all other Americans of his era, as a synonym for terrible despotism, hardly better than the "oriental despotisms" that Enlightenment thinkers were wont to ridicule. But the predicament for all states, and particularly for free states, was scarcely resolved by the recognition that resistance was demanded to the ambitious monarchs who aspired to the palm of universal empire: "not the less true is it that the liberties of Rome proved the final victim to her military

40

triumphs; and that the liberties of Europe, as far as they ever existed, have, with few exceptions, been the price of her military establishments."[1]

Madison's analysis in this passage is recognizably modern; in it are clearly stated the two central themes that have run "like a red skein" throughout the history of American reflection on the modern state system, and that are central to the unionist paradigm.[2] On the one hand, there is the danger that "universal empire" would extinguish the liberty and independence of states; on the other hand, the no less pronounced worry that the necessary resistance to this danger would entail the acquisition of institutions—standing armies, powerful executives, enormous debts and taxes—that would destroy "liberty" through a different route. The same polarity, expressive of a fundamental predicament, that informed the American understanding of the lessons held out by antiquity, and by the contrasting experiences of Greece and Rome, also informed the American understanding of the modern European system. Neither universal monarchy, whose aspirants promised peace and order yet whose inordinate power would inevitably degenerate into despotism, nor the balance of power system, which maintained "the liberties of Europe" in one sense (the independence of states) but had destroyed them in another, offered a resolution.

Madison's account of the emergence of the European state system closely followed in most respects that of the Scottish historian William Robertson, as well known in his day as David Hume or Adam Smith. "Universal monarchy" and the balance of power were the two fundamental poles in Robertson's *History of the Reign of the Emperor Charles the Fifth*.[3] Like Madison, Robertson dated the emergence of that system from the introduction by Charles VII of France of a "body of troops, kept constantly on foot, and regularly trained to military subordination." Such a standing army, Robertson noted, "was so repugnant to the genius of feudal policy, and so incompatible with the privileges and pretensions of the nobility, that during several centuries no monarch was either so bold or so powerful as to venture on any step towards introducing it." Charles VII, flush from victory over the English, "and taking advantage of the impressions of terror which such a formidable enemy had left upon the minds of his subjects," at last did so, an event that "occasioned an important revolution" in the affairs and policy of Europe. By forming "the first standing army known in Europe," a "deep wound was given to the feudal aristocracy." With it, France "acquired such advantages over its neighbors, either in attack or defence, that self-preservation made it necessary for them to imitate its example. Mercenary troops were introduced into all the considerable kingdoms on the continent. They gradually became the only military force

that was employed or trusted." Charles VII was not only the first to introduce a standing army; he was also the "first monarch of France who by his
royal edict, without the concurrence of the states-general of the kingdom,
levied an extraordinary subsidy on his people. He prevailed likewise with
his subjects to render several taxes perpetual which had formerly been imposed occasionally and exacted during a short time." Standing armies and
perpetual taxes—no eighteenth-century republican could doubt the significance of this military revolution.[4]

The military revolution introduced by Charles VII at the beginning of the
fifteenth century found its logical terminus in the diplomatic revolution
begun by Charles VIII at century's end. His expedition into Italy in 1494
was "the first great exertion of those new powers which the princes of Europe had acquired and now began to exercise." It "occasioned revolutions
no less memorable; produced alternations, both in the military and political system, which were more immediately perceived; roused the states of
Europe to bolder efforts, and blended their affairs and interests more
closely together." Charles at first met with no resistance, but the Italians
"quickly perceived that no single power which they could rouse to action
was an equal match" for such a powerful monarch, "but that a confederacy might accomplish what the separate members of it durst not attempt,"
and to this expedient they had recourse. The success of this confederacy in
forcing the return of Charles to France "instructed the princes and statesmen of Italy as much as the eruption of the French had disconcerted and
alarmed them. They had extended, on this occasion, to the affairs of Europe, the maxims of that political science which had hitherto been applied
only to regulate the operations of the petty states in their own country.
They had discovered the method of preventing any monarch from rising to
such a degree of power as was inconsistent with the general liberty, and had
manifested the importance of attending to that great secret in modern policy, the preservation of a proper distribution of power among all the members of the system." During all the subsequent wars in Italy, "the
maintaining a proper balance of power between the contending parties became the great object of attention to the statesmen of Italy. Nor was the
idea confined to them. Self-preservation taught other powers to adopt it. It
grew to be fashionable and universal. From this era we can trace the
progress of that intercourse between nations which has linked the powers
of Europe so closely together, and can discern the operation of that provident policy which during peace guards against remote and contingent dangers, and in war has prevented rapid and destructive conquests."[5]

Rooted in Robertson's celebration of the balance of power was a detestation of "universal monarchy." That detestation, to which a wide range of

voices in the eighteenth century gave expression, was not a discovery of the Enlightenment. The main features of the critique of "Monarchia Universalis" were advanced by a remarkable group of Spanish writers, including Vitoria, Las Casas, and Soto, two centuries earlier.[6] These views, though not representative of opinion at the Spanish court, had become conventional opinion by the eighteenth century. So convinced was Vattel of the necessity of avoiding concentrations of power that would deliver "all Europe into servitude" that he authorized, in certain circumstances, preventive war to avert the danger.[7] Fénelon had come to the same conclusion: even supposing that a particular succession or donation was lawful, one that threatened to set up a universal monarchy "can be no other than unjust" and could "never prevail over the sovereign and universal law of nature for the common security and liberty, engraven in the hearts of all the nations of the world." Such power would inevitably be abused; a prince that did not do so would be "the ornament of history, and a prodigy not to be looked for again."[8] Gibbon, too, found that "the division of Europe into a number of independent states . . . is productive of the most beneficial consequences to the liberty of mankind. A modern tyrant, who should find no resistance either in his own breast or in his people, would soon experience a gentle restraint from the example of his equals, the dread of present censure, the advice of his allies, and the apprehension of his enemies." Far otherwise, thought Gibbon, was the case when "the empire of the Romans filled the world": "when that empire fell into the hands of a single person, the world became a safe and dreary prison for his enemies."[9] Hume believed resistance to any power "formidable to the liberties of Europe" to be just and necessary; "the maxim of preserving the balance of power is founded so much on common sense and obvious reasoning" that it could not have escaped antiquity; the burden of his essay "Of the Balance of Power" was the demonstration that ancient writers and statesmen had made refinements on this principle as extensive as those "that ever entered into the head of a Venetian or English speculatist." Montesquieu doubted that Louis XIV, accused "a thousand times . . . of having formed and pursued the project of universal monarchy," had really done so; but had the Sun King been successful in the pursuit of that objective, Montesquieu held, "nothing would have been more fatal to Europe, to his first subjects, to himself, and to his family."[10] That universal monarchy threatened fundamental interests and values was acknowledged by all; and so thoroughly had the repugnance of it entered into European speculation that even the aspirants to it were normally to be found denying that any such intention had ever entered into their heads. Their reply, and defense, was simply to charge that malignant aim upon those powers who had made the accusation against them. By the

1740s, if not earlier, the charge and countercharge that was to be so characteristic of the subsequent history of the European system—with Britain and her allies charging upon their enemies the objective of "universal empire," and those same enemies charging upon Great Britain the objective of an atrocious maritime dominion that necessitated a continental bloc in opposition to the "tyrant of the ocean"—had become routine in political discourse.

Universal empire, however, was not just thought dangerous; it was, by the best writers, also considered as unnatural and artificial. "There is nothing more contrary to nature than the attempt to hold in obedience distant provinces," Gibbon declared, and he was joined in this perception by a host of others.[11] "Enormous monarchies," Hume wrote, "are, probably, destructive to human nature; in their progress, in their continuance, and even in their downfall, which never can be very distant from their establishment." Hume traced out, as had Montesquieu, a natural process by which aggrandizement turned on itself: "Thus human nature checks itself in its airy elevation: Thus ambition blindly labours for the destruction of the conqueror, of his family, and of every thing near and dear to him."[12] Rousseau reached a conclusion very similar to that of Hume: "[I]f the princes who are accused of aiming at universal monarchy were in reality guilty of any such project, they gave more proof of ambition than of genius. How could any man look such a project in the face without instantly perceiving its absurdity . . . ?" A host of forces operated to frustrate any such attempt: the relative weakness of would-be conquerors in relation to the rest of Europe, the general diffusion of military knowledge and discipline, "the maxims of European policy."[13]

The dismissal of the danger of universal monarchy might be taken as a sign that all was well with the world; such, however, was emphatically not the case. Among a diverse set of thinkers, the remedy for universal monarchy—the balance of power system—was also seen to carry with it a host of pernicious consequences. Though the balance of power might still be held up as a progressive principle in contrast with either the dreaded specter of universal monarchy or the no less distasteful prospect of utter anarchy, and be closely identified with the public law of Europe, there lay alongside this perception considerable anxiety over the operation of the balance in practice.[14] Wrote Montesquieu:

A new disease has spread across Europe; it has afflicted our princes and made them keep an inordinate number of troops. It redoubles in strength and necessarily becomes contagious; for, as soon as one state increases what it calls its troops, the others suddenly increase theirs, so that nothing is gained thereby but the common ruin. Each monarch keeps ready all the armies he would have if his peoples were in danger of being exterminated; and this state in which all strain against all is called peace. Thus Europe is so ruined that if individuals were in the situation of the three most opulent powers in this part of the world, they would have nothing to live on. We are poor with the wealth and commerce of the whole universe, and soon, as a result of these soldiers, we shall have nothing but soldiers and we shall be like the Tartars.[15]

Rousseau gave a second to this judgment as well. If the European system seemed to him unshakable, and the possibility of universal monarchy more ludicrous than dangerous, the system was "for that very reason the more liable to constant storms. Between the powers of Europe there is a constant action and reaction which, without overthrowing them altogether, keeps them in continual agitation. Ineffectual as they are, these shocks perpetually renew themselves, like the waves which forever trouble the surface of the sea without ever altering its level."[16] Hamilton would later describe the European state system in almost identical terms: "The history of war in that quarter of the globe is no longer a history of nations subdued and empires overturned, but of towns taken and retaken, of battles that decide nothing, of retreats more beneficial than victories, of much effort and little acquisition."[17] Both peoples and princes were inevitably ground up in the maws of this system. The result was well summarized by Alexander Pope, whose 1715 couplet said it all:

> Now Europe's balanced, neither side prevails;
> For Nothing's left in either of the scales.[18]

The rejection of universal monarchy in the eighteenth-century republic of letters was thus attended by the somewhat unnerving reflection that the remedy—in the form of the balance of power system—had brought consequences nearly as bad as the disease. No commonwealth, to be sure, could ignore the balance, and indeed Madison would observe in the federal convention that it was to the operation of that principle, in the form of the rivalry between Britain and France, that America owed her liberty.[19] But the larger judgment of the Americans in 1787 reflected the same dour portrait to which enlightened observers had increasingly been drawn during the two great wars of midcentury. Writing anonymously in the *Annual Register,* Edmund Burke commented, "The balance of power, the pride of modern policy, and originally invented to preserve the general peace as well as freedom of Europe, has only preserved its liberty. It has been the original of innumerable and fruitless wars."[20] It was the contrast between the pretended virtues of the balance of power system and the way it subjected Europe to a "reign of violence" that led Rousseau, writing contemporaneously with Burke, to a similar conclusion. In his *Abstract of the Abbé de Saint-Pierre's Project for Perpetual Peace,* Rousseau noted the elements of interdependence among the inhabitants of Europe that made it "a real society." The ease of communications, the rise of a community of knowledge and studies, the complicated ties of commerce that rendered each nation necessary to the others—all had produced in Europe "not merely, as in Asia and Africa, an ideal collection of people, who have nothing in common but a name, but a real society, which has its religion, morals, customs, and even its laws, from which none of the people composing it can separate without causing an immediate disturbance." Far from producing peace, however, the intimacy of their connections had only made their dissensions more fatal:

> To behold . . . the perpetual dissensions, depredations, usurpations, rebellions, wars, and murders, which are constantly ravaging this respectable abode of philosophers, this brilliant asylum of the arts and sciences; to reflect on the sublimity of our conversation and the meanness of our proceedings, on the humanity of our maxims and the cruelty of our actions, on the meekness of our religion and the horror of our persecutions, on a policy so wise in theory and absurd in practice, on the beneficence of sovereigns and the misery of their people, on governments so mild and wars so destructive; we are at a loss to reconcile these strange contrarieties, while this pretended fraternity of European nations appears to be only a term of ridicule, serving ironically to express their reciprocal animosity.[21]

8

Républiques Fédérative *and Machiavellian Moments*

OF ALL THE HISTORICAL analogies that appeared of relevance to the Americans of 1787, probably the most direct were to those modern confederations that had sought to join various states and commonwealths into a union. Italy, Switzerland, Germany, and the Netherlands had all been held together by confederal arrangements of various sorts; they each shared a recognized cultural unity; and they had often found themselves the cockpit of international rivalry.

These precedents were often discussed in the debates in Congress over the terms of confederation, and it was by no means anomalous that John Adams should, in recommending to his son a course of reading, draw attention "above all others" to "the History of the Flemish Confederacy, by which the seven united Provinces of the Netherlands, emancipated themselves from the Domination of Spain."[1] In the early years of the American Revolution, the Dutch experience seemed particularly close, and Adams recurred frequently to the parallel in his correspondence. It had it all: united provinces striving to protect their corporate liberties from a despotic tyrant panting after universal monarchy; the confederates seeking common cause at home and abroad to defeat that nefarious project; a federal government dependent on unanimous consent and voluntary contributions among provinces disparate in size and wealth—hence sometimes prone to breakdown; the danger that not all would make it through the struggle. It was, at the beginning, seen as a source of inspiration and emulation. "It is very similar," wrote Adams, "to the American Quarrell in the Rise and Progress, and will be so in the Conclusion."[2] In a speech on foreign affairs in 1779, John Dickinson justified his principles of conduct by invoking the example "of those great Statesmen and excellent Patriots whose Prudence and Virtue . . . established the Freedom, Sovereignty and Independance of the united provinces of the Low Countries."[3] This positive view, however, became more measured over time. Having formed the Articles of Confederation "on the Dutch model," and having witnessed its severe deficiencies in practice, many Americans began to see negative rather than positive examples in the Dutch experience. Madison drew attention to the fact that the Dutch constitution seemed workable only because its provisions were frequently disregarded by the stadtholder of Holland, the largest province. It

47

was, in any event, the Dutch struggle for liberty rather than the experience of Holland in the eighteenth century that had always been held closest in American thought, and here the parallel often seemed exact. Wrote John Adams to James Burgh, the author of the "invaluable" *Political Disquisitions,* in late 1774: "We are in this Province, Sir, at the Brink of a civil War," beset by "Our Alva, Gage."[4]

One difference that separated the American confederation from all other confederated republics was relative size. "The United States," as Adams noted in 1787, "are large and populous nations in comparison with the Grecian commonwealths, or even the Swiss cantons; and they are growing every day more disproportionate." That comparison was not necessarily favorable to the American states, since their greater size was likely to increase the centrifugal forces tearing at their union. As Adams went on to note, "Countries that increase in population so rapidly as the States of America did, even during such an impoverishing and destructive war as the last was, are not to be long bound with silken threads; lions, young or old, will not be bound by cobwebs."[5]

A second point of difference concerned the character of the "republicanism" that the American states had embraced in the course of their Revolution. A principal theme of Adams's *Defence* of the American constitutions was that the most discerning of those commonwealths, and above all that of Massachusetts, had internal forms that reflected a balance among the three different orders of the community; those governments were animated by the rule of law, and they protected rights to life and property. The governments of Florence, to which Adams devoted long attention in his *Defence,* were by contrast destitute of these qualities. Commenting on "Machiavel's" treatment of the Florentine rebellion against Gaultier, duke of Athens, in which Machiavelli traced the outrages that made the duke's rule "as wild, cruel, and mad as all other tyrannnies have been which were created on the ruins of a republic," Adams criticized Machiavelli's comment that the duke's outrages had roused the Florentines because they "'neither knew how to value their liberty nor to endure slavery.'" In truth, said Adams, "they had no liberty to value, and nothing but slavery to endure; their constitution was no protection of right; their laws never governed. They were slaves to every freak and passion, every party and faction, every aspiring or disappointed noble. . . . If the word *republic* must be used to signify every government in which more than one man has a share, it is true this must be called by that name; but a republic and a free government may be different things." While Adams's views on the best form of government were idiosyncratic in the American context of 1787 (and particularly in his insistence that the three different orders in the community should be "acknowledged in any constitution of government"), his distinction between the republics of "the Italian middle age" or of antiquity and the free governments of America was widely accepted and understood.[6]

Despite these animadversions on the character of the Italian republics, their experience could not but appear as especially poignant to a denizen of the American states. If, after Athens and Rome, there was not "a more interesting city" than Florence, there was no more interesting time in Florentine history than the age of Machiavelli and Guicciardini—two authors, Adams said, "who may be compared to any of the historians of Greece or Rome." That was a city and an age responsible "in a great degree for the resurrection of letters, and a second civilization of mankind." Yet the fair promise of the age had been wrecked in the years that followed the intervention of Charles VIII of France in 1494, a time of troubles that had left in Florence not even "the shadow of a free government."[7]

The contrast between the golden age before 1494 and the stark brutalities and crushing humiliations of the years thereafter had been the great theme in the opening pages of Guicciardini's *History of Italy*. Italy, which before that year had "deservedly held a celebrated name and reputation among all the nations," was plunged thereafter into "the most terrible happenings" and calamities. The Italian commonwealths had been kept in a certain state of balance by Lorenzo de Medici, a condition that "could not be achieved without preserving the peace and without being diligently on the watch against every incident, even the slightest." The intervention of the French king into this well-ordered system—too dependent, it was soon revealed, on the skill and moderation of the recently deceased Lorenzo— "opened the door to innumerable horrible calamities, in which, one could say, for various reasons, a great part of the world was subsequently involved." Charles's entry into Italy "not only gave rise to changes of dominions, subversion of kingdoms, desolation of countries, destruction of cities and the cruelest massacres, but also new fashions, new customs, new and bloody ways of waging warfare, and diseases which had been unknown up to that time." Above all, the French incursion "introduced so much disorder into Italian ways of governing and maintaining harmony, that we have never since been able to re-establish order, thus opening the possibility to other foreign nations and barbarous armies to trample upon our institutions and miserably oppress us."[8]

Historians continue to treat the dividing line of 1494, with Guicciardini, as one of profound significance. In the four decades from the Peace of Lodi in 1454 to the French intervention and Florentine Revolution of 1494, Italy had known a condition of general peace. The 1454 treaty—initially founded on compact among Milan, Florence, and Venice—was seen to offer a framework by which the Italian states might settle disputes among themselves and guard against the intervention of foreign powers. With the subsequent adhesion of Naples, the pope, and lesser Italian states, Italy acquired "a peace-keeping organization that was unique to Europe. Its members pledged that for twenty-five years in the first instance they would respect one another's borders, consult fellow members before taking any military or diplomatic initiative that might threaten the common interest, and maintain a force to be added to those of other members to use against any signatory who broke the terms of the agreement."[9] This common front, precariously but on the whole successfully maintained in the four decades before 1494, was thereafter broken into pieces. The French intervention of 1494, at the instigation of Ludovico Sforza, duke of Milan, was followed by the formation of the League of Venice in 1495, also dependent on the support of foreign powers, a confederation that included among its members the pope, the king of the Romans (Maximilian I), the king of Spain, the Venetians, and the duke of Milan (who by this time, and not for the last time, had switched sides). The disunion of the Italian commonwealths—above all their willingness to call in the aid of foreign powers as a means of furthering their ambition or assuaging their fear—made Italy the cockpit of a European-wide system that now suddenly crystallized, with the four powers of France, Spain, Germany, and England forming an unprecedented constellation of power. The submission of Florence and Rome, the capture of Naples, and the pillaging of the countryside were, as Quentin Skinner has commented, but the first fruits of the disorder. Louis XII, the successor of Charles, "mounted three further invasions, repeatedly attacking Milan and generating endemic warfare throughout Italy. Finally, the greatest disaster of all came when the Emperor Charles V decided in the early 1520s to contest the French control of Milan, a decision which converted the whole of the *Regnum Italicum* into a battlefield for the next thirty years." In all these years of fluctuating fortune, one trend remained constant: "the extension and consolidation of increasingly despotic forms of princely rule."[10]

A view interior to and sympathetic with the Italian experience could hardly draw the conclusion that the balance of power, as it had operated in the affairs of the Peninsula, was the wise and provident system that Robertson had made it out to be. The disunion of the Italian commonwealths, together with the emergence of Italy as the theater of a system that, in its larger balances, now suddenly extended to the whole of western Europe, had placed Italy in the folds of a deadly embrace and showed that the balance of power could have disastrous implications for any country unfortunate enough to be the prize in the struggle. Though Madison did not mention the Italian experience in his summary of the vices of the ancient and modern confederacies, it pointed to the same lesson that he drew from the failure of confederal experiences in Greece and Germany. A tendency toward dissolution, hastened by foreign intrigue and ambition, seemed woven into the inner fabric of these federative systems.[11]

Machiavelli would advise in *The Prince* that only a strongman willing to act decisively and, if necessary, with disregard of conventional legal and moral restraints, could beat the broken states of Italy into some kind of rough union. That was an expedient against which the American states instinctively shuddered—it would be better, remarked Adams, "to ring all the changes with the whole set of bells, and go through all the revolutions of the Grecian states, rather than establish an absolute monarchy among them, notwithstanding all the great and real improvements which have been made in that kind of government."[12] Such, however, was the sense of crisis by the winter of 1786–87 that the comparison began to seem more and more plausible to many observers in America: the press in the eastern states had begun speculating in earnest about a reversion to monarchy and a division of the states into three separate confederacies; Spanish intrigues blossomed in the West (with even Andrew Jackson on the Spanish stipend); some Virginians espied a plot by John Jay to dismember the union in his negotiation ceding use of the Mississippi for twenty-five years to Spain; and in the North, Britain was widely suspected of having a hand in Shays's Rebellion and the prospective independence (outside the American union) of Vermont.[13] Though the American founders were obliged to castigate the idea that the health of republics might be served by the dose of poison that Machiavelli had recommended, they were coming to understand that they stood in danger of duplicating the circumstances that had produced those recommendations.[14] If an American of that generation were told that "the Machiavellian moment," in J. G. A. Pocock's words, denoted "the moment in conceptualized time in which the republic was seen as confronting its own temporal finitude"; and if this mythical American were asked to explain how his republic, or republics, might experience that moment, there can be little doubt that his answer would mark out, in the first instance, this trajectory of internal disunity and external intervention. "The Consequences of a Division of the Continent," wrote Adams in 1787, "cannot be foreseen fully, perhaps by any Man: but the most short sighted must perceive such mannifest danger both from foreign Powers, and from one another as cannot be looked upon, without terror."[15] The fatal link between disunion and foreign domination—first demonstrated among the republics of ancient Greece, and sadly confirmed in the experience of the Italian commonwealths—seemed self-evident to the Federalists, and they repeatedly warned their compatriots to treat these lessons with the utmost gravity.[16]

Many Americans greatly admired Machiavelli as a writer "most favorable to a popular government," who was "even suspected of sometimes disguising the truth to conceal or mollify its defects." But the larger judgment of Machiavelli was far more guarded. "The best part of his writings," Adams observed, "he translated almost literally from Plato and Aristotle, without acknowledging the obligation; and the worst of the sentiments, even in his *Prince,* he translated from Aristotle, without throwing upon him the reproach. Montesquieu borrowed the best part of his book from Machiavel, without acknowledging the quotation. Milton, Harrington, Sidney, were intimately acquainted with the ancients and with Machiavel. They were followed by Locke, Hoadley, &c."[17] This passage is interesting not only as a somewhat crooked commentary on the numerous borrowings in the history of political thought on the theory and practice of the balanced constitution (plagiarists take heart!) but also as placing Machiavelli in a context—emphasizing both the best and the worst of his sentiments—that allows for a more measured view of his significance. While admiring his discernment and his sincere devotion to his native city, and while sharing to a large degree the Florentine's intense distrust of human nature, the consensus of opinion in the late eighteenth century also knew "Machiavellism" as a term of reproach.[18] By that date, indeed, Machiavellism had come to be a subject of regular denunciation even by its most avid practitioners, and Americans were unlikely to be outdone in their disapproval of such wickedness by any European monarch, be he ever so enlightened.[19]

Americans, who saw themselves in significant respects as bearers of a "new diplomacy," and who eagerly embraced the writers on the law of nations like Grotius, Pufendorf, and Vattel, took a dim view of the breaches of faith and unmatched cruelties in the name of reason of state with which Machiavelli's name had, fairly or not, become closely identified. Those atrocities and assassinations formed part of the "dark ages" of European statecraft that, in Jefferson's estimation, had been "exploded and held in just horror in the 18th century."[20] In Henry Wheaton's later assessment: "Unfortunately for [Machiavelli's] own fame, and for the permanent interests of mankind, this masterly writer, in his patriotic anxiety to secure his country against the dangers with which it was menaced from the *Barbarians,* did not hesitate to resort to those atrocious means already too familiar to the domestic tyrants of Italy. The violent remedies he sought to apply for her restoration to pristine greatness were poisons, and his book became the manual of despotism, in which Philip II. of Spain, and Catherine de Medici found their detestable maxims of policy." No Protestant of the eighteenth century would forget the role these maxims had played in the sudden and brutal destruction of French Huguenots in the Saint Bartholomew's Day Massacre. Opposing Machiavelli, Wheaton observed, was Grotius, "whose treatise on the *Laws of Peace and War,* produced a strong impression on the public mind of Christian Europe, and gradually wrought a most salutary change in the practical intercourse of nations in favor of humanity and justice."[21]

As Wheaton indicated, the publicists had indeed made Machiavelli an object of repeated attack, and the great conflict between Grotius and Machiavelli became symbolic of a fundamental division in Western political thought. The American response to this battle among the titans was not unambiguous, for there are various marks of an affinity between Machiavelli's outlook and that of the Americans of 1787. The dark pessimism and historical realism that informed much of the American outlook (and above all in the thought of John Adams and Alexander Hamilton) is certainly Machiavellian in tenor, as is the oft-encountered rallying cry of a return to first principles. Most Americans, too, would probably have accepted the old Roman (and Machiavellian) doctrine of *salus populi suprema lex est.* "A strict observance of the written laws," wrote Jefferson, "is doubtless *one* of the high duties of a good citizen, but it is not the *highest.* The laws of necessity, of self-preservation, of saving our country when in danger, are of higher obligation."[22]

But if these points of contact do exist with Machiavelli, it is also true that in other respects Americans took sides unreservedly with Grotius and his followers. "Machiavellism," certainly, was firmly rejected. The humane expositors of the law of nature and of nations in Holland, France, and Switzerland had, in the American estimation, "held up the torch of science to a benighted world," in the words of Patrick Henry. From 1776 onward, appeal to the law of nature and of nations—and to "these kind instructors of human nature"—was woven closely into the fabric of the American position, and might even be mistaken for *being* the American position. "Ever since we have been an Independent nation," as Hamilton once summarized the question, "we have appealed to and acted upon the modern law of Nations as understood in Europe. Various resolutions of Congress during our revolution—the correspondences of Executive officers—the decisions of our Courts of Admiralty, all recognized this standard." The law of nations set important limits on the exercise of a traditional reason of state. It was founded "by nature" on the principle, in Montesquieu's words, "that the various nations should do to one another in times of peace the most good possible, and in times of war the least ill possible, without harming their true interests." It taught that the mutual recognition of the independence and sovereignty of states was imperative were the system to avoid a war of all against all. It set forth the criteria by which certain wars were adjudged just, and others unjust, and certain means in war permitted, and others placed outside the pale. It dictated the duties that a nation owed to itself (considered primary) and those it owed to others. Crowning this architecture was the conviction, as Hamilton put it, that "faith and justice between nations are virtues of a nature the most necessary and sacred."[23]

The embrace, at independence, of this Grotian (or Vattelian) world was not, it should be emphasized, a heroic act of self-denial. The law of nations, save in unusual circumstances, did not require such self-abnegation. The restraints that it did mandate, in any case, were barriers that mostly favored the interests of the weak confederation among the American states, and were certainly useful in rallying other European powers against the imperious acts of Great Britain. If the embrace of Grotius did not require the repudiation of self-interest, the rejection of Machiavellian remedies could not provide an immunity from the occurrence of Machiavellian moments. In fact, when one considered the life of republics as they had really been in history, unfavorable auguries abounded, and none more so than in the dreadful repetitive sequence by which republics, consumed in internecine strife, and incapable of farsighted cooperation, yield freedom and independence to foreign masters. Time alone could reveal whether Americans could escape that fate, and whether, in attempting to escape it, they could avoid the compounding with evil that Machiavelli had seen as embedded in political life "as it really was."[24]

9

The British Setting: Continental Connections and the Balanced Constitution

THERE IS ONE FINAL CONTEXT that may be considered in this sketch of the historical analogies to which the American mind of 1787 was drawn. Rather close to home, it was provided by the way the concepts of universal monarchy and the balance of power had figured in the wide-ranging debate over "continental connections" and the "mercantile system" that occurred in Great Britain in the eighteenth century. Nearly all the positions in this great debate had been sketched out in the course of the long series of wars against Louis XIV. The pamphlet wars of an earlier era—pitting Jonathan Swift's *The Conduct of Allies,* for example, against the polemical writings of Daniel Defoe in support of Britain's continental strategy—raised questions that would perplex Englishmen throughout the century. The conception of the European system that divided Defoe from Swift, or Marlborough from Bolingbroke, during the War of the Spanish Succession, also set continentalists and anticontinentalists apart during the two great wars of the mid–eighteenth century.

One side, initially identified with the Whigs and Hanoverians, emphasized the reality of the concert and of the public law of Europe the concert was brought into being to defend. It saw a genuine threat to the balance of power from the pretensions of France to "universal monarchy" and believed an active British role was of critical importance in preventing it. Its "legitimating language," as J. G. A. Pocock has well said, was based not only on Britain's role as the organizer of resistance to Spanish and French designs after universal monarchy but also on "its replacement by a concert of Europe held in being through commerce, the balance of power, and the great treaties which had begun with the Peace of Westphalia."[1]

The other side, initially identified with the Tories, was far more skeptical of European involvement and argued that British security would be better provided for through maritime war and extra-European empire. Both outlooks could stress the critical importance of the balance of power—the prevention of dominance by a single power over Europe and its resources—but the latter was more receptive to the view that the balance of power would take care of itself, more disposed to see a conflict of interest with its part-

ners, and given to a keener eye as to the distribution of benefits and burdens within the "grand alliances" that British ministries were perennially
cobbling together. The set speech of the continentalists was that Britain
owed it to her own interest, and to the safety and liberty of Europe, to play
an active role upon the continent; the composite speech of the opposition
ran along different lines: "You, the ministry, aim to take advantage of your
allies, whereas the obvious fact is that they are taking advantage of you.
You claim to be serving both the particular interest of England, and the general interest of Europe; in fact your policy is at war with both. You celebrate
the balance of power, which is admittedly a good thing, but your interventions are either unnecessary, because the balance of power will take care of
itself, or counterproductive, because you are subsidizing the wrong party."[2]

That the safety of Britain required a balance of power on the continent
was a proposition that all sides in the eighteenth-century debate acknowledged. In one of the treaties of Utrecht, in 1713, the balance of power appeared for the first time in a treaty of settlement. In order "to settle and
establish the peace and tranquillity of Christendom, by an equal balance of
power (which is the best and most solid foundation of a mutual friendship,
and of a concord which will be lasting on all sides)," the treaty between
"the Most Serene and Most Potent" Princess Anne of Great Britain and
"the Most Serene and Most Potent" Prince Philip V of Spain stipulated that
the kingdoms of France and Spain should never be united under the same
dominion.[3] English policy was at this time directed by Henry St. John, Viscount Bolingbroke, who had broken from the policy of Marlborough, and
of England's allies on the continent, and made a separate peace with France
and Spain. Bolingbroke's subsequent writings on the balance of power,
mainly in his *Idea of a Patriot King, Letters on the Study and Use of History,* and his contributions to the *Craftsman,* reflected in part the furious
controversy that arose over this action, deemed a stupid treachery by some
and by others as reflecting the "true interest" of Great Britain. That "true
interest," Bolingbroke thought, required acknowledging that Britain, as an
island, need not, like European nations, "watch over every motion of their
neighbours; penetrate . . . every design; foresee every minute event; and
take part by some engagement or other in almost every conjuncture that
arises." Its detached situation invited a different posture, one that made
"the general interest of Europe" the sole desideratum that should "call our
councils off from an almost entire application to their domestick and
proper business." "It may be our interest," he acknowledged, "to watch
the secret workings of the several councils abroad; to advise, and warn; to
abet, and oppose; but it can never be our true interest easily and officiously

to enter into action, much less into engagements that imply action and expense." Britain should look upon "the powers of the continent, to whom we incline, like the two first lines, the principes and hastati of a Roman army: and on ourselves like the triarii, that are not to charge with these legions on every occasion but to be ready for the conflict whenever . . . necessary." Such was "the post of advantage and honour" to which Bolingbroke called England and her "Patriot King": "By a continual attention to improve her natural, that is her maritime strength, by collecting all her forces within herself, and reserving them to be laid out on great occasions, such as regard her immediate interests and her honour, or such as are truly important to the general system of power in Europe; she may be the arbitrator of differences, the guardian of liberty, and the preserver of that balance, which has been so much talked of, and is so little understood."[4]

Bolingbroke's identification of the "true interest" of Great Britain with the "general interest of Europe" was not as implausible as it may at first seem. The proposition was credited by observers who had no motive for exaggerating in this respect; there was, it seemed to many, a happy coincidence that the nation which had, in its own constitution, perfected the mechanisms of balance and equipoise, should have been accorded by nature a status by which it might pursue the same objective in Europe. The two phenomena were in fact related: it was its insular position that spared Britain the necessity of maintaining large standing armies, the curse of free government on the continent. Vattel, after noting that the large standing armies that had arisen in Europe to preserve the balance had also deprived "the soil of cultivators," checked "the growth of population," and could "serve to oppress the liberties of the Nation which maintains them," exclaimed: "Happy England! whose situation relieves her of the necessity of maintaining at great expense the instruments of despotism."[5] Admirers of the British constitution abroad, like Montesquieu and Vattel, together with its celebrants at home, understood that the justifications for the "balanced constitution" in England and the "balance of power" in Europe were, at a certain level of reasoning, identical. Writing in the midst of the War of the Spanish Succession, and on behalf of the Whig policy of continental involvement, Daniel Defoe argued that "Every Power, which over balances the rest, *makes itself a Nuisance* to its Neighbours. *Europe* being divided into a great Variety of separate Governments and Constitutions; the Safety of the whole consists in a due Distribution of Power, so shared to every Part or Branch of Government, that no one may be able to oppress and destroy the rest."[6] The same fear of unchecked power that justified resistance to the Stuarts at home justified resistance to the Bourbons abroad; and it was not

unusual, as Defoe's example suggests, for the language and images associated with the maintenance of the balanced constitution of England to be
employed to justify the maintenance of a balance of power for the "constitution of Europe." The interlocking language of equipoise, stability, and
liberty that men employed in discussions of the British constitution was the
same language they used to describe the European system.[7]

Bolingbroke, a once-neglected figure whom Americans looked upon as
one of the giants of the age, wrote at length about both the balanced constitution and the balance of power. He saw threats to the balanced constitution at home, however, just as he insisted that the policy of the balance
of power in Europe, so wise in theory, had "hardly ever been truly and
wisely pursued." "The principle of our conduct has been right," the manner of pursuing it often wrong. It was right and proper to check the power
of France and to enter, as William did, into a coalition for the maintenance
of the European balance; but his successors erred when, flush with victories, they "judged that the balance of power could not be effectually restored, unless we wrested the whole Spanish monarchy from the house of
Bourbon, to give it to the house of Austria." This was a fatal error, and it
badly confused the true object of British participation. To "set the Imperial and Spanish crowns on the same head" was as much against "the common interest of Europe, and the fundamental principle of the war," as was
the danger that France and Spain, each of whom previously had aimed separately, and in opposition, at universal monarchy, should join together in a
union. "We acted like men who thought that the exorbitant power of one
family could not be reduced, unless a power as exorbitant was raised in another, and who never looked back to preceding centuries to consider the
usurpations, the tyranny, and the bigotry that the house of Austria had exercised in the fulness of her power, and would exercise again if she was ever
restored to the same." Ambition began the war on the side of France but
continued it in the foolish war aims of "the grand alliance."[8]

Such was Bolingbroke's defense of his role in the making of the peace of
Utrecht. Its deficiencies—he acknowledged that there were such, French
power having not been checked as much as was desirable—were attributed
by him to the factious opposition of the Whigs, whose domestic opposition
encouraged the break with Austria and gave France an opening for better
terms. The return to power of the Whigs after the death of Anne left him
in exile, where he took up, briefly, with the pretender; but upon his renunciation of that tie, then punishable as treason, he returned to England in
1723 and began a fabled career of opposition to Walpole and the Whig establishment. By comparison with what came before and after, Walpole's

foreign policy was remarkably pacific; but Bolingbroke and his circle detected in it sinister threats to the true interest of Great Britain and the balance of the constitution. The Glorious Revolution of 1688 had not simply set right the balanced constitution, though in Bolingbroke's estimation it had done that; it had also introduced a set of institutions that, under Whig patronage, constituted a threat to its first principles. For many opponents of continental measures, an active policy in Europe was strongly associated with these interlocking institutions. What Jefferson would later call the "paper system, stockjobbing, speculations, public debt, moneyed interest, etc."[9] expressed one aspect of a transformation that, when it began occurring in the 1690s, and grew in strength thereafter, was thought by the opposition writers to be corrupting the balanced constitution of England. Subsidy treaties with German princes were just a different manifestation of a policy that at home took the form of the artful management of positions, places, and elections—a practice, its defenders said, that was necessary to make the British constitution practicable, but which was thought a corruption of it by the opposition. Domestic institutions and practices were seen as interlocking with foreign policy; they were two peas in a pod. What is meant today by the term "military-industrial complex" is suggestive of what the opposition saw. Standing armies that only a despot could want, and sinking funds that never sunk, were the results of a policy pursued by men "who succeeded to the name rather the principles" of Whiggery.[10]

Bolingbroke's treatment of the balance of power in Europe was not without ambivalence. The principle itself he treated with as much respect as Fénelon; he saw in its proper observance the key to the safety, tranquillity, and prosperity of Europe. It might be suspected that a policy wise in theory that managed invariably to be mangled in practice might not qualify as a great discovery in political science, but Bolingbroke did not draw this conclusion; the right application only awaited a change of ministry, and a better king. There was, nevertheless, in his treatment of the proper lines of British policy a recognition that participation in the interstices of the European system would be fatal to Britain's free institutions, and the whole tenor of his policy was directed toward avoiding those perils if possible.

Bolingbroke's ambivalence toward the balance of power is also reflected in the distinction (drawn by others as well) between the "particular interest" of England and the "general interest of Europe." Though Bolingbroke insisted that the "true interest" of Great Britain was virtually identical with the general interest of Europe, it was the particular interest of Great Britain that he thought ought to be, but had not been, controlling. To adopt a different standard, he said, "would be nothing better than setting up for the

Don Quixotes of the world, and engage to fight the battles of mankind."
The state that kept its own interest in view had "an invariable rule to go
by; and this rule will direct and limit all its proceedings in foreign affairs;
so that such a state will frequently take no share, and frequently a small
share in the disputes of its neighbors, and will never exert its whole
strength, but when its whole is at stake. But a state, who neglects to do this,
has no rule at all to go by, and must fight to negotiate, and negotiate to
fight again, as long as it is a state; because, as long as it is a state, there will
be disputes among its neighbors and some of these will prevail at one time,
and some at another, in the perpetual flux and reflux of human affairs."
This frank acknowledgment of what was primary, and what secondary, in
the proper direction of British policy could only feed suspicions on the continent that the boasted high-mindedness of Great Britain was to be heard
through ears properly attuned to hypocrisy and cant. In Bolingbroke's estimation, nevertheless, the right policy was one that made Britain's "particular interest" wholly in tune with the general interest of Europe. And in
this assumption he differed not one whit from the Whigs.[11]

The ideas that Bolingbroke unfolded became the stock-in-trade of opposition to continental measures from the Peace of Utrecht to the two great
wars of the mid–eighteenth century. William Pitt's comment of 1755 (on the
eve of assuming power and pursuing the war vigorously in all theaters) is il-
lustrative of a pervasive attitude: "We have suffered ourselves to be deceived
by names and sounds, the balance of power, the liberty of Europe, a common cause, and many more such expressions, without any other meaning
than to exhaust our wealth, consume the profits of our trade, and load our
posterity with intolerable burdens."[12] Pitt, like Bolingbroke, had always
been identified with maritime as opposed to continental war; with the
proposition that the true element of Great Britain was the water, not the
land, and this whether the object in view was the preservation of a balance
of power in Europe or the expansion of British possessions overseas. Pitt's
statement of 1761—"that America had been conquered in Germany"—was
not something the Great Commoner would have ever said previously; the
anticontinentalists had always taken the view that France and Spain could
best be struck by striking at their colony trades. "The water," as Bolingbroke had put it, "is more properly our element," and if England, "like
other amphibious animals," had occasionally to "come on shore," to do so
frequently meant wasting herself "by an improper application of our
strength in conjunctures, when we might have served the common cause far
more usefully, nay with entire effect, by a proper application of our natural
strength."[13] Until Pitt's efforts on all fronts during the Seven Years' War,

maritime war was deemed less expensive than continental fighting; Bolingbroke, like Pitt, was hot for war with Spain in 1739 but did not associate
that with funding systems and taxes. On the contrary, he imbibed (to a fault)
the eighteenth-century catechism: "[T]rade gave us wealth, wealth gave us
power, and power raised our island to be, at one time, a match for
France."[14] Maritime war, in some estimations, would virtually pay for itself,
in the double operation it worked on its magnifications of British commerce,
and the fatal blows to wealth and power inflicted on the French or Spanish.

Most of the anticontinental pamphleteers, therefore, were by no means
pacifists; they just looked with coldness and contempt on European quag-
mires. In the most famous of anticontinental pamphlets published during
the Seven Years' War—Israel Mauduit's *Considerations on the Present
German War* (1760)—the same complaint that Pitt had brought against
British policy in the past was now brought against Pitt himself. Like Bolingbroke, Mauduit did not deny that the European balance of power was
a legitimate object of British concern. His contention was that such an objective had been "made a pretence for so many meaner purposes." He
strongly attacked the support that Britain gave to Prussia during the war
and compared it to the support Britain had given Austria during the War
of the Austrian Succession. In that previous war, instead of making the
maritime conquests that would have made the great expense of the conflict
worthwhile, "we at last forgot both the Spanish war and the French, and
spent our money in Germany against the king of Prussia; for fear he should
get, what we are now spending still more millions to prevent his losing."[15]

David Hume also shared in the profound unease over the direction of
British foreign policy. "To mortgage our revenues at so deep a rate in wars
where we were only accessories," Hume wrote of Britain's continental wars
to maintain the balance and prevent universal monarchy, "was surely the
most fatal delusion, that a nation, which had any pretensions to politics
and prudence, has ever yet been guilty of. That remedy of funding, if it be
a remedy, and not rather a poison, ought, in all reason, to be reserved to
the last extremity; and no evil, but the greatest and most urgent, should
ever induce us to embrace so dangerous an expedient." Hume's essay "Of
the Balance of Power," in which this passage appeared, was first published
in 1752, a few years before the outbreak of another war that would entail
expenditures, and debts, far in excess of those incurred during the War of
the Austrian Succession. Britain's conduct in the Seven Years' War, under
the leadership of William Pitt, drove Hume further to despair, and he
thought Pitt wicked and mad for pursuing without limit a war whose victories would prove of illusory benefit.[16]

The financial revolution that had begun in the 1690s and that had permitted these profligate expenditures was thus, in Hume's eyes, very much a double-edged sword. That revolution had afforded Great Britain, the state where it was made, with enormous resources, enabling it to outstrip its rivals in war; but also raised the danger that the state that had carried the revolution furthest would sink the fastest when the bubble inevitably burst. That onerous public debts would diminish trade and fatally undermine national strength—would destroy, in short, the wealth on which British power was erected—was the continually recurring theme; it was a point, moreover, on which the staple contentions of opposition country ideology coincided with most sophisticated economic thought of the age. Hume's close friend and student, Adam Smith, also believed that the "enormous debts which at present oppress . . . all the great nations of Europe" would probably ruin them in the long run. The ease with which such debts were contracted helped explain the readiness with which European nations resorted to arms; and Smith argued that "were the expence of war to be defrayed always by a revenue raised within the year," wars "would in general be more speedily concluded, and less wantonly undertaken." Because of the ability to borrow, "In great empires the people who live in the capital, and in the provinces remote from the scene of action, feel, many of them, scarce any inconveniency from the war; but enjoy, at their ease, the amusement of reading in the newspapers the exploits of their own fleets and armies." That a less ruinous form of entertainment was advisable was among his deepest convictions.[17]

There are striking parallels between early American thinking on foreign policy and many prominent themes in the eighteenth-century British debate. Madison, for example, would take up Smith's idea in his essay "Universal Peace" (1792), focusing on the insidious role of debt in tempting states, even republican states, toward war.[18] Indeed, the larger contours of the great debate of the late 1790s—with the high Federalists charging upon France the objective of a universal empire and appealing to the importance of the balance of power, and the Republicans declaiming against an insidious plot against liberty made up of standing armies, funding systems, and threats to the balance of the Constitution—form a nice parallel to the eighteenth-century British debate, differing mainly in its greater intensity. When John Adams revolted from his counselors in 1799 and sent a peace mission to France, the visions that danced in his mind were all drawn from the ideological terrain marked out in these eighteenth-century debates: "[A]ll the declamations, as well as demonstrations, of Trenchard and Gordon, Bolingbroke, Barnard and Walpole, Hume, Burgh, and Burke, rush upon my memory and frighten me out of my wits."[19] Indeed, the way in which Adams thought about foreign policy more generally shows strong marks of Bolingbroke's influence, hardly surprising in a man who read Bolingbroke all the way through five or six times in his life. Adams's concern over the excessive weakening of Britain during the Revolution—"the time might come when we should be obliged to call upon Britain to defend us against France"—is very Bolingbrokean, as are his reasons for preferring a navy to an army: "a naval power," as Jefferson expressed their common sentiment in the 1780s, "can never endanger our liberties, nor occasion bloodshed; a land force would do both."[20] Finally, the tenor of Washington's advice in the Farewell Address, urging detachment from the European system, is also very similar to the counsel that Bolingbroke gave England, only more so: whereas Bolingbroke conceded that Britain did have a limited role to play in the maintenance of the European balance of power, Washington stressed the dangers of any such role: "Europe," he observed, "has a set of primary interests which to us have none or a very remote relation. Hence she must be engaged in frequent controversies, the causes of which are essentially foreign to our concerns. Hence, therefore, it must be unwise in us to implicate ourselves by artificial ties in the ordinary vicissitudes of her politics, or the ordinary combinations and collisions of her friendships or enmities. Our detached and distant situation invites and enables us to pursue a different course." That different course was "to steer clear of permanent alliances with any portion of the foreign world, so far . . . as we are now at liberty to do it" and to "safely trust to temporary alliances for extraordinary emergencies."[21]

I shall return to the development of American ideas on foreign policy in due course, but my primary purpose has been to understand the ideological background to the American perception, circa 1787–88, that they stood amid the competing dangers of "consolidation" and "anarchy," one of which conjured images of Rome and "universal monarchy," the other of which was suggestive of the experience of ancient Greece, the Italian res publicas, various confederate republics, and of the balance of power system in Europe. These lessons, of course, did not point to any predetermined conclusion: the Anti-Federalists were not bereft of powerful examples to buttress their case. At the same time, it is not difficult to see why the Federalists should have been struck by a kind of mortal terror when they realized the American states were on the verge of replicating the experience of the European state system. For them, the great question was not simply whether they could maintain their distance from the European system but whether they would themselves *become* the European system; when that possibility dawned on them, it shook them with a kind of volcanic force. The perception made real and vivid a "train of causes" and "series of influences" that would convert these Americans into ardent "Unionists."[22]

These perceptions of the lessons of history began reaching maturation only with the end of the War of American Independence in 1783. Two decades earlier, the outlook of the American colonists, on the morrow of the great war that ended with the removal of French power from North America, was vastly different. The controversy that in England had attended the dispute over continental versus maritime warfare reached a climax in the final two years of the "Great War for the Empire," and it was resolved in a way that testified to the vast importance now vested by Great Britain in the American colonies. The American colonists had shared in this victory and took the measure of their importance from the fact that the war in Europe had ended in stalemate, whereas in America the great adversary had been swept from the field to secure continental colonies that were seen to make a vital contribution to British wealth and power. Further revolutions of power awaited them, and if these would find them, in the early 1780s, beginning to draw the lessons from history that we have described, it was because the lessons from their own experience had already prepared the ground.

PART THREE
The British Empire
and the American Revolution

10

From War to War

THE FACTORS THAT LED to the disruption of the First British Empire and to the independence of the American colonists are, like any great movement in history, highly complex. The outline of the story, however, is simplicity itself. In the aftermath of the war that drove the French from North America, a British ministry led by George Grenville imposed direct taxes on the colonies, both in its 1764 reform of the regulations governing the trade of the empire and in the 1765 Stamp Act. The American continental colonies rose up in unison against a change in policy they regarded as highly threatening to their traditional liberties, and with the Stamp Act Congress of 1765–66 agreed to stop all importations from Britain until the offending measures were repealed. They achieved partial satisfaction from another ministry led by Lord Rockingham, which repealed the Stamp Act and reduced to a nominal level the taxes imposed in the Sugar Act, but which coupled this retreat with a 1766 Declaratory Act affirming the sovereignty of Parliament over the colonies "in all cases whatsoever." The repeal quieted the colonies—temporarily. Many colonists had distinguished between "internal" and "external" taxes in their opposition to the Grenville reforms; seeing an opening, Charles Townshend, Chancellor of the Exchequer in yet another ministry, introduced further taxes in 1767 on imports into the colonies, measures that provoked another wave of colonial opposition. All but one of these taxes—that on tea—were repealed in 1770 by a new ministry led by Lord North. This, too, quieted the colonies, but the calm was deceptive. The British measures, and the colonial opposition, had raised, and dramatically so, the issue of sovereignty; a further reform of the East India trade in tea in 1773, undertaken for reasons having nothing to do with America, was thought by Americans to constitute a symbolic reaffirmation of parliamentary sovereignty. Further resistance followed, particularly in Massachusetts Bay, where colonials threw the tea into Boston Harbor, denying through this symbolic act the authority of Parliament over the colonies. The ministry of Lord North responded with "Coercive Acts" intended to single out Massachusetts for punishment and teach the Americans a lesson; her sister colonies rallied to her defense and demanded, through the First Continental Congress, a repeal of the obnoxious measures recently passed, together with a recognition of the equal authority of

American parliaments with that of Great Britain. The refusal of either side to retreat from its claims then produced the war.

In the longer run of things, the War of American Independence appears as a denouement of powerful forces unleashed by what Lawrence Henry Gipson called the "Great War for the Empire" from 1754 to 1763. This is so not simply with respect to the removal of French power from North America, a victory so sweeping that it profoundly altered the security position of the colonies, and particularly of Massachusetts and Virginia, which had seen vital interests threatened by France's position in Canada and the Mississippi basin. As important as victory was in altering colonial perceptions of the benefits and burdens of membership within the empire, the significance of the experience and the outcome of the war reach far beyond that. That peace also gave the defeated power, France, a motive to side with the American colonists in any future quarrel; the intractable issues that arose as a consequence of the war would give her an excellent opportunity. The war heightened Britain's resolve to set its American affairs in order, while the peace settlement decreased the ability of the metropolis to do so effectively. The war and the peace settlement confirmed, in the minds of all participants, the enormous importance of North America as the holder or makeweight of the European balance of power. For the Americans, this growing sense of self-importance contributed immensely to their desire to establish their relationship with Britain on the footing of equality; for the British, it underlined the importance of maintaining the colonists in their traditional status of dependence.

Most of all, the experience and outcome of the war deranged the extant moral order within the empire. Really for the first time, Britain had expended enormous sums on behalf of America, with hardly a thought given to how this would affect the division of powers and responsibilities within "the constitution of the British empire." This experience gave the political nation in Britain a keener sense of possession and entitlement. The Stamp Act crisis was a rude shock to British opinion; and in the heat of that crisis nothing stung more deeply than the American claim that the war was fought for *British* and not *American* interests.[1] To the common appreciation that the Americans were deadbeats was now added the view that they were ingrates, and that perception erected a profound barrier to a policy of conciliation. The Americans, on the other hand, rejected entirely the assumption that they were now to be proceeded against as delinquents, and wanted from Britain a full recognition of what they conceived to be their traditional rights and privileges.[2]

For all the flaws attributed generally, and rightly, to historical determinism, the conclusion seems just that fortune had, by 1763, written the lines of the drama that would unfold over the next decade and more. The experience and outcome of the war made a fight over the imperial constitution inevitable, and it very nearly made inevitable the resolution that followed: that Britain would fight, and then lose, the War of American Independence. It was truly a case, as Hume had written in 1752, and as he understood again in 1776 as he lay dying, of "human nature check[ing] itself in its airy elevation," of "ambition blindly labour[ing] for the destruction of the conqueror." The great victors of 1763, in Josiah Tucker's words, had only prepared "a more magnificent Tomb for their own Interrment."[3]

I I

Constitutional Crisis

As THE AMERICAN COLONISTS inquired into the principles on which to properly rest their resistance to British measures, they were led to stake out ground that represented an advance over that which they had taken initially. The Stamp Act Congress had affirmed that Parliament enjoyed a general superintending power over the colonies and acknowledged that, as British subjects, the colonists owed a "due subordination" to measures that fell within that ambit of authority. As the controversy advanced, however, leading men in many of the colonies concluded that the attempt to trace the line between the "general" authority of Parliament and the internal autonomy of the colonies was futile and would simply provide an opening for British ministries they had learned to distrust, if not loathe. John Adams in Massachusetts, James Wilson in Pennsylvania, Thomas Jefferson in Virginia, and Alexander Hamilton in New York all reached the same conclusion: far from having authority over the colonies "in all cases whatsoever," Parliament enjoyed this authority in no cases whatsoever. As Wilson wrote in the "advertisement" to the pamphlet announcing this conclusion:

> Many will, perhaps, be surprised to see the legislative authority of the British parliament over the colonies denied *in every instance.* Those the writer informs, that, when he began this piece, he would probably have been surprised at such an opinion himself; for that it was the *result,* and not the *occasion,* of his disquisitions. He entered upon them with a view and expectation of being able to trace some constitutional line between those cases in which we ought, and those in which we ought not, to acknowledge the power of parliament over us. In the prosecution of his inquiries, he became fully convinced that such a line does not exist; and that there can be no medium between acknowledging and denying that power in all cases.[1]

The colonies, in this view, still owed an allegiance to the king—an allegiance founded, as Wilson put it, "on protection." Parliament's authority, however, rested "on representation," and because the colonies were not represented in Parliament, they were not bound by its acts. John Adams took essentially the same ground but mischievously advanced a bit further by insisting that what had been called the British Empire throughout the long debates, in both America and Britain, was not really an empire at all. For Adams, an empire was "a despotism, and an emperor a despot, bound by no law or limitation but his own will: it is a stretch of tyranny beyond absolute monarchy." A monarch had to have his edicts "registered by parliaments," but even this formality, Adams thought, "is not necessary in an empire." The American colonists belonged to no such association; they were not "a part of the British empire. Because the British government is not an empire . . . it is a limitted monarchy."[2]

Once the king, acting upon his oath of office, took side with Parliament in the assertion of its authority, the Americans concluded that they had no better ground to go on than that the king had thrown them out of his protection. As for "the people or parliament of England," said those pushing for an immediate declaration of independence in 1776, "we had alwais been independant of them, their restraints on our trade deriving efficacy from our acquiescence only & not from any rights they possessed of imposing them, & that so far our connection had been federal only, & was now dissolved by the commencement of hostilities."[3] A federal relationship was one evidently based on compact and agreement among authorities equivalent in their formal powers, and could be entered into only by a body, or bodies, that held what Locke had called "the federative power."[4] There are hints of such a position in the early pamphlets opposing the Stamp Act: the colonies, Richard Bland argued in 1766, were distinct states, "independent, as to their *internal* government, of the original Kingdom, but united with her, as to their *external polity, in the closest and most intricate* LEAGUE AND AMITY, under the same allegiance." But it was only with the final crisis in 1774 and 1775 that this doctrine was readily avowed, and then acted on.[5]

From the beginning, the controversy between metropolis and colonies had reflected, and really grown out of, a constitutional crisis within the British Empire. The essence of the colonial claim was that successive British ministries had transgressed their authority in imposing direct taxes on the colonies to fund a new program of imperial defense, that they had crossed long-established constitutional boundaries in the changes made in the laws and administrative practices governing the system of trade and navigation, and that with these and other measures they had struck at the autonomy previously enjoyed by the American assemblies in the direction of their internal affairs. A return to this constitutional standard was the perpetually recurring refrain of the Americans. Responding in 1769 to the plaintive cry "Can nobody propose a Plan of Conciliation?" Franklin wrote, "My Answer was, 'Tis easy to propose a Plan; mine may be express'd in a few Words; *Repeal* the Laws, *Renounce* the Right, *Recall* the Troops, *Refund* the Money, and *Return to the old Method of Requisition.*"⁶ Even after the Continental Congress had advanced to the complete denial of parliamentary authority over them, they still held out the prospect of a reconciliation on the basis of a return to the status quo. "Place us in the same condition that we were at the close of the last war," the Congress declared, "and our former harmony will be restored."⁷

The Grenville ministry, of course, denied these claims at the outset of the controversy, and its partisans would continue to do so throughout the dispute. They insisted that the direct taxation of the colonies was made necessary by the inadequacies of the system for obtaining colonial contributions for their own defense; that experience had pointed to serious violations of the laws governing trade and navigation; and that in taking measures to address these problems they were only exercising their undoubted authority to superintend the general purposes of the British Empire, not encroaching on the admittedly legitimate internal powers of the colonial legislatures. According to Thomas Whately, who mounted the most elaborate apologia for the measures of the Grenville ministry, both the "national Parliament" and the "provincial Legislatures" were representative of the people and were vested with "equal legislative Powers." The difference was that the one was "exercised for local and the other for general Purposes." Far from being incompatible, the two were complementary and would seldom "interfere with one another: The Parliament will not often have occasion to exercise its Power over the Colonies, except for those Purposes, which the Assemblies cannot provide for. A general Tax is of this Kind; the Necessity for it, the Extent, the Application of it, are matters which Councils limited in their Views and in their Operations cannot properly judge of." Whately acknowledged that the authority of the British Parliament rested on representation, and that the colonists were not actually represented there; they were "virtually" represented, however, because parliamentary members took seriously their obligation to consider the interests of the whole empire in their deliberations. "All *British* subjects are really in the same [circumstances]; none are actually, all are virtually represented in Parliament; for every Member of Parliament sits in the house, not as Representative of his Own Constituents, but as one of that august Assembly by which all the Commons of *Great Britain* are represented."⁸

In the decade-long controversy over the constitution of the British Empire, we thus find Americans and Englishmen arguing over (1) the location and origin of sovereignty within this system, and hence wrestling with a language of inferiority, equality, and supremacy; (2) the authoritative boundaries that ought to exist between one legislature acknowledged to have "general" or "external" responsibilities, and other legislatures acknowledged to have "local" or "internal" responsibilities; (3) the proper requirements of representation, acknowledged by all to be an indispensable requirement for the legitimation of authority; (4) the accurate description of a set of governing arrangements that were sui generis, not easily comparable to any other European monarchies or colonial empires then extant; (5) the benefits, whether one-sided or reciprocal, that the relationship brought to each of the parties; and (6) the allocation of the burdens associated with the running of the system. With due appreciation of the varying significations of the word, it may be said that they found themselves in a recognizably federal situation. At the least, this search between 1763 and 1775 for the elusive basis of the relationship between Great Britain and America strongly prefigures the debate, from 1776 onward, over the conditions, features, and problems of the federal union among the American states. In what follows, we want to understand how Americans reasoned about these questions in their first great grappling with them; how the British, whose nation was the fount of the constitutional liberties to which the colonists laid claim, saw the same questions; why these clashing perspectives produced what was, depending on one's angle of vision, a rebellion, a war of independence, a civil war, or a revolution (it was, of course, all four); and how the decade-long debate affected the nature and character of the association the Americans would make among themselves when they declared their independence.

In undertaking such a survey, it needs to be recalled that American and British opinion was not unanimous. There were "friends of America" in Great Britain who sympathized with colonial views and made claims on behalf of the colonies that the colonists would have blushed to make on behalf of themselves, as well as loyalists in America who, though largely sympathetic to the colonial case, feared a controversy that might end in rebellion and war. The friends of America in Britain fared rather better than the friends of Britain in America. The former group briefly returned to power in 1782, after a long period in the political wilderness, long enough to make a generous peace with the United States; large numbers of the latter group fled or were expelled, in distressful circumstances, to Canada, there to preserve in arctic solitude the values of peace, order, and good government. So, too, the Americans themselves were a diverse lot, their identities confused, their loyalties mixed. They hailed from colonies that had enjoyed little commercial contact with one another in the past; before the 1765 Stamp Act Congress, they had never gathered together in an intercolonial parliament or assembly of any kind, save the sparsely attended Albany Congress in

1754, whose recommendations were rejected by every assembly that bothered to consider them. Most of these provincials knew more of metropolitan culture and politics than they knew of one another; what they did know they did not necessarily like, for they were of distinct religious sects, cultures, and ways of life.[9] Still, they were soon to discover that, for all their differences, they had certain vital things in common. As Englishmen, they agreed that they were "entitled to all the inherent rights and liberties of his natural born subjects within the kingdom of Great Britain"; as American colonials, they were also distinct from the body politic that existed in Great Britain, and were as one in thinking it "unreasonable and inconsistent with the principles and spirit of the British constitution, for the people of Great Britain to grant to his Majesty the property of the colonies."[10] Despite their internal diversity, therefore, it is reasonable to speak of an American outlook, for a rough consensus would be achieved in the course of the decade-long controversy on certain crucial points; just as it is reasonable to speak of a British outlook, for there, too, a radically different consensus would harden on certain fundamentals.

In Great Britain, the main lines of division formed between "New Tories" and "Old Whigs."[11] Under the Grenville and North administrations (in 1764–65 and 1770–82, respectively), the more hawkish position was advanced by Thomas Whately, Soame Jenyns, William Knox, and Samuel Johnson in pamphlets in support of these respective ministries. On the other, more dovish, side, the Rockinghamites and the Chathamites represented the Whigs, who were broadly receptive to colonial complaints and who urged a conciliatory policy toward America. Burke, the most obedient and humble servant of Lord Rockingham, provided the main intellectual candlepower of that "party."[12] The Chathamites had at their head the formerly great and formerly common Great Commoner himself—William Pitt—as well as a few other noble lords, including Shelburne. Because Pitt had always stood above party, the Chathamites were not quite a party; Horace Walpole said of Pitt, when he arrived in power in 1757, that he "wanted friends for places, more than places for his friends."[13] Though the British political nation was thus riven into hawks and doves on the American question, there was an insistence among both Tories and Whigs over parliamentary sovereignty that attested to the larger consensus within which the debate proceeded. Chatham seemed willing to give up the right of taxation as early as 1766 and was a hero throughout the colonies; but when he collapsed in the House of Lords in 1778, as John Adams observed, he "fell a martyr to his idol," dying "with the sovereignty of parliament in his mouth."[14]

12

Burden-Sharing and Representation

THE DEBATE OVER benefits and burdens revealed certain points of agreement on both sides of the Atlantic, while also exposing profoundly different readings of what was fair and equitable that played a crucial role in the unfolding controversy. Observers were agreed that the system of trade and navigation was the basis on which British wealth and power rested; Britain's trade with her North American colonies, as Adam Smith complained in 1776, had raised "the mercantile system to a degree of splendour and glory which it could never otherwise have attained to."[1] It was a short step from the acknowledgment of such immense benefits to the conclusion that what Britain had gained the colonies had lost; such was the conclusion that Jefferson drew, writing in 1774 that the British "have indulged themselves in every exorbitance which their avarice could dictate or our necessity extort: have raised their commodities called for in America, to the double and treble of what they sold for, before such exclusive privileges were given them, and of what better commodities of the same kind would cost us elsewhere; and at the same time, give us much less for what we carry thither, than might be had at more convenient ports."[2] No colony felt its grievance as deeply as Virginia, whose interior system of rivers had operated, menacingly, to prevent the emergence of a native commercial center that might speak for the interests of tobacco farmers and which found herself deeply enmeshed in a transatlantic system of debt and dependency.[3] This broad sense of exploitation was crucial to the colonial outlook, and it convinced Americans that every tax or requisition upon them was a burden loaded on a yet greater burden. It convinced them also that, as the cause of British wealth and power, they might, through economic sanctions, be the cause of its undoing.

Neither point was lost on the British political nation. That the Acts of Trade and Navigation imposed burdens, even onerous burdens, on the colonies was admitted by both government and opposition in the parliamentary debate over the American question. These burdens were thought to be compensated for by the benefits the colonies gained through membership in the empire, but the existence of the burden was conceded. If the burden was great, so, too, was the temptation to evade it, and ministerial spokesmen reasoned from this premise to the conclusion (for which they had considerable evidence) that smuggling had been and continued to be rife. The reforms reflected in the extension of Vice-Admiralty jurisdiction in 1764 and the creation of an American Board of Customs Commissioners in 1767 proceeded from that recognition. The opposition, too, shared the view that the colony trade was responsible for British wealth and power; Burke never failed to pore over in his American speeches the statistics from the customs service, and it was his complaint that British taxes and other officious regulations would kill the geese that laid these golden eggs. Neither hawks nor doves denied the second conclusion from this premise: that the colonies, if united, could inflict a devastating blow on British wealth and power. "In the total exclusion from the colony market, was it to last only a few years," as Adam Smith summarized this consensus, "the greater part of our merchants used to fancy that they foresaw an entire stop to their trade; the greater part of our master manufactures, the entire ruin of their business; and the great part of our workmen, an end to their employment."[4] This dependence was highly paradoxical, indeed shocking, for it cast a strange light on all the past efforts made on behalf of America: concentrating all their trade within the confines of the mercantile system, far from relieving Britain's dependence (its ostensible object), had in fact heightened it. The American colonists drew quickly the obvious conclusion as to who now held the upper hand. The perception had formed even before the crisis brought on by the Stamp Act; the repeal of that measure simply confirmed the lesson in their eyes. "Elevated with the advantage they had gained," wrote the first distinguished historian of the Revolution, David Ramsay, "from that day forward, instead of feeling themselves dependent on Great Britain, they conceived that, in respect to commerce, she was dependent on them. It inspired them with such ideas of the importance of their trade, that they considered the Mother Country to be brought under greater obligations to them, for purchasing her manufactures, than they were to her for protection and the administration of civil government. The freemen of British America . . . conceived it to be within their power, by future combinations, at any time to convulse, if not to bankrupt, the nation from which they sprung."[5] This imbalance of power was equally well understood in Britain, but Whigs and Tories drew very different conclusions therefrom. For the friends of America, it showed the necessity of concession; for hard-liners, it showed that concessions made on this ground would beget further concessions. It was an argument, Lord North warned, "which might be applied upon every occasion." If Parliament yielded to such pressure, it "would find that in future, whenever any act of Parliament was made not perfectly agreeable to the Americans, they would constantly go into the same measures to obtain a repeal, and in the end, by the same means, get rid of all acts of Parliament, even that essential one, the Act of Navigation, the basis of the wealth and power of Great Britain."[6]

The question of burden-sharing also arose over the measures of taxation taken to defray partially the costs of the British army stationed in North America after the Peace of 1763. These taxes, considering the expected proceeds from the Sugar Bill and Stamp Act, amounted to about 100,000 pounds. The cost of the army was over three times that, and this did not include expenditures for "Indian extraordinaries" that, as a consequence of Pontiac's "rebellion" and the subsidies incident to the pacification that followed, were also in excess of 300,000 pounds from 1764 to 1767. The justification for imposing the taxes proceeded from minimal considerations of equity; the Americans gained the benefits of these expenditures; they should, it was thought, also share in the burdens. And yet the system by which such supplies were traditionally afforded had demonstrated severe weaknesses in the recent past. Benjamin Franklin's was the classic statement. In 1754, in justifying the Plan of Union, he wrote that great were

> the difficulties that have always attended the most necessary general measures for the common defence, or for the annoyance of the enemy, when they were to be carried through the several particular assemblies of all the colonies; some assemblies being before at variance with their governors or councils, and the several branches of government not on terms of doing business with each other; others taking the opportunity, when their concurrence is wanted, to push for favourite laws, powers, or points that they think could not at other times be obtained, and so *creating* disputes and quarrels; one assembly waiting to see what another will do, being afraid of doing more than its share, or desirous of doing less; or refusing to do anything, because its country is not at present so much exposed as others, or because another will reap more immediate advantage; from one or other of which causes, the assemblies of six (out of seven) colonies applied to, had granted no assistance to Virginia, when lately invaded by the French, though purposely convened, and the importance of the occasion urged upon them.[7]

Grenville's calculations in 1764 and 1765 on the inadequacies of the requisition system reiterated the concerns that Franklin had raised a decade earlier, and they closely foreshadowed the route that would be taken by many Revolutionary leaders during the War for Independence. The Americans were then fighting for their lives, their fortunes, and their sacred honor; still the old requisition system would prove a bust. These experiences show well enough that Grenville was right in thinking that requisitions would be wholly inadequate as a means of maintaining the army, and the conclusion is reinforced if we register the facts (for facts they are) that much American opinion was of the view that the army was unnecessary; that the territories the army garrisoned had nothing to do with their interests, and everything to do with British interests; that they were already groaning under the intolerable burdens imposed by the Acts of Trade and Navigation; and that, besides, they had no specie to pay taxes that were unconstitutional, inexpedient, unfair, unnecessary, and obnoxious. Burke's subsequent claim that the colonies would have contributed "at least a million of free grants" since 1763—indeed, "a great deal more"—was more pure fantasy than the "moral certainty" he took it to be.[8]

To acknowledge the predicament of British officialdom is not to deny that the Americans had good grounds for fearing the consequences that might ensue were the power of direct taxation granted. The colonies were never asked to shoulder the burdens of the debt contracted in the Great War for the Empire, but the debt, at the end of that war, stood at 137 million pounds, the interest on which consumed five-eighths of Britain's annual budget. A few opposition figures apart, British opinion did not doubt that the war had been fought on behalf of the continental colonies; the same argument from equity that justified direct taxation for the support of an army in North America might also justify taxation to relieve the burden of a debt that not only was seen as oppressive but really was. So the colonists denied the claim in toto, demanded a return to requisitions, but also gave every indication that they would look upon such requests to their assemblies with the utmost suspicion.[9]

The Americans founded their immunity from direct taxation on "the undoubted right of Englishmen, that no taxes should be imposed on them, but with their own consent, given personally, or by their representatives." Representation, then, was vital, yet "the people of these colonies are not, and from their local circumstances, cannot be represented in the House of Commons in Great Britain."[10] No one in Britain denied the requirement of representation: the British government, as one discerning observer put it, attempted to justify its measures of taxation "by admitting the Principle but denying the Consequence," holding that the colonies were virtually represented in Parliament.[11] Though the doctrine of virtual representation has often been subjected to considerable ridicule, it was not devoid of merit as a practical matter. The American assemblies maintained colonial agents in Britain that represented their viewpoint; the interests of British manufacturers and merchants—well represented in Parliament—made them sympathetic to colonial claims; and the Americans had in the parliamentary opposition to ministerial measures men who might fairly be counted among the most splendid oratorical talents of this or any age.[12]

Despite these considerations, virtual representation was not actual representation. Particularly on the point of taxation, there was no question but that British and American interests were diametrically opposed; the landed interest in the two "countries," who might well reason about the balanced constitution in identical terms, had interests that, on this point, were utterly irreconcilable. The inadequacies of virtual representation led some observers in Britain to the conclusion that Americans would have to receive representation in Parliament; only with such a representation, Governor Pownall concluded, might America join with Britain in forming "A GRAND MARINE DOMINION . . . UNITED INTO ONE EMPIRE, IN ONE CENTER, WHERE THE SEAT OF GOVERNMENT IS." In taking this step, Adam Smith would add, "a new method of acquiring importance would be presented to the leading men of each colony. Instead of piddling for the little prizes which are to be found in . . . the paltry raffle of colony faction . . . they might then hope, from the presumption which men naturally have in their own ability and good fortune, to draw some of the great prizes which sometimes come from the wheel of the great state lottery of British politiks." Most Americans, however, were unmoved by such proposals and believed that "in the nature of the case" they could not gain a useful representation in the British Parliament.[13] Besides, when Smith made his argument (1776), events had already transformed the little prizes to be won in the paltry raffle of colony faction into something considerably greater, as he was ruefully to acknowledge. "From shopkeepers, tradesmen, and attornies," he noted, "they are become statesmen and legislators, and are employed in contriving a new form of government for an extensive empire, which, they flatter themselves, will become, and which, indeed, seems very likely to become, one of the greatest and most formidable that ever was in the world."[14] Though the British political nation was not keen on the prospect, which Pownall had raised, of being governed in the future by Americans, Grenville indicated his willingness to bring forward such a plan of representation if the colonies expressed a disposition to receive it. No such offer was forthcoming: Americans well understood that colonial representation in Parliament would severely weaken their claim to an immunity from parliamentary taxation and other obnoxious measures, while not appreciably increasing their effective political power in the deliberations of the metropolis.

13

Plans of Union and the Imperial Predicament

IF PLANS FOR colonial representation in Parliament stood no chance in the decade before the war, neither was there a serious prospect of an intermediate type of imperial constitution, such as that called for in the Albany Plan of Union of 1754, many of whose features would be revived in the proposals for conciliation and constitutional reconstruction put forward by Joseph Galloway of Pennsylvania in 1774. The 1754 Plan of Union had called for the establishment, by act of Parliament, of "one general Government" for the colonies, consisting of a president general to be appointed and supported by the Crown, and a "Grand Council to be chosen by the Representatives of the People of the several Colonies met in their respective Assemblies." The initial allocation of seats in this forty-eight-member body gives an indication of the population and wealth then prevailing (very different from what we might imagine today): Virginia and Massachusetts got seven, Pennsylvania six, Connecticut five, New York and the two Carolinas four apiece, "New Jerseys" three, and lowly New Hampshire and Rhode Island two. Subsequent allocations were to be based on the moneys that each colony contributed, via taxation by the Grand Council, to the general treasury. The Grand Council was to be a legislative body "empowered to make general laws to raise money for the defence of the whole," addressing matters too general to be considered by the provincial assemblies, yet too provincial to be addressed by Parliament (though the authority of each of these bodies in their respective spheres was both implicitly and explicitly acknowledged in the Albany Plan). Its laws required the assent of the president general, who was accorded an absolute negative on its proceedings.[1]

The Albany Plan had been proposed, in 1754, against the backdrop of the threatened defection of the Iroquoian Confederation to the French; its most urgent matter of business was settling on an agreement with the representatives of the Six Confederated Nations, including the Mohawks, the Oneida, the Onondaga, the Tuscarora, the Cayuga, and the Seneca. That the Six Nations "held the balance" in the competition between the English-speaking colonies and France was widely acknowledged; no eighteenth-century official of the British Empire doubted their importance. Though in 1754 comprising only ten to twelve thousand souls, they commanded the Mohawk River and the Finger Lakes region, hence also the western approaches to the Great Lakes and the source of the Ohio-Allegheny system; their disposition was also of crucial significance in determining who would control two other water systems—the Hudson River heading south to New York City, Lake Champlain and the Richelieu River heading north to the St. Lawrence—that had long made this region the pivot of Anglo-French rivalry in North América. They would be weakened during the French and Indian War, as they would be weakened in every subsequent one: time would show that it was "possible to hold the balance of power and be at the same time the corn between the millstones." But in 1754 they remained a force to be reckoned with, and the speech of Chief Hendrick to the Albany commissioners, complaining of the injustice of the English traders, showed evidently enough that their reckonings had taken most of them into the arms of the French.[2]

The commissioners at Albany had sent the plan to the colonial assemblies "to receive such alterations and improvements as they should think fit and necessary; after which it was proposed to be transmitted to *England* to be perfected," and established there by act of Parliament. Franklin, who in 1751 had thought a voluntary union among the colonies might be possible, had concluded by 1754 that it was "impracticable to obtain a joint agreement of all the colonies to an union." The same basic causes that made requisitions infeasible applied even more strongly to the act of union itself, and it seemed to Franklin and the other commissioners to require a parliamentary first mover to set the machine in motion. The great merit of the scheme, in Franklin's view, was that it would draw resources from a body in which the colonial assemblies had a fair representation, and he argued that any schemes that did not respect the "undoubted Right of Englishmen not to be taxed but by their own Consent given thro' their Representatives" would be doomed to fail. By such a connection, he hoped and believed, the colonies might "learn to consider themselves, not as so many independent states, but as members of the same body; and thence be more ready to afford assistance and support to each other."[3]

The reception accorded the Albany Plan of Union in both England and the colonies throws a powerful light on the constitutional predicament of the British Empire. Only in Massachusetts Bay did it receive extensive consideration, but it was firmly rejected by the General Court after having received a warning from its London agent that the plan evinced "a Design of gaining power over the Colonies" by the British Parliament. The Massachusetts General Court objected to the "perpetuity of the proposed Union; the great sway which the Southern Colonies (the Inhabitants whereof are but little disposed to and less acquainted with affairs of war) would have in all the determinations of the Grand Council, etc. But the great and pre-vailing reason urged against it" was that this "new Civil Government . . . would be subversive of the most valuable rights & Liberties of the several Colonies included in it . . . and would be destructive of our happy Consti-tution." In the rest of the colonies, in Gipson's summation, "the Albany Plan was either treated contemptuously or placidly ignored after either a half-hearted defence of the work of the commissioners or the expression oᴸ vague sentiments in favour of some sort of union." The plan fared not much better in England. If the colonial assemblies feared the creation of a body that would encroach upon their cherished freedom of action, impe-rial officials also saw danger. The Grand Council seemed to Governor Shirley of Massachusetts, in its powers of defense and taxation, to put "a great strain upon the prerogative of the Crown." Even the plan of union proposed by the Board of Trade, which went much less far than the Albany Plan in the powers vested in the common council, had been thought objec-tionable by the Speaker of the House of Commons, who pointed to "the Independency upon this country to be feared from . . . uniting too closely the northern colonies with each other." Whether because the plan seemed certain to elicit the opposition of the colonial assemblies, or because it would unite colonies in a manner potentially prejudicial to the British in-terest, or because the exigencies of the crisis with France seemed too press-ing, the plan was never submitted to Parliament. Acting on the presumption that the colonies could not in any eventuality be abandoned, the British government put off efforts at constitutional reform until after the war and sought instead to draw support from the colonial assemblies by offering partial reimbursements for their efforts.[4]

The obstacles confronting the Albany Plan of Union, though formidable, seem minor by comparison with those that greeted the similar plan offered by Joseph Galloway twenty years later. Galloway himself privately believed that a colonial representation in Parliament would be "the only effectual Remedy for the present Evils . . . notwithstanding the many Difficulties and Objections made thereto, on both Sides of the Water," but when he offered his proposals of reconciliation in September 1774, he had reaffirmed the premise of the Stamp Act Congress that "the Colonies from their local Cir-cumstances cannot be represented in the parliament of Great Britain." He had instead brought forth a plan avowedly modeled on the Albany pro-posals and disclaimed any "design of taking from Doctor Franklin, or the Congress of 1754," the merit of prior discovery. Like the Albany propos-als, Galloway's provided for a "president General to be appointed by the King and a Grand Council to be chosen by the Representatives of the people of the several Colonies in their respective Assemblies, once in every three years."

Galloway's plan, however, differed in three important respects from that of the Albany commissioners. In the first place, his Grand Council had much wider responsibilities. The responsibilities of the general government under the Albany Plan were limited to defense, whereas Galloway's joint body was to hold all powers "necessary for regulating and administering all the general Police & Affairs of the Colonies." Second, though styled as "an inferior and distinct Branch of the British Legislature united and incorporated with it for the aforesaid general purposes," it was to have a veto on all acts of the British Parliament that concerned the colonies. Its leading principle, wrote Galloway twenty years later, was "that no law should bind America without her consent." Finally, Galloway's plan was also more emphatic than the Albany Plan on the principle of internal autonomy, though both plans recognized it. Whereas the Albany Plan had provided "[t]hat the Particular Military as well as Civil Establishments in each colony" were to "remain in their present State, this General Constitution notwithstanding," Galloway declared that "each Colony shall retain its present Constitution and powers of regulating and governing its own internal Police in all Cases whatsoever." In the extension of its authority beyond defense to "the general Affairs of America," in its embrace of the principle of concurrent majority, and in its reaffirmation of colonial autonomy in studied mimicry of the Declaratory Act, Galloway's plan was far in advance of the Albany proposals of 1754 but far in arrears in 1774 so far as New England and Virginia were concerned.[5]

It was indicative of how deep an impasse had been reached in 1774 that a majority of the delegates to the First Continental Congress showed little interest in pursuing any such plan of conciliation, and Galloway's proposal was expunged from the record a month after its offering. Though it attracted the support of Duane and Jay of New York, and of Rutledge of South Carolina, the republicans denounced it as "an idle, dangerous, whimsical, ministerial plan" that would be "big with destruction to the Colonies." By characterizing the unified body of the colonial assemblies as an "inferior and distinct branch of the British Legislature," Galloway had rejected the view of the imperial constitution (as articulated by Wilson, Adams, Jefferson, and Hamilton) to which the majority of the Continental Congress was now wedded. Parliament, in their view, had *no* authority over America: "By the law of GOD in the Old and New Testament, it has none. By the law of nature and nations, it has none. By the common law of England, it has none. . . . By statute law it has none, for no statute was made before the settlement of the colonies for this purpose; and the declaratory act, made in 1766, was made without our consent, by a parliament which had no authority beyond the four seas."[6]

The Galloway Plan offered no resolution of the immediate controversy between Britain and the colonies—whether she should prevail in her "Coercive Acts" against Massachusetts Bay—and it was destined to irrelevance. While the American secretary, Lord Dartmouth, showed mild interest in some plan of union, his government rejected the authority of the only such union then extant—the Continental Congress. Galloway, who doubtless hoped to hear from his old friend Franklin an endorsement of what he might suppose to be their common handiwork, instead received a ringing denunciation. Considering "the extreme corruption prevalent among all orders of men in this old, rotten state, and the glorious public virtue so predominant in our rising country," Franklin saw "more mischief than benefit from a closer union. . . . It seems like Mezentius' coupling and binding together the dead and the living."[7]

If there was a time for such a plan, it lay in the years before the Great War for the Empire. The one surviving description of the deliberations of the Albany Congress said that this assembly, whose speakers "delivered themselves with singular energy and eloquence," was to be "compared to one of the ancient Greek conventions, for supporting their expiring liberty against the power of the Persian empire, or that *Lewis* of Greece, Philip of Macedon." Despite all the obstacles then existing to any such plan of union, the basis for it in common enmity and mutual need was more strongly felt in 1754 than at any other time before or since in the life of the old empire. Franklin doubtless exaggerated when he mused, late in life, that the adoption of the Albany Plan would have put off the independence of America for another century, but it certainly was true that the failure to address these delicate balances among representation and burden-sharing before making the great effort to expel the French was an error in policy for which succeeding British governments would pay a very heavy price.[8]

It had become a maxim among imperial officials, bred in the Anglo-French wars of midcentury, that the American colonials were incapable of united effort. In striving to bring a semblance of order and common effort to the ragged edges of this system, they were also conscious of the danger of any plan that threatened to institutionalize colonial unity, as any American parliament would certainly have done. The problem of policy centered on how to find the basis for unified action among the colonies that would be sufficiently strong to contend with external enemies and equitably share the burden, yet not *so* strong as to acquire an "equal force, which might recoil back on the first mover." As these great lines of policy contradicted themselves, it seems not too surprising that the dilemma was never resolved, or rather was resolved by throwing the burden on the British Parliament, whose votes of men and money made up the deficit. After the Peace of 1763, it was with surprise and anger that Britain saw her colonies uniting, for the first time, against the mother country herself. If this perverse squaring of the circle brought any consolation, it was that America's unity was more apparent than real, and that the natural antagonisms and jealousies so often displayed in the colonies' past conduct would render them incapable of resisting the enforcement of British authority in America. In 1774, this was a potent and winning argument for the party in Great Britain favoring coercive measures against Massachusetts Bay.[9]

14

"The Great Serbonian Bog"

THE FRIENDS OF America in Britain who resisted the drift toward war felt acutely the larger dilemma of British policy. "To prove that the Americans ought not to be free," Burke once ruefully noted, "we are obliged to depreciate the value of freedom itself; and we never seem to gain a paltry advantage over them in debate, without attacking some of those principles, or deriding some of those feelings, for which our ancestors have shed their blood."[1] This was undoubtedly the case, and it badly weakened the British position. Though Burke himself acknowledged and even insisted on certain ideas closely bound up with "virtual representation"—the representatives of Parliament were to serve the general interest, not particular interests, and to act upon their conscience, and not upon instruction—he rejected the appeal to "virtual representation" in the case of the colonies. That argument appealed to the "shameful parts" of the British constitution, giving "our weakness for their strength," "our opprobrium for their glory," "the slough of slavery, which we are not able to work off, to serve them for their freedom."[2]

The whole thrust of Burke's thinking on the American question was that it must be possible to escape this cul-de-sac, which he sought to do by describing the lineaments of an imperial constitution that would preserve both empire and liberty, that would be rooted in consent yet would also retain sovereign power in Parliament. No other system was possible: "If that sovereignty and their freedom cannot be reconciled, which will they take? They will cast your sovereignty in your face. Nobody will be argued into slavery."[3] Though pleading for the removal of all the taxes that had occasioned the dispute, he acknowledged that there would be circumstances in which Parliament might resort to taxation against a colony whose assembly failed to make fair contribution under the old system of requisition. Under such circumstances, Burke held in 1774, "surely it is proper, that some authority might legally say—'Tax yourselves for the common supply, or parliament will do it for you.'" Burke, however, believed that "this ought to be no ordinary power; nor ever used in the first instance." It was to be avoided if at all possible, and was certainly to be avoided in 1774. In the spring of 1775 he refused to even discuss the question of right, consigning it to the domain of a "metaphysical" distinction. The deep metaphysical question then at issue was whether the power to tax was inseparable from the power of legislation generally. Here, he said, "reason is perplexed, and an appeal to authorities only thickens the confusion. . . . This point is the *great Serbonian bog betwixt Damiata and Mount Casius old, where armies whole have sunk.*" He did not intend, he insisted, "to be overwhelmed in that bog, though in such respectable company."[4]

It is, alas, in the nature of Serbonian bogs that they exert a magnetic power of attraction, and it is possible to get into them, as Americans have more than once subsequently discovered, even if the desire to stay out is felt profoundly. Once in, moreover, it is useless to say that a withdrawal from the bog that concedes the practical issue to the adversary will not have profound consequences. Burke's whole position was centered on the proposition that by withdrawing all taxes the *"former unsuspecting confidence of the colonies in the mother country"* might be restored. He ignored the impressive consensus gathering in the colonies that Parliament was destitute of authority over them. Here lay the serious weakness of his position in the final crisis before the outbreak of war. Britain and America had been disputing the location of sovereignty for a decade; and it was a peculiar blindness that held that the parties to the controversy should all graciously forget that they had been mucking about in this Serbonian bog for what, in politics, is an eternity. *They were in it.* They could not get out without resolving the central issue—of colonial subordination or equality—that every discrete controversy had been raising and symbolizing for a decade. The issue facing Britain in 1774 was whether to acquiesce in the loss of empire or to fight for it.

In his depiction of "the constitution of the British empire," Burke sketched out a system that recognized what would later be called a "federal" division of responsibility. As we have seen, however, a federal relationship was then considered as one among equals who had entered into a treaty or compact, and Burke did not use the word "federal" to signify the relationship he had in mind. "The Parliament of Great Britain sits at the head of her extensive empire in two capacities: one as the local legislature of this island, providing for all things at home . . . ; the other, and I think her nobler capacity, is what I call her *imperial character,* in which, as from the throne of heaven, she superintends all the several inferior legislatures, and guides and controls them all, without annihilating any. As all these provincial legislatures are only co-ordinate to each other, they ought to be subordinate to her; else they can neither preserve mutual peace, nor hope for mutual justice, nor effectually afford mutual assistance." In order for Parliament to answer these ends, he said in 1774, "her powers must be boundless."[5]

Burke's theory of the "constitution of the British empire"—his phrase—was very close to the government he was attacking, and quite distant from the American colonials he was defending. As much as he wanted to give satisfaction to the colonists and return to the state of putative Edenic innocence that had existed before 1763, when such questions had slept in oblivion, he still maintained in 1774 the boundless supremacy of Parliament because he understood that without such a point of authoritative decision within the imperial constitution this association would cease to be an empire. It would become the "limited monarchy" that John Adams insisted, in 1775, it had always been.

The attitude taken by the British political nation on the question of sovereignty has normally been treated roughly by historians, from the beginning to the present day. The British, these historians say, were their own worst enemies in insisting on parliamentary sovereignty. It was a fatal error to have asserted "a theory of centralized legislative omnipotence" after the Seven Years' War that challenged profoundly the existing "principle of differentiation" within the empire. The Americans, in the conventional account, were guilty of no such sin but instead had sought to define a recognizably federal line—between general and local, external and internal, "imperial" and "provincial"—in the early years of the controversy. It was only when Parliament "insisted on the existence of unlimited power—asserted, one might not unjustly say, that Parliament was above the law," that the Americans were driven to stake out an equally extreme position. The American utterances that sought to "divide sovereignty" and that thus anticipated the theory and practice of American federalism broke down before the "inflexible" and "rigid" character of the opposing parliamentary claim.[6]

These depictions mischaracterize the British position and the nature of the issue at stake in 1774. The Grenville program of 1764 and 1765, as Whately's apologia shows, was not based on a repudiation of a "federal" division of responsibility between the "general" and "local" legislatures. Nor is it reasonable to lay this charge at the feet of the Rockingham Whigs. In seeking the repeal of the Stamp Act and the confirmation of parliamentary supremacy "in all cases whatsoever" in the Declaratory Act, the Rockingham Whigs evinced their desire to preserve not only the "authority" but also the "equity" of Great Britain, and they would have denied with indignation the charge that they sought to encroach on the autonomy of the colonial assemblies or that they claimed "centralized legislative omnipotence." The burden of the British case rested not on the proposition that Parliament was to decide everything, but that it was to decide where everything was to be decided. It seemed to a consensus of British opinion that a final, authoritative power whose function it was to decide the relation between superior and inferior legislatures must exist *somewhere* in the imperial constitution.[7] If that authority were lodged in Parliament, the empire would continue to exist; if lodged in the American Parliaments, the empire would cease to exist. On this crucial point, the position taken by Americans in 1774 was a virtual replica of that taken in Great Britain; the colonists just located this point of decision in a different place. Both sides saw that an "imperium in imperio," a final power to decide wrapped within another such power, could not be, once events had thrust the question to the center of the controversy; and the hard-liners on either side paid mute tribute to the mental powers of their adversaries. If the colonial position is considered dispassionately, moreover, the conclusion is difficult to resist that Americans had located that point of decision in provincial institutions from the very beginning of the crisis. There was little change in the colonial position from 1766 to 1774: the movement from "the rights of Englishmen" to the "rights of man," or from the "federal" vision of 1766 to the denial in 1774 of any authority in "the national Parliament" is to be measured in centimeters, not kilometers. At the beginning, the Americans had defined what lay in the external arena—and hence was subject to the "superintending care" of Parliament, to which they professed a "due subordination"—in such a way as to leave virtually everything, including the Acts of Trade and Navigation, subject to an "internal" veto by provincial institutions: assemblies with the power to refuse requests from the king's representative for men and supplies, juries with the power to acquit smugglers. They claimed, as John Dickinson put it in 1767, the right "that all free states have, of judging when their privileges are invaded, and of using all prudent measures for preserving them." Though they dotted a few "i's" and crossed a few "t's" along the way, the rough draft of their position was virtually complete at the outset and needed only a committee of detail to work out the right phrasing.[8]

15

Rights and Wrongs, Prophets and Seers

THE HISTORIOGRAPHICAL CONTROVERSY over the coming of the Revolution has always centered on certain basic questions: Who started it? Was there a reasonable compromise between the parties? Was the difference between them as wide as the Atlantic Ocean—as a comparison of the positions taken in 1774 would indicate—or did it amount to something paltry and insignificant, the uncollectible proceeds from a miserable tax on tea? Who most displayed the will to power—the ungovernable urge to dominate—that led to the war? One side? Both sides? Neither? The question of responsibility for the war is important, for its consequences were, for many of the peoples of North America, damaging in the extreme. It meant displacement for a significant class of the colonial population who were exiled to Canada or Britain, and it damaged badly the prospect of peaceful relations between whites and Indians, now identified with the hated British enemy. By giving the southern gentry an example of the dreaded prospect of slave revolt, it retarded the prospect of peaceful emancipation even as it convinced many slaveholders that such an emancipation was incumbent upon them. Like other wars, it brought the usual toll of mangled bodies and deranged minds, and it led men on both sides to justify acts inconsistent with "the laws of nature and of nature's God."

Since World War II, American historians have with few exceptions favored an account that places primary, if not indeed exclusive, responsibility for the conflict on British shoulders, reviving a "whiggish" view that had arisen at the outset but that was largely disputed among the "imperial historians" who commanded attention in the first half of the twentieth century. The impulse is understandable: if we think one side to a conflict is good, the temptation to designate the other as bad is difficult to resist. So, too, if one side is acknowledged to stand for liberty, it seems a logical deduction that the other side must stand for tyranny. If there are heroes on one side—and who can deny that the men of the American Revolution had a heroic cast about them?—there must, after all, be villains on the other.[1]

Such treatments, however understandable, are nevertheless profoundly unhistorical; they lead, often unconsciously, to a narrative line in which the motives of one side come to be known through the ungenerous and often quite ridiculous representations of the other; and so have Americans often been taught to understand the motives and intentions of those who, in Britain, launched the reform program of 1764 and 1765 and then settled on a war to keep their rebellious colonies within the British Empire. That the war was lost—that it ended with a British army listening, at Yorktown, to "The World Turned Upside Down"—seemingly provides further support for the common judgment that British ministers capped their evil intent with the unforgivable sin of stupidity. They were, in this writer's opinion, neither wicked nor stupid. They may, however, have been deluded in two important respects—in their belief that force might be employed successfully to keep the Americans within the empire, and in their estimate of the contribution made by the colonies to British wealth and power.

It may thus be contended, in the first place, that Britain's war was basically unwinnable, that victory in the field would yield a balance sheet with more liabilities than assets. The opponents of war in Britain hammered away on this theme, and did so with considerable force. Military power, Burke held, was to be considered not as an "odious" but as "a feeble instrument," for "a nation is not governed which is perpetually to be conquered." He doubted that "fighting a people be the best way of gaining them" and insisted that the object for which Britain proposed to fight—the wealth and power that her supremacy over the colonies gave her—would not be the thing that was recovered: a prostrated America would be "depreciated, sunk, wasted, and consumed in the contest." Victory, even if possible, would produce in the Americans "nothing but the meditation of revenge."[2] Nearly a decade before, the opposition had sounded the same charges. Still more alarmingly, they warned throughout that success, in such a case, would be "hazardous" because "America, if she fell, would fall like a strong man. She would embrace the pillars of the state, and pull down the constitution along with her."[3]

Were the case against British ministries to rest on the unprofitability of force, or the dangers its use would pose to the balance of the constitution, it would be difficult, and perhaps impossible, to rebut. It was the peculiarity of the opposition's argument, just as it has been the peculiarity of the whig historiography that has followed them, that these far-reaching objections to the utility of force were not thought incompatible with the preservation of the British Empire.[4] Surely, however, we are not to deduce from the proposition that America could not be governed by force the proof of the theorem that it could be governed without force; that the old policy of "salutary neglect" was a viable one in 1774, as Burke was forever urging; or that the constitutional settlement the Americans proposed, recognizing only a common king, would have borne the faintest resemblance to the empire that Englishmen thought they had. It had been the very debility of the position of the colonial governors that had led to recognition of the need for parliamentary legislation, even before the Great War for the Empire. The colonial assemblies had won this contest, and won it completely, even before 1763. The royal governors were the merest ciphers in colony after colony; they could do almost nothing without the consent of the colonial assemblies, and they had at their disposal precious few "places and positions" by which they might manage their little houses of commons, certainly nothing approaching that which the monarchy still enjoyed in Great Britain. Thomas Hutchinson's position as governor of Massachusetts Bay in the final years of the crisis—besieged, bothered, and bewildered—was symbolic of a larger pattern in which "swollen claims and shrunken powers" had existed side by side, fueling the receptiveness of Americans to an outlook that saw the wicked hand of power in every step and misstep of the colonial governors, and progressively depriving these governors of the capacity to act save with the consent of the assemblies.[5]

There were a few observers at the time in Britain who achieved a real understanding of what was at stake, including Josiah Tucker and Adam Smith, in their different ways the two most perceptive observers of the American question at the time. Tucker was as emphatic as Burke on the disutility of force. He conceded that the government, if it acted speedily, "might prevail, and *America,* however unwilling, be forced to submit." But the blood and treasure that would be spent in that eventuality, the damage to commerce and manufactures that a hostile spirit would produce, and the impossibility of maintaining "a Superiority in it afterwards for any Length of Time" all argued for the absurdity of the attempt. In the event of a successful war, Britain would face the alternative of "permitting the Colonies to enjoy once more those Advantages of *English* Liberty, and of an *English* Constitution, which they had forfeited; or else a Resolution to govern them for the future by arbitrary Sway and despotic Power." Tucker showed either alternative to be inadmissible, lamenting in the latter case the "baleful Influence this *Government a la Prusse* would have on every other Part of the *British* Empire" and in the former the return to the very situation—their ungovernability—the use of force was expected to resolve.[6]

Tucker also rejected the idea of combining colonial representation in Parliament for the purpose of incorporating "*America* and *Great-Britain* into one common Empire." Far from "proving a Means of Reconciliation, and a Center of Union," the measure would instead "have a Tendency to beget endless Jealousies, Quarrels, and Divisions, between the Mother-Country and the Colonies." Tucker saw two great difficulties from this measure: it would, in the first place, import into the British constitution doctrines of representation that would be inimical to the right understanding of parliamentary duty. Tucker shared with Burke and Whately the view that a member of Parliament was obliged to "to take Care of the Interests of all the People in general," and that he could not, consistently with that duty, "pay any Deference to the Request, Instruction, Remonstrance, or Memorial, of his particular Electors, except in such Cases only herein he is convinced in his Conscience, that the Measures, which they require him to pursue, are *not incompatible with the public Good*." Instructions sent by sovereign bodies were characteristic of diplomatic assemblies, but a similar procedure in the case of parliaments threatened basic values of deliberation for the sake of an acknowledged common good; it seemed plain to Tucker that American notions of representation would challenge the normative order of the British Parliament and perhaps lead subjects at home into disobedience to the laws (since they had not, after all, actually consented to them).

Tucker's second objection was directed against the assumption that colonial representation in Parliament would establish the legitimacy of parliamentary measures over America. That sanguine view ignored the evident difficulties of dividing powers between the national Parliament and colonial legislatures, based on what was external and internal, and what general and provincial: "who is to judge between the *British* Parliament and the Provincial Assemblies" when conflicts arose, as they surely would? The "very same Things justly pass under both Denominations, according as they are seen from different Points of View." Barracks and fortresses necessary for defense were of a general nature, yet from another view every barrack might be denominated "as an odious Badge of slavery," and every magazine "a Monument of Tyranny and despotic power, and Prerogative for destroying the few Liberties that were left."[7]

The proposals for colonial representation in Parliament had carried with them the evident implication, occasionally acknowledged, that "America should become the general Seat of the Empire." Tucker was at his most mischievous in showing the absurdity of this scheme. "[W]hatever Events may be in the Womb of Time, or whatever Revolutions may happen in the Rise and Fall of Empires, there is not the least Probability, that this Country should ever become a Province to *North-America*." The English would rather be governed by the French than the Americans. He acknowledged that his foresight was limited, but he thought "this Island would rather gravitate towards the Continent of *Europe*, than towards the Continent of *America*; unless indeed we should add one Extravagance to another, by supposing that these *American* Heroes are to conquer all the World. And in that Case I do allow, that *England* must become a Province to *America*." There was, in fact, as much probability of America governing England as of England governing America, and his demonstration of the impossibility of the one gave strength to his condemnation of the other. Having surveyed the extant options, and readily shown the defects of them all, Tucker arrived at his astonishing conclusion: "For if we neither can govern the *Americans,* nor be governed by them; if we can neither unite with them, nor ought to subdue them;—what remains, but to part with them on as friendly Terms as we can?" Those terms were to declare "them to be a free and independent People, over whom we lay no Claim" and to offer "to guarrantee this Freedom and Independence against all foreign Invaders whatever." The relationship would be reconstructed on the basis of mutual interest and beneficial exchange rather than obedience.[8]

Tucker disposed readily of the proposition that the surrender of sovereignty would mean the sacrifice of the American trade. The reverse was true. The British could have it when it was in the interest of the Americans to do so, and those were, as a practical matter, the very terms on which they enjoyed it now. Besides, there was no better motive for denying Great Britain a trade prompted by interest than the injuries and retaliations incident to a war. Britain had already "become a Kind of a general Mart" for most commodities, and from an economic perspective it was clear that the colonies could not "trade with any other *European* State to greater Advantage than they can with *Great-Britain*." As for fears that the French would take possession of the colonies, Tucker deemed them "very wild, very extravagant, and absurd." The notion supposed that the colonists, "who cannot brook our Government, would like a *French* one much better," and that "our mild and limited Government, where Prerogative is ascertained by Law, where every Man is at Liberty to seek for Redress, and where popular Clamours too often carry every Thing before them,—is nevertheless too severe, too oppressive, and too tyrannical for the Spirits and Genius of *Americans* to bear; and therefore they will apply to an arbitrary, despotic Government" for their remedy. It was not only that the Americans would not submit to this inglorious yoke; the French themselves should certainly think thrice about it. Could an arbitrary government, Tucker asked, "dispose with such Liberties as a republican Spirit will require"? Could it incorporate, and still remain itself, "[a]n absolute Freedom of the Press! No controul on the Liberty either of Speaking or Writing on Matters of State! Newspapers and Pamphlets filled with the bitterrest invectives against the Measures of Government! Associations formed in every Quarter to cry down Ministerial Hirelings, and their Dependents! The Votes and Resolutions of the Provincial Assemblies to assert their own Authority and Independence! No landing of Troops from *Old France* to quell Insurrections! No raising of new Levies in *America!* No quartering of Troops! No Building of Forts, or erecting of Garrisons!" All this fun was to show that France could not turn the balance of power in her favor by seeking dominion over the colonies; at all events, Great Britain, with her superior marine, would have in her hands the means to prevent such an acquisition if it seemed that a revival of French ambitions in America "would really and truly be an Addition of Strength in the political Balance and Scale of Power."[9]

Tucker's sketch of the consequences such an abdication would have on the political relations between Great Britain and the American states emphasized the parlous unity of the colonials. "The Moment a Separation takes Effect," he wrote, "intestine Quarrels will begin: For it is well known, that the Seeds of Discord and Dissention between Province and Province are now ready to shoot forth; and that they are only kept down by the present Combination of all the Colonies against us, whom they unhappily fancy to be their *common enemy.*" Renounce the claim of authority, and "the weaker Provinces will intreat our Protection against the stronger; and the less cautious against the more crafty and designing." Tucker's vision of Great Britain—serving, in effect, as the holder of the balance in America, and being found useful by Americans as "their general Umpires and Referees"— was a highly plausible projection from his line of policy and bore out his larger argument that the renunciation of all authority over the Americans would actually increase rather than diminish British influence with them. That it would have had momentous consequences for the political structures that emerged in North America after 1776 seems evident, for the centripetal forces operating on the American states after that date were almost all owing to the exigencies, oaths, sacrifices, and common institutions that emerged from the vortex of the War of Independence. That struggle cast its shadows long after its thunders were hushed in peace. For a generation and more, the great thing that Americans could agree on, when they could agree on almost nothing else, was that the British state, led by wicked and designing ministers, had conducted an infamous attack against the liberties of the American colonies. The development of the American union and the sentiment of American nationalism was bound part and parcel with the divorce from the British nation, and from the bitter passions that engendered.[10]

Tucker shared in many respects Burke's appreciation of "the spirit of liberty" that animated the American colonists, though he readily distinguished, as all observers did, between the northern and southern continental colonies. Burke had attributed that spirit in northern colonies to their religion. While all varieties of the Protestant religion were "a sort of dissent," New England offered a refinement on this principle: it was "the dissidence of dissent and the Protestantism of the Protestant religion." In the southern colonies, by contrast, where "the Church of England forms a large body and has a regular establishment," the "spirit of liberty" was "still more high and haughty" than in the North. To Samuel Johnson's famous taunt—"How is it that we hear the loudest yelps for liberty among the drivers of Negroes?"—Burke answered that where slavery existed

> those who are free are by far the most proud and jealous of their free-dom. Freedom is to them not only an enjoyment, but a kind of rank and privilege. Not seeing there that freedom, as in countries where it is a common blessing and as broad and general as the air, may be united with much abject toil, with great misery, with all the exterior of servitude liberty looks amongst them like something that is more noble and liberal. I do not mean, Sir, to commend the superior morality of this sentiment, which has at least as much pride as virtue in it; but I cannot alter the nature of man. The fact is so; and these people of the southern colonies are much more strongly, and with a higher and more stubborn spirit, attached to liberty than those to the northward.

Tucker accepted this basic portrait, though he reminded Burke that the first settlers in New England, conceiving *"that Dominion was founded in Grace,"* were of that strain of Republicans who thought "that they had the best Right in the World both to *tax,* and to *persecute* the *Ungodly.* And they did both, as soon as they got Power into their Hands, in the most open and atrocious manner." Tucker acknowledged that the "present Dissenters in *North-America* retain very little of the peculiar Tenets of their Fore-fathers, excepting their Antipathy to our established Religion, and their Zeal to pull down all Orders in Church and State, if found to be superior to their own." But these surviving traits raised strong doubts over the desirability of continuing "a Connection with a People who are actuated by Principles so very repugnant to our own Constitution both in Church and State, and so diametrically opposite to the Spirit of the Gospel."[11]

Nor did Tucker dispute Burke's contention that the Americans' "ungovernable Spirit" of liberty was derived, in the southern colonies, from the "Domination of the Masters over their Slaves." "For it seems, he that is a Tyrant over his Inferiors is, of Course, a Patriot, and a Leveller in respect to his Superiors." Tucker did not let pass the opportunity of condemning the institution of *"domestic* or *predial"* slavery: it was "the most onerous and expensive Mode of cultivating Land, and of raising Produce, that could be devised." Much to be preferred, in point of economy and morality, was "the Method of hiring free Persons, and paying them wages," a fact that demonstrated that the "Laws of Commerce, when rightly understood, do perfectly co-incide with the Laws of Morality." But his larger point was that the very spirit that made slave masters "haughty, insolent, and impe-rious in private Life" also made them "turbulent and factious in respect to the Public." Republican governments, whether ancient or modern, were consequently "the most insolent and tyrannical upon Earth"; their subjects retained "less of Liberty, both in Form and Substance, than most of the Subjects even of monarchical Governments." It was useless to appease such people in the hope of keeping them within the British Empire, and all the characteristics to which Burke had pointed in showing the necessity of gov-erning them mildly showed to Tucker, and not unreasonably, that the British could not govern them at all. A man, he said, must have a high opin-ion of his eloquence who should think he should bind these "High Might-inesses" further than they wished to be bound.[12]

Tucker's animadversions on the American character, though unkind, were not terribly unjust. The leveling, intolerant, and fanatical ways of New Englanders, imbibed from their Puritan fathers; the haughty, insolent, and imperious ways of the southern gentleman, molded from birth by the institution of slavery—these cultural traits not only were real but also showed little sign of disappearing. Though Tucker took perverse delight in dwelling on the "refractory Behavior" of the colonies, he was far from charging them "with being Sinners above others." On the contrary, it was the nature of all colonies "to aspire after Independence, and to set up for themselves as soon as ever they find that they are able to subsist, without being beholden to the Mother-Country. And if our *Americans* have ex-pressed themselves sooner on this Head than others have done, or in a more direct and daring Manner, this ought not to be imputed to any greater Malignity, or Ingratitude in them, than in others, but to that bold free Con-stitution, which is the Prerogative and Boast of us all." Employing the fa-milial analogy so characteristic of discourse on the empire, Tucker recognized that America had come of age; for the parents to continue treat-ing the young man like a child would simply confirm him in his childish be-havior. Better to throw him out, and then reestablish the relationship on the basis of equal respect and mutual interest.[13]

In terms of immediate policy, Tucker was not as far from Burke as his polemic might indicate. When Burke made his plea for peace—"Not Peace thro' the Medium of War; not Peace to be hunted thro' the Labyrinths of intricate and endless Negotiations; not Peace to arise out of universal Discord, fomented from Principle, in all Parts of the Empire"—Tucker had asked: "[W]hat is this Heaven-born pacific Scheme, of which we have heard so laboured an Encomium? Why truly; *if we will grant the Colonies all that they shall require, and stipulate for nothing in Return; then they will be at Peace with us.* I believe it; and on these simple Principles of simple Peace-making I will engage to terminate every Difference throughout the World." Yet Tucker's plan was vulnerable to the same satire, and in fact his real quarrel with Burke was that he and the Rockingham Whigs would *not* grant the colonies the freedom and independence they really wanted but rather continued to solicit from them an acceptance of their subordination to Parliament.[14]

Closest to Tucker's perspective was the view advanced by Adam Smith in his *Inquiry into the Nature and Causes of the Wealth of Nations.* Like Tucker, Smith combated the myths, widely held in both Europe and America, regarding the relationship between the production of wealth and the strictures of the "mercantile system" and sought to show that "the effects of the monopoly of the colony trade . . . are, to the great body of the people, mere loss instead of profit." Pointing, also like Tucker, to the immense expense to which Britain had been put in the two previous wars on behalf of her American colonies, he wrote in the concluding passages of *The Wealth of Nations,* "The rulers of Great Britain have, for more than a century, amused the people with the imagination that they possessed a great empire on the west side of the Atlantic. This empire, however, has hitherto existed in imagination only. It has hitherto been, not an empire, but the project of an empire; not a gold mine, but the project of a gold mine; a project which has cost, which continues to cost, and which, if pursued in the same way as it has been hitherto, is likely to cost, immense expense, without being likely to bring any profit." If the project could not be completed, "it ought to be given up."[15]

As much as Smith's vision in *The Wealth of Nations* displayed an acute understanding of the real relationship among colonies, commerce, and national power, it was extravagant in one respect. It was excessive to say that the project of empire had, "for more than a century," brought all loss and no gain. Britain had grown prosperous within its exclusive system of trade and navigation, and had discovered within it a source of strength that overthrew previous calculations of the balance of forces in Europe. Smith himself had recognized that the Act of Navigation had contributed mightily to Britain's naval power and security, and that act was tied closely to many of the provisions he identified with "the mercantile system." The decisive change had come with the two great wars of the mid–eighteenth century—fought, as Smith had said, "on behalf of the continental colonies." Of these two wars, it was the last where North American aims were most pronounced: the settlement in 1748 had obliged New England to surrender its Canadian conquests; whereas that in 1763 had resolved every debate—Europe versus America, Canada versus Guadeloupe—in favor of the continental colonies in North America. This entailed, as Smith would later note, an epochal change from the past. Whereas the British, during the reign of the first two Georges, "used to complain, that our connexion with Hanover deprived us of the advantages of our insular situation, and involved us in the quarrels of other nations, with which we should, otherwise, have had nothing to do," they had "much more reason to complain, upon the same account, of our connexion with America."[16]

In the *Wealth of Nations,* Smith still clung to a vision by which empire might be pursued. His proposed means of completing the project called for colonial representation in Parliament and direct taxation to ensure colonial contributions for "the support of the whole empire." As we have seen, such proposals were universally reprobated in the colonies and had no chance of acceptance. At least, however, he had stated the obvious alternative. Though he ended on a pessimistic note—awakening from her golden dream, Britain would have to accommodate herself "to the real mediocrity of her circumstances"—his larger argument was such as to show that the means toward wealth and power could be recovered after a loss of the colonies. As such, he and Tucker were raging optimists in comparison with their compeers, who glimpsed a miserable future for Britain were she to stand bereft of her empire and dominion.[17]

It was on this point that Tucker and Smith split most deeply from the prevailing consensus within Great Britain. Whereas these seers were looking for ways in which Britain might give up her empire without the sacrifice of wealth and power, the great debate between Tories and Whigs in Parliament had revolved around the ways in which Britain might keep it. It was the recognition by Tucker and Smith that the project of empire was incoherent and based on mistaken premises that made them see most deeply into the web of time; but it was, by the same token, their belief that it could be given up without danger, and that it ought to be given up in certain circumstances, that made them appear as voices crying in the wilderness. Even those who followed them in their course of argument, and admired their skill and learning, could not but gag on the conclusion. Adam Ferguson, a member of Parliament and the republic of letters, responded to their proposals by noting that a few had said "that it would be no such fatal stroke to Britain as it generally imagined, were America to be abandoned altogether." He declared that "he had not opinion enough of his own foresight to say with certainty what the consequences would be, but so much benefit had he reaped from these speculations as to hope that the prosperity of Great Britain would not be desperate even were such an event to happen. But who would be bold enough to advise such a measure? and who could, with certainty, answer for the effects of it? If no person would, what remained, but they should exert every nerve to reduce their rebellious subjects to obedience?"[18]

This larger consensus on the need to maintain parliamentary sovereignty, and the concomitant rejection of a voluntary surrender of empire, may make the great debate over America appear as something of distinctly limited value, and the image of the British as lemmings plunging unthinkingly into the sea has consequently appeared to match perfectly the summary judgment of historians as to the folly and madness of the mother country. From a different perspective, however, the debate generated a set of perspectives that would not die out and that would be transferred across the Atlantic and form part of the argument over America's own union. For all the flaws inherent in the position that Burke took in 1774 and 1775, he had nevertheless called forth a vision of empire thoroughly informed by federal values; and it lay there waiting for subsequent appropriation. His American orations evoked ideas and sentiments that would later find fertile ground in American thought, among them his celebration of peace and his skepticism that force could preserve an empire that was "the aggregate of many states under one common head"—"I do not know," he said, "the method of drawing up an indictment against a whole people." Burke's image of an empire held together by the silken cords of affection—ties as light as air but strong as links of iron—might be satirized as an impossibility masquerading as a coherent policy, but some such an idea was part and parcel of American conceptions of union from the beginning. No American, too, could fail to be struck by his evocation of imperial distances, whether oceanic or continental, and the implications this had for the relationship between center and periphery: "Three thousand miles of ocean lie between you and them. No contrivance can prevent the effect of this distance in weakening government. Seas roll, and months pass, between the order and the execution, and the want of a speedy explanation of a single point is enough to defeat a whole system." If even despotism were obliged to "truck and huckster," the same should surely be so for a constitutional state, which ought not "to fret and rage, and bite the Chains of Nature." "The Sultan gets such obedience as he can. He governs with a loose rein that he may govern at all; and the whole of the force and vigour of his authority in his centre is derived from a prudent relaxation in all his borders. Spain, in her provinces, is, perhaps, not so well obeyed as you are in yours. She complies too, she submits, she watches time. This is the immutable condition, the eternal law, of extensive and detached empire."[19] Though Tucker would cast his animadversions on this passage as well, Burke was right to think that "[i]n large Bodies, the Circulation of Power must be less vigorous at the Extremities," and that distance was a factor that ought to limit, and did limit, the arrogance of power.[20]

But if Burke's vision emphasizing the decentralized and noncoercive character of extended and detached empire might get registered in subsequent American thought, the vision of the new Tories also found ready adherents, though the latter were admittedly not keen to advertise the resemblance and for the most part did not see it themselves. Still it is a fact: those "ministerial hirelings" and "fawning and bigoted Tories" had shown why a large collection of discontented provinces needed a hand on the tiller; they had demonstrated why these independent bodies could not be expected to generate cooperation among themselves, however sincere the will; they had recognized that in certain areas, such as the relations maintained with the aboriginal inhabitants of the continent, it would be neither just nor expedient to entrust responsibility with the separate provinces, for that meant certain depredations of whites on reds, and therefore certain war; they saw that, in questions relating to commerce and currencies, some general authority was needed to manage the joint affairs of provinces that were resistant to external direction and jealous of their powers. They did not propose the annihilation of these local authorities, recognizing them as valuable, if refractory, parts of the imperial constitution. The general powers they wanted to exercise were very close to those that were accorded the federal government under the Constitution of 1787—much closer, indeed, than the allotment of authority to the federal government provided for in the Articles of Confederation. If a continental perspective is admitted to have validity—and who among American nationalists can deny it?—it must be conceded that the vision had plausibility and coherence, that they had seen things that the Americans themselves would later come to see. They were wrong in only one thing, and a very big thing it was: they would not be the ones to direct and manage the general concerns of the new empire arising on the western shore of the Atlantic.

Does a portrait that makes intelligible, and therefore humanizes, the fears and calculations of the demons of the story—the Norths, the Grenvilles, the wicked though not yet fully mad king—necessarily dehumanize the other side? There is no reason why it should. The colonials may have painted the motivation of their enemies in fanciful colors, but these dark imputations are a feature of all conflicts—discreditable and often dangerous, certainly, but hardly unusual. The Americans might fairly be charged with ingratitude for the efforts Britain had made on their behalf; and if the rule is good that gratitude is owed in the affairs of states they surely did violate it. At the same time, all the decisions taken on behalf of their security had been made in London. A few intrepid provincial leaders apart, the colonists would have remained passive spectators of the Great War for the Empire had the British government, then led by Pitt, not generated military power from them by promising to reimburse their efforts (though even with such forces the colonial contribution, in comparison with that of regular British forces, had been slight). In the midst of these vast imperial doings the American assemblies had surrendered exactly nothing of their traditional rights and privileges; it was no secret that they wished the least restraint possible.[21] They would have been less, or more, than human had they not sought to register explicitly the new facts that the war had brought about, above all the fact that the British Empire rested on them, and not they on the British Empire.

Nor does the plausibility, or lack thereof, of the contentions made in the debate that preceded the Revolution detract from the vast historical importance of what was now to be attempted in North America. Held in the eye of these refractory republicans, their declaration of independence having been made, was the ideal of free government, a government without kings or hereditary aristocracies that would be popular in its foundation and limited in its objects. Jefferson in the Declaration of Independence may have characterized the motives of George III and his ministers in a way that no dispassionate historian can credit, but the beginning and ending paragraphs of this state paper, in which the purpose and justification of freedom were proclaimed, were, after all, sublime. Americans knew the common opinion that the ancient and modern republics, borne aloft on the rights of the people, had always ended their flight in a wreck. It was given to them, therefore, to show that republican government could also be free government, giving the lie to the belief, widespread in Europe, that to vest the sovereign power exclusively in the people would end by making citizens less free than subjects. The language the Americans used to describe this mission shows that it touched them to the very quick, stirred their deepest emotions. The desire to show the world that republican government was possible, that it could be made to serve both individual and collective freedom, was felt to be exhilarating in the opportunities it offered, awe-inspiring in the responsibilities it imposed. And they held this grand idea before them knowing that, were they to fail, the halter awaited, followed by deserved historical execration.[22]

16

Independence and Union

IT WAS, therefore, a consciousness of acting in a drama of world historical importance, and of vindicating the idea of free government against its calumniators, that found expression in the "spirit of '76." But devotion to free government was only one half of that spirit; the other half expressed itself in the belief that the experiment in republican liberty could only be carried through on the basis of the enthusiastic concordance of the new state governments then forming. That unity would be the basis of their strength these Americans well understood. Alone each colony was a nullity; if these provinces were to become free and independent states, they could only do so together. Independence and union hence advanced arm in arm—mutually dependent, the realization of either unthinkable without the other.

In back of this codependence lay a simple recognition of political realities. From the beginning of the crisis that produced the American Revolution, British ministers had watched keenly for signs of division among the colonies. They had sought to single out New York for punishment in 1767 and then had gambled that Massachusetts Bay might suffer the closure of her port and the abrogation of her charter in lonely isolation from her sister colonies. This expectation of the divisions that would prevent concerted action among the colonies was a deeply held article of faith in Great Britain, which contrary indications barely disturbed. Tucker and Smith prophesied it; republicans like Richard Price feared it; the old Whigs urged it as a complaint against the ministry; and ministers made it the basis of their policy. In 1776, as David Ramsay recalled two years later, "Our enemies seemed confident of the impossibility of our union; our friends doubted it; and all indifferent persons, who judged of things present, by what has heretofore happened, considered the expectation thereof as romantic." Long after the war, long, indeed, after the making of the federal constitution, whose perpetuity they did not credit, many Englishmen would derive wry consolation from the thought that America's union would soon fracture, appearances would give way to realities, political artifice would succumb to nature. Americans knew that the belief had a genuine basis, and they are often to be found indulging the same prophecies; but they also knew that the poison might be counteracted, that a remedy for it was discoverable and lay within their grasp.[1]

When the First Continental Congress convened in September 1774, it did so with the purpose of displaying unified resistance to the acts of the British Parliament. Since the colonists still looked toward a constitutional settlement within the British Empire, any moves toward a more formal union among themselves were generally seen as wholly premature. Nevertheless, the congress had to decide on a fair method of voting, and this immediately provoked disagreement. In Patrick Henry's first speech to the congress, in which he had gloried in the name of America, he had raised the question of the "weight" to be assigned each colony. In affirming that he was "not a Virginian, but an American," he did not neglect to propose a rule of voting in which Virginia's importance would be acknowledged, and the great mischief avoided of "an Unequal Representation." Indeed, his famous observation—"All Distinctions are thrown down. All America is all thrown into one Mass"—was clearly made for the purpose of establishing a rule of representation that would give "each Colony a Just weight in our deliberation" in proportion to its wealth and numbers. Though Henry was willing to throw slaves "out of the Question," other southern delegates were not: Lynch of South Carolina differed from Henry "in thinking that Numbers only ought to determine the Weight of Colonies." On the contrary, "Property ought to be considered," and the "Weight" of each colony "ought to be a compound of Numbers and Property." To the claim of the Rhode Island delegate, Samuel Ward, that each colony ought to have one vote because the weakest colony "would suffer as much as the greatest" in the event of calamity, Benjamin Harrison of Virginia said that his constituents would censure him severely for the injustice of this arrangement, and he feared "we should never see them at another Convention" were the one colony–one vote rule agreed upon.[2]

Despite these warnings, congress decided "that the Sense of the Congress shall be taken by Voting in Colonies each to have one Vote." One reason given at the time for adopting the one colony–one vote rule was that there were no materials at hand to make a more equitable determination, and that objection proved "unanswerable." In acquiescing in this inequitable arrangement, as Henry had intimated his willingness to do, the delegates of the larger colonies did not surrender their claim for a more equitable representation in the future. With all eyes riveted on the marshaling of support for New England, and with the colonists still holding out to the mother country a return to the status quo of 1763, that question was not yet ripe. Still, the fragmentary evidence of these initial debates shows clearly enough that all the main positions in the subsequent debate over representation got canvassed immediately. As these showed profound disagreement over the equities of the case, they stored up much trouble in the future.[3]

The larger principle of union was nevertheless confirmed and consecrated by the first congress, and Massachusetts, though favoring the case of the larger states, was certainly not disposed to complain of the result. The principal uncertainty surrounding the congress was whether it would lend its aid to the support of Massachusetts Bay, and that answer had come through loud and clear. "The spirit, the firmness, the prudence of our province are vastly applauded," Adams wrote, "and we are universally acknowledged, the saviours and defenders of American liberty." "One of the happiest days of my life" was how Adams characterized (to his diary) the moment when it became clear "that America will support the Massachusetts or perish with her." Such an outpouring of emotion was "enough to melt a heart of stone. I saw tears gush into the eyes of the old grave pacific Quakers of Pennsylvania."[4]

This union of sentiments in the first congress was perhaps most marked in the relationship that developed between Massachusetts and Virginia. In its larger signification, this presented a sectional alignment that pitted New England and the South against the four middle colonies, where the fear of the consequences of a separation with the mother country ran deepest. New York and Pennsylvania, the two most important middle colonies, had long been at odds with New England, their hinterlands clashing at several points; both displayed "Fears and apprehensions from the Temper of her Neighbors, their great swarms and small Territory."[5] This split between New England and the middle colonies entailed a significant ethnic differentiation. John Adams, in recounting "that overweening Prejudice in favour of New England" that he very often felt and sometimes feared, gave five reasons why "New England has in many Respects the Advantage of every other Colony in America, and indeed of every other Part of the World," the first of which was that "[t]he People are purer English Blood, less mixed with Scotch, Irish, Dutch, French, Danish, Sweedish &c than any other."[6] The five southern colonies also had a higher proportion of English than the middle colonies, which were mixed in the fashion that Adams described, but the southern colonies were vastly different in social organization from New England. Some 60 percent of South Carolina were African slaves, and some 40 percent of Virginia. In decided contrast to New England, with its egalitarian ethos, South Carolina presented a social organization in which a handful of "opulent and lordly planters" ruled, as Josiah Quincy Jr. remarked, over "poor and spiritless peasants and vile slaves." Among these gentlemen, "Cards, dice, the bottle and horses engross prodigious portions of time and attention."[7] Southerners were well aware of this radical social differentiation, and indeed conservatives from both Virginia and South Carolina, like Carter Braxton and Edward Rutledge, objected as much to the egalitarianism of New England as Quincy had done to the massive social inequalities of South Carolina. Events would show, however, that neither Braxton nor Rutledge spoke for Virginia and South Carolina in the developing crisis, or at least that the fears they expressed did not constitute a barrier to collaboration between North and South. Virginia, on the contrary, emerged as the fast friend of Massachusetts, and even South Carolina, under the insistent prodding of Christopher Gadsen and Henry Laurens, was not backward in her support.

In the first congress, as Dickinson would recall in 1775, the "balance" had lain with Carolina. With New England and Virginia largely in accord, their relationship cemented by the blossoming relationship between the Adamses and the Lees, and the middle colonies taking up the rear, the attitude of Carolina had proved crucial. The same pattern presented itself in the Second Continental Congress, which convened on May 10, 1775, to consider the British response to the American platform of the previous year. Yet it would be misleading to conclude that any narrow majority felt itself in a position to press its advantage or decide for the others. Their rule of decision more closely approximated, in practice, the idea of a concurrent majority, and on important questions a rule of unanimity prevailed. "We have no coercive or legislative authority," said Edward Rutledge in the first meeting of the congress. "Our Constituents are bound only in Honour, to observe our Determinations."[8] That the American colonies gathered in something called a "congress" rather than a "parliament" was surely not adventitious: in the law of nations, "congress" was a diplomatic term signifying an assembly of states or nations, such as Westphalia, Nimeguen, Ryswick, or Utrecht, in which no state was understood to have bound itself by its mere appearance: it would be bound only by that to which it gave its formal consent.[9] Even in diplomatic assemblies, of course, to be a minority of one may require acquiescence from a practical standpoint, and other states do not need a legislative authority to exert pressure on isolated malcontents. Economic sanctions and the withholding of recognition are among the "unfriendly, though vigorously legal" instruments they may employ. Nevertheless, the rule of unanimity does confer a blocking power on recalcitrants, and the delegates to congress recognized that that was the rule they were obliged to follow. The "great, unwieldy body" of America, in Adams's words, was "like a large fleet sailing under convoy. The fleetest sailors must wait for the dullest and slowest."[10]

Adams often bristled at the lengths to which more moderate voices wished to go in reaching for an accommodation with Great Britain, but he acknowledged that there was no alternative but to acquiesce in their slug-gishness. "We ought to have had in our Hands a Month ago," he wrote on July 24, 1775, "the whole Legislative, Executive and Judicial of the whole Continent, and have compleatly moddelled a Constitution." John Dickin-son thought otherwise and proposed instead "to hold the sword in one hand and the olive branch in the other." Dickinson's objections carried the day. When Adams's letter calling for this bold program was captured by the British and published, his animadversions on Dickinson—"a piddling Ge-nius whose Fame has been trumpeted so loudly"—caused embarrassment to the congress and were thought in Britain to give an increased probabil-ity of success to the plan of the Howe brothers "to sow dissensions among the Provinces." Adams was determined not to let that happen. Though he dreaded "like Death" Dickinson's proposed petition to the king, fearing that the colonies might be "deceived, wheedled, threatened or bribed out of our Freedom," he thought it unavoidable: "Discord and total Disunion would be the certain Effect of a resolute Refusal to petition and negociate." And so went forward the second petition to the king, which appealed to the memory of George's royal ancestors, "whose family was seated on the British throne, to rescue and secure a pious and gallant nation from the popery and despotism of a superstitious and inexorable tyrant." Adams signed despite considering the whole performance "imbecilic." "Unite or die," under the circumstances, was always a clinching argument for acqui-escing in the stubborn determination of a minority of the congress, even if you had to put your name to barefaced falsehoods and unmanly prevari-cations; that consideration, rather than harmony on the merits of the mea-sure itself, explains such unanimity as the congress possessed.[11]

From mid-1775 to mid-1776, the fear of the New Englandmen was that futile efforts at reconciliation would foreclose the necessary and even vital effort to prepare for the inevitable war. With Boston beseiged, and her del-egates burdened with the thought of her suffering, this presented a delicate set of problems. Twenty thousand men, gathered from the New England countryside, stood athwart a much smaller British force encamped in Boston. Seeking support from the outside, the New Englanders knew that there was a "strong jealousy" of New England in general and Massachu-setts in particular. "Suspicions entertained of designs of independency; an American republic; Presbyterian principles, and twenty other things" were picked up by Adams's sensitive ear, but perhaps the greatest suspicion cen-tered on the possibility of "a New England army under the command of a New England General." This entailed "a Southern party against a North-ern" one, stemming from the fears—"some plausible, some whimsical"—

that New England would "soon be full of Veteran Soldiers, and at length conceive Designs unfavourable to the other Colonies."

Adams cut through these difficulties with his magnanimous, and thoroughly unexpected, resolution that "Congress should adopt the army before Boston, and appoint Colonel Washington commander of it." This bold stroke felled three birds: it allowed Massachusetts to warmly acknowledge the generous assistance and leadership of "our sister colony of Virginia, which ranks highest in numbers"; it allayed the jealousies that "an enterprising eastern New England general proving successful, might with his victorious army give the law to the Southern and Western gentry"; and it exerted civilian control over the military, as the Massachusetts Provincial Congress had urged the Continental Congress to do. Despite grumblings in both New England and Virginia—Pendleton of the latter state thought it bad precedent to force a command on a soldiery perfectly content with its existing officers—the resolution was adopted unanimously. It was the first great sectional compromise in American history.[12]

Unanimity in council, however, did not translate readily into unity in the camp. Once Washington arrived in Massachusetts to take command, he let loose in his private correspondence with a steady stream of prejudicial remarks regarding the New Englanders, finding "an unaccountable kind of stupidity in the lower class of these people which, believe me, prevails but too generally among the officers of the Massachusetts *part* of the army who are *nearly* of the same kidney with the privates!" Adams, whose apparent masterstroke had elevated Washington, learned of these comments and was now driven to ask if "every Man to the Southward of Hudsons River behave like a Hero, and every Man to the Northward of it like a Poltroon." The reverse seemed the case to one of Adams's correspondents, who told him of a group of riflemen "from the Southward" who were "as Indifferent men as I ever Served with, their Privates, Mutinous and often Deserting to the Enemy, Unwilling for Duty of any kind, Exceedingly Vicious . . . [but] Truth may not best go from me any further." No, indeed. Washington, stung by the leaks in what he had supposed to be a privileged correspondence with friends in Virginia, reached a similar conclusion and from thereon righteously eliminated such aspersions from his private letters. All could see the merit of Witherspoon's observation that "if local provincial pride and jealousy arise, and you allow yourselves to speak with contempt of the courage, character, manners, or even language of particular places, you are doing a greater injury to the common cause, than you are aware of." Still, it was mighty difficult to keep these things down; the sense of heterogeneity, of regions that differed "as much as several distinct Nations almost," bespoke the plain facts of the situation, and from the very beginning it was understood that without consideration and forbearance the divisions among these proto-nations would certainly be fatal.[13]

In the months leading up to the Declaration of Independence, these provincial rivalries weighed heavily on the delegates, mostly from the middle states, who urged caution in moving toward a formal break with the mother country. John Dickinson was at the head of this group, and the warnings he uttered on the eve of independence reflected worries of long standing. He had, as early as 1765, espied a whole series of frightful consequences that lay in wait if the controversy between the mother country and her colonies were to be resolved through war. In a letter to William Pitt in 1765, he had expressed no "doubt in the least" that the colonies would prevail in such a struggle, but he warned that there would follow a "Multitude of Commonwealths, Crimes, and Calamities, of mutual Jealousies, Hatreds, Wars and Devastations; till at last the exhausted Provinces shall sink into Slavery under the yoke of some fortunate Conqueror. History seems to prove, that this must be the deplorable Fate of these Colonies whenever they become independent." The intervening years served, if anything, to deepen his sense of the dangers of going it alone. For "about seven years past," Dickinson wrote in 1774, the "passions of despotism raging like a plague . . . have spread with unusual malignity through Europe. Corsica, Poland, and Sweden have sunk beneath it." The European powers would keenly eye America as a potential spoil in their partitioning system, and Britain, once the protector of America's liberties, would be ruined by independence and in no condition to any longer afford that aid. "France must rise on her Ruins. Her Ambition. Her Religion. Our Danger from thence. We shall weep at our victories."[14]

Dickinson's fears were also those of the loyalists. Were America to become independent, Daniel Leonard thought, she would become an "easy prey, and would be parcelled out, Poland like." The colonists, certainly, would have to arm for their protection. "As matters are now circumstanced throughout Christendom," wrote Charles Inglis, "no state can preserve its independency without a standing army. The nation that would neglect to keep one, and a naval force, if it has any sea coast, must infallibly fall a prey to some of its ambitious and more vigilant neighbors." Prophecies of the intestine wars and foreign domination that awaited the colonies, if independent, were the common theme of loyalist pamphleteers, and on the other side of the Atlantic the same portrait was deeply etched in the political consciousness of the British nation. "Fire and water are not more heterogeneous," wrote Andrew Burnaby in 1775, "than the different colonies of North America." Such were their differences in character, manners, religion, and interest that "were they left to themselves, there would soon be civil war, from one end of the continent to the other; while the Indians and Negroes would, with better reason, impatiently watch the opportunity of exterminating them all together."[15] Virginia had gained a taste of that impatience in the decision of her royal governor, Lord Dunmore, to enlist both slaves and Indians to put down the rebellion. In November 1775 he had offered freedom to all slaves and servants who would join his cause. Fear of servile rebellion did what massive indebtedness to British merchants could not do: it united the southern gentry on the cause of independence.[16]

Even as the tide rolled on toward independence, the most serious reservations were expressed with respect to the prospects of a durable union among themselves. "We should know on what Grounds We are to stand with Regard to one another," Dickinson argued on July 1, 1776: "The Committee on Confederation dispute almost every Article—some of Us totally despair of any reasonable Terms of Confederation."[17] "Nothing but present danger will ever make us all agree," worried Abraham Clark of New Jersey, "and I sometimes even fear that will be insufficient." "We shall remain weak, distracted, and divided in our councils," fretted Samuel Chase of Maryland: "[O]ur strength will decrease; we shall be open to all the arts of the insidious Court of Britain, and no foreign Court will attend to our applications for assistance before we are confederated. What contract will a foreign State make with us, when we cannot agree among ourselves?"[18] A good question that, which shows that the American search for foreign assistance from France had also managed to get itself entangled in the indissoluble knot between independence and union. The difficulties the congress faced in agreeing upon the articles, not submitted to the states until November 1777, confirmed the worries that had led Dickinson to urge a delay of the Declaration of Independence, and that persisted and even deepened after the Declaration was made. Still, the fear of disunion was insufficient to block the movement forward. It was the theory of the Tories that the Americans would fall out among themselves and blow up their experiment through division; at the time, these American whigs, while fearing that internecine quarrels would hurt them, were also tempted to consider that idea a near synonym for tyranny, for it was the ever-recurring refrain of those who now made war against them. To vindicate free government against its enemies, and to confound the prophets of inevitable division, was their dual task and mission as they launched themselves into the world of independent states.

PART FOUR
Articles of Confederation and Perpetual Union

17

Problematics of Union

THE STORY OF America has been told many times as a loss of innocence, and it sometimes seems that, as a people, we are perpetually fated to undergo a cycle in which innocence is lost and then recovered only for the purpose of losing it again. A cycle in which hope thus perpetually, though temporarily, gains a triumph over experience seems deeply embedded in the American cultural pattern and is rooted in the inescapable disjunction between the ideals of our national life and the realities that taunt them. Lady Liberty has lost her innocence many times over, and though ravished by experience survives to think innocently again. Nature mischievously sends the lessons of experience to the grave; a new generation arises that laughs at the tired warnings of its elders, that knows it must learn for itself, and that manages to intuit, even in its innocence, how preferable it is to know the experience of disillusion than never to have dreamed at all.

The first great loss of innocence in the nation's history—symbolic of many others to come—occurred before there was a nation; when there were many peoples, not one. It occurred, in time, in the aftermath of the hopeful and heroic days of 1776; the locale where it was most detectable was the meeting place, or places, of the Continental Congress. There had unfolded, from 1774 to 1776, the encounter between American colonials who hardly knew each other, nearly all of whom were meeting for the first time. They were hesitant and distrustful at first, fearing that bad impressions would be taken or gotten; but as friendships formed and as the crisis with the mother country rolled to its fateful terminus, they had been struck over how much alike they thought; how the crisis with Great Britain had found their minds in tune, having independently arrived at the same conclusions, made the same calculations, reasoned from the same premises. They calculated rightly that they need only form a union to prevail. They were, most of them, as yet not fully conscious of how difficult the making of this union would prove to be.

Auguries of disillusion had, to be sure, disclosed themselves in the minds of some well before the Declaration of Independence, but nothing prepared them for the grim descent to follow. Armies were raised that dissolved on expiration of the enlistments, the terms of which were liberally interpreted by volunteer militia. Disputes over command—largely sectional in basis—

troubled the congress throughout the war; Washington was not yet the acknowledged hero he became and was described in 1777 as the "most to be pitied of any man I know."[1] Continental currency poured from the presses and became "as worthless as a Continental"—its depreciation being almost Weimar-like in its rapidity and completeness. There were momentary victories that made the prospects seem bright, like the battle of Saratoga in 1777, which brought the French, with new moneys and supplies, into the war. But the respite was short-lived. The Continental army, ill clothed and ill fed, fought every winter a desperate battle with the elements. Valley Forge was not atypical. The years 1779 and 1780 were dark, the war turning uglier in its methods, as the British carved a path of desolation through the South. By that time, many observers had reached the conclusion that the union would not survive the exigent circumstances that had brought the American states together. Deflated expectations and blasted hopes had become the bitter fruits of time; experience was one long declension from the hopeful and heroic days of 1776.

The decision to move to independence has always been seen, and rightly so, as a momentous act, a discontinuity or break from the past that rivals any other. In certain respects, however, there was no discontinuity at all. As they had done as members of the British Empire, Americans during and after the making of independence found themselves arguing over (1) the location of sovereignty in the new association they made among themselves, and doing so in the familiar language of equality, supremacy, and subordination; (2) the authoritative boundaries that ought to exist between one institution ("the united states in congress assembled") and the new state governments formed after independence—an argument, as before, that they conducted in the familiar language of "internal" and "external," "general" and "local," while substituting "union" and "states" for "empire" and "provinces"; (3) the proper requirements of representation, acknowledged by all to be an indispensable requirement for the legitimation of authority; (4) the accurate description of a set of governing arrangements that were sui generis, comparable to, yet at the same time different from, every other "firm league of friendship" known to history; (5) the benefits, whether one-sided or reciprocal, that the union brought to each of the parties; and (6) the allocation of the burdens associated with the running of their new association.

As before, all these questions were hopelessly mixed up with one another, and it is a serious mistake—often made—to believe that the question of sovereignty, for example, was considered apart from the question of representation or burden-sharing or indeed any of the other matters then agitated. Thomas Burke's comment of 1777—that the "same persons who on one day endeavour to carry through some Resolutions, whose Tendency is to increase the Power of Congress, are often on an other day very strenuous advocates to restrain it"[2]—was right. It was possible to look with suspicion on the congress and jealously guard the prerogatives of the states while thinking it utterly absurd that the control of the western lands should be left in the hands of those states with "sea to sea" charters; so, too, it was possible to glimpse the glories of the common cause and to think even of the national character America might one day have, while threatening the withdrawal from the confederacy unless the issue of representation was fairly settled. Though these multifarious and diversely interconnected positions, of which many more examples might be given, challenge the plausibility of the labels that historians have fixed upon the factions and parties, there was no contradiction in holding to such carefully qualified views. The issues *were* interrelated, and where the line of sovereignty was drawn or federal responsibilities allocated did rest vitally upon the related issues of burden-sharing and representation. No one doubted the necessity of union; no one approached it without conditions and reservations. In making these conditions and reservations, moreover, Americans did not split nicely into two parties. Coalitions continually formed, dissolved, and re-formed: there were multiple lines of distinction. Though the divisions between north and south, "carrying" and "non-carrying," landless and landed, commercial and planting, expressed the enduring and basic division, there were others that crossed and complicated the great sectional divide. Those related to the settlement of accounts were a particularly fertile source of cross-sectional concert and dissensus, as was the conflict between those states with, and those states without, commercial ports. We shall return to these various divisions, because they tell us something very important about the structure of American politics on the eve of the Philadelphia convention. But first we need to look closely at the instrument of union itself. It gave a preliminary, though in many respects incomplete and tentative, answer to all six questions we have raised, though in a fashion fully acceptable to nobody.

In coming to an understanding of the Articles of Confederation, it is important to bear in mind that Americans were not exactly beginning everything all over again, in the portentous phrase of Thomas Paine. In the years from 1774 to 1777—from the time of the First Continental Congress and the Continental Association to the submission of the Articles of Confederation to the states—they did certainly find themselves in a state of nature,[3] and they were badly in need of establishing a constitutional authority in the states and for the union; but they stood behind no "veil of ignorance." Not for nothing had they, over the preceding decade, torn apart the justifications for the sovereignty of Parliament over their assemblies. In considering what they did, that experience—fresh, immediate, and compelling—is of great import. So, too, in considering the articles, attention needs to be given to the various alternatives before them. Of these alternatives, the plan of confederation that Benjamin Franklin laid before congress in the summer of 1775 is perhaps the most revealing. Franklin, as we have seen, did not approach his task as a novice, and his proposal of 1775 makes an instructive contrast with the plan of the Albany Congress. John Adams, too, gave serious thought to the problem of confederation and provides an important clue to what was done. Finally, there is the draft of the articles that a committee of the congress, in the pen of John Dickinson, prepared in June 1776. Stripped of some of its provisions, and its language sometimes altered, the Dickinson draft formed the base of the proposal that congress ultimately submitted to the states in November 1777. Let us look at each of these plans in turn, preparatory to considering the question of what rough beast, its hour come round at last, was slouching toward York to be born.[4]

Franklin's 1775 proposal was titled "Articles of Confederation and perpetual Union, entered into by the Delegates of the Several Colonies." Under this association, *"The United Colonies of North America"* were to "severally enter into a firm League of Friendship with each other, binding on themselves and their Posterity, for their common Defence against their Enemies, for the Security of their Liberties and Propertys, the Safety of their Persons and Families, and their mutual and general welfare." Each colony was to "enjoy and retain as much as it may think fit of its own present Laws, Customs, Rights, Privileges, and peculiar Jurisdictions within its own Limits; and may amend its own Constitution as shall seem best to its own Assembly or Convention" (Article 3). Delegates were to be annually elected to meet "in General Congress," at a place that would be "in perpetual Rotation" among the colonies. The "Power and Duty of the Congress" extended to war and peace, sending and receiving ambassadors, entering into alliances, settling all disputes and differences between colony and colony about limits, and "the Planting of new Colonies when proper." The congress was to appoint "all Officers civil and military, appertaining to the general Confederacy," and was also empowered to "make such general Ordinances as tho' necessary to the General Welfare, particular Assemblies cannot be competent to; viz., those that may relate to our general Commerce or general Currency; to the Establishment of Posts; and the Regulation of our common Forces." All general charges incurred by the congress were to be defrayed out of a common treasury in proportion to the number of male polls aged sixteen to sixty, and "the Taxes for paying that proportion are to be laid and levied by the Laws of each Colony." Franklin did not fix the number of delegates "to be elected and sent to the Congress by each Colony" but provided instead that one delegate be allowed "for every 5000 Polls." Out of this body, far larger in number than the Continental Congress, was to be appointed an "executive Council" consisting of twelve persons with a rotating membership. In "the recess of Congress," this council was "to execute what shall have been enjoin'd thereby; to manage the general continental Business and Interests, to receive Applications from foreign Countries, to prepare Matters for the Consideration of the Congress; to fill up (*pro tempore*) continental Offices that fall vacant; and to draw on the General Treasurer for such Monies as may be necessary for general Services, and appropriated by the Congress to such Services." Each colony was forbidden to "engage in an offensive War with any Nations of Indians without the Consent" of congress or its "great Council." The control of Indian relations more generally was also placed in congress, and authority was granted to establish "as soon as may be" a "perpetual Alliance offensive and defensive" with the Six Nations. All other British colonies "upon the Continent of North America" might join "the said Association"—"viz. Ireland the West India Islands, Quebec, St. Johns, Nova Scotia, Bermudas, and the East and West Floridas." This "Constitution" might be amended by the congress so long as such amendments were approved by a majority of the assemblies; failing reconciliation with Great Britain, "this Confederation is to be perpetual."[5]

The circumstances of 1754 and 1775 were very different, and these differences in context must be borne in mind in any comparison between the two plans Franklin produced in those years. Perhaps the most basic difference between the two was that the Albany Plan had provided for a "General Government," whereas the 1775 plan was a confederacy or "firm League of Friendship." In keeping with this fundamental distinction, Franklin proposed in 1775 that all necessary taxes were to be raised in each colony, whereas the Albany Plan had vested this vital adjunct of the legislative power in the Grand Council. Whereas the architects of the Albany Plan had concluded that it could be established only through an act of Parliament, and left ambiguous the formal role enjoyed by the assemblies in approving or reprobating the plan, the 1775 plan vested the constituent power in the separate assemblies or conventions of the colonies. The executive council Franklin called for in 1775, which he almost certainly envisaged as being made up of representatives of each of the twelve colonies, was a very different animal from the president general that was proposed in the Albany

Plan. Whereas the president general, appointed and supported by the crown, was to have an absolute veto on "all Acts of the Grand Council," the 1775 council was clearly subordinate to congress as a whole, even if it might conduct the continental business when congress was in recess. In the 1775 plan, the evident check on the power of congress lay with the colonies. This check was not entirely lacking in the Albany Plan, for that charter forbade the impressment of men for military duty without the consent of the colonial assemblies. At the same time, however, the Albany Plan had conferred on the president general and Grand Council everything requisite to raise such forces, and for its general purposes of defense it would enjoy the power to make laws and lay and levy "such General Duties, Imposts, or Taxes, as to them shall appear most equal and just."

If by virtue of its power of taxation the 1754 Grand Council would have enjoyed more inherent powers than the congress projected in 1775, in respect to authority it enjoyed less. The Grand Council's responsibilities were limited to defense, and even in that important area its authority was limited to raising forces and to making peace or declaring war "with the Indian Nations." This proviso was evidently included to preclude a declaration of war aimed at France, which only the king might do. In the 1775 plan, by contrast, the power of congress over peace and war was plenary, and its authority extended as well to a wide range of objects, including "those that may relate to our general Commerce or general Currency," that the Albany Plan had implicitly left with Parliament.

Despite these differences, there were certain respects in which the two plans were very much alike.

1. The Albany Plan did not call, as the 1775 plan did, for "a perpetual Alliance offensive and defensive" with the Six Nations, but the necessity of reaching an agreement with that distinguished council had been the immediate cause of drawing the delegates to Albany in the first place.
2. Both plans, too, vested in the general body extensive powers over the disposition of unsettled territories in the West. In enabling congress to settle "all Disputes and Differences between Colony and Colony about limits" and to plant "new Colonies when proper," Franklin clearly contemplated a general authority that would deny the authority of the "sea-to-sea" charters and enable congress to reduce them "to more Convenient Dimensions," as the 1754 Plan of Union had put it.
3. Both plans recognized the integrity of the existing colonial constitutions. If this principle was rather more emphatically stated in the 1775 constitution, the Albany Plan had also recognized that "the Particular Military

as well as Civil Establishments in each Colony remain in their present State, this General Constitution notwithstanding." In both cases, substantial numbers of Americans thought this seeming reassurance over the integrity of their charters, if that is indeed what Franklin's phraseology signified, was in flat contradiction with provisions allowing the general body to prescribe their limits, and the furor in 1775 over the 1774 Quebec Act—in which the British Parliament sliced away and awarded to the Canadian province land which many colonists thought belonged to them under their charters—showed that these controversies would continue to be fertile sources of discord.

4. Both plans, finally, recognized that the principle of representation and burden-sharing would have to be proportional to the numbers and wealth of each colony, though they served this idea in different ways. The Albany Plan had provided that its initial allocation of forty-eight seats would be readjusted once it was determined in what proportion the colonies had contributed money to the general treasury, though with the number of representatives never to be "more than Seven nor less than Two." In the congress, by contrast, representation was not made subordinate, even partially so, to the "proportion" of contribution, but the formulas were otherwise identical in practice by virtue of their appeal to the number of male polls.

Franklin's plan was not recorded in the official journals of the congress, but it was apparently completed on May 10, 1775, and submitted to congress on July 21. Because many members believed it premature to advance toward formal union, Franklin's plan lay fallow. When debates over the confederation did arise, however, many of Franklin's proposals were highly controversial and by no means reflected a consensus of the delegates. Interestingly, it was in those areas of his 1775 plan that were most like the Albany Plan—and particularly in matters of proportional representation and the control of western territory—that Franklin's views aroused the most serious opposition, and neither provision made its way into the Articles of Confederation. In other respects, however, and above all in his depiction of the confederation as a "firm league of friendship," the final product bore signal marks of Franklin's influence, or at least showed how far Franklin's first precocious thoughts had simply expressed a larger consensus regarding the purposes and limits of the American confederation.

Franklin was not, of course, alone in considering the problem of confederation. As the decision on independence neared in the spring of 1776, John Adams threw off in several places succinct expressions of the frame of the association that ought to be made. Adams, oddly, seemed to approach the problem of union with a certain trepidation. As with the *Defence* of 1787, discussed in chapter 8, his *Thoughts on Government* in 1776 touched but briefly and almost tangentially on the problem of union, with Adams devoting the lion's share of his attention to the forms of government best suited to the American states. But whereas his *Defence of the Constitutions* fell upon an uncomprehending country, his *Thoughts on Government* was highly esteemed as a first draft of American constitutionalism, and it was probably his most popular production. In this pamphlet—originally written to a gentleman in North Carolina who had made inquiries—Adams gave to republican government the mechanisms of check and balance that distinguished the English constitution. "A MAN," he wrote, "must be indifferent to the sneers of modern Englishmen to mention in their company the names of Sidney, Harrington, Locke, Milton, Nedham, Neville, Burnet, and Hoadley. No small fortitude is necessary to confess that one has read them." Read them Adams evidently had, and he carefully applied the precepts of the English republicans to constitution-making in the American states, establishing the importance of bicamericalism, an independent executive, a separate judicial power operating as a check on the legislative and the executive, and representative assemblies that should be, "in miniature, an exact portrait of the people at large." Adams was not dogmatic about the precise form and indeed was quite insistent that each colony should do that which most suited it. Republican governments had an "inexhaustible variety, because the possible combinations of the powers of society, are capable of innumerable variations," and each colony would have to decide for itself, in "constituting the great offices of state," what would be most "productive of its ease, its safety, its freedom, or in one word, its happiness." It was only at the end of this pamphlet, and almost as an afterthought, that Adams addressed the problem of union. "If the Colonies should assume governments separately, they should be left entirely to their own choice of the forms, and if a Continental Constitution should be formed, it should be a Congress, containing a fair and adequate Representation of the Colonies, and its authority should sacredly be confined to these cases, viz. War, trade, disputes between Colony and Colony, the Post-Office, and the unappropriated lands of the Crown, as they used to be called. THESE Colonies, under such forms of government, and in such a union, would be unconquerable by all the Monarchies of Europe."[6]

Adams amplified on his conception in several letters in the approach to independence. In a fulsome and giddy letter to Patrick Henry, Adams had praised "the Author of the first Virginia Resolutions against the Stamp

Act" and thought Virginia lucky in having "So masterly a Builder" (Governor Henry) to frame its constitution. "It has ever appeared to me," wrote Adams, "that the natural Course and order of Things, was this—for every Colony to institute a Government—for all the Colonies to confederate, and define the Limits of the Continental Connection—then to Declare the Colonies a sovereign State, or a Number of confederated Sovereign States—and last of all to form Treaties with foreign Powers." When this was written (June 3), it had become apparent that no such systematic procedure was possible. "We Shall be obliged," Adams told Henry, "to declare ourselves independant States before We confederate, and indeed before all the Colonies have established their Governments. It is now pretty clear, that all these Measures will follow one another in a rapid Succession, and it may not perhaps be of much Importance, which is done first."[7]

Adams's belief that the natural order of things was to institute constitutional government in the states before defining the limits of the continental connection was surely significant, though he was probably right in thinking that it was of little importance which was done first—assuming, as he did, that each would be done expeditiously. As his comments make clear, the issue of the proper sequence reached beyond the formation of the union and the states. It was also closely entangled with the ongoing decisions over independence and foreign alliance. It is apparent that the congress, with four different balls in the air, had worked itself into a fine tangle in reasoning about these issues. A year before, the delegates who had opposed the uncompromising program of New England and Virginia, led by John Dickinson, had believed that any move toward union would be equivalent to a declaration of independence, and they wanted to delay that step as long as possible. This in effect made union hostage to a prior decision on independence, and probably accounts for the decision to lay aside the Franklin plan when offered in the summer of 1775. In the spring of 1776, however, Dickinson and his friends reversed tack and now made independence hostage to union. As the move toward independence began to look irresistible, they warned against leaving one protective relationship forever and aye without any assurance that the American colonies would successfully form another one among themselves. We must have a union before we have independence, they said. For this reason, Carter Braxton thought it in April 1776 almost a matter of scientific proof that a Declaration of Independence lay far in the future, because intestine wars would follow inexorably from a failure to observe the proper sequence.[8]

Those on the other side of this argument, by contrast, thought that independence was a necessary prerequisite of foreign assistance. Though they acknowledged that the making of a durable union would be crucial both in obtaining foreign aid and in prosecuting the war, they did not see how it was possible to make progress on the union without first instituting government in the states. If the parties to the union were to be the free and independent states of America, their chances of making a durable union would be greatly diminished if they themselves were not constituted on good authority. But that in turn required independence. By reasonings not terribly implausible, it was in fact possible to argue a kind of logical precedence for each of the steps—new state constitutions, federal union, independence, and foreign assistance—that had to be taken.[9]

Faced with this Gordian knot, congress boldly cut through it by in effect waiving the question of precedence and agreeing to do all four things together and at once. That was the essential meaning of the triple resolution calling for independence, foreign alliances, and confederation introduced by Richard Henry Lee in early June 1776, followed shortly thereafter (June 12) by the appointment of committees to consider each of these three subjects, and then (on June 15) by the call to the states to form new governments.[10] The realization that these things would have to be done together dawned simultaneously in Philadelphia and Williamsburg, and when Adams recalled, late in life, how "thirteen clocks were made to strike together," he doubtless remembered his elation on learning of the coincidence.[11] "The colonies had grown up under constitutions so different, there was so great a variety of religions, they were composed of so many different nations, their customs, manners, and habits had so little resemblance, and their intercourse had been so rare, and their knowledge of each other so imperfect, that to unite them in the same principles in theory and the same system of action, was certainly a very difficult enterprise. The complete accomplishment of it, in so short a time and by such simple means, was perhaps a singular example in the history of Mankind. Thirteen clocks were made to strike together. A perfection of mechanism, which no artist had ever before effected."[12] This well describes the kind of unity that Americans possessed in 1776, something very inadequately conveyed by later ideas of "the nation." Their unity expressed itself not in their similarities—they were, on the contrary, profoundly conscious of their differences—but in their commitment to the same principles of government, their common detestation of the British ministry, and their deep-seated fear of the consequences of disunion.

This meeting of the minds led directly to the Declaration of Independence, voted July 2, to be proclaimed on "the glorious fourth." "When in the course of human events," ran the preamble, "it becomes necessary for one people to dissolve the political bands which have connected them with another, and to assume among the powers of the earth the separate & equal station to which the laws of nature and of nature's God entitle them, a decent respect to the opinions of mankind requires that they should declare the causes which impel them to the separation." After stating those causes in the body of the document, it was declared in the conclusion, in the name of "the representatives of the United States of America in General Congress assembled, . . . and by the authority of the good people of these colonies . . . that these united colonies are & of right ought to be free & independent states; that they are absolved from all allegiance to the British crown, and that all political connection between them & the state of Great Britain is, & ought to be, totally dissolved; & that as free & independent states they have full power to levy war, conclude peace, contract alliances, establish commerce & do all other acts & things which independant states may of right do." The signers of the Declaration, in support of this end, mutually pledged to one another "our lives, our fortunes, and our sacred honor."[13]

It is symbolic of an entire history that the two great competing claims over which men and women would quarrel for generations—that Americans were one people, and that they formed a neighborhood of independent and sovereign states—were thus announced in this fundamental testament of the American Revolution. The emphatic concluding statement declaratory of the powers that these free and independent states might exercise, it is true, would seem to carry more force than the invocation of "one people" at the beginning; if the drafters of this document intended to establish a sort of plenary power in this one people, making it a single body politic that possessed national sovereignty, it would seem rather strange that they should employ language so unambiguously affirming that the American states were now possessed of the rights that all states had in a state of nature. It seems most improbable as well that the author of those lines, Thomas Jefferson, intended with this language to constitute such a single body politic; the conclusion seems wholly inconsistent with everything we know about his characteristic mode of constitutional reasoning. It is nevertheless the case that alongside these free and independent states now possessing full and unvarnished sovereignty there was also the claim that Americans constituted, in some sense, a single people. So, too, it was the case that these states were now solemnly pledged to secure their independence in common. Could they now claim in good faith that they were free to go it alone? If not, was their sovereignty not thus sharply qualified at the outset? At a minimum, the fact must be acknowledged that the document could be, and was in the future, read in different ways. Whatever the right interpretation is (and what, after all, is an "is"?), it seems clear enough that the delegates in congress were not then looking to the Declaration to discover the proper relationship between the union and the states. It was in the committee on the confederation established for this purpose in June 1776 that congressmen would begin the task of defining the nature and hammering out the terms of their continental connection.[14]

Jefferson would recall, late in life, that the Declaration of Independence was the fundamental act of union of these states.[15] It would probably be more accurate to say that it was the fundamental act that committed Americans to making the union of the states; certainly by itself it could not resolve the ambiguities inherent in both disuniting from Britain and uniting among themselves. Because the confederation had not yet been made, July 4, 1776, may perhaps best be regarded not as their day of betrothal but as their night of forbidden passion, a glorious consummation to the warm embraces of the previous two years yet an act that fell well short of a regular marriage. The final line of the Declaration was a pledge that they would see each other through the making of the union and the winning of independence, but it was not yet an achievement of either. In a technical sense, therefore, they were living in sin. If the fond hope of British strategists was to catch these Americans in flagrante delicto—that is, without the union—American whigs were just as determined to proceed rapidly to the formalization of their vows.

18

The "Dickinson Plan"

THE CONGRESS entrusted the task of drawing up articles of confederation to a committee of twelve. John Dickinson was chosen as member from Pennsylvania, and we know the work of this committee almost entirely from his surviving draft. There was undoubtedly much conflict in the committee: when Dickinson said in his speech of July 1 that the committee on confederation disputed almost every article, he presumably knew whereof he spoke. Though a rough draft was probably drawn up by June 17, the fair copy of the Dickinson draft was not submitted to congress until July 12, and by then Dickinson had left the congress. The interim period had been dominated by the vote to declare independence (on July 2) and, for Dickinson, by the call for the Pennsylvania militia to meet Howe's movements in New York and New Jersey. When congress received the committee's report on July 12, Dickinson was gone, the draftsman standing instead at the head of his battallion in Elizabethtown, New Jersey.[1]

All historical narratives of the drafting of the confederation are hobbled by the extreme paucity of accounts, and firm conclusions must be advanced with circumspection. When John Adams reviewed the making of the confederation in his autobiography, he lamented the "profound Secrecy" with which it was done. The "whole Record of this momentous Transaction" was very sparse indeed: "No Motions recorded. No Yeas and Mays taken down. No Alterations proposed. No debates preserved. No Names mentioned." Adams objected to this at the time, as did James Wilson, but was overruled. As a result, "Nothing indeed was less understood, abroad among the People, than the real Constitution of Congress and the Characters of those who conducted the Business of it. The Truth is, the Motions, Plans, debates, Amendments, which were every day brought forward in those Committees of the whole House, if committed to Writing, would be very voluminous; but they are lost forever." The results are not quite as bad as Adams indicated: he and Jefferson made useful notes of the debates in the late summer of 1776, and there is enough surviving evidence to reconstruct the main lines of the story. There remain, nevertheless, serious gaps in the record—Charles Thomson, the secretary of the congress, was no James Madison—and historians have been unavoidably reduced to abject speculation at many a turn in the story.[2]

One such speculation that appears particularly questionable is the widely held assumption that the surviving initial draft of the articles, which was marked up in numerous interpolations and deletions in Dickinson's hand, was "the Dickinson plan." Most authorities appear to have envisaged a sequence in which Dickinson's proposal, independently drawn, was submitted to the committee's scrutiny and then amended and revised.[3] That assumption, for a variety of reasons, appears eminently implausible. Dickinson no doubt believed strongly in some of its provisions—for example, the authority it gave congress to fix the limits of the landed colonies—but the draft in certain places reads more like an agenda for discussion than a finished product. We know that there were bitter conflicts within the committee, and that these emerged before the first draft was produced. It seems plausible to assume that Dickinson, seeking a consensus within the committee, would include in his draft language suggested by members that the committee would then accept or delete according to its pleasure. Even if the draft drawn by Dickinson, as Edward Rutledge remarked, had "the Vice of all his productions to a considerable Degree; I mean the Vice of refining too much," it seems doubtful that all this sinning was attributable to his prolix pen alone.[4] Even in his initial draft, Dickinson was obliged to harmonize sentiments and in keeping with that duty might well have included provisions with which he himself disagreed, or language that was seen by him as being internally inconsistent, but which the committee and not the penman needed to resolve.

The mysteries of the Dickinson draft are not fully plumbed unless we see its production against the background of Dickinson's peculiar political situation in June 1776. Congress had deferred to Dickinson's judgment in 1775 but in the year to follow would do so less and less frequently. His advice and alarums were politely heard but gleefully overridden, and no more so at any moment than during the month preceding the Declaration during which the articles were drafted. His political position in Pennsylvania was also sinking rapidly. He and his friends were left out of the new Pennsylvania delegation elected in early July, as Adams noted, "because they opposed Independence, or at least were lukewarm about it. Dickinson, Morris, Allen, all fallen, like Grass before the Scythe notwithstanding all their vast Advantages in point of Fortune, Family and Abilities."[5] Dickinson's declining political fortunes also reinforce the likelihood that he presented himself to the committee as its servant rather than its master.

One fact seems clear: in the period of his seminal contribution, the father of the confederation was very much a hounded man. Overruled by the congress, and scorned by his countrymen in Pennsylvania, Dickinson was then handed the perfectly hopeless job of reconciling differences that he had publicly predicted were irreconcilable. He himself experienced his departure from congress as a liberation, and he wanted the world to know that he had resigned before he had been fired. "No youthful Lover," he told his close friend Charles Thomson on August 7, 1776, "ever stript off his Cloathes to step into Bed to his blooming beautiful bride with more delight than I have cast off my Popularity. You may recollect circumstances that are convincing, that my resignation was voluntary, I might have said ardent." Dickinson's own interpretation of his departure from congress was perfectly sincere, but the plain meaning of events was that he had been publicly reprobated and humiliated—cut down like grass before the scythe. Samuel Chase was doubtless speaking not entirely abstractly when he wrote, contemporaneously with Dickinson's departure from congress, that "Cursed be the Man that ever endeavors to unite Us," for Dickinson, at that moment, undoubtedly appeared to himself and to others as having been cursed by an inordinately malicious fortune.[6]

In what follows, the material that is italicized and enclosed in brackets was considered but deleted by the committee, and the remainder was submitted to the congress on July 12. After styling the confederacy, in the first article, "The United States of America," the draft made rapid descent into prolixity in Article 2:

> The said Colonies unite themselves *[into one Body politic]* so as never to be divided by any Act whatever *[of the Legislature of any Colony or Colonies, or of the Inhabitants thereof]* and hereby severally enter into a firm League of Friendship with each other, for their Common Defence, the Security of their Liberties, and their mutual & general Wellfare, binding the said Colonies *[and all the inhabitants, & their Posterity,]* to assist one another . . . against all Force offered to or Attacks made upon them or any of them, on account of Religion, Sovereignty, Trade, or any other Pretence whatever, *[and faithfully to observe and adhere to all & singular the Articles of this Confederation.]*

This article, as it ultimately appeared in the version submitted to the states, was positively lean and mean by comparison. "The said states hereby severally enter into a firm league of friendship with each other, for their common defence, the security of their Liberties, and the mutual and general welfare, binding themselves to assist each other, against all force offered to, or attacks made upon them, or any of them, on account of religion, sovereignty, trade, or any other pretence whatever." While most of these deletions seem insignificant, in that their purport was stated elsewhere in the draft or they were redundant, surely the choice between "body politic" and "firm League of Friendship" was quite significant. Nowhere else in the draft was the body politic language revived, signifying the conscious choice that the confederation was to be the one thing and not the other.[7]

Like the constitution of the United Provinces, on which it was in many respects closely modeled,[8] the Dickinson draft divided powers and authorities into two great classes. One was of those things given to the congress, and the other powers not given, which were to remain with the states. Article 2 laid the groundwork for this procedure by styling the association a firm league of friendship into which the states severally entered; Article 3 affirmed it by providing that "Each Colony shall retain and enjoy as much of its present Laws, Rights & Customs, as it may think fit, and reserves to itself the sole and exclusive regulation of its internal Police, in all Matters that shall not interfere with the Articles of this Confederation." These two provisions established the rule that whatever was not granted to the union was retained by the states. Instead of immediately enumerating what these powers were to be, however, the Dickinson draft laid the foundation for congressional authority by enumerating the powers that the states were to give up. Article 5 mandated that "No Colony or Number of Colonies without the consent of the union shall send any Embassy to or receive any Embassy from" either the British government or any foreign state. Nor might any colony or its servants "accept of any Present, Emolument, Office or Title of any kind whatever" from any foreign state. Article 6 forbade separate agreements among the states outside the machinery of the union: "No two or more Colonies shall enter into any Treaty, Confederation, or Alliance whatever between them without the previous and free Consent & Allowance of the Union." One of the curiosities of the Dutch confederation was that it allowed for separate embassy by the respective provinces, while also forbidding any alliances or confederations with foreign powers without the consent of the generality. The ferocious controversy that arose over Holland's separate treaty with Great Britain in 1654 showed that there might be sufficient elasticity in those clauses, or of temptation in the members, to make this a dangerous loophole, and the authors of the American confederation closed it: separate state embassies were forbidden.[9] These provisions, like the Union of Utrecht, did not forbid separate treaties, confederations, or alliances among the states, or with foreign states, but by making such arrangements contingent on "the previous and free Consent & Allowance of the Union," the renunciation of this power by the states was pretty much complete.

The power over commerce was handled differently, and in a way that suggested conflict within the committee. While "The Inhabitants of all the united Colonies" were to "enjoy all the Rights, Liberties, Privileges, Exemptions & Immunities in Trade, Navigation & Commerce in every Colony, and in going to & from the same, which the Natives of such Colony enjoy," the next provision forbidding each colony from laying duties or imposts on the productions or manufactures of another colony was deleted (Article 8). Under the committee plan, therefore, the power to regulate commerce, and to impose the duties and imposts incident thereto, lay with the states, and the only restraint under which they were laid was the provision (in Article 9) stipulating that such duties or imposts "do not interfere with any Stipulations in Treaties hereafter entered into by the Union, with the King or Kingdom of G.B. or with any foreign Prince or State."[10]

In its allocations of authority over the military, the Dickinson draft followed the basic lines of the compromise of 1775. For troops raised "in any of the Colonies for the Common Defense," the general officers would be appointed by congress, but each state legislature would otherwise enjoy full discretion in choosing officers. Here, too, there were to be restraints upon the states: "No *[standing]* army or Body of Forces shall be kept up by any Colony or Colonies in Time of Peace *[or War without the Approbation of the Union]*" except those requisite for garrisoning forts. Every colony, however, was obliged to "always keep up a well regulated & disciplined Militia," suitably armed and equipped. The committee considered, but deleted, a provision stating that it was *"the Intent of this Confederacy, Notwithstanding the powers hereafter given to the Union in Genl. Congress, that all Resolutions of Congress for raising Land Forces, should be executed by the Legislature of each Colony respectively where they are to be raised, or by persons authorized by such Legislature for that purpose."* The intent stated here largely conformed to current and subsequent practice—the Continental army was nothing other than state lines that had been "adopted" by congress—and the states continued to be responsible for maintaining both those continental lines and their state militias. It seems likely that the provision was deleted because it might be read as excluding such support for those continental forces—in the way of ordnance, clothing, and other essentials—as the united states in congress assembled might secure through currency emission or foreign loan.[11]

Article 12 provided that "All Charges of War and all other Expences that shall be incurr'd for the general Wellfare and allowed by the Union in General Congress, shall be defrayed out of a Common Treasury." This was to be supplied by the colonies in proportion to the number of all inhabitants, except Indians not paying taxes. A triennial census would be held, and the taxes necessary to pay the congressional quotas were to be laid by the respective colonies. In agreeing to terms of confederation, the states obliged themselves to "abide by the Determinations of the Union in general Congress." No colony, "in any case whatever," might seek "by Force to procure Redress of any Injury or Injustice supposed to be done by the Union to such Colony" in the settlement of accounts (Article 13).[12]

Having obliged the states to renounce many of the rights and powers that free and independent states enjoyed in a state of nature, the Dickinson draft finally reached, in Article 19, the class of powers for which congress enjoyed "the sole and exclusive Power & Right." These included authority to raise naval and land forces for the defense and security of the colonies but did not include the right to levy taxes or duties for this purpose, which was specifically forbidden. Congress was also given "the sole and exclusive Power & Right of determining" on war and peace and on the complicated rules of maritime law bearing on prizes and letters of marque and reprisal. Congress's "sole and exclusive Power & Right" also extended to "sending and receiving Embassadors under any Character; entering into Treaties & Alliances; establishing a sameness of Weights & Measures throughout all the united Colonies; coining Money and regulating the Value thereof; establishing and regulating post offices throughout all the united Colonies."[13]

None of these provisions seem to have been particularly controversial, or at least they survived the criticism that a few delegates would raise against them.[14] The case was otherwise with the extensive powers that the Dickinson draft gave congress in "settling all Disputes and Differences now subsisting or that hereafter may arise between two or more Colonies concerning Boundaries, Jurisdictions, or any other Cause whatever; . . . superintending all Indian Affairs, & regulating all Trade with those Nations; assigning Territories for new Colonies either in Lands to be separated from Colonies the words of whose Charters extend to the South Sea, or from the Colony of New York, heretofore purchased by the Crown." Essentially, it was proposed that congress should have unbounded authority in cutting off the extravagant claims of certain colonies, in selling such lands "for the general Benefit and advantage of all the united Colonies," and in giving to these new colonies "convenient and moderate Boundaries," with forms of government animated by "the Principles of Liberty." Significantly, the decisions on these latter questions did not require the affirmative vote of nine states, a procedure that was mandatory for the powers of war and peace, alliances, raising military forces, emitting bills, or borrowing money.[15]

Perhaps the most controversial feature of the Dickinson draft was its provision according one vote to each colony (Article 18). This vital provision flew squarely in the face of the view that Pennsylvania had always maintained in continental councils and Franklin found highly objectionable the rule according one vote to each colony. In the two other respects in which the committee's proposal proved highly controversial—the proportion of contribution and the control of western territory—the July 12 report stood not too far from Franklin's proposal of the previous year. Instead of a formula based on male polls from sixteen to sixty, the July 12 draft would apportion the common expenses according to the number of all inhabitants, "except Indians not paying taxes." With respect to the control of western lands, and the vesting in congress of a right to pass on the validity of charters, the Dickinson draft was at one with Franklin's in purpose and intent, even if it varied in the language. They both looked toward a great domain in the West, providing both a common fund for the union and a plan to lay out new colonies in the western territories founded on "Principles of Liberty."[16]

The various changes that occurred to this first rough draft on its submission to congress have invited the thesis that the confederation underwent a drastic change in character over the next sixteen months. Apart from the loss of the provision over the western territories, however, it is the continuities rather than the changes that are most pronounced. One continuity was registered in the use of the term "firm league of friendship"—which Franklin had also used in 1775—to describe the association they hoped to constitute. That terminology was not adventitious. In calling it that, the authors of the articles were, it must be presumed, not ignorant of prevailing usage among expositors of the law of nations or taxonomists of political forms. These leagues may certainly have had anomalous features if compared with the distribution of powers in a nation, state, or body politic constituted by a single people, but the form was hardly unknown to political taxonomists. In the perceptive summary of Rufus Davis: "To Polybios, [such an association] would be an example of *sympoliteia;* to Bodin, *foedus aequum;* to Althusius, *confoederatio non plena;* to Pufendorf, *systema civitatum irregulare;* to Hugo, it would be of the same genre as the Achaean, Swiss, and Netherlands leagues, a union 'so close as to exceed the bounds of the usual treaty'; to Montesquieu, it would be a *[republique fédérative];* and to Rousseau, a Helvetic or Germanic type of confederacy, kin to but more highly developed than the Greek leagues."[17]

Nor was this central feature of the instrument changed in any respect in its passage through the congress. Most authorities place an altogether implausible emphasis on Thomas Burke's amendment of April 1777, which provided that "Each state retains its sovereignty, freedom, and independence, and every Power, Jurisdiction, and right, which is not by this confederation expressly delegated to the United States, in Congress assembled."[18] Two distinguished interpreters, Merrill Jensen and Richard Morris, both write as if this amendment, incorporated as Article 2 in the 1777 text, effected a fundamental transformation in the purposes of the instrument—changing it, in Jensen's estimation, from a centralized national government with virtually unlimited discretion to one that "gave to the states the field of undefined authority."[19] The amendment, in fact, was supremely unimportant and simply restated the intention of the congress with respect to the sources and limits of its authority. That is why it was approved with near unanimity. The thrust of the amendment was not contrary to Adams's previously articulated understanding: he, too, had written in *Thoughts on Government* that the authority of the continental councils should be "sacredly confined" to certain objects, and this certainly presumed a whole and entire sovereignty in whatever had not been expressly granted.[20] Burke's language simply restated, though with greater emphasis, the paragraphs (Articles 2 and 3 in the Dickinson draft) that had defined the association as a "firm league of friendship" and that secured the right of each state to pass on the adequacy of its own constitution and government. These provisions established the rule that whatever was not granted to congress was retained by the states. Nor was Burke's language stressing the retention by the states of their sovereignty, freedom, and independence contrary to the essential character of the "firm league of friendship" as this had been understood in public law. This was also the language of Burlamaqui, Vattel, Pufendorf, and Montesquieu, who each had written in a similar vein: when several commonwealths joined together in a confederate republic or firm league of friendship, they surrendered only that portion of their sovereignty, freedom, and independence which they had expressly committed to their common councils.[21]

This formula, to be sure, did not resolve all the muddy areas that might exist between what belonged to congress and what belonged to the states, and indeed every month would bring a new and unexpected twist on that familiar problem. Burke's amendment, however, brought no such clarification either. It did not reach those powers that had been granted, and it took an inordinate faith in the force of the word "expressly" to believe that it would confound those who wished to probe the implications of those grants. Could it really put the war power in a cage? Those supporters of expanded powers in the congress would in later years always reason downward from the specific and ample grants of authority allotted to congress under the confederation, and Burke himself acknowledged the legitimacy of that procedure when he wrote that "the United States ought to be as One Sovereign with respect to foreign Powers, in all things that relate to War or where the States have one Common Interest." The obstacle to any effective expansion of congressional power, as subsequent events would show, had nothing to do with Burke's amendment and everything to do with the provision requiring the unanimous consent of all thirteen states for an amendment to the Articles to take effect. That provision, however, existed in all the drafts of the confederation from July 1776 to November 1777.[22]

Continuities between the first and final drafts are also marked with respect to the larger distributions of authority and power that they contained. Both bore a curious resemblance to the "constitution of the British empire" as the Americans had come to understand it. That mixture of executive, judicial, and "federative" powers that, in the American theory, had belonged to king and council, was basically given to "the united states in congress assembled"; those powers that belonged to the legislatures of the provincial colonies passed to the newly founded states.[23] In the traditional theory of the British constitution, the king enjoyed the powers of war and peace and of leagues and alliances that Locke had identified with the "federative power." This authority went to the Continental Congress under all drafts of the articles, which excluded the states from everything touching on foreign relations. By the same token, the arrangement the Americans made among themselves displayed the same dependence on the provincial legislatures that, in their view, had characterized the imperial constitution. While congress was to propose, the states were to dispose. Congress was given no formal power of compulsion in either the Dickinson draft or the perfected instrument, and it is highly doubtful that any such provision would have gained the assent of a majority of the states (to say nothing of the needed unanimous concurrence) had it been proposed. In agreeing to the "great Compact," the states would place themselves under both a moral and a legal obligation to submit to the determinations of congress—so long, at least, as others performed their part of the bargain—and in that sense the obligation entered into was more onerous than that which the colonial assemblies had to the king's representatives. But if in this respect the congress contemplated by the Dickinson draft enjoyed more authority than the king, in another respect it enjoyed less. Unlike king and council, it had no general power of disallowance or veto over the acts of provincial institutions. Unlike king and council, it lost its claim (to the great and evident dissatisfaction of the landless states) to the ungranted lands that lay within the charters of the landed colonies.

Though it is customary to see the articles as a precursor to the federal constitution of 1787, and though they did mark out an allocation of authority very similar to that of 1787, it is misleading to describe "the united states in congress assembled" as a national government. It had no distinct executive, judicial, or administrative departments, though it would soon enough appreciate the need for them. It is best thought of as a "plural Executive" or "deliberating Executive assembly," formed to coordinate rather than direct the exertions of the states, and with primary responsibility for deliberating on war, peace, treaties, and alliances. Much of this can be plausibly explained as a consequence of American expectations of a short war, but it also owed greatly to prevailing conceptions of legitimacy.[24]

That the congress was seen as acting in an executive capacity is the reason why proposals to take the sense of the states by a majority of states and people, in the manner of the constitution of 1787, were turned aside in 1777, and it is highly probable that the committee on confederation saw this quandary at the outset. They resolved it not by introducing into this executive body an unwieldy bicameral arrangement but by requiring the votes of nine states on all important matters. This meant that the states in the antipodes that felt themselves to be, and in fact were, the most different from the rest need only find a handful of allies elsewhere to protect their vital interests, but the protection was general and gave solace to any state and people who saw the danger of a continental coalition against them. Even under those circumstances, some observers considered the protection insufficient—William Henry Drayton of South Carolina would later suggest that eleven rather than nine out of thirteen was the better rule. Wrote Drayton:

When I consider, the extent of territory possessed by the thirteen states—the value of that territory; and that the three most southern, must daily and rapidly increase in population, riches, and importance. When I reflect, that from the nature of the climate, soil, produce of the several states, a northern and southern interest in many particulars naturally and unavoidably arise; I cannot but be displeased with the prospect, that the most important transactions in congress, may be done contrary to the united opposition of Virginia, the two Carolinas, and Georgia: States possessing more than one half of the whole territory of the confederacy; and forming, as I may say, the body of the southern interest. If things of such transcendent weight, may be done notwithstanding such an opposition; the honor, interest and sovereignty of the south, are in effect delivered up to the care of the north. Do we intend to make such a surrender? I hope not.

Despite Drayton's anxieties, which were shared by other South Carolinians as well, the three-fourths rule adopted by the committee in June 1776 survived the bitter debates over representation that were to follow over the next sixteen months. It also provided a greater measure of veto power to minority states or sections—and greater difficulties in the search for a congressional consensus—than the various formulas for a concurrent taking of states and peoples that some observers proposed in these years.[25]

That congress was a committee and not a king, while enjoying certain kingly responsibilities, gave it a peculiar character that is certainly anomalous if seen from the standpoint of 1787. As a deliberative body with executive responsibilities, it would have need of both the secrecy of executive deliberation and the courtesies of parliamentary assemblies, and the mixture thereof would cause much inconvenience and confusion. Experience, indeed, would show it to be ill formed for the regular pursuit of an immense press of business. Americans, nevertheless, did have a closely held theory as to why it should work. The colonists had repeatedly claimed, in the previous decade, that they were willing to support any fair and reasonable request from the king's representatives, and they had acknowledged the importance of the unifying role that king and council played in settling boundary disputes and organizing united action. In the American interpretation—and particularly that of Massachusetts and Virginia—colonial troops, raised in this fashion, had played a valuable, even critical, role in the great victory over France in 1763; the lavishness of their contributions, they insisted, had been attested by the willingness of Parliament to reimburse them for their expenditures. Their "narrative" of these events, it might be said, was both partial and inflated; but it was theirs, and it was not without supporting evidence: they *had* contributed, Parliament *had* reimbursed them; the war *had* been won. In entering into these arrangements—contested, in fact, in none of the plans for union then broached in congress, including Franklin's—Americans were to be given the opportunity of demonstrating that their theory of the imperial constitution had been a workable one, and that a political machine so configured could be run effectively on the basis of the faithful cooperation of the "free, independent, and sovereign states" making it up. They could not make their own union on the principle that such cooperation would not succeed without severely undercutting much of what they had been saying to the British over the past decade.

19

Deadlock and Compromise

NEITHER THE ABSENCE of a power of taxation over individuals, nor the absence, more generally, of a power of compulsion, nor even the confederation's status as a "firm league of friendship" reached the real source of disagreement that the Dickinson draft met with on its presentation to congress. Those disagreements centered instead on the equities of the arrangement as they were to be established in the related provisions for representation, control of the western lands, and the allocation of the burdens to be assumed by each state. The first great blows in this controversy were struck in the heated exchanges that occurred in the summer of 1776; the lines of the controversy were identical to those that, a decade later, almost tore apart the Philadelphia convention. The article on voting, as Chase observed, was the most serious, for "the larger colonies had threatened they would not confederate at all if their weight in congress should not be equal to the numbers of people they added to the confederacy; while the smaller ones declared against an union if they did not retain an equal vote for the protection of their rights." Chase believed that many delegates did not appreciate that it was of the "utmost consequence" to bring the parties together: no foreign power would ally with them at all, the different states would form separate alliances, and this state of "separation & independence" would bring on the horrors of civil war. In light of the fact that "our importance, our interests, our peace required that we should confederate, and that mutual sacrifices should be made to effect a compromise of this difficult question," Chase proposed a compromise that would reach both contested articles: in all questions relating to "life and liberty," the states would have an equal vote; in all questions relating to "property," the voice of each colony would be proportional to the number of its inhabitants.[1]

Franklin thought both contributions and votes should be proportioned according to the number of inhabitants. "He thought it very extraordinary language to be held by any state, that they would not confederate with us unless we would let them dispose of our money." If we vote equally, he said, we should pay equally. While one might submit to a representation made unequal by time and accident, it would be "very wrong to set out in this practice when it is in our power to establish what is right." In the case of the union between England and Scotland of 1707, the Scottish had voiced the same fear as the smaller states now did in America, but experience had shown them often in "possession of" the English government. Whereas Scottish critics, fearing this incorporation, had prognosticated "that the whale would swallow Jonas," as in times of old, Franklin observed that the reverse occurred: "Jonas had swallowed the whale." A confederation formed upon such iniquitous principles, Franklin held, could not last.[2]

John Adams also spoke on behalf of proportional representation. There was no danger that the large states would swallow up the smaller in those circumstances. Considering the distance from one another of Virginia, Pennsylvania, and Massachusetts, and considering, too, "their difference of produce, of interests, & of manners," the large states would never have an interest in oppressing the smaller. What was likely to happen (and what largely did happen) was that regional blocs would form, with "Jersey, Delaware & Maryland" generally pursuing the same objects as Pennsylvania, Virginia in leadership of the southern states, and Massachusetts carrying the banner for New England. Like Franklin, Adams stressed the inequity of allowing one vote to each state. If A contributed £50, B £500, and C £1000 in partnership, would it be just that they should "equally dispose of the monies of the partnership"? To the argument that the states were individuals and as such entitled to an equal vote, Adams held that "the question is not what we are now, but what we ought to be when our bargain shall be made. The confederacy is to make us one individual only; it is to form us, like separate parcels of metal, into one common mass. We shall no longer retain our separate individuality, but become a single individual as to all questions submitted to the Confederacy."[3]

Equally strong objections were raised against the rule of contribution according to the number of inhabitants, including slaves. The southern states were uniformly opposed to any such rule. Chase of Maryland, a slaveholder, favored fixing the quotas by the number of white inhabitants. Harrison of Virginia, also a slaveholder, proposed a compromise in which two slaves would be counted as one freeman. John Adams and James Wilson delivered stinging rebukes to both proposals. If Harrison's amendment took place, Wilson observed, "the Southern colonies would have all the benefit of slaves, whilst the Northern ones would bear the burthen." Wilson's objections were cast in such a way as to raise a question in the mind of Lynch of South Carolina whether "their Slaves are their Property." If that were debated, said Lynch, "there is an End of the Confederation." To Lynch's argument that slaves were their property and ought not to be taxed more than "Land, Sheep, Cattle, Horses, &c.," Franklin replied that "Slaves rather weaken than strengthen the State, and there is therefore some difference between them and Sheep. Sheep will never make any Insurrections." Harrison's amendment being put, it was rejected by the votes of New Hampshire, Massachusetts, Rhode Island, Connecticut, New York, New Jersey, and Pennsylvania, against those of Delaware, Maryland, Virginia, and North and South Carolina. These debates were focused on the quota of contribution and not the proportion of representation, but the two questions were inextricably bound up with one another, as Franklin had always insisted. And there were corollary advantages of an arrangement prompted by simple equity. Voting by the number of free inhabitants, as Benjamin Rush observed, would have the "excellent effect" of "inducing the colonies to discourage slavery & to encourage the increase of their free *inhabitants.*"[4]

Closely related to the issue of both representation and burden-sharing was the question of whether congress would have the authority to pass on state claims to western lands and to control relations with the Indians. Of all the "landed" states, Virginia had the largest claim. Hers not only stretched to the South Sea but also squinted at the North Pole, as it embraced most of the area out of which the states of Kentucky, Ohio, Indiana, Illinois, Wisconsin, and Minnesota were later made. These claims were in stark conflict not only with the states that had no charter claims to the western territory—Pennsylvania, Maryland, Delaware, New Jersey, and Rhode Island—but also with Massachusetts and Connecticut (both of which, if the charters were the rule, had good claims to territory within New York and Pennsylvania, and thence westward to the Pacific Ocean). Despite New England's conviction that she might have a lawsuit, to be settled for a consideration, in these claims, the real force of the proposal to cut off the sea-to-sea charters fell on the southern states, and Virginia above all. Jefferson said there was no doubt the colonies would limit themselves, but the virtually unlimited discretion vested in congress meant that Virginia and the other landed states could have no assurance that congress would not curtail their existing settlements.[5]

Virginia's apparent willingness to cede, under conditions determined by herself, was not enough for the delegates from the landless states. "No colony has a Right to go to the South Sea," claimed Chase. "They never had—they can't have. It would not be safe to the rest. It would be destructive to her Sisters, and to herself." Wilson was even more scornful of these "extravagant" claims, which were made by mistake, and in total ignorance of geography (since the grantees believed the South Sea to be within one hundred miles of the Atlantic Ocean). Pennsylvania, Wilson said mockingly, "has no Right to interfere in those claims. But she has a Right to say, that she will not confederate unless those Claims are cut off." Though the attitude of the landless states has sometimes been ascribed to the control exercised over them by members of the great land companies, there were interested parties on both sides of the dispute. The larger problem was political. Without the possibility of sharing in the revenues of the western domain, and with the landed states controlling a vast source of wealth and potential revenue, the landless states faced the serious prospect of higher levels of taxation that would provide a powerful incentive for their states to be depopulated—a vicious circle that time would make worse rather than better. This prospect was particularly onerous for those states, like New Jersey and Delaware, whose commerce passed through the ports of neighboring states. What sort of common cause was it, their delegates asked, that required them to fight and sacrifice to secure territorial claims that, if devolving solely upon the states with western lands, threatened to ruin those states without?[6]

These fierce denunciations of the injustice of the committee draft, and the reiterated threat of a refusal to confederate, may leave the impression that the confederation as proposed had no defenders, only critics. Yet that impression is misleading. Of all the speakers in the controversy, none gave so thorough and complete a defense of the committee draft as John Witherspoon. As delegate from New Jersey, Witherspoon was enamored of two provisions—of equal state voting, and of congressional control of the West—and he has customarily been seen (insofar as his presence has been noticed at all) as one among a host of small-state and landless-state advocates. While he was that, he also emerged as the philosopher of confederation; he certainly gave to that instrument its most profound exposition.

Witherspoon took note of the unanimous opinion that union was an absolute necessity in the achievement of independence; even those "who have expressed their fears or suspicions of the existing confederacy proving abortive, have yet agreed in saying that there must and shall be a confederacy for the purposes of, and till the finishing of this war." Giving up hopes of a "lasting confederacy," however, would fatally undermine any such temporary union. Not only would it "greatly derange the minds of the people" and undermine the war effort; the failure to confederate would also doom the peace to follow independence and would raise the certain prospect, as soon as peace was restored, "of a more lasting war, a more unnatural, more bloody, and much more hopeless war, among the colonies themselves." If it were impossible to reach agreement now, "when the danger is yet imminent," it would be madness to suppose it might be done thereafter, when the sense of common danger had slackened. Would not subsequent congresses display the same jealousies, "the same attachment to local prejudices, and particular interests," that this one displayed? The making of the union, Witherspoon remarked, was just like "the repentance of a sinner—Every day's delay, though it adds to the necessity, yet augments the difficulty, and takes away from the inclination."[7]

Pursuing this keen speculation, Witherspoon held that he was not one "of those who either deny or conceal the depravity of human nature, till it is purified by the light of truth, and renewed by the Spirit of the living God," and he conceded the force of the proposition "that from the nature of men, it is to be expected, that a time must come when it will be dissolved and broken in pieces." But what, he asked, was the consequence: "Shall we establish nothing good, because we know it cannot be eternal? Shall we live without government, because every constitution has its old age, and its period? Because we know that we shall die, shall we take no pains to preserve or lengthen our life? Far from it, Sir: it only requires the more watchful attention, to settle government upon the best principles, and in the wisest manner, that it may last as long as the nature of things will admit."

Witherspoon had no monopoly on the belief that one of the greatest dangers the colonies faced was of "treachery among themselves, augmented by bribery and corruption from our enemies." Yet he made this danger serve the interests of the smaller states. If they could say that the consequence of their independence from Great Britain would be to subject them "to the power of one or more of the strongest or largest of the American states," they would be strongly tempted to withdraw from the confederacy. Would not those states, Witherspoon asked, "prefer putting themselves under the protection of Great Britain, France, or Holland, rather than submit to the tyranny of their neighbors, who were lately their equals?" It was no argument that these "rash engagements" might issue in "their own destruction"; the "mixture of apprehended necessity and real resentment" might nevertheless produce it. Those states knew that "in all history we see that the slaves of freemen, and the subject states of republics, have been of all others the most grievously oppressed." The same argument "which we have so often used against Great Britain" was also applicable to the subjection of the small states by the larger. "I do not think the records of time can produce an instance of slaves treated with so much barbarity as the Helotes by the Lacedemonians, who were the most illustrious champions for liberty in all Greece; or of provinces more plundered and spoiled than the states conquered by the Romans, for one hundred years before Caesar's dictatorship."

We have already had occasion to cite the passage, from the peroration of Witherspoon's address, in which he affirmed the possibility of "great improvements" in "human knowledge" and "human nature," and placed the founding of the American confederation in a line of progress that began with "the disunited and hostile situation of kingdoms and states" two centuries previously and had ended, thus far, with the firm establishment in Europe of "that enlarged system called the balance of power." The step from the balance of power to federal union, in Witherspoon's estimation, had to cover an even lesser distance than that earlier leap, and he deemed it "not impossible, that in future times all the states on one quarter of the globe, may see it proper by some plan of union, to perpetuate security and peace; and sure I am, a well planned confederacy among the states of America, may hand down the blessings of peace and public order to many generations." The "quarter of the globe" to which Witherspoon referred was Europe; and here he was paying his respects to the tradition of inquiry that had sought to provide a federal constitution or plan of peace for that long-divided continent. Experience showed, if only on a small scale, that such federal experiments might well bear fruit. "The union of the seven provinces of the Low Countries, has never yet been broken; and they are of very different degrees of strength and wealth. Neither have the Cantons of Switzerland ever broken among themselves, though there are some of them protestants, and some of them papists, by public establishment. Not only so, but these confederates are seldom engaged in a war with other nations. Wars are generally between monarchs, or single states that are large. A confederation of itself keeps war at a distance from the bodies of which it is composed."

In justifying equal voting by the states, Witherspoon appealed to the practices of the modern confederations. In the "Belgic confederacy" (the name sometimes used to designate the United Provinces of the Netherlands), voting was done by provinces. Equality was the appropriate rule in a federal union, such as America proposed to make; this association was radically distinct, in Witherspoon's estimation, from the "incorporating" union that had occurred in 1707 between Scotland and England. "Equality of representation," he acknowledged, "was an excellent principle, but then it must be of things which are co-ordinate; that is, of things similar and of the same nature: that nothing relating to individuals could ever come before Congress." Stephen Hopkins of Rhode Island chimed in to similar effect. Too little was known of the ancient confederations, observed Hopkins, "to say what was their practice," but the Belgic confederacy, the "Germanic body," and the "Helvetic body" all voted by states. Advocates of proportional representation, including Benjamin Rush and James Wilson of Pennsylvania, retorted that it was that very feature that made them weak and imperfect. "The Germanic body is a burlesque on government," said Wilson, "and their practice on any point is a sufficient authority &

proof that it is wrong." Like Rush, Wilson insisted that "the greatest imperfection in the constitution of the Belgic confederacy is their voting by provinces." That had ensured, particularly during the war in the reign of Queen Anne, that the interest of the whole was "constantly sacrificed to that of the small states."[8]

Of all the speakers from the larger states, it was Benjamin Rush who made the most eloquent appeal to the idea that "we are now One people— a new nation"—a fate, he averred, that "heaven intended." It would be madness, Rush believed, to introduce within the American confederation "the very evil We fled from Great Britain to avoid—taxation without *representation.*" Like Franklin, he warned that a disease introduced at the outset of the confederation "'would grow with its growth, strengthen with its strength,'" ending finally in its ruin. The people, Rush conjectured, were to have allegiances to two legislative bodies: every man deposited "his property, liberty & life with his own State, but his trade *[and]* Arms, the means of enriching & defending himself & his honor, he deposits with the congress." If voting were by states, Rush argued, faction would gain a ready foothold: "a majority of the people, not states, will determine questions out of doors, and wherever we go contrary to their sentiments they will resent it—perhaps with arms." Rush dilated on the obstacles to effective action congress would face if its members remained bound to the wishes of their masters in the state assemblies. Pennsylvania, Rush's home state, was interested in a rule of proportional representation, but Rush professed not to be pleading the cause of Pennsylvania. Imagining expansion on a north-south rather than westerly direction, he argued that New Hampshire and Georgia would probably receive greater benefit from such a rule. But his larger plea was not for the interest of any state but for "the cause of the Continent—of mankind—of posterity." Fixing such an unequal rule upon congress would guarantee that America should introduce at her birth "the principal cause of the downfall of liberty in most of the free States of the world." If voting were by the number of free inhabitants, Rush averred, then "we cannot deposit too much of our liberty & safety in the hands of the congress. . . . But if we vote by colonies I maintain that we cannot deposit too little in the hands of the congress." Rush would not refuse to sign the confederacy if voting were by states—"but I will say that every man who does, signs the death warrant of the liberties of America."[9]

Despite Rush's eloquent appeal to the idea of a common American nationhood, it is clear he and Pennsylvania lost out on the bid to define the emerging association as a body politic and on the great claim—proportional representation according to numbers—with which that contention was invariably paired. The choice, as we have seen, was posed in committee in the deliberations on the Dickinson draft; Rush in effect sought to reopen that question, and he lost. What he said this association ought to be, and what it in fact was, were vastly different. It is also the case that the large-state delegates who spoke of the principle of nationality, or of melding the colonies into one united mass, did so for the purpose of achieving an equitable representation: they were looking not to draw the federal line between congress and the states in a particular way—that was a separate question—but to establish a fair rule for the direction of the partnership.

The general appreciation that effective representation and power within the union were inextricably linked with the powers that could be safely entrusted to the union subverts any clear alignment of "nationalists" against "federalists" in 1776. There was no such cohesive alignment.[10] Even for Rush, it is doubtful if he himself saw the full implications of the idea that he had stated for the distribution of authority between congress and the states—his peculiar enumeration of loyalties gives evidence of not having fully digested the question. Taking him at his word, however, it is surely significant that he thought congress ought to have as little power as possible were congress to vote by states. The "nationalist-federalist" distinction also breaks down if we consider the positions of other delegations. Witherspoon and other landless state delegates who wanted congressional control over the West can scarcely be considered nationalists, and had that claim of congressional power been retained, it would not have meant that their association was an "incorporating" as opposed to a "federal" union. Virginians who argued for representation according to numbers did not believe that they would thereby establish a consolidated government with the power to define or to cut off Virginia's own boundaries. In 1776 and 1777 (as well as a decade later), the southern states were most interested in a rule of population for representation, because it was widely expected that the future growth of population would be "to the southward." At the same time, those same southern states generally displayed the most anxiety over the need to closely limit the powers of the union.[11]

Perhaps most remarkable, and certainly of solace to the author of this book, is that from these fragmentary and incomplete records we may discern virtually all the leading elements of the unionist paradigm stated with great precision and candor:

1. The union is seen as a species of international cooperation, its historical significance as a successor to and elaboration on the peace plans that

had sought to take the vital and not impossible step from the balance of power to federal union over an area of continental dimensions.

2. This aspiration for peace and security over half a continent was stated alongside the recognition that Americans had a serious security problem, one represented by the likely interaction of the ambitions of foreign powers and the internal divisions among the American states. Americans would hear much more of that analysis in coming years.

3. Despite a developing consensus that there was no real alternative to permanent union, we find the repeated prediction that the union will dissolve if made on an unjust basis. Every great question touching representation and burden-sharing was considered in these terms, and there was always a delegate ready to proclaim that a wrong turn on representation, or control of the West, or the rule for apportioning expenditures among the states would send the confederation over a cliff.

4. There is, finally, the repeated invocation of arguments "so often used against Great Britain," making the Americans' understanding of their rights and grievances under the British Empire—also a "union" in the American estimation—a template by which to assess the wisdom and fairness of their own association. In the course of the proceedings, it became apparent that any principle of representation or burden-sharing they chose would be found by some group of states to undermine a crucial fount of legitimacy, implicating the union in a violation of the very principles they had taken up arms to oppose.[12]

The immediate result of these heated debates was to strip from the Dickinson draft a provision that he, along with Franklin, had thought indispensable: that to congress should fall the right to cut off the western territories of the landed states, and to appropriate the proceeds thereof to the common purposes of the union. That right was never successfully revived over the next year—though the division on it proved very close—and the Articles as submitted to the states in November 1777 were absent all these crucial provisions. Though the confederation retained authority "as the last resort on appeal in all disputes and differences now subsisting or that hereafter may arise between two or more states concerning boundary, jurisdiction or any other cause whatever"— and the Articles described a complicated process of arbitration by which that result was to be achieved—it provided also "that no state shall be deprived of territory for the benefit of the united states." As the landless states claimed the western domain as devolving upon congress from the rights of the British Crown, and not because they had a charter claim to any of it, this provision sunk the prospect of any relief for them from this procedure.[13]

The closely related issues of representation and burden-sharing were resolved in a way that caused equally dire prophecies of inevitable dissolution. It was Witherspoon, stung by the defeat over the western territories, who introduced the formula congress ultimately agreed upon, which made the rule of contribution dependent on "the value of all land within each state" granted or surveyed, together with the value of buildings and improvements, according to a mode that congress would subsequently determine. Experience would show, as Roger Sherman observed at the time, "that the States can neither agree to nor practise the mode voted by Congress, & nothing effectual can be done to fix the Credit of the currency or to raise necessary supplies until some Rule of proportion is adopted."[14] Indeed, about the only thing Witherspoon's hopeless formula had going for it was that it had avoided direct confrontation over slavery, the heated discussion of which had disclosed fundamentally incompatible perspectives in North and South. It was only in a situation of deadlock—arising from the inability of the northern and southern states to reach a compromise on how to count slaves—that Witherspoon's proposal could find adherents.[15] He found none of them, however, in the eastern states. Because those states had more in the way of buildings and improvements, this provision favored the South, as did the rule that established the quota by which congress might requisition soldiers from the states according to the number of white inhabitants.[16]

The years 1776 and 1777 are not known in history as ones of any great compromise; that a series of important compromises took place, however, would seem indisputable. "In this great business," wrote Richard Henry Lee, "we must yield a little to each other, and not rigidly insist on having every thing correspondent to the partial views of every State. On such terms we can never confederate."[17] For Lee and the Virginians, the great compromise consisted of their having given up an equitable rule of voting in exchange for two equivalents: the reservation of their rights in the West, and the rules adopted for the apportionment of contributions. The fact that the landless states never accepted Virginia's claim as valid was felt as a betrayal by Virginians in later years. They had felt themselves entitled to compensation in 1777 and believed that they had gotten it; the discovery that they had successfully reserved nothing provoked dismay and outrage in the Old Dominion.[18]

Up to and beyond the time when the Articles were submitted to the states for ratification, there were almost none who expressed their wholehearted approval of the shape it had taken, and a majority of the states were on record as prophesying that the confederation was tainted with an obvious injustice that would threaten its hoped-for perpetuity. Most of those who felt this way, however, signed anyway. From mid-1776 to late 1777 the inability to reach agreement on the contested articles was seen as severely weakening the common cause, and the conviction that the union must be made despite its imperfections was the preponderant sentiment. This sense of urgency is well conveyed in the letter, drafted by Richard Henry Lee, that was sent along with the printed articles to the states. Appealing to "the difficulty of combining in one general system the various sentiments and interests of a continent divided into so many sovereign and independent communities," congress found ratification indispensable "to confound our foreign enemies, defeat the flagitious practices of the disaffected, strengthen and confirm our friends, support our public credit, restore the value of our money, enable us to maintain our fleets and armies, and add weight and respect to our councils at home and to our treaties abroad." Without that instrument of cooperation—"essential to our very existence as a free people" —the inhabitants of the United States might "bid adieu to independence, to liberty, to safety."[19]

Congress intimated its willingness to hear fully and fairly the objections the states might enter to the perfected instrument,[20] but so sturdy was this belief in the vital significance of ratification that congress rejected all the amendments—some one hundred in number—subsequently proposed by the states in 1778 and 1779. Open up one provision, the reasoning went, and you would have to open up all of them. The inability of the congress to secure the assent of Maryland, which held out until 1781, should not obscure the existence of this larger consensus on the view that any union, even a radically imperfect one, was better than none at all. It was this conviction that produced a reasonably prompt ratification in ten states, and this conviction that lay at the core of the great compromise effected in these years. At the same time, it is equally apparent that the bitter debates launched in the summer of 1776 had revealed profound disagreements over the equity of the union's central provisions; those bitter pills, though largely swallowed, did not go away. If some delegates went further than others in their menaces—Pennsylvania's warning of disunion did not pass from the mouth of a Massachusetts man, nor South Carolina's defiant position on slavery from the lips of a Virginian—all approached the union with reservations and, typically, a keen sense of dissatisfaction with the emerging instrument. When Paine declared in *Common Sense* that 1776 would be "the seedtime of continental union, faith, and honor," he had warned that the "least fracture now will be like a name engraved with the point of a pin on the tender rind of a young oak; the wound will enlarge with the tree, and posterity read it in full-grown characters." That the American confederacy had sustained many such fractures was evident for all congressmen to see; whether it would kill the tree, or merely disfigure it, was a question that only time could answer.[21]

20

The Basis of Congressional Authority

WHEN JOHN ADAMS conceived his idea of waiving the problem of proper precedence and marching forthwith toward new state governments, federal union, independence, and foreign alliance, he expected that the problem of confederation could be rapidly dispatched. The idea that it would drag on interminably—though expressed by those opposed to an immediate declaration—was not one that had appeal to the band of brothers that led the march to independence in the summer of 1776. The skeptics, alas, had been proved right: it would take sixteen months from the committee report of July 12, 1776, to the submission of the Articles to the states in November 1777. Ten ratifications had followed by the summer of 1778, but three states—Maryland, Delaware, and New Jersey—were particularly aggrieved with the massive reservation of the "rights" of the landed states contained in the Articles. New Jersey came in in the fall of 1778, Delaware in the spring of 1779; Maryland, thinking that if she withheld signature she might establish her claims, and if she signed that the door would be forever locked against her, did not accede until February 1781, with the perfected ratification occurring on March 1, 1781. Since her signature was obtained through the good offices of the minister of France, with whom the delegates of Maryland had formed close ties, this was a doubtful symbol of perpetual union.[1] By the time it occurred, indeed, the mutual cooperation foreseen in 1776 had already broken down, the universe of assumptions on which the states had originally acted—a short war, valiant effort for the common cause—blasted to the four winds. Congress was bankrupt, its credit exhausted. It had confessed to the states in 1779 that all exertions for the war effort fell on the states individually. While the final act of ratification, up until the last moments, was deemed of vital significance by congress, the results were meager and even, in one crucial respect, perverse. As of March 1, 1781, the rules of voting foreseen in the now perfected instrument would have to be scrupulously observed: that meant that "not less than two nor more than seven delegates" could represent a state; it meant that seven votes were needed to decide any question, and nine to decide any question of importance, and it meant that, starting now, members would have to rotate out after a period of three years. While congress would usually manage over the next two years to constitute a quorum of nine states, the habitual nonattendance of various delegations set congress in practice under the hopeless rule of the Polish Diet—a *liberum veto*.[2] The several states in congress assembled remained in that condition until the new government was inaugurated in 1789.[3]

During the war, the congress had conducted its votes with a fluctuating set of rules. In late 1777, Burke noted that the congress "now determines by a majority which need not be more than five, and which seven is always conclusive."[4] Later, complaining of the "arbitrary and uncertain" rules of order, over which there were frequent disputes, he noted that the rules established for "deliberating Legislative assemblies" could not be applied "without manifest Inconvenience," because congress was a "deliberating Executive assembly." Any given majority was quick to observe that the utility of the case must govern: "So whatever rule appears to a Majority to be Contrary to utility must Necessarily be rejected as not order."[5] While unanimity was always sought for and the public face of it preserved until 1779, there were countless votes on which the majority had prevailed by the slimmest of margins—with four or five votes in favor, three to four opposed, and one to two divided. States with one delegate sitting were allowed to cast their vote, and to be counted for purposes of a quorum. James Lovell, for example, served continuously for five and a half years, at great personal sacrifice, often maintaining solo the duties of a foreign correspondence.[6] Even with these rules of order, congress still had trouble maintaining a quorum of nine states during the war. Nor could it maintain a permanent residence. Driven from Philadelphia to the mud of Baltimore in the winter of 1776, it returned to Philadelphia in 1777, only to flee to York, Pennsylvania, on the approach of Howe, and it was not yet done with its "*vagabondizing* from one paultry village to another."[7] Despite these manifold dangers and obstacles, by the date of ratification in 1781 it had sat in continuous session for the six previous years. What, it may be asked, was the basis of its authority during that time?

This question has both a short and a long answer, the short one being that there was no consensus on the point. "Lord though knowest whereof we are made," sighed the president of congress, Henry Laurens, in 1779, employing what he called "the facetious Sterne exclamation." Alas, the "great Governor of the world," as he was styled in the Articles, was probably unsure himself. Though doubtless attracted to a distinction between the *body* and the *spirit* to indicate the distribution of authority between the states and congress, the manifest division of his flock made it prudent to await such further clarification as events might provide. Several states, in ratifying the Articles, had held that it would not be obligatory on them until all the states had ratified, and if those reservations meant anything they meant that the terms of confederation were not yet obligatory. "The band of national union, the Confederation," observed Gouverneur Morris in 1779, "is not yet agreed to by all, nor binding on any."[8] Yet the unratified articles were appealed to by Virginia at the end of that year in assessing what congress might legitimately do. "When Virginia acceded to the Articles of Confederation," said the General Assembly, "her Rights of Sovereignty and jurisdiction within her own territory were reserved & secured to her, & cannot now be infringed or alterd without her Consent." Were congress to assume such a "Jurisdiction, and arrogate to themselves a Right of Adjudication not only unwarranted by, but expressly contrary to the fundamental principles of the Confederation, . . . it would be a violation of public faith, introduce a most dangerous precedent which might hereafter be urged to deprive of Territory, or subvert the sovereignty and Government of any one or more of the United States, and establish in Congress a power which in process of Time must degenerate into an intolerable despotism."[9]

Whereas Virginia considered herself bound *and* protected by the terms of the confederation, even before ratification, and took the reasonable position that the powers of congress could not be greater than those spelled out in the Articles, other states seemed to deny this authority altogether, or at least to assume that their obligations to the union were something that only they could know. It became a habit in them "to exercise a right of judging in the last resort of the measures recommended by Congress, and of acting according to their own opinions of their propriety."[10] "Some States," as Thomas Burke characterized the constitutional crisis of 1779, "seem not very clear that they are bound by any thing which has hitherto been done, and others Scruple not to declare that if Congress Should, on a Question for agreeing to Terms of peace decide in a manner Contrary to the Sense of those States they will Neither Submit or Confederate."[11] Burke wanted a clear avowal from New England on the latter question—was she in or out of the union?—but as to the former did not doubt that the states were so bound: "That for every purpose of common defence and common Exertions in the progress of the present War and for the conclusion thereof, the States are unquestionably, united by former acts of the Several States."[12] The same position was stated yet more emphatically in a circular letter from congress to the states, drafted by John Jay:

For every purpose essential to the defence of these States in the progress of the present war, and necessary to the attainment of the objects of it, these States are as fully, legally, and absolutely confederated as it is possible for them to be. Read the credentials of the different delegates who composed the Congress in 1774, 1775, and part of 1776. You will find that they establish a Union for the express purpose of opposing the oppressions of Britain, and obtaining redress of grievances. On the 4th of July, 1776, your representatives in Congress, perceiving that nothing less than unconditional submission would satisfy our enemies, did, in the name of the people of the Thirteen United Colonies, declare them to be free and independent States; and "for the support of that declaration, with a firm reliance on the protection of Divine Providence, did mutually pledge to each other their LIVES, their FORTUNES, and their SACRED HONOUR." Was ever confederation more formal, more solemn, or explicit? It has been expressly assented to, and ratified by every State in the Union. Accordingly, for the direct support of this declaration, that is, for the support of the independence of these States, armies have been raised, and bills of credit emitted, and loans made to pay and supply them. The redemption, therefore, of these bills, the payment of these debts, and the settlement of the accounts of the several States, for expenditures or services for the common benefit, and in this common cause, are among the objects of this Confederation; and, consequently, while all or any of its objects remain unattained, it cannot, so far as it may respect such objects, be dissolved consistently with the laws of GOD or MAN.[13]

Everything to which the states had unanimously bound themselves by that date—the joint winning of their independence, the joint prosecution of the war, the joint payment of the debt—might be considered as falling within the terms of their original compact, and it was readily deducible from their prior commitments that a right of sovereignty or of supremacy in the congress followed inexorably. Those former acts, as Burke wrote in a congressional resolution in April 1779, meant that congress was "invested with the supreme sovereign power of war and peace," and it meant further that no state had a right to nullify an act of congress within its sovereign jurisdiction, which Pennsylvania had sought to do by giving its state juries an unreviewable authority to determine the legality of captures at sea.[14]

Jay and Burke, so often taken as polar opposites in the heat of their nationalism, were in entire concord. They agreed that the authority of the congress rested on the prior acts of the several states, to which the states gave their voluntary consent, and until those obligations were fulfilled, neither nullification of the authority of congress, exercising its due powers, nor secession from the compact itself was consistent with the terms of their original pledges. Neither Jay and Burke nor the rest of the congress believed that by so insisting they were also denying the importance of achieving the ratification of the Articles. They all felt in very bad need of it, believing to a man that it would improve, rather than undermine, their claim to authority. Nor did they rest the authority of congress on the idea that "we are become one Nation"—the notion for which Rush had pleaded in vain in 1776. It was the plighted faith of the several states that was controlling and that generated such authority as congress possessed. It was on that authority that the debt had been contracted and the war had been fought, and it was good for as long as those obligations had not been discharged. Nor, finally, was the claim of congress unlimited in scope. In thus insisting on the supremacy of congress, neither Jay nor Burke contended for an unlimited power of sovereignty in the congress. Its domain embraced the power to make war and peace and to contract treaties and alliances, but it did not generally extend beyond the exercise of the federative power. The supremacy contended for was an avowedly limited sovereignty, reaching to those objects, largely external, to which the faith of the confederated states was pledged.

The same conclusion as to the legitimacy of nullification—or, conversely, the legitimacy of congressional compulsion—was reached in later years with respect to the powers granted to congress under the Articles of Confederation. Jefferson's is the classic statement: "It has been often said," he wrote in 1786, "that the decisions of Congress are impotent because the Confederation provides no compulsory power. But when two or more nations enter into compact, it is not usual for them to say what shall be done to the party who infringes it. Decency forbids this, and it is as unnecessary as indecent, because the right of compulsion naturally results to the party injured by the breach. When any one state in the American Union refuses obedience to the Confederation by which they have bound themselves, the rest have a natural right to compel them to obedience."[15]

It is notable that these declarations from Jay, Burke, and Jefferson are inconsistent with the theories of the origins of the union that in later periods of American history would excite the rapt attention of millions, and over which historians still argue today. From some nationalist interpreters in the 1830s, and most authoritatively by Joseph Story, came the avowal that the authority of congress during the war rested on the grant of the sovereign American people, whose consent through the separate states was irrelevant to the national sovereignty this body politic possessed and exercised in 1776, whence it followed that neither secession nor nullification was allowable under the constitutional system of the United States. From many "compact theorists," but by no means all, came the declaration that the union was always in a nature of a compact, that the states so acceding did not surrender their right to interpret the extent of their obligations, whence it followed that both nullification and secession were permitted. These rival theories lay along the outer limits of the subsequent constitutional argument, but it is striking how inconsistent they both were with the interpretation of the union given at the beginning. On the evidence presented here, Story was wrong in his assumption that the union was not a compact, but right in his denial of nullification or secession; Calhoun was right in his assumption that the union was a compact, but wrong in his support of a right of nullification and succession. The great idea that many of the rival combatants of the 1830s shared—that if it is a compact, then nullification and secession follow inexorably—was precisely that which was denied in 1779 by Jay and Burke, and in 1786 by Jefferson. Far more consonant with the original understanding was the view taken during that later controversy by James Madison. Writing of the "Constitutional compact" of 1788, but in words that applied just as readily to the compact of 1781 or the sacred vows of 1776, he insisted that its nature precluded "a right in any one of the parties to renounce it at will, by giving to all an equal right to judge of its obligations; and, as the obligations are mutual, a right to enforce correlative with a right to dissolve them." It gives some measure of Madison's despair in his dying years that this historically more accurate and logically more compelling account should have been rejected at that time by both extremes of the argument, for in that rejection he saw grave peril to the union.[16]

Despite these avowals of an implied right of compulsion in the congress both before and after 1781, there was a vast gap between the authority congress might claim in theory and what it could actually exercise in practice. Hamilton might find in the powers granted to congress a "full power *to preserve the republic from harm*," but he well knew that the delegates to congress had in practice displayed a "diffidence . . . of their own powers, by which they have been timid and indecisive in their resolutions, constantly making concessions to the states, till they have scarcely left themselves the shadow of power."[17] The several states, in 1779, might be obligated to the debt contracted in their name, but they could not reach agreement on an equitable way of apportioning the shares, nor on the two most eligible sources of general revenue (imposts and the western lands). The Articles might speak of perpetual union, and Jay invoke a certain kind of perpetuity in 1779, but many Americans presumed in 1780 and 1781, with Madison, "that the present Union will but little survive the present war." Already observers were estimating as the more likely reality that the "several states would ultimately form several confederations rather than a single nation."[18] Though aiming at union, and cherishing the idea of it as a sacred necessity on which everything depended, this association of bodies politic found itself before and after 1781 very nearly in a condition of disunion. The stark contrast between the claimed authority and real power of congress, and the concomitant and numerous violations by the states of their obligations, could not, moreover, but weaken the practical force of the argument appealing to an implied power of congressional compulsion. Was one obliged to fulfill the terms of a contract if the other parties to it were not fulfilling theirs? Was this the rule of the law of nature and of nations?[19]

However compelling contemporary observers or subsequent historians might find the case for congressional compulsion of refractory states, that authority was not exercised during or after the war. The states may have been obligated to fulfill the requisitions of congress, but those obligations were not fulfilled in the nullifications that occurred almost from the first moments of the war, and that continued until 1787. From 1779 to 1781, that situation was particularly desperate, the sheer destitution of congressional power the omnipresent reality. Everything now depended on the exertions of the states individually—they had no credit or resources collectively—but experience had shown that while some states might strain their nerves, others would sit on their hands. Congress, in the artful summary of one historian, "could not pass effective laws or enforce its orders. It could ask for money but not compel payment; it could enter into treaties but not enforce their stipulations; it could provide for raising of armies but not fill the ranks; it could borrow money but take no proper measures for repayment; it could advise and recommend but not command."[20] There was a flurry of interest in reversing this situation in 1781, prompted by the ratification of the Articles, but it went nowhere. Madison, who then promoted the idea of a power of compulsion in the congress that was implicit in their compact, nevertheless thought that basic principles of constitutionalism required that such a power be explicitly authorized, and his amendment to this effect disappeared in committee.[21] Instead of claiming such a right, congress instead embarked on an amendment to the Articles allowing it to raise money through an impost. The failure of that and subsequent amendments—defeated ultimately by the *liberum veto*—would set them on the road to the Philadelphia convention.

Even before the Articles had been ratified, Americans found themselves in a most peculiar and indeed strange situation. They had agreed to cooperate but could not agree on the terms of that cooperation. They knew they had to share the burdens equitably but could not agree on what that entailed. They saw that congress, to be legitimate, must be representative, but they could not agree on what or who it should represent. They had constituted a government whose efficiency would rest on "a disposition of accommodation in the States to each other, and of Congress to all,"[22] but then found themselves ill disposed to make the necessary accommodations. In explicating the nature of the federal bond to an Indian leader, Jefferson remarked that Virginia was "but one of thirteen nations, who have agreed to act and speak together. These nations keep a council of wise men always sitting together, and each of us separately follow their advice."[23] Yet experience was daily showing that the wise men were often thought foolish, their advice neglected. More in keeping with the understanding of white men (which they kept to themselves when addressing the Indians) was the observation of one of Jefferson's congressional correspondents in 1777: "Rely on it our Confederacy is not founded on Brotherly Love and Able Statesmen are Surely wanting here."[24]

PART FIVE
A Foreign Policy of Independence

21

Foundations of the New Diplomacy

THE YEARS FROM 1776 to the Peace of Paris in 1783 not only saw the first great attempt to establish a workable compact of union among the American states; they also witnessed the elaboration of the key ideas that provided the foundation of American foreign policy. Union and independence were, as we have emphasized, closely linked ideas that ran on parallel paths. Like the story of the union, the struggle for an independent foreign policy is, in many respects, a story of lost innocence. Here, too, a gap opens between aspiration and reality in the course of the war—a simultaneous and parallel discovery of how difficult it is for independent states to cooperate in the achievement of an objective they all regard as vital, and how difficult it is to pursue a policy of independence in a threatening and dangerous world. As always, each of the separate strands of union and independence vitally affected the other, with the weakness of the union threatening the objective of independence, and the practical dependency on foreign assistance threatening to undermine the union. Historians have a tendency to regard these dual aspirations to union and independence as settled facts from the first moments of the American Revolution. They are, I think, better seen as fixed aspirations. At a certain level of generality, a deep consensus existed on both points. Descending to particulars, however, Americans found themselves in their usual condition of bitter conflict and dissensus.

In the years and months leading up to the Declaration of Independence, the common lament of the hesitant and fearful was that independence promised a terrible future for the independent colonies. Vulnerable to foreign predation and in danger of dividing among themselves, they would soon fall victim to internecine conflict and ultimately to some fortunate conqueror. These terrors were felt very widely, and not simply by loyalists. It was one of the great contributions of Thomas Paine's *Common Sense*— a wildly successful pamphlet that first appeared on January 10, 1776—that its author sought to demonstrate that these fears were without foundation. In dispelling these fears, Paine not only reconstructed the past relationship between Britain and the colonies in a way that sharply diminished the advantages that America derived from its connection with Great Britain; he also set forth a new vision of the role that America would play in the world that expressed vital features of the developing American consensus.

Paine's reconstruction of the colonial past emphasized that "France and Spain never were, nor perhaps ever will be our enemies as *Americans,* but as our being the *subjects of Great Britain.*" In the past, Britain "did not protect us from *our enemies* on *our account,* but from *her enemies* on *her own account.*" That assessment held peril for the future because "any submission to, or dependence on Great-Britain, tends directly to involve this continent in European wars and quarrels, and sets us at variance with nations, who would otherwise seek our friendship, and against whom, we have neither anger nor complaint." America had no interest in being dragged into the wars of Britain; her "true interest," on the contrary, was "to steer clear of European contentions, which she never can do, while by her dependence on Britain, she is made the make-weight in the scale of British politics." America had very little to do with such connections. "Our plan is commerce, and that, well attended to, will secure us the peace and friendship of all Europe; because, it is the interest of all Europe to have America a *free port.*" As the supplier of "necessaries," America would "always have a market while eating is the custom in Europe." Strategically placed along vital trade routes, moreover, her position was such that Britain's own valuable trade to the West Indies was entirely at her mercy.[1]

Paine placed no credence on the oft-repeated observation that the colonies would fall into war themselves were they to become independent. The reverse was true. It was only "independence, i.e. a continental form of government," that "can keep the peace of the continent and preserve it inviolate from civil wars." Thus far, the colonies had "manifested such a spirit of good order and obedience to continental government, as is sufficient to make every reasonable person easy and happy on that head. No man can assign the least pretence for his fears, on any other grounds, than such as are truly childish and ridiculous, viz. That one colony will be striving for superiority over another." It was the monarchical and aristocratical governments of Europe that were continually throwing that continent into violent contests; republican governments, by contrast, were inherently pacific: "Where there are no distinctions there can be no superiority, perfect equality affords no temptation. The republics of Europe are all (and we may say always) in peace. Holland and Swisserland are without wars, foreign or domestic." The horrors of civil war were not discounted by Paine, but he found the danger of them to lie wholly in a "patched up connexion" with Britain, for it was "more than probable" that such a reconciliation would "be followed by a revolt somewhere or other, the consequence of which may be far more fatal than all the malice of Britain."[2]

In thus dismissing the prospect of internecine wars among the American states, Paine went further than the developing American consensus, for the prospect of such wars, as we have seen, would be repeatedly invoked in 1776 and 1777 as a potent argument for completing the American confederation. So, too, the fear that Paine had deemed "childish and ridiculous"—that one or more American states would strive for superiority over the others—was in fact gravely urged by a host of delegates in the debates over their charter of union. But if in these respects Paine's views commanded nothing approaching a consensus, in other respects he captured perfectly the prevailing American outlook in 1776. "Peace and commerce with all nations, entangling alliances with none," is an expression of Jefferson's First Inaugural in 1801, but Paine had clearly caught the spirit of that outlook in *Common Sense*.

John Adams had arrived, independently, at a very similar conception. Though keen on the idea that "God helps those who help themselves,"[3] and anxious that foreign countries not rob Americans of the glory of securing their own liberties, Adams earnestly solicited a connection with France, through whom America might gain desperately needed military supplies. The fears that such a connection with France would "put us in the Power of foreign states" were dismissed by Adams on the grounds that he was not "for soliciting any political Connection, or military assistance, or indeed naval, from France. I wish for nothing but Commerce, a mere Marine Treaty with them."[4] In the Plan of Treaties he drafted in the summer of 1776, he had set forth the provisions that ought to govern a future treaty between the United States and France, and he wanted it to be shorn of a political commitment. France would make no treaties unless the colonies declared themselves independent, Adams argued, but he was confident she would do so once they did. The plan he drafted set forth principles of the treatment of neutral shipping in war, and of commercial comity among the signatories, that were to be a model for other such treaties with European powers, including Britain. These provisions, Adams expected, would be seen as consonant with the "true interest" of both France and America, and he believed that the offer America made was one that no European power would spurn.

The 1776 Model Treaty was in most respects entirely consistent with the diplomatic spirit of the time. The reluctance of the Americans to tie themselves to French direction, their desire to maintain their freedom of action, and their fear of exchanging one master for another were not generally felt with the same heat in the southern colonies as they were in New England, but all the colonists seemed to grasp that their interest lay in a policy of nonentanglement toward Europe. Nor did Americans depart from the accepted maxims of the age in the great value they attached to their commerce. If the "true balance of power really resides in commerce and America," as Choiseul had affirmed in 1759, it was scarcely anomalous that Americans should believe that "whatever European Power possess the presumption of [the commerce of this country] must of consequence become the richest and most potent in Europe."[5]

In one critical respect, however, the American attitude toward commerce was vastly different from the outlook prevailing in European courts. It was pointedly "liberal" rather than "mercantilist"—in favor of removing the fetters and restraints on commerce that dictated the policy of European nations. Though Americans were understandably sensitive on the point of declaring their desire to break free of the fetters imposed by the Acts of Trade and Navigation—such, Lord North argued, had been their real motivation in the controversy with Britain—they certainly agreed with British opinion in thinking that such restrictions imposed onerous hardships on the colonial economy. Once independence was declared, they looked forward to the day when they could explore the advantages of a free commerce with all the world, and they believed devoutly that they would be the gainers from this policy. "The sweets of a free commerce with every part of the earth," wrote the congress in a May 1778 address to the inhabitants of the United States, "will soon reimburse you for all the losses you have sustained. The full tide of wealth will flow in upon your shores, free from the arbitrary impositions of those, whose interest and whose declared policy it was to check your growth." It did indeed require but a "moment's reflection," wrote David Ramsay in the same year, to demonstrate "that as we now have a free trade with all the world, we shall obtain a more generous price for our produce, and foreign goods on easier terms, than we ever could, while we were subject to a British monopoly."[6]

The debate over the Model Treaty was not over the general desirability of a free trade with all the world—that was an aspiration that Americans, despite differing regional economies, could generally share. The question, rather, was whether the American offer to France would be sufficient. While Adams was intent, as he later recalled, on avoiding "every thing that could involve us in any alliance more than a commercial friendship," others were not so sanguine. Two of his intimate friends, Samuel Adams and Richard Henry Lee, "thought there was not sufficient temptation to France to join us. They moved for cessions and concessions, which implied warranties and political alliance that I had studiously avoided."[7] Though Adams recalled that he had "carried every point" in this first great discussion of the foundations of American foreign policy, he did not do so for long. Over the course of the next year, congress progressively cast aside its reluctance to offer political warranties and guarantees to France, and when the great bargain was made, in February 1778, there were two treaties, not one. In addition to a treaty of amity and commerce, concluded largely on the terms of Adams's initial draft, there was a treaty of alliance that forbade the parties to "conclude either truce or peace with Great Britain without the formal consent of the other first obtained" (Article 8).

It was an American triumph that the "essential and direct end of the present defensive alliance" was declared to be the maintenance of "the liberty, sovereignty, and independence absolute and unlimited, of the said United States, as well in matters of government as of commerce" (Article 2). At the same time, the treaty contained an entanglement: the United States undertook to guarantee "from the present time and forever against all other powers . . . the present possessions of the Crown of France in America, as well as those which it may acquire by the future treaty of peace" (Article 11). Though Adams would claim in 1780, largely on the basis of Article 2, that the treaty of alliance was to last "no longer than this war," the plain meaning of Article 11 was that certain of its stipulations were to last forever. Franklin pithily summarized its moral and political significance by noting, in a letter written four days after the conclusion of the treaties, that America had been "a dutiful and virtuous daughter" when subordinate to Britain: "A cruel mother-in-law turned her out of doors, defamed her, and sought her life. All the world knows her innocence and takes her part, and her friends hope soon to see her honourably married. . . . I believe she will make as good and useful a wife as she did a daughter, that her husband will love and honour her, and that the family from which she was so wickedly expelled will long regret the loss of her." Anticipating the coming war between France and Britain, Franklin wrote soon afterward to a British agent that America would stand loyally by the alliance: "[W]e are bound by ties stronger than can be formed by any treaty to fight against you with them as long as the war against them shall continue."[8]

Adams would later complain bitterly of Franklin's "dogmatical" attachment to a system of policy opposite to his own, but his initial reaction to the treaty of alliance was one of fervent support. In the negotiations for the alliance, the American side was quite aware that France's great fear was that of a rapprochement between Britain and the United States, and it was in anticipation of such an offer from Britain that France had signed the treaty of alliance that brought her into the war.[9] Adams never had much use for such demeaning suggestions, which implied a weakness of will he thought it bad policy to advertise, and which for New England was certainly untrue.

When the prospect of such an offer arose in 1778—entailing a British acceptance of American independence on the condition that the United States would renounce her alliance with France—Adams fervently rejected it as "a modest Invitation to a gross act of Infidelity and Breach of Faith." "This Faith is our American Glory, and it is our Bulwark, it is the only Foundation on which our Union can rest securely, it is the only Support of our Credit both in Finance and Commerce, it is our sole Security for the Assistance of Foreign powers. If the British Court with their Arts could strike it or the Confidence in it we should be undone forever." As vital as these considerations were for an infant state struggling to establish its good character, Adams also insisted that the alliance was founded in mutual interest: in his estimation, France was "the natural Ally of the united States," and this for two reasons. So long as Britain retained Canada, Nova Scotia, and the Floridas, "or any of them," Britain and America were fated to be enemies. "It is not much to the Honour of human Nature, but the Fact is certain that neighbouring Nations are never Friends in Reality." Added to the likelihood of future territorial disputes was a second great fact of mutual interest: both France and America had strong reason to detest "the rapacious Spirit of Great Britain against them," and in particular to wish a curb upon British naval power.[10]

Adams amplified on these conceptions in letters written in 1780, and subsequently published in Great Britain. The great point he contended for in these essays was that the "true interest" of both America and Europe was that "America should have a free trade with all of them, and that she should be neutral in all their wars." Were America's trade to fall again under a British monopoly, it "would establish an absolute tyranny upon the ocean." That fact established, in Adams's view, "that the other maritime powers ought to interfere in assisting America to maintain her independence, and also to maintain her true system of neutrality in future, that the blessings of her commerce may be open to all." Britain herself, as she had done in every war for the last hundred years, was then pointing at "the ambition of France, for universal monarchy," as the basis of her system of policy, but Adams thought that "a chimera," fit only "to amuse the madness of Britains." Much as Englishmen might delude themselves with what, in the final analysis, were mere phantoms, the rest of the world needed to take their pretensions seriously: "Universal Monarchy at land is impracticable; but universal Monarchy at sea has been well nigh established, and would before this moment have been perfected, if Great Britain and America had continued united." Were Britain and America to be "again united under one domination, there would be an end of the liberty of all other nations upon the seas. All the commerce and navigation of the world would be swallowed up in one frightful despotism. The Princes of Europe, therefore, are now unanimously determined that America shall never again come under the English government."[11]

The princes of Europe, as events would show, were not so terribly keen on that determination as Adams affected to believe, but Americans were generally convinced that a genuine mutuality of interest existed between themselves and those nations of Europe that had groaned under Britain's maritime despotism. Such had been the basis of the "militia diplomacy" that had sent American ministers abroad with careless abandon in the first years of the war to solicit aid and recognition (and from which, as Franklin had warned, there would be little or worse to show). Expectations of a fundamental change in the maxims of European politics and of the structure of interstate relations were not, however, merely the preserve of Americans anxious to demonstrate that whatever they received from foreign nations was certainly in the best interests of those nations to bestow. Thomas Pownall had also foreseen that American independence, which he thought in 1780 was as "fixed as fate," would "change the system of Europe." However long Britain and the House of Bourbon continued the war, "to their mutual ruin," in order to decide "to which of them *as allies, fœdere inequali,* the Americans shall belong," the Americans would belong to neither. Establishing themselves instead as a great commercial and naval power, they would "oblige the nations of Europe to call forth within themselves such a spirit, as must change entirely its commercial system also." The "Political Founders of the old system in the old world were totally ignorant" of the spirit of commerce, and "it was wisdom with them to render their neighbours and customers poor." The three great wars of the mid–eighteenth century, of which the War of American Independence was the last, were but the latest demonstration that commerce had been "a never-ceasing source of war for many of the latter ages of the world." Its true nature, however, was quite otherwise: it was in fact "an equal, equable, universal operation of communion, which concenters the enjoyments of all regions and climates, and consociates men of all nations, in a one mutual communion of all the blessings of Providence." The meaning of the American Revolution was that it would exert profound pressures on the nations of Europe such that they would see, finally, their true interest: "[A]ny one of those Powers of Europe, who would aim to deal with the rest of mankind with an unequal balance; who would endeavour to pile up the flow of their commerce in a channel above the level of the circumfluent commerce; will only find in the end, that they have raised amongst their neighbour nations, a spirit of jealousy, a revulsion, and a temper of universal rivalship, that shall conspire to wrest that false balance out of their hands, and to depress them down again, to a level with the rest of the world."[12]

Adams thought so highly of Pownall's pamphlet that he sent to congress and published a shorter *Translation* of it in which he condensed and digested the author's main ideas. It was indeed flattering to be informed that America, "as an Independant State," would "become the principal leading Power in Europe," but the concordance between Adams and Pownall went far beyond that point. Adams, too, believed that "America will grow with astonishing Rapidity and England France and every other Nation in Europe will be the better for her prosperity. Peace which is her dear Delight will be her Wealth and Glory, for I cannot see the Seed of a War with any part of the World in future but with Great Britain, and such States as may be weak enough, if any such there should be, to become her Allies."[13]

In assessing the efficient cause of the change from the old system to the new, Pownall had identified not simply the force of the commercial pressure America would exert. He also expected, as many Americans hoped and most Englishmen feared, that the conclusion of the war on the basis of American independence would be followed by "an almost *general Emigration to that New World.*" A few years previously, David Ramsay had celebrated the prospect that America's extent of territory "would be sufficient to accommodate with land thousands and millions of the virtuous peasants, who now groan beneath tyranny and oppression in three quarters of the globe." In celebrating the majestic cities that would rise "on those very spots which are now howled over by savage beasts and more savage men," Ramsay had concluded that "the thrones of tyranny and despotism will totter, when their subjects shall learn and know, by our example, that the happiness of the people is the end and object of all government." It was that fact that made the cause of America "the cause of human nature," for the tyrants of the old world "will be obliged to relax of their arbitrary treatment, when they find that America is an asylum for freemen from all quarters of the globe." Indeed, American independence would be a boon not only to "human nature" but also to true philosophy. "Large empires are less favorable to true philosophy," Ramsay explained, "than small independent states. The authority of a great author is apt, in the former case, to extinguish a free enquiry, and to give currency to falsehood unexamined. The doctrines of Confucius were believed all over China, and the philosophy of Descartes, in France. But neighboring nations, examining them without partiality or prepossession, exploded them both. For the same reason, our separate states, jealous of the literary reputation of each other, and uninfluenced by any partial bias, will critically pry into the merit of every new opinion and system, and naught but truth will stand the test, and finally prevail."[14]

Americans are accustomed in the twentieth century to arguing about foreign policy in terms of the opposition between "realists" and "idealists," and so have historians tended to see the intellectual framework of early American foreign policy. In many ways, however, that opposition is a misleading vantage point for identifying the elements of consensus and conflict within the early American outlook. While the tension between realism and idealism is an enduring feature of political life, a better depiction of the early American outlook would be on the order of "we are all realists, we are all idealists." It was not difficult at all for colonial Americans "to comprehend the importance of the power factor in foreign relations."[15] The record shows that they were quite fluent in calculations of power and interest.[16] In their hierarchy of values, as in the law of nations generally, there was no expectation that states would or should do anything other than pursue their own interest, subject to the limitations of justice and good faith. An eminent task of political science was to find where that true interest lay, because without it all political constructions would be built on sand. At the same time, Americans also felt deeply about the justice of their cause and continually avowed the importance of pursuing the aims of statecraft within a recognized moral and legal framework. "Practical idealism," in other words, was the American leitmotif, and this is as true for Adams and Hamilton as for Franklin and Jefferson. All knew the language of interest; all spoke in morally freighted terms. If the latter two figures appealed sometimes to gratitude and friendship as a basis for interstate relations (and both did so in the context of the alliance with France, eliciting objections from Adams and Hamilton), the latter two figures by no means depreciated the idea that America ought to act in a morally upright fashion, and they, too, sought "progress" and "improvement." While appealing to the expected benefits of the American Revolution to other states and peoples, no American leader expected that it would bear unfavorably on the former colonists themselves. Americans, it would appear, have always believed that what they do for themselves they do for others, and the first breath of an American diplomatic outlook shows they believed that proposition heartily at the beginning.[17]

Rather than viewing the intellectual framework of early American diplomacy in terms of the tension between realism and idealism, it is more revealing and profitable to situate it within the context of a larger body of reflection on the world of states—what might be termed "the whig or constitutional tradition in diplomacy." In American thinking about commerce, the balance of power, and the law of nations—and, more broadly, in the emphasis placed on good faith—we find a set of interlocking concerns that may best be described as Grotian or internationalist.[18]

Commerce, certainly, is one area where Americans hoped to make a new departure in the customary practices of states. "I have seen so much Embarrassment and so little Advantage in all the restraining & Compulsive Systems," as Franklin observed, "that I feel myself strongly inclined to believe that a State which leaves all her Ports open to all the World upon equal Terms, will by that means have foreign Commodities cheaper, sell its own Productions dearer, and be on the whole the most prosperous."[19] Americans readily imbibed what Smith, Tucker, Price, and Pownall were saying on the mistaken premises of the mercantile system. A candid view of their own interest prompted them to this conclusion, but they were not averse to anticipating the beneficial effects it would have on the world of interstate relations. This vision of a liberal trading regime based on mutual interest and reciprocal benefit, and excluding all ideas of domination, would certainly seem to qualify as internationalist, and it was a pronounced feature of the early American outlook.[20]

American policy was also internationalist in its call to the nations to resist Britain's "universal monarchy" upon the ocean, which was also an appeal to the norm that a balance of power would be far more consistent with the liberty and independence of states than a system of maritime domination. For Adams, this was in some respects an awkward adjustment. He was told by a Dutch merchant in 1778 "that they in Holland had regarded England as the Bulwark of the Protestant Religion and the most important Weight in the Ballance of Power in Europe against France." Adams said that he had been educated from the cradle in the same opinion and had read enough in the history of Europe to be still of the same view. But whether the Protestant cause would be weakened, or the balance of power deranged, depended on Britain's own conduct. If she forced America "against our inclinations into permanent and indissoluble connections with one Scale of the ballance of Power," that would be "a misfortune to Us, but not our fault." Though America's plan was to avoid the politics and wars of Europe, if she could, "it ought not to be expected that We should tamely suffer Great Britain to tear up from the foundations all Governments in America, and violate thirteen solemn and sacred Compacts under which a Wilderness had been subdued and cultivated."[21]

Given the passions engendered by the conflict with Britain, it is remarkable that at its outset Adams should have emphasized that she should not be weakened too severely, and is perhaps accountable only on the assumption of a close familiarity with Bolingbroke. Even so, that was a difficult posture to maintain in the heat of war. Adams's friends in the states were instead hoping "to hear that, you have lighted up a Fire, not only to roast, but absolutely to consume, the whole House of Hanover. Little less will satisfy our sanguine Countrymen, and nothing less will be its Fate, unless the other Powers of Europe should interpose their Influence, and preserve the Remains of a shatter'd Empire."[22] In 1778, at least, Adams was tempted to a similar conclusion: "The longer I live in Europe and the more I consider our Affairs the more important our Alliance with France appears to me. It is a Rock upon which we may safely build, narrow and illiberal prejudices peculiar to John Bull with which I might perhaps have been in some degree infected when I was John Bull, have no influence with me. I never was however much of John Bull. I was John Yankee and such I shall live and die." Adams found little signs of superstition and zealotry in "papist" France, and it was England, not France, that now manifested the spirit of unbounded power and of universal dominion. For Adams, the proper course to follow in the face of this dilemma was a difficult one, and he resolved it in a different way after 1778. Nevertheless, the recognition by him and others that universal monarchy constituted a profound danger for which the balance of power provided a salutary, if imperfect, remedy also qualifies as internationalist.[23]

There is a third respect in which early American opinion qualifies as internationalist: in its recognition of the authoritative character of the law of nations. As we have seen, the "illustrious" and "celebrated" writers on the law of nations were highly admired by Americans. All throughout the war the charge was rung against the Court of Great Britain of "how little Avail in their Estimation are the Laws of Nations, sacred throughout all the rest of the civilized world."[24] Americans, by contrast, professed fidelity to those sacred laws. The publicists had described an international system in which the solemn stipulations of the law of nations were seen as binding the states of Europe in a durable union for the purpose of the joint protection of their independence. Insofar as it was observed by those Christian princes, it justified to many observers the description of the European system as "one Republic," "one great nation composed of several," "one great republic whose inhabitants have attained almost the same level of politeness and cultivation," "virtually one great state."[25] In 1776, when Americans made their revolution, they did not repudiate this world of public law—as would be done, a generation later, by the Jacobins of France. They sought rather to join it, enlisting the protections it accorded all states, especially weak and fledgling states, while also seeking its reform.

The reform of the law of nations was sought in various ways but perhaps most revealingly in the American attempt to secure a different code for the conduct of war. As Benjamin Franklin opined to Edmund Burke: "Since the foolish part of mankind will make wars from time to time with each other, not having sense enough otherwise to settle their differences, it certainly becomes the wiser part, who cannot prevent these wars, to alleviate as much as possible the calamities attending them."[26] That aspiration was registered in the article that Franklin drew for inclusion in a treaty of peace with Great Britain, which would have committed the parties to a far-reaching code of noncombatant immunity in the conduct of war on land and sea. This provision, though rejected by Great Britain, would later be incorporated in the 1785 Treaty of Amity and Commerce between the United States and the Prussia of Frederick the Great. John Adams, who signed along with Franklin and Jefferson for the United States, was distressed that "other courts and states" faltered in grasping this instrument of progress, but "charmed to find the King do us the honor to agree to the platonic philosophy of some of our articles, which are at least a good lesson to mankind, and will derive more influence from a treaty ratified by the King of Prussia, than from the writings of Plato or Sir Thomas More."[27]

The basis of this disavowal of the barbarities so often practiced in war, as Adams well knew, lay less in the "platonic philosophy" than in the doctrines of Christianity. American reflection on this subject often dilated on the barbarous code of antiquity, contrasting it with the more elevated sentiments of modern times. Throughout "the whole Roman History," as Adams summarized the question in 1777, revenge

was esteemed a generous, and an heroic passion. Nothing was too good for a Friend or too bad for an Enemy. Hatred and Malice, without Limits, against an Enemy, was indulged, was justified, and no Cruelty was thought unwarrantable. Our Saviour taught the Immorality of Revenge, and the moral Duty of forgiving Injuries, and even the Duty of loving Enemies. Nothing can shew the amiable, the moral, and divine Excellency of these Christian Doctrines in a stronger Point of Light, than the Characters and Conduct of Marius and Sylla, Cæsar, Pompey, Anthony and Augustus, among innumerable others. Retaliation, we must practice, in some Instances, in order to make our barbarous Foes respect in some degree the Rights of Humanity. But this will never be done without the most palpable necessity. The Apprehension of Retaliation alone, will restrain them from Cruelties which would disgrace Savages. To omit it then would be cruelty to ourselves, our Officers and Men.[28]

The law of nations did indeed permit retaliation for the purpose of enforcing respect for the offended principle, even if the consequence was to drive a stake in the heart of a humane code of war, and the passions of the war were such as to make difficult the adherence to that code. The confiscation of loyalist estates, the hanging of Africans who took up the British offer of liberation in exchange for war against their masters, and plundering expeditions into Indian country were all justified on the principle of retaliation. Much as many Americans might wish, with Henry Laurens, to uphold the contrast between "American Humanity" and "British Ferocity," the logic of retaliation exerted its usual power. Responding to a parliamentary bill that would have allowed the apprehension of Americans suspected of high treason or piracy to be brought to England, to be tried at the convenience of the British court, Richard Henry Lee thought it would be necessary to ensure "that every Tory may be precisely in the same situation if we succeed in this war, that we undoubtedly shall be if the enemy prevail."[29]

Perhaps the central principle of the law of nations was the maxim that the pacts the nations made among themselves were to be religiously observed. The emphasis placed from the outset on establishing the "good character" of the United States meant, in the first instance, establishing its reputation for good faith—a reputation that was vital, as Adams indicated, for a whole host of purposes. The importance attached to good faith established a moral undertone to a whole range of issues, but it also had central political importance. It was an inescapable fact that the way the United States dealt with one would inevitably affect their perceived ability to make good on the others. The making of the union, as we have seen, was deemed necessary for the French alliance; the ability to preserve the value of the currency was a barometer of confidence in the union. The emphasis on good faith occurs repeatedly in the correspondence of the delegates to congress and of American ministers abroad, and in a variety of contexts. The American belief that compacts were sacred is not to be confused with the judgment over whether in any particular instance they observed them; in fact, with respect to each of the great issues that Adams had identified—the maintenance of the currency, fidelity to the French alliance, and adherence to the articles of union—there were always those ready to proclaim, and not without considerable evidence, that good faith was a chimera in their hands. At the same time, good faith might fairly be considered as the linch-pin of the normative order that Americans recognized, and there was no great political issue they confronted in which it was not deeply enmeshed.[30]

Did, then, the appearance of the United States in the community of na-tions represent a new diplomacy? In vital respects, it did. So far as Europe was concerned, however, it was not so much how America was to act as what it was to be that excited optimistic visions of the structural transfor-mation of the European system, or at least of a new order of things on the ocean. These expectations were reducible to four propositions: (1) that the failure of British arms would demonstrate the folly of seeking commerce by conquest; (2) that the achievement of an independent United States holding the commerce of the new world meant that the exclusive possession of their wealth could not plausibly be aimed at by any European power, thus elim-inating a potent source of war for that object; (3) that the establishment of free republican governments in the new world, by offering an attractive place of emigration to European peasants and laborers, would force im-provement on those rulers, since they could prevent such emigration only through mild government; and (4) that independence would bring rapid strides in mechanic arts and true philosophy, because the separate Ameri-can states would "critically pry into the merit of every new opinion and system, and naught but truth will stand the test, and finally prevail." Taken together, these hopes pointed to a different logic of interstate relations that, if realized, would constitute something new—and better—under the sun. So at least this hardy band of revolutionaries believed.

While true philosophy doubtless made rapid strides as a consequence of the independence of the American states, these optimistic assessments of the likely impact of the Revolution were otherwise not borne out at the end of the war. The European powers, including France, held fast to the old sys-tem, especially in their treatment of American commerce, and the op-pressed peasants and laborers of Europe did not suddenly decamp en masse on the shores of the new empire. For the next generation, the pressures of European war and the maxims of European policy stopped cold the prospects of a general European emigration and confirmed the basic fea-tures of the old commercial system. The blasting of those hopes "for a *ref-ormation,* a kind of *protestantism,* in the commercial system of the world," was a rude shock that would call for adjustments in American policy, the nature of which in turn caused bitter strife between the sections.[31] Never-theless, these confident views are significant as barometers of early Ameri-can opinion, and for showing how it was possible to believe that America, though detached from the European system, might nevertheless exert a profound impact on it over time. Attitudes, in other words, that would later be contrasted as "isolationist" and "internationalist"—the one signifying detachment from the European system, and the other its reform—were broadly shared and were not seen at this time as standing in mortal antagonism to one another.

The greatest immediate impact of the American Revolution on the European order came not from new systems of commerce or new channels of emigration but from the tie the War of American Independence bore to the subsequent revolution in France. While Ramsay and others had suspected that the regimes of Europe might totter as a consequence of the American Revolution, no one foresaw the conflagration that actually ensued, and yet it bore a direct relation to France's role in support of America. The collapse of French finances, which Turgot had foreseen and warned against before the outbreak of the war against England; the return of French officers from America, whose impact on public opinion was profound; the obvious and radical inconsistency between the principles of the Americans and the practices of Louis XVI, operated together with the enfeeblement of the old regime to produce the spark that set Europe afire for a generation.[32] But the American Revolution, though productive of revolution abroad, was itself conservative in many respects, and thus sharply distinguishable from the French version. The appeal to "thirteen sacred compacts" or to "a liberty which is founded not upon the capricious will of an unstable multitude, but upon immutable statutes and tutelary laws," made considerations of legality crucial for the Americans. The distance Americans traveled from colonial self-government to independent self-government was not very great—"the freest of peoples was the first to rebel"—whereas the gap between old and new in France turned out to be enormous, and set the course of the Revolution on a path that smashed the icons of legitimacy and swept away the past.[33] Whereas the European sympathizers of the French Revolution threw into disrepute "the sorry comforters" of Grotius, Pufendorf, and Vattel, the American revolutionaries elevated these authorities and wanted to enter the international society the publicists had described.[34] Though Americans of all persuasions might heartily concur in the liberal tenor of the Declaration of the Rights of Man and the Citizen (1789), the French rejection of American ideas of constitutional balance marked a fundamental difference between the two revolutions. The self-evident truths announced in the Declaration of Independence, which placed no limitation of place or time on the doctrine that legitimate government rests on the consent of the governed, thus gave hope and solace to Dutch patriots and French revolutionaries, and Americans, too, believed at the outset of independence that a successful experiment on their part would do wonders for the cause of republican government in Europe. But there was no thought of going abroad in search of monsters to destroy.

If Americans represented a new diplomacy that looked toward a new system of interstate relations, they did so most completely in their hopes for the union. Opinion in the American states, in other words, was most "internationalist" not with respect to their relationship to the European system but with respect to the relations among themselves. With the construction of their federal union, Americans proposed to take a step beyond the balance of power, as John Witherspoon had urged them to do. If the balance of power, in this understanding, represented a progressive principle, federal union was yet more progressive. The construction of that union was a profound necessity, for few Americans believed their independence could be secured without it, but at the same time it represented a generous ideal, for if realized it promised to establish an American system based on perpetual peace and free trade among the confederating states. Paradoxically, it was the imperious needs associated with the construction of an American system based on such ideals that, more than any other factor, dictated separation from the European system. From an early date it was understood that any continental connections they formed with Europe threatened to undermine the great "Continental Connexion" they wished to form in America; "internationalism" was, in this sense, not simply compatible with but a potent auxiliary and abettor of "isolationism."

To anxious friends of America in Europe, the belief that such a system might be created appeared as speculative as any theory of the pacific effects of commerce, and not any more plausible. Could thirteen states, hitherto lacking a constitutional connection with one another, and so different in size, climate, resources, and ways of life, find together a common bond of power and of peace? Were not neighboring nations natural rivals? Did not the Americans propose something that had never been done well and, if history and human nature were any guide, could probably not be done at all? In 1776 and beyond, those were still questions to which it was difficult to venture a confident answer, even in the United States. Americans had a considerable distance to travel before convincing themselves, to say nothing of a skeptical Europe, that their experiment in federal union was anything other than a pleasing illusion.

22

States, Sections, and Foreign Policy

THE POLITICAL COALITION that led the march to independence was an alliance between New England, led by Massachusetts, and the southern states, led by Virginia; it joined the antipodes against the middle colonies, where the strength of the loyalists was greatest and which were plagued by internal divisions unknown to New England republicans or the Virginia gentry. The central thread of American political history from 1776 onward is an account of how that coalition got disrupted. What rapidly emerged in its place, and was starkly apparent by 1779, was a political division in which the "Eastern party" was locked, on issue after issue, in political combat with "the southern interest," each of which found allies in the middle states. By 1779, those terms also designated what the French minister Gerard called an "English" party and a "French" party. Why this sectional split, whose inner core was an estrangement between Massachusetts and Virginia, took place and why easterners and southerners came to have such radically opposed perspectives on foreign policy are two questions we shall try to explain. But our larger purpose is to show why these developments helped produce the alarums that the Federalists would so vividly call forth in the debate over the federal constitution, and that had begun to be expressed with increasing frequency in the early 1780s. At the core of the Federalist argument was one great proposition: that divisions among the American sections, fueled by the rivalries of European powers, would lead in the absence of ratification to the emergence of a system of regional confederacies, and thence on to anarchy, war, and despotism. Though these dark specters have often been dismissed as clever propaganda by twentieth-century historians, and were even at the time occasionally considered as the product of deranged minds, our working assumption has been the unconventional and daring view that the Federalists of 1788 said what they meant, and meant what they said. What political forces, we may inquire, had been set loose on the continents of Europe and America such that this analysis would seem compelling to them?[1]

In considering the emergence of sectionalism as a potent force in the American system, a few words must be said concerning the larger structure of loyalties, identities, and interests that Americans felt in the early years of their struggle. In a basic sense, independence immediately constituted white

Americans into five different kinds of communities: locality, state, section, union, and nation. The relationship among these various loyalties, identities, and sisterly feelings is a very complicated problem, in large part because there were many different ways in which any individual might add up this jumble of loyalties into a clearly intelligible pattern. Certain generalizations, however, can be advanced with confidence. It was when they looked to Europe that Americans most wished to act "in a national character." Whereas the idea of an American nation suggested a certain homogeneity (they were all different from Europe in certain basic respects), the idea of the American union suggested heterogeneity or the reconciliation of difference. Everyone realized that if they were to have a national character, they had to have the union; the union, in turn, rested on the consent of the states, as the authority of the states rested on the consent of their people. The union was more than a means—it also proposed, as Witherspoon had suggested, a great and glorious end—but at the same time it had to be a means (i.e., an instrument by which states and sections might achieve their goals) if it were to be successful. Purely instrumental considerations thus mingled with aspirations of a most lofty character from the beginning.

While loyalties to particular states, a basic division between the eastern and the southern states, and a felt need for the union as a fundamental necessity were all present at the outset of independence, the experience of war and revolution, which forced them to work together in all sorts of unprecedented ways, also had vital effects on the way this cluster of identities, loyalties, and interests was understood. It not only forced them—really for the first time—to "think continentally," producing in some the sentiments of nationalism and in most a keen sense of "the safety of the Union" as a fundamental desideratum of policy. It also confirmed the historic sense of particularism founded on loyalty to individual states and produced a much sharper sense of the political meaning of America's regional diversity, in particular a deepened sense of the division between the northern and the southern states. That division got registered in many different ways, but perhaps above all with respect to the emergence of profoundly different attitudes between East and South over the fundamental interests of the American states in foreign policy.

Though it is customary—and indeed even useful—for historians to try to understand which of these various loyalties were most important at any given time, and to measure their relative temperature against the others, it is probably more accurate to say that they were all important all the time. When John Dickinson returned to congress in 1779 after three years in the political wilderness, he wrote the governor of Delaware that "the Interests of each State" were "Objects comprehended within the Confederation" and were "to be regarded as the Interests of the whole." As a delegate, Dickinson was pledged to contend for and defend those interests, but he noted that "beyond those Limits" difficulties might arise. He was certainly bound "to prefer the general Interests of the Confederacy to the partial Interests of Constituent Members" but also thought himself bound "to prefer the particular Interests of the State that honours Me with her Confidence & invests Me with a share of her power, to the particular Interest of any other State on this Continent."[2] Probably most delegates understood their obligations in a similar sense; the formulation had the merit of recognizing that distinct loyalties to state and union were blended in certain vital respects yet opposed on others. Thomas Burke also knew the importance of the common cause, but when Burke examined the loyalties of Americans in 1777, he placed the accent on the loyalties to the states. "The virtue most cultivated" in congress "will be that which will most distinguish a man in the State in which he resides. The grandeur & preeminence of that State will be the favourite passion of every man in it." In insisting that "patriotism in America must always be partial to the particular States," and that it would "never be cherished or regarded, but as it may be conducive or necessary to the other," Burke pointed to the fact that no man could "rise to eminence or distinction but through the favor of his particular State," and that no man could "acquire that favor by any other means than convincing them that their wishes will always be the first object of his attention." If one added to that the "natural prejudice which every man living has in favour of his own country," something which "the most attentive & liberal education is not able wholly to remove," the conclusion was inescapable that "all men are & ever will be national," which in America meant a partiality to their own state and "country."[3]

Burke had lately arrived in congress, and in speculating on "the delusive intoxication which power naturally imposes on the human mind"—a favorite subject—he was not under any "apprehensions from the New England States." Their detached situation, and their dependence on commerce and the fisheries, which they could not fully pursue without the assistance of the other states, would "prevent their becoming formidable if uncombined with others." The real danger, Burke thought, lay in a combination of Massachusetts, Pennsylvania, and Virginia. The natural sway that these large states might exercise over the smaller states in their vicinity was such that their concurrence on any point "must be carried into effect, even if it tended to annihilate the Independence of other States, & divided their territory." As a partial remedy to this danger, it seemed to him that North

Carolina ought to feel herself obliged "to check the ambition of Virginia."[4] Two years hence, Burke was not writing in a similar vein. He then was impressed with the fact that "Sister Virginia" had "Interests, habits, Manners and Inclinations" that were "so similar and consenting with ours."[5]

The contrast between the fear of Virginia Burke expressed in 1777 and the identity of interest he felt for her in 1779 shows clearly enough that the political meaning of America's regional diversity was not something that immediately impressed itself on the American imagination, or at least that did so in commonly accepted ways. It took time and experience under the wholly unprecedented situation in which they found themselves for the lineup of interests, identities, and inclinations to sort itself out. A broad division into three distinct sections—of eastern, middle, and southern—was of course well known to observers from the colonial period, and this tripartite division continued to be employed after 1776 as a way of differentiating the sections, but it was more common for the political divisions in congress to be described in bilateral terms—pitting the "Eastern states," often described as a party, a squadron, or a junto, against "the Southern States" or "the southern interest" (also similarly described). If it is remembered that political assemblies, even of the "deliberating Executive" variety, have no choice but to decide questions on the basis of yeas and nays, this bilateral division makes sense, but it also introduces a source of confusion. Geography, as it were, is fixed, but political coalitions change, and when geographic terms are used to describe political divisions—as was overwhelmingly the case in this period—it is necessary for us to get used to a variety of usages. New England always considered Virginia as a southern state, but Virginians could sometimes think of themselves, and not unreasonably, as part of the middle. Pennsylvania might appear northern to a Carolinian, but from the vantage point of Massachusetts it was just one of many states "to the southward." When William Henry Drayton of South Carolina looked at the political map in 1778, he said that four southern states—Virginia, the Carolinas, and Georgia—formed the "body of the southern interest." Everything else was "eastern," and there were nine of them. When New Englanders considered their interest in the fisheries, however, they knew very well that four eastern and nine southern states was a more apt—and alarming—depiction of the political realities.[6]

In the debates over the Articles of Confederation, as we have seen, the institution of slavery emerged as a vital line of distinction, and of starkly incompatible perspectives, between the five southern states and all the rest. The difference transcended the question of representation or contribution. For the northern states—and on this point there was little discrimination between New England, New York, and Pennsylvania—the promise of the American Revolution came to mean very rapidly a commitment to the abolition of slavery, and by 1786 most northern states had put it on the road to extinction.[7] For the northern states, slavery was never embedded in their systems of land and labor use, whereas for the South it was. This gave the southern states a distinct interest on all the continental questions of contribution and representation, and they voted as a block on these from the very outset. But there was a very significant difference of opinion between Virginians and South Carolinians on the slavery question, one made manifest in the drafting of the Declaration of Independence. In his first, tumultuous, draft of the Declaration, Jefferson had execrated "the CHRISTIAN king of Great Britain" for his complicity in violating "the most sacred rights of life and liberty in the persons of a distant people who never offended him, captivating & carrying them into slavery in another hemisphere, or to incur miserable death in their transportation thither." That the king had "prostituted his negative for suppressing every legislative attempt to prohibit or to restrain this execrable commerce" was bad enough; that he had then excited "those very people to rise in arms" against those on whom he had inflicted the wrong was, for Jefferson, the last stab to agonized affection and a key cause of the unity of the southern gentry in 1776. Jefferson's heated condemnation of slavery and the slave trade did not appear in the final version of the Declaration but was struck out "in complaisance to South Carolina and Georgia, who had never attempted to restrain the importation of slaves, and who on the contrary still wished to continue it."[8] This division between upper and lower south was very important and would persist for another generation, and one way of expressing it is to say that a majority of the Virginia gentry, albeit a slight one, wanted to become more like Pennsylvanians.[9] Carolinians and Georgians wanted nothing of the kind. Jefferson also recalled that his clause reprobating the slave trade and slavery aroused anxiety in New England, "for tho' their people have very few slaves themselves yet they had been pretty considerable carriers of them to others."[10] That made it hypocritical to charge upon the king of Great Britain entire responsibility for the evil, which Jefferson had undoubtedly done. New England's consciousness of guilt did not inhibit—on the contrary, it most certainly advanced—the cause of emancipation in Massachusetts, a bill for which was introduced in 1777. Already the sensitivities that would define the place of slavery in the politics of American union for the indefinite future were in place: James Warren, then governor of Massachusetts, wrote to John Adams in congress: "We have had a Bill before us for freeing the Negroes [in Massachusetts], which is ordered to lie, [lest] if passed into an Act it should have had a bad effect on the Union of the Colonies. A letter to congress on that subject was proposed and reported, but I endeavoured to divert that, supposing it would embarrass and perhaps be attended with worse consequences than passing the Act." Adams agreed with Warren's judgment: "The Bill for freeing the Negroes, I hope will sleep for a Time. We have Causes enough of Jealousy, Discord, & Division, and this Bill will certainly add to the Number."[11]

Whereas the South was both united on some questions and divided on others in the early years of the war, the northern states were fractured by the line of Biram's River along the boundary between New York and Connecticut.[12] The rivalry and distrust between New England and New York was an often-remarked and well-understood division, and it was deeply rooted in colonial history. They were different peoples but had a common hinterland, and this made for manifold sources of collision.[13] They were divided throughout the war on all questions relating to the army—New York was stalwart for Washington and Schuyler, whereas in New England the former was distrusted and the latter loathed; New York was keen on "half-pay" and other expedients by which Washington sought to secure a stable officer corps, whereas New England saw in those proposals the odious signs of an aristocratic conspiracy. In the first years of the war, New York also formed a close connection with "the body of the southern interest" on the issue of the western lands. When Gouverneur Morris became a delegate from New York in 1778, he was considered by New Englanders as the leader of the southern junto; it would take time and the slow working of events to make Morris realize that he was a northerner.[14]

Despite the existence of a southern interest and a northern interest, a "New England standard" and a "southern scale," the first years of the resistance appeared to show that the basic division between North and South was not insurmountable. The great symbol of this was the concord with which the representatives of Massachusetts and Virginia had acted in congress, and its epicenter in the congress was the relationship between Samuel Adams and Richard Henry Lee. These fast friends saw eye to eye on several critical questions in 1776 and 1777—on the need to march to independence, to raise ample military forces, to secure aid from France, and to complete the confederation. Adams's assessment of the military contributions of the states in 1777 placed critical importance on the efforts and valor of "my Countrymen of Georgia, So. & No. Carolina, Virginia & Jersey."[15] With New York City under British occupation, and Pennsylvania and Delaware incapable of generating military power (whether from rampant Toryism, Quaker pacifism, or sheer disorganization and internal conflict), the military contributions of the southern states had been crucial in that year.[16]

Lee's enthusiasm for eastern politics, however, began to cause problems for him in Virginia. By late 1776, the charge arose that Lee had "favored New England to the injury of Virginia." Lee responded to that "contemptibly wicked" accusation with a flood of acrimony that laid bare the motives for his policy, as well as the nature of the coalition that formed in the first year of the war:

> Our enemies and our friends too, know that America can only be conquered by disunion. The former, by unremitting art had endeavoured to incite jealousy and discord between the Southern and Eastern Colonies, and in truth Sir they had so far prevailed that it required constant attention, and a firmness not to be shaken, to prevent the malicious art of our enemies from succeeding. I am persuaded as I am of my existence, that had it not been for Virginia and Jersey, with Georgia sometimes, that our Union would eer now have been by this means broken like a Potters vessel dashed against a rock and I heartily wish that this greatest of all political evils may not yet take place before a safe and honorable peace is established.

One thing he thought certain: "that among the Middle and Southern states Virginia had many Enemies, arising from jealousy and envy of her wisdom, vigor, and Extent of Territory. But I have ever discovered, upon every question, respect and love for Virginia among the Eastern Delegates. Folly and ingratitude would have marked the Representatives of Virginia had they shown disesteem for the latter, and attachment to the former." In the end, however, it was not gratitude but interest on which Lee rested his vindication. "I defy the poisonous tongue of slander to produce a single instance in which I have preferred the interest of New England to that of Virginia. Indeed I am at a Loss to know wherein their interests clash."[17]

Increasingly, however, Virginians did know where their interests clashed with those of Massachusetts. The collaboration between Virginia and Massachusetts was already on the ropes in 1778, but the bitter debate over foreign policy that erupted in 1779 was what really finished it off as a working coalition. Lee saw a common American interest in the fisheries—were not the southern states equally interested in a merchant marine and a naval force?—and he supported the strong claim that New England wished to register to them, but that was a stance that left him isolated in Virginia. Soon after becoming governor of Virginia, Jefferson wrote to William

Fleming, a delegate in congress: "We have lately been extremely disturbed to find a pretty general opinion prevailing that peace and the independence of the thirteen states are now within our power, and that congress have hesitations on the subject, and delay entering on the consideration. It has even been said that their conduct on this head has been so dissatisfactory to the French minister that he thinks of returning to his own country, ostensibly for better health, but in truth through disgust. Such an event would be deplored here as the most dreadful calamity."[18] Nothing more disgusted the French minister, Gerard, than New England's obstinate attachment to the fishery. Nothing, in turn, disgusted New England more than the disposition in the southern states to view the claim to the fisheries as a "particular" interest bearing only on three states. Gerard wanted the congress to place its peace commissioners under the guidance of France, and in that discretion New England saw grave peril. John Adams thought such instructions equivalent to the Declaratory Act.[19] "If it could be supposed," said Elbridge Gerry of Massachusetts in congress, "that any obstruction to our rights originated in the policy of our ally, it would diminish the affection with which our great friend is now cherished in the hearts of our people. But before France had given us one encouraging word, the people of New-England had poured out their blood like water in defence of their rights; they had been cheered also by their southern friends, but at first they had stood alone; and by God's blessing they would stand alone again without allies or friends, before they would barter away their rights."[20]

In 1779, as later, the vital interests of the sections were those that, if bartered away or abandoned, would be held to justify a secession from the confederacy. But the southern states felt a sense of imperious necessity too, particularly in 1779. After the defeat at Saratoga in 1777, the British ministry had abandoned the prospect of recovering New England, and in the second half of the war concentrated its full might on the project of conquering the southern states.[21] It was not only Lee who now felt the force of southern resentment. Henry Laurens, a South Carolinian who had joined with Lee in supporting the claim to the fisheries, felt it, too. "The eastern States are charged with wanting what they have no Right to," wrote Lovell of Massachusetts, and Lee and Laurens "are squinted at as two monsters on the other Side of the Susequehanna, who can be found to pursue points in which the southern States have *no* Interest."[22] Laurens was gravely threatened by the North Carolina delegation, which wrote to him that unless he rescinded his vote in favor of the fisheries, South Carolina could expect no aid from her sister state. The right of fishing claimed was "more Extensive than can with Justice be insisted on, and which our

Allies by their engagements are not bound to assist us in Contending for, and which the Minister Plenipotentiary of France assures us his Court can not agree to continue the war for." Given the French declaration that no aid would be forthcoming to support a war for this object, the delegates told Laurens that he "relies on a degree of Strength and resources in your State which is unknown to us, or on a mistaken Idea of the strength and resources of North Carolina." If Laurens persisted in his attitude, North Carolina would not lift a finger for her defense, and he was advised to consider the calamities that would inevitably ensue "from an Insolent, Relentless, Iritated, and Rapacious enemy, from your own Slaves armed against their former Masters, from the Savages excited to more bloody and merciless dispositions."[23]

If North Carolina might point its finger at Laurens as a betrayer of regional interests, the real force of the southern resentment fell on the northern states. Christopher Gadsen, then desperately attempting to organize the defense of Charles Town, recalled to Samuel Adams how South Carolina had always been "particularly attentive to the Interest and feelings of America," and how she had, in the Stamp Act crisis of 1765, listened to the call and rushed to the aid "of our Northern Brethren in their Distresses." Boston would have been ruined without that response from Carolina, Gadsen averred, because without it there would have been no congress. "In every stage of her Misfortunes we . . . felt at every Pore for her. Now the Tables are turn'd, and we in far greater Distress than New England ever was. . . . But who feels for us? We seem to be entirely deserted, even the Continental Troops of our Neighbours are retained with the grand army and denied us. Where are our Frigates? From these Carolina has a right to claim assistance as from her great Distance from Congress." Proclaiming himself "an American *at large,* anxiously wishing for the Happiness and confirmed Independency of the Whole, not having, indeed scorning a Thought in Favor of *any one* State to the prejudice of the rest," Gadsen could only conclude that though he had remained the same man, with the same principles he "set out with at first," others had changed. Where was the fairness, where the equity, in that? Apprehending the fall of the southern states due to Britain's recruitment of backcountry bandetti and New England's readiness "to leave them in the Lurch," Gadsen warned that the consequences to New England "at a not very future Day" were "not very difficult to grasp."[24] To New Englanders, however, all this came with very ill grace. The idea that they had been backward in their contributions to the common cause seemed little short of ludicrous. They had raised the first army, had driven the British from Boston and then defeated them at

Saratoga, were convinced in 1777 that Howe's invasion would have failed had there been any virtue in the people of the middle states,[25] had taxed themselves heavily in 1778 when the southern states did comparatively nothing on that score. They could only discern in the support to the southward for the French propositions a dislike of the political principles and manner of New England, and an attitude intent on reducing "their trade, and consequently their power and influence. What could more effectually do that than by ceding all right and claim to the fishery to get a Peace rather than see us Flourish?"[26] The response of Massachusetts to Gadsen's frantic plea was to marshal its resources for an attack in the summer of 1779 on a new British post in Penobscot. Charles Town fell the following year.

From the first moments of the resistance, as Gadsen's letter indicates, there had been a contest among the states to demonstrate who displayed most virtue in the common cause. That the states would readily compete in this sprint, and give their all to show which among them were the keenest, was the expectation that made sense of their first continental constitution. John Adams's letters reflect tremendous anxiety on this score. He was devastated by the initial failure of Massachusetts to fulfill its continental quota in 1777. He believed that Massachusetts had to set the tone, to do more than the others, to set a glorious example, but stood badly chastened by the event and demanded in one letter that he be either supported or recalled.[27] This proved but a momentary panic—the victory at Saratoga in 1777 made the New England troops "stand high in the Estimation of all sensible and impartial Men"—but before that event it was the southern states that had seemed most deserving of the palm of virtue.[28] The stresses and hardships of the war over the following two years, however, had turned the contest into something rather different. The war turned out to be a grueling marathon rather than a sprint. No one had doubted at the beginning that a settlement of accounts would have to be made, nor that this could only really occur after the war had been concluded: "neither Equity nor sound Policy," as the Massachusetts delegates put it, "will admit that different States, contending in the same common Cause, having in View the same common Benefit, should be unequally loaded with Expence, or suffer disproportionate Losses. But as it is impossible to foresee what Course the War will take, or what State will be the greatest Sufferer, it is probable this Question will be postponed untill the End of the War."[29] The Massachusetts delegation was responding to a request from their state that congress offer compensation for British depredations against Charlestown, Massachusetts, but congress was deeply fearful of the "monstrous demands that would be made from Virginia, New Jersey, New York and elsewhere, if a

Precedent should be once set."[30] The question of compensation, however, was but one of a dozen closely connected with the settlement of accounts; so numerous were the disagreements on this vital and delicate question that it was beginning to seem obvious to many observers that a settlement of accounts might never be made. Once that realization was made, it had a fatal effect on contributions to the common treasury.

It is customary to see the collapse of the requisition system, very nicely foretold by George Grenville in 1764 and by Benjamin Franklin in 1754, as an issue between congress and the states, but it was as much and perhaps more importantly an issue between the sections. Both the eastern states and the southern states felt keenly a sense of mutual betrayal. From New England's vantage point, she was being asked to give up her livelihood and to accept a peace of penury. From the vantage point of southerners, however, the inattention of New England to their plight reflected an odious and sniveling particularism. It was the existence, rather than the livelihood, of the southern states that was now in question, and the sense that they had been left in the lurch felt like an aggression.[31]

Wars are seldom launched with a full appreciation of the consequences they will bring and the new choices they will pose, and the War of American Independence is no exception. Events, however, had conspired to produce in both eastern and southern states a profoundly different relationship to the two principal European powers, Great Britain and France. When the British turned south after Saratoga, they abandoned all thought of conquering New England.[32] Uncannily, however, and certainly unexpectedly, this threw New England into a dependence on Great Britain. In order to secure access to the fisheries, she needed a peace treaty with Britain that acknowledged her right. France might take the fisheries from her in peace negotiations, but only a treaty with Great Britain would secure her claim and render it safe from the depredations of Britain's maritime power. The southern states, by contrast, were now most threatened by British arms, and they desperately needed French aid in the here and now. When the French minister told them that obstinacy on the fisheries would lead to his withdrawal, they were mortified. What New England needed, in short, was something only Britain could confer; and what the South needed was something only France could confer. This was the strategic basis that gave the eastern party an English coloration, and that made the southern interest wish for concord with France. It was an alignment, moreover, that survived the particular issues that brought it into being. Deepened by the varying commercial interests of the eastern and the southern states after the war, reinforced by various propinquities and antipathies in culture and religion, and then given yet more purchase by the outbreak of the French Revolution, the same basic alignment persisted until the conclusion of the War of 1812: New England was partial to Old England and was certainly strong in its anti-Gallicanism. The South, by contrast, was friendly to France and certainly hated the British with surpassing ardor.

The bitter debate in 1779 over peace instructions was harrowing because it threatened the principle of equal benefits that had always lain at the heart of the union. The most agreeable procedure in ensuring respect for this principle was simply to add up the vital interests of the states and sections and to pronounce them all as American ultimatums, but that produced results that France—on whom the United States were increasingly dependent for aid—found absurd in their grandiosity. And so there occurred a considerable contraction of aims to south and north, with the one affecting the other. With Britain in possession of Georgia and much of South Carolina in 1779, and with Spain now being solicited for aid and recognition, all thought of the possession of Florida was at an end. Based on Georgia's title, America might claim only to the thirty-first parallel, and had to hope that a European mediation would not be based on the principle of *uti possidetis*.[33]

By 1779, Canada had also become a distant objective that was not worth the expenditure of scarce resources. In the beginning stages of the war, congress had immediately conceived the desire to kick the British government out of all of North America and had labored to convince the French Canadians to join the American union. In a letter to the inhabitants of Quebec, congress had defied them "to discover a single circumstance" promising "the faintest hope of liberty to you or your posterity, but from an entire adoption into the union of these Colonies." In a contemporaneous address to the people of Great Britain, however, congress had declared that the Quebec Act of 1774 had opened the door to a Canada "daily swelling with Catholic emigrants from Europe" and had professed its astonishment that "a British Parliament should ever consent to establish in that country a religion that has deluged your island in blood, and dispersed impiety, bigotry, persecution, murder and rebellion through every part of the world."[34] The Quebecois, though insular, were not oblivious to the hostility of the Protestant colonies, and they were grateful for the establishment of their religious practices that the Quebec Act had accorded them. They showed no interest in the offer from congress to "unite with us in one social compact, formed on the generous principles of equal liberty, and cemented by such an exchange of beneficial and endearing offices as to render it perpetual."[35] Despite the indifference and hostility of the French Canadians, hopes for the incorporation of Canada were not entirely vanquished in the early years of the war, but the desire owed more to security considerations than territorial cupidity. "The Union is yet incompleat," wrote George Mason in 1778, "& will be so, until the Inhabitants of all the Territory from Cape Briton to the Mississippi are included in it; while Great Britain possesses Canada & West Florida, she will continually be setting the Indians upon us, & while she holds the Harbours of Augustine & Halifax, especially the latter, we shall not be able to protect our Trade or Coasts from her Depredations."[36] Even as Mason was writing, however, the wisdom of taking Canada by force had become less and less compelling. Lafayette's projected invasion in 1778 fizzled for want of any soldiers, and by 1779 it was far down the list of American strategic objectives. Washington was not willing to pursue it at the expense of the southern states; the French government, looking to keep the British in Canada, was opposed as well.[37]

Even in New England, the aspiration for Canada now ran cool. Saratoga had shown that the British possession of Quebec was not quite the dagger it had seemed to be, and had proved to be a trap rather than an opportunity for Burgoyne. New England was also ambivalent on the point of absorbing the French population in Canada—Lovell, for example, saw in 1777 the problems posed by that aspiration—and her objective now ran more toward assuring security along her northern coast, in the direction of Nova Scotia, than providing for the safety of her rear. Access to the fisheries, the incorporation of Nova Scotia, and the absorption or neutralization of Canada, in descending order of importance, remained her objectives in 1779, but the first was by far the most important, the second had merit mainly as insurance for the first, and the last was more a dream for the future than a need of the present. These priorities were registered in Sam Adams's resolution of August 1780 that would have allowed Washington to act to the northward in conjunction with a French general against the common enemy, which he urged on the French minister in the following terms: "We do not know whether the General will in fact take advantage of it to shift the theater of war to enemy territory, but if he judges that the English can be attacked there with advantage, he need not hesitate to do so. The result can only be useful to the Thirteen States. The worst would be to exchange Nova Scotia or any other place conquered by our arms for Georgia or South Carolina at the time of the peace negotiations."[38]

The states to the southward reasoned about their objectives in very different fashion. That neither Georgia nor South Carolina would be given up at the peace—nay, that such a settlement would be utterly inconsistent with the mutual pledges of the Declaration—was axiomatic to the southern interest. For those southern states with charter claims to the western territory—Virginia, the Carolinas, and Georgia—the order of strategic priorities might fairly be stated as follows: first and foremost, the independence of all thirteen states, Georgia and South Carolina included, even at the expense of claims to the transmontane region; territorial claims to the Mississippi as a close second; and, third, the right to navigate its waters so as to render the western region fit for commerce. From this vantage point, Canada and Nova Scotia were objectives entirely peripheral and indeed positively threatening insofar as any move in that direction would draw off desperately needed resources. Even with a worsening military situation, as Luzerne discovered in early 1780, delegates from the "South" and "Center" were firm in the persuasion that they had an indisputable claim to the Mississippi, and he noted that the states regarded it "as an act of moderation" that they did not claim to the Pacific Ocean.[39]

The strategic priorities of the middle states cannot be so concisely described—they were, as usual, full of contradictory perspectives and alignments. Perhaps their great vital interest was simply the assurance that the strategic claims made by the northeast and southwest not imperil the safety of the union. Congressmen from the middle states were the ones who mediated these conflicting objectives in the 1779 wrangle over peace instructions, and such a role would fall on them frequently in the future. In part this was purely a function of geographic happenstance, but the nature of their own countries—frequently riven on religious, ethnic, and class lines—well fitted them for a mediating role. The middle states, however, had interests of their own. Pennsylvania looked to the Ohio Valley for future expansion and was thought to have as keen an interest as the southern states in the navigation of the Mississippi, though she and other landless states wrangled repeatedly with Virginia over the terms of the West's settlement.[40] But it was New York's position that was in many respects most important. In the early years of the war, New York was aligned with the southern states on the belief "that by the confederation, the United States" could set up no claim to territory "as a *joint interest*"; her paper claim, based on suzerainty over the Iroquois, reached to the borders of the Province of Quebec as established in 1763, and as far to the west as fancy might dictate, but by 1779 and 1780 her priorities were changing. By that time, New York leaders had decided their claim to Vermont would probably be impossible to sustain, and they had never really looked at Canada save for security reasons. The claim, however, to Oswego and Niagara on the Great Lakes was crucial. During the 1782 peace talks, John Jay proposed the line of the lakes as a happy solution to the problem of the northern boundary, and his leading contribution to the negotiation lay in his machinations to create a joint Anglo-American interest (directed against Spain) in the free navigation of the Great Lakes and the Mississippi. His conduct in that negotiation suggests that some New Yorkers espied early on their future role as the great entrepôt of the western trade, a glittering prospect that gave them a perspective more continental and national than their brethren to the east and south. Jay's strong support of both the fisheries and the western claims in that negotiation also reinforces the proposition that the basic interests of the middle states were resolvable to the proposition that the claims to northeast and southwest not imperil the safety of the union.[41]

After months of bitter wrangling in 1779, congress had, in deference to the French minister, made New England's claim to the fisheries a condition of a commercial treaty, rather than a peace treaty, with Great Britain.[42] While this was at best half a loaf, and not at all satisfactory to New England, she obtained a security for cod and haddock nearly as good by winning the appointment of John Adams as sole plenipotentiary of the projected peace talks. This proved, however, but a temporary victory, as Adams soon made himself obnoxious in France. When the issue of peace terms arose again in 1781, the French insisted on either Adams's removal or a broadening of the peace delegation. Congress agreed to a broadening, and the five-man delegation appointed was nicely balanced on sectional lines. (The commissioners appointed were Adams, Jay, Franklin, Jefferson, and Laurens, though Jefferson declined to serve.) Much more significantly, the French got congress to agree to instruct the commissioners, on June 15, 1781, that "you are to make the most candid and confidential communications upon all subjects to the ministers of our generous ally, the King of France; to undertake nothing in the negotiations for peace or truce without their knowledge and concurrence; and ultimately to govern yourself by their advice and opinion."[43] The United States agreed to that humiliating instruction partly from an inability to reach consensus on how to ratchet down their own aim, but fundamentally from a keen sense of their dependence on the aid of France, whose representative hinted that they were always free to seek their objectives alone.[44] The tenor of French thinking at the time—as indeed of all other potential European mediators—is well indicated by Vergennes's dispatch to Luzerne of June 30, 1781. Noting that it was "an established fact that the United States have the greatest interest in maintaining the integrity of their union," and that a separation of any would be a "sensible loss," Vergennes nevertheless held that "it happens too often that circumstances make the law for the most powerful Sovereigns." While the king of France, Louis XVI, would change his resolution to maintain the independence of the thirteen states only "when he sees the absolute impossibility of arriving at a reasonable peace without some sort of sacrifice," such sacrifice had now become first in the "order of probabilities." If it became necessary, Vergennes wrote, "it will be necessary to be resigned to it: most of the Belgian Provinces had shaken off the Spanish yoke; however, only 7 have preserved their independence."[45]

Cornwallis's defeat at Yorktown in October 1781—what Madison called "the glorious victory of the combined arms at York & Glocester"[46]—assured all thirteen states that the treaty of peace would ensure their independence; but that they would be able to obtain access to the fisheries and a boundary to the Mississippi was still very much in doubt. France had to satisfy not only her American allies but also Spain, who had joined the war in 1779, and American and Spanish objectives were deeply opposed. France's desire to hold all the threads of the negotiation in her hands bore adversely on American interests, and she made no attempt to conceal her idea that American claims to the fisheries and the West were well in excess of what might be reasonably expected in a final treaty. French ideas of an equitable peace at least had the advantage of bearing adversely on all states and sections; it was the prospect of an unequal sacrifice that threatened to drive a stake in the union. That such would be the result of peace parleys, however, was a clear and present danger from 1779 to 1782.

The emergence of sectionalism as a potent force and danger in the struggle over peace objectives had a parallel in the emerging division over the ownership of the western territories. For the first three years of the war, New York had been aligned with the southern states on that question. She was locked in bitter rivalry over the "New Hampshire Grants," the territory in eastern New York or western New Hampshire claimed by the Green Mountain Boys as their own. Massachusetts, Connecticut, and Rhode Island sought to vindicate the pretensions of Vermont to an independent status in the American union on grounds of natural right, but New York was deeply opposed to independence, as were the southern states, who saw clearly enough that the real intention was to add another vote to the New England bloc in congress while simultaneously establishing the precedent that any other state might be broken by revolution into little parts. When New York leaders broke from the Virginians in 1780, they did so as part of a scheme that would confirm their own remaining title (to the extreme prejudice of Virginia) and worked up a coalition in the congress in which the northern states lined up squarely against the claims of "the body of the southern interest." By 1780 and 1781, there had already appeared the glimmerings of a northern interest that might make the interests of New

York and New England coincide on the admission of another northern state and on other questions of great moment.[47] In his revealing assessment of the play of congressional forces over this question, Madison noted the peculiarities of the sectional lineup. The "general interests and policy" of Pennsylvania and Maryland "are opposed to the admission of Vermont into the Union, and if the case of the Western territory were once removed, they would instantly divide from the Eastern States in the Case of Vermont." The same was true of New York: "If this Cession should be accepted, and the affair of Vermont terminated, as these are the only ties which unite her with the Southern States, she will immediately connect her policy with that of the Eastern States; as far at least, as the remains of former prejudices will permit."[48]

The effect of six years of war, then, was to increasingly divide the delegates to congress on a geographic line. Richard Henry Lee, now out of congress, felt that pull as much as anyone, and in 1783 is to be found worrying that the 5 percent impost proposed by congress would "strangle our infant commerce in its birth, make us pay more than our proportion, and sacrifice this country to its northern brethren."[49] Carolinians saw the danger of such a sacrifice, too: Pierce Butler lamented in 1782 that "The *Northern Interest* is all prevalent; their members are *firmly united,* and carry many measures disadvantageous to the *Southern interest.* They are laboring hard *to get Vermont established as an independent State,* which will give them *another vote,* by which the balance will be *quite destroyed.*" This polarization did not reach all issues, nor did it eliminate the propensity for compromise within the congress, but everyone saw its primordial force. It was sufficiently alarming to justify to many observers the sense that the union might not survive either the war or the peace, and that a division into two or three confederacies, themselves the dependents and playthings of the European powers, foretold an increasingly probable future.[50]

23

The Armistice of 1783

ON NOVEMBER 30, 1782, the preliminaries to a peace agreement were signed by the representatives of Great Britain and the United States. The peace exceeded, "in the goodness of its terms, the expectations of the most sanguine."[1] Instead of a boundary to the watershed of the Alleghenies, Britain recognized American claims to the Mississippi. Instead of crimped restrictions on fishing rights, or a wholesale denial thereof, Britain conceded a generous allotment of cod and haddock. Even on the question of restitution to those who had taken up arms for the king, and had paid for that by the confiscation of their estates, the British negotiators accepted a provision merely recommendatory, obliging the congress to "earnestly recommend it to the Legislatures of the respective States" that such restitution be provided.[2] In the negotiations for a settlement, the tenor of which was wholly unknown to the French, Jay had remarked to the British negotiators that "as every Idea of Conquest had become absurd, nothing remained for Britain to do, but to make friends of those whom they could not subdue: That the way to do this, was by leaving us nothing to complain of either in the negotiation, or in the Treaty of Peace, and by liberally yielding every point, essential to the Interest and Happiness of America."[3] Though the provisions regarding the fisheries and the northeast and northwest boundaries were sufficiently inexact as to leave much to complain of on both sides, Jay's simple principles of simple peacemaking had largely been followed by the earl of Shelburne and his negotiators. Shelburne's private opinion was "to go a great way for Fœderal Union," by which he meant a great free trade area underpinned by a defensive alliance, but he knew that the initial treaty would fall short of that aspiration.[4] He hoped, nevertheless, for a revival of alienated affections and sought a "system upon which the *china vase*, lately shattered, may be cemented together, upon principles of compact and connexion, instead of dependence."[5] Not less important, Shelburne had seen and acted on what Jay called "the obvious interest of Britain": "immediately to cut the Cords, which tied us to France."[6]

No one was more chagrined by what Adams called "the unravelling of the Plot" than the Comte de Vergennes. The French minister had known and approved of the separate negotiation between Britain and the United States, but he was astounded by the generous terms Britain had offered.

The English, he remarked to a subordinate, "are purchasing the peace rather than making it," their concessions on the boundaries, the fisheries, and the loyalists exceeding all he had thought possible.[7] Vergennes was deeply offended that the nature of the British offer had been kept secret from the French, and that the American ministers had signed the preliminaries without consultation, presenting him with a fait accompli that complicated his larger aims.[8] "You have concluded your preliminary articles without informing us," he told Franklin, "although the instructions of Congress stipulate that you do nothing without the participation of the King. You are going to hold out a certain Hope of peace to America without even informing yourself of the State of our negotiation."[9] Vergennes did not respond to American actions by breaking relations and would in early 1783 approve another loan of six million livres (out of twenty million requested) as insurance against the formation after the war of an Anglo-American entente. But there is no doubt that he felt betrayed, and with a resigned air he told Luzerne that "if we cannot steer [the Americans] according to the grand principles which have served as the basis of our alliance with them," there would yet be time to take "the measures necessary not to be the dupes of their ingratitude and of their false policy." The American negotiations with England had been "terminated in a manner most brusque, most unexpected and, I may say, most extraordinary." It was "a breach of procedure and of respect of which there exist few examples," an opinion, he averred, he had no doubt congress would share. Though he claimed not to have ever based the policy of France on American gratitude—that was a sentiment "infinitely rare" among sovereigns and unknown among republics—he had in fact done something very close to that; at a minimum he had conferred, before receiving, the mutual exchange of benefits his policy had contemplated. He urged Luzerne, in the latter's explanations to congress, to take the line that France had not restrained the Americans in any way, but the defense was reducible to the proposition that the American negotiators had kept him entirely in the dark. How he might have acted had he been asked was conveyed in his comment to Luzerne that the boundaries "must have caused some astonishment in America; for it was surely not expected that the English Ministry would go beyond the watersheds of the chain of mountains which border the United States."[10]

The decision of the American commissioners, led by Jay, to break from the advice and opinion of the French court was a risky one. If it were a trick, it provided the British government with much good material to drive a stake into the Franco-American alliance, for Jay had intimated his willingness to accept a total break with France as the price of a generous treaty from Great Britain. The risk, nevertheless, seemed well worth taking, for it had become starkly apparent to him, and to John Adams, who joined him at a relatively late stage in the negotiations, that the French were "endeavouring to deprive Us of the Fishery, the Western Lands, and the Navigation of the Mississippi. They would even bargain with the English to deprive us of them. They want to play the Western Lands, Mississippi and whole Gulph of Mexcio into the Hands of Spain."[11] Convinced of French duplicity, Jay and Adams held that they could not be bound to the letter of their instructions. Neither could see any way of doing their duty to congress "but to interpret the instruction, as we do all general precepts and maxims, by such restrictions and limitations, as reason, necessity, and the nature of things demand."[12] In other words, they proposed to ignore it. In a long letter to congress of November 17, Jay had poured out his suspicions of the French and justified his decision to proceed separately by highlighting the difference in essential interest that had clearly emerged between America and France. The French, he conceded, were interested in ensuring a separation between America and Great Britain, "but it is not their Interest that we should become a great, and formidable People, and therefore they will not help us to become so." It was not their interest that an Anglo-American treaty should produce "Cordiality and mutual Confidence" between the United States and Great Britain, and they had rather finagled to ensure that "Seeds of Jealousy, Discontent, and Discord" would be planted in the treaty so as to keep up America's dependence on France. Finally, it was clearly in the French interest to delay an Anglo-American settlement until the end of the war, "and thereby keep us employed in the War, and dependent on them for Supplies."[13] This contrariety of interest dictated independent action by the United States, and once the commisioners went down that road, there was no turning back. To submit the preliminaries to French approval, they believed, would risk the entire settlement. With a Franco-Spanish fleet set to sail within the month (certain to prolong the war another season), and the renewal of Parliament likely to threaten Shelburne's precarious hold on power, the American commissioners concluded, as Adams concisely put it, that "the peace depended on a day." "We must have signed or lost the peace."[14]

It is difficult to dispute the soundness of Adams's judgment, for in the mysteries and labyrinths of the negotiations for a final settlement a different turn might well have been made. There was nothing inevitable about the outcome. Shelburne's subsequent fall over the concessions made in his separate treaties with America and France—indeed, the whole tenor of British policy for the next decade—indicates well enough the latent obstacles to a policy not merely conciliatory toward America but extravagantly so in the eyes of Europe. Had the British negotiators acted on a more realistic assumption as to the possibilities of an Anglo-American reconciliation, they would doubtless have proceeded in a far stingier vein.

It is also evident that had Britain taken a harder line, the Americans had no French card to play: the French government had no intention of exerting serious pressure on Britain to accept more generous terms. It is not that the French were anxiously seeking to betray the American commissioners—for in their own minds they had amply fulfilled their part of the bargain—but rather that their ideas of an equitable peace, or what it was they had agreed to in committing themselves to the independence of the United States, were hundreds of miles apart from American conceptions of vital interest. Until the preliminaries were signed, it was always in the option of the British government to get out of the war by conciliating France and Spain at the expense of the United States, rather than the other way around. Their taking of the former route was critically dependent on their expectation that they would gain a sundering of the Franco-American alliance. Had the preliminaries been presented by the American commissioners for French approval, it would have gravely challenged that assumption and immediately collapsed the case for a generous peace with the United States. Initially, at least, Britain was not disappointed in her belief that she had made a separate peace. The discord between Vergennes and the American commissioners, wrote one British negotiator, must reassure "such persons in England as were apprehensive that the hostilities committed against America by Great Britain and the friendship & protection she met with at the same time from France would rivet her for ever in an inveterate animosity against the former Kingdom, and a firm alliance and union with the latter, since it manifest that even now, when the war cannot be said to be finished, we stand to the full as well with them, as their allies here."[15]

Franklin, the great symbol of and believer in the alliance between America and France, consented to this break with France with reluctance, though he did consent. To Vergennes, he pleaded the technicalities of the case, insisting, "Nothing has been agreed in the Preliminaries contrary to the Interests of France; and no Peace is to take Place between us and England till you have concluded yours." Vergennes, of course, was quite convinced of the contrary, and he could hardly accept, as Franklin had put it, that the American commissioners were only "guilty of neglecting a point of bienséance." Franklin had no alternative but to put as good a light on the transgression as he could, but he surely knew that Vergennes would find these explanations unconvincing. His larger and more important plea was that Vergennes not make the preliminaries the basis of a rupture. England thinks she has done this, he said; let us show that she has not.[16] Franklin made that appeal sincerely, for he still felt his country in dire need of the French connection as protection against the duplicity of England. That indeed was the key to his whole line of policy. The British government, as he would later observe, "is not in Truth reconciled either to us or to its Loss of us; but still flatters itself with Hopes that some Change in the Affairs of Europe or some Disunion among ourselves, may afford them an Opportunity of Recovering their Dominion."[17]

In these sentiments he spoke the views of Madison and Jefferson as well, and indeed of a larger southern interest. For them, the alliance with France continued to be a rock of safety, and the prospects for a secure independence would be badly injured without it. All three worked to smother the evidence of Franco-American discord, gave fair-minded rather than malicious renderings to such conflicts as existed with France, and were deeply angered by Adams's contemptuous and scathing depiction of French motives.[18] Writing to congress, Franklin characterized thusly the opinions that Adams had been publicly expressing in Paris, "sometimes in the presence of the English Ministers": "He thinks the French Minister one of the greatest Enemies of our Country, that [Vergennes] would have stratned our Boundaries to prevent the Growth of our People, contracted our Fishery to obstruct the Increase of our Seamen, & retained the Royalists among us to keep us divided; that he privately opposes all our Negociations with foreign Courts, and afforded us during the War the Assistance we received, only to keep it alive, that we might be so much the more weaken'd by it: that to think of Gratitude to France is the greatest of follies, and that to be influence'd by it, would ruin us." All this was preparatory to Franklin's famous judgment of Adams: "he means well for his Country, is always an honest Man, often a Wise One, but sometimes and in somethings, absolutely out of his Senses."[19]

Adams, though happy to concede the deserved preeminence in the negotiation to Jay, believed that he had done well for his country and was content with asserting the prior discovery of the principles that animated the negotiation. He often recalled in his letters of 1783 the principles he had set forth in 1776. "Gentlemen," he said, "can never too often [be] requested to recollect" the debates that had arisen in congress when the French treaty was in contemplation. "The Nature of those Connections, which ought to be formed between America and Europe, will never be better understood than they were at that time. It was then said, there is a Ballance of Power in Europe. Nature has formed it. Practice and Habit had confirmed it, and it must exist forever. It may be disturbed for a time, by the accidental Removal of a Weight from one Scale to the other, but there will be a continual Effort to restore the Equilibrium."[20] The "first principle" of policy in such a world was

> that we should calculate all our measures and foreign negotiations in such a manner, as to avoid a too great dependence upon any one power of Europe—to avoid all obligations and temptations to take any part in future European wars; that the business of America with Europe was commerce, not politics or war; and, above all, that it never could be our interest to ruin Great Britain, or injure or weaken her any further than should be necessary to support our independence, and our alliances, and that, as soon as Great Britain should be brought to a temper to acknowledge our sovereignty and our alliances, and consent that we should maintain the one, and fulfill the others, it would be our interest and duty to be her friends, as well as the friends of all the other powers of Europe, and enemies to none.[21]

This retrospective fudged things a bit, because in 1775 and 1776 America had made no alliances, and it was not clear in 1783 whether Great Britain, or indeed Adams himself, believed the alliance with France to be still intact. Nor was the aspiration to be friends to all, and enemies to none, a particularly apt summation of his deeper fears, which were "that France and England both will endeavor to involve us in their future wars." In either light, the great line of policy for America was clear: "to be completely independent, and to have nothing to do with either of them, but in commerce."[22]

Jay's course in the negotiations came as a surprise to both Vergennes and Adams. When he was chosen in 1781, the expectation of congress, and the French, was that he would reinforce Franklin's system rather than Adams's. Instead, Jay and Adams found themselves in entire concord during the secret parleys with England. Adams was amazed that there should be such an "entire Coincidence of Principles & Opinions between him & me."[23] It was unexpected that he should either distrust the French so completely or contend so vigorously for New England fishing rights, and Hamilton would later kid him that the people of New England were thinking of making him an "annual *fish-offering*."[24] That a New Yorker should emerge as a champion of the fisheries reflected New York's ongoing gravitation to the northern interest and was in keeping with the entente between New York and New England that was occurring simultaneously on other issues, but New York's riverine system and the potential it afforded her of serving as the leading entrepôt of the western trade also gave her an interest in the claims to the western territories and the navigation of the Mississippi. Jay folded all this into a nice package with his acceptance of the line of the lakes and his underhanded attempts to get Britain to attack Spain in the southwest—an audacious plan that would have sent Vergennes through the roof had he known of it. On balance, Jay steered a middle course in 1782 and 1783 between Adams's anti-Gallicanism and Franklin's Francophilia, and he managed to maintain good relations with both men despite their mutual estrangement. The French also thought him immune from the anti-French sentiments they espied in Adams. The emerging role of the middle states as the mediators between the antipodes, and the holders of the balance in the union, was thus registered in his conduct in Paris.[25]

The definitive treaty (identical to the preliminaries) was signed on September 3, 1783, and was ratified by the congress in January 1784. By the time that ratification took place, however, it was already apparent that the achievement of the negotiators in November 1782 was far less brilliant than it first had seemed. The first shock had come in July 1783, when by order-in-council Britain imposed severe burdens on American shipping. Instead of acting on Shelburne's ideas, the British government repudiated them as a dangerous threat to the Act of Navigation and national security. Under the influence of Lord Sheffield's ideas, a line of policy far different from Shelburne's now took shape. In this scheme, Canada would supply lumber and foodstuffs to the West Indies, displacing the exports of the United States; those American goods for which there was no adequate Canadian replacement could come to the West Indies only on British vessels. The direct trade between Britain and America—which sent tobacco, rice, iron, and other products to the former mother country in return for manufactures—was also to be reestablished on a basis favorable to British navigation, and American ships were duly placed under onerous restrictions in British ports. British merchants and Scottish factors returned to the colonies in force after the war, and the old pattern of debt and dependence—particularly in the southern colonies—reasserted itself. Britain refused to evacuate its military position along the lakes in the northwest, arguing that the unwillingness or inability of the United States to execute the treaty of peace (particularly with respect to debts owed to British merchants from before the war) relieved it of any obligation on this score. Not much better were relations with Spain and France. Spain kept the West Indies shut to American shipping, closed the Mississippi in 1784, still claimed western territory up to the Ohio, and fostered numerous intrigues with westerners. France made clear that no further loans would be forthcoming and accounted the Americans as unreliable in the event of new troubles with England. The hopes of Franklin that the more enlightened and generous views of commerce would be translated into policies that allowed a greater trade with the French sugar islands were also disappointed. In 1784, France sharply restricted American trade to the islands in both flour and sugar, and the direct trade between America and France hardly developed at all, a sharp blow to the Virginians, who saw in the development of this trade the only means to escape the damnable web of debt and dependency that ensnared them in the British mercantile system.[26]

In considering the status of American diplomacy in the aftermath of the War of Independence and the treaty of peace, these disappointments must be recalled. It is a remarkable fact that virtually all the leading principles of American diplomacy in the coming century are stated with candor and precision in the course of the War of American Independence. Those foundational principles are rendered in figure 6 of the appendix. Union and independence were at the core, and from those two fundamental imperatives a set of logical deductions, implications, and commitments followed. Political isolation and nonentanglement in the European system; neutrality in Europe's wars; freedom of commerce; territorial expansion; fidelity to the law of nations; an American system capable of bidding defiance to the potentates of Europe; and a belief in the radiating power of the American example are all given expression in this early period. Like union and independence themselves, however, all were deeply problematic and represented aspiration rather than fact:

1. The desire to steer clear of the entanglements of European politics and to remain neutral in all her wars was deeply felt; no less evident was that America was deeply entangled in the European system. If the past were any guide, America would remain what she had been in the past, the "football" of the European powers.[27]
2. The desire to throw open the doors of commerce and to enjoy a free trade with all the world was also deeply felt; the reality was that the European powers remained hostile to the idea and were all returning with a vengeance to the ideas of commercial jealousy that Americans had hoped would be exploded by British defeat in the war.
3. The desire to be independent, and to "move like a Primary & not like a Secondary Planet . . . in the Political System of the World,"[28] was belied by various dependencies that threatened to severely compromise this objective. That the war against Britain could not have been won without French moneys and French arms was one obvious dependency, but such dependencies reached as well to all issues of commercial access. New

England needed badly to regain the shipping routes she had enjoyed as part of the British Empire; only Britain could confer that. The southern states felt themselves in desperate need of breaking free from the commercial connection with Great Britain; they could get that only by complaisance to France.

4. The desire to calculate America's policies in relation to the European balance of power, avoiding commitments that would "infallibly make enemies of those" in the opposite scale, had promised a world in which America would be "friends to all, and enemies to none." The reality of her relationships with Britain, France, and Spain in 1783 was more prosaic, and "enemies to all, and friends to none" might stand as a fairer depiction of her situation.

5. The desire to calculate America's measures on a plan immune from European influence developed alongside the suspicion that some individuals and factions were under the influence, and possibly in the pay, of a foreign court. The salient fact is not so much that many individuals had taken emoluments from France, Spain, or Britain, for corruption of this sort explains little of the divisions in continental politics. The more significant consideration is that the suspicion was widely shared.[29]

6. The desire to expand America's territories, seemingly gratified by the Peace of Paris, now stood thwarted by a ring of hostile powers. Canada was being reconstituted by peoples with good cause to bear a grudge against the United States and was backed by a nation that hated the Americans "universally, from the throne to the footstool."[30] The Indian nations that held the transmontane territory were hostile to an expansion that would mean their dispossession, and they stood to find backers from Spain in the southwest and Britain in the northwest. Spain still held the keys to the Mississippi and wanted to keep it locked. Britain still held the northwest posts and vowed to keep them forever if the Americans did not fully execute the treaty of peace. Britain evacuated New York, Charles Town, Penobscot, and a few other posts; apart from that, however, the idea so often feared during the war—a peace based on *uti possidetis*—turned out to be pretty much the peace the Americans got. The treaty of 1783 was less a peace than an armistice.

7. The desire to establish America's good faith, so central to the development of a national character, stood in tatters. The debts of the union had not been discharged, and there was a whole class of disaffected soldiers and unpaid creditors, foreign and domestic, who were cursing that good faith. The separate negotiation with Britain, even if thought justifiable for reasons of state, was part of this larger pattern and was not without

its costs. The commissioners might plead that they were guilty of no breach of faith against the alliance, but Vergennes knew, and Europe knew, that the marriage arranged by Franklin in 1778 between France and the virtuous but estranged daughter of England had ended in an infidelity. On one view, America was wiser for the experience, having learned from the peace negotiations "that gratitude, friendship, unsuspecting confidence, and all the most amiable passions in human nature, are the most dangerous guides in politics."[31] On another view, however, she had shown herself in possession of "all the follies of youth and all the vices of old age."[32]

The contrast between aspiration and reality was no less marked with respect to the union, and indeed the foregoing contrasts between hope and fact were all ultimately traceable to the weaknesses and "imbecilities" of the confederation. "Our prospects are not flattering," wrote Hamilton in 1783. "Every day proves the inefficacy of the present confederation, yet the common danger being removed we are receding instead of advancing in a disposition to amend its defects. The road to popularity in each state is to inspire jealousies of the power of Congress, though nothing can be more apparent than that they have no power." Charles Thomson saw in the "underhand workings" of the congress a resemblance to "the mountain in Germany mentioned in a late paper. Inward grumblings are heard; The head is covered with clouds & darkness. Vapours burst through apertures which destroy the trees and herbage and every thing denotes an approaching irruption which may involve the neighbourhood in one common ruin and calamity."[33] Thomson believed, with others, that disunion would be a disaster: "It cannot admit of a doubt that the peace, happiness and prosperity of these new and rising republics depend greatly on a close and intimate Union. And yet the temper, disposition and views of the inhabitants are so discordant, that I have serious apprehensions they will not be long kept together & that the predictions of our enemies will but too soon be verified in the dissolution of our Confederacy."[34] Writing from London, and despairing of the settlement of his accounts and of the larger American cause, Silas Deane had come to a similar conclusion: "That union which subsisted between the several States during the war, but especially that between the Northern and the Southern States, was in too great a degree an union from the necessity of the time, from the war existing in the country. The cause (and with it, unhappily, the effect) has ceased, and old partialities and jealousies and local prejudices are reviving, and threaten to operate with additional force. Hence men of observation and of cool reflection in America

. . . [see no alternative but to divide them] into two new confederations, the Northern and the Southern."[35]

The danger to the union was not lost on the American commissioners in Europe. Though Franklin, ever alert to the impact of opinion on policy, told Hartley that the views of an impending disunion widely circulated in ministerial newspapers were a figment of their malicious imagination— "most are mere London fictions"—he also believed that their widespread circulation showed that the British ministry "wish the reality of what they are pleased to imagine." "In those circumstances we cannot be too careful to preserve the friendships we have acquired abroad, and the Union we have establish'd at home, to secure our Credit by a punctual discharge of our obligations of every kind, and our Reputation by the wisdom of our councils: since we know not how soon we may have a fresh occasion for friends, for credit, and for reputation."[36] "Were it certain," wrote the commisioners, "that the United States could be brought to act as a Nation," it was probable that other nations would make extensive concessions in trade. If not, however, "we shall soon find ourselves in the Situation in which all Europe wishes to see us, viz., as unimportant Consumers of her Manufactures & Productions, and as useful Labourers to furnish her with raw Materials."[37] Congress, however, had no power to regulate trade, and attempts to give it that power kept running aground on the *liberum veto*. When Adams went to London as minister to negotiate a commercial treaty, he was informed that there was nothing to discuss so long as the United States did not abide by the peace treaty. He had nothing to do in a diplomatic vein and so gave himself over to composing his *Defence* of the American constitutions during his paid sabbatical.

Those who speculated on a potential separation of the states did not doubt that it would place the northern and the southern states in separate confederacies. "Time will discover," wrote Samuel Osgood, "whether our Union is natural; or rather whether the Dispositions & Views of the several Parts of the Continent are so similar as that they can & will be happy under the same Form of Government. There is too much Reason to believe they are not."[38] To many New Englanders, proposals to strengthen the confederacy seemed to augur a loss of the independence so bravely won in the war. The United States, wrote William Gordon, had to "remain a collection of Republics, and not become an Empire . . . [because] if America becomes an Empire, the seat of government will be to the southward, and the Northern States will be insignificant provinces. Empire will suit the southern gentry; they are habituated to despotism by being the sovereigns of slaves: and it is only accident and interest that had made the body of them the temporary sons of liberty."[39] This disenchantment in New England reached to those southern republicans who had once seen eye to eye with the eastern provinces in the beginning stages of the war. In the nature of things, wrote Osgood, it was impossible that the southern states "should be democratic. It is also impossible that there should be a Coincidence of political Views, in some matters of very great Importance to the Eastern States: for those who have appeared to be honest Republicans, of which Number I have had the Misfortune to find not more than two or three, have uniformly depreciated our Exertions, & denied to us that Justice, which is clearly due." New England had gotten the right to take fish by the treaty but was as yet without a market, and it was obvious that the southern republicans, like all other descriptions of southerners, would do their best to ensure that a commercial treaty with Great Britain not be formed.[40]

Suspicions cast southward were fully reciprocated in those climes. The "uniform conduct" of the eastern states, wrote one North Carolinian, "has been to Weaken the Powers of the union as much as possible, & sacrifice our national strength & dignity in hopes of rendering themselves more conspicuous as individual states. . . . I do not think they wish for a dissolution of the Confederacy, but they press so extremely hard on the chain that unites us, that I imagine it will break before they are well aware of it."[41] Disunion, Spaight warned, "may be thought distant," but unless the easterners changed, "it will happen in a very short period." Southerners had numerous sources of complaint, among them the location of the capitol and New England's obstruction on the army and the impost, but the issue from 1783 to 1787 that most galvanized the southerners was John Jay's discussions with the Spanish minister Gardoqui in 1786. In requesting authority to yield the right to navigate the Mississippi for twenty-five years in exchange for commercial privileges in Spanish ports of primary benefit to the northern states, Jay provoked vast upheavals and writhings in the body of the southern interest. Monroe thought that back of it lay a plot to dismember the union. Pennsylvania had joined with the rest of the north, the five southern states dissenting, in approving Jay's request for a change of instructions, and Monroe was keen that Virginia should prepare herself to prevent the specter of a northern confederation with Pennsylvania in it. "If a dismemberment takes place, that State must not be added to the eastern scale. It were as well to use force to prevent it as to defend ourselves afterwards."[42] Madison did not join Monroe in that speculation, but he, like most other southerners, was outraged that the northern states should seek "a voluntary barter in time of profound peace of the *rights* of one part of the empire to the *interests* of another part. What would Massachusetts say to a proposition for ceding to Britain her right of fishery as the price of some stipulations in favor of tobacco?"[43] The controversy over Jay-Gardoqui in 1786 was the crisis of 1779 all over again, but with the roles reversed. The suspicion that the purpose of a congressional majority was to thwart the growth of a minority section was reiterated frequently in both episodes. Both demonstrated that unequal sacrifices dangerous to the union would ineluctably be called forth from a position of weakness. Jay's negotiations of 1786 also throw an interesting posterior light on the peace negotiations of 1782. The dog that did not bark in that negotiation was a conflict among the plenipotentiaries over terms that would entail an unequal sacrifice to northeast or southwest. It was a piece of great good luck, in the person of the earl of Shelburne, that that tension did not get seriously registered in the negotiations.

We are not to draw from these depictions the conclusion that the situation facing the American states was hopeless, though the conclusion is surely just that such hopes as did exist had come to rest more and more on a future convention of the states. In assessing the prospects for such a convention, there were some bright spots in the general gloom. Over the previous decade, congress had often come to compromises between the sections; and if the American states could find a way round the *liberum veto,* a way might be found to prevent the dissolution of the union. In 1776 and 1777, they had agreed to the principle of concurrent majority as a middle term between a numerical majority and unanimity; might they not do so again? So, too, any division of the states posed formidable dangers and obstacles. The four New England states and the five southern states were the two clear cores of separate confederacies, but where the middle states might end up was anybody's guess. Would Pennsylvania choose north or south? Would New York choose New England or Pennsylvania? Those were among the considerations that made observers speak inexactly of a division into two or three confederacies. They also help explain why the middle states should be so averse to a disunion in 1786 and 1787, as before they had been averse to a disruption of the British Empire. With the union, they were the holders of the balance; without the union, they were the corn between the millstones. This situational disability made the middle states the incubator of nationalism, as it had previously made them the incubator of loyalism.[44]

If these considerations might augur well for a reinvigorated union, there was also certainly a well-founded basis for pessimism. Factors that in later periods of American history operated to bind the union together were often seen in this period as threatening to tear it apart. The incorporation of new states, for example, threatened to multiply the parts of a machine; that it would work better as a consequence seemed a dubious proposition to James Madison. Nor did the multiplicity of conflicts among the states and sections operate before 1787 as a centripetal rather than centrifugal force. With a new government, pluralism might operate as a force for stability, but every one of those conflicts was also a potential source of blockage to whatever compromise might come from a new convention. The very factors that made for stability in a large commonwealth, as David Hume observed, also operated to prevent its creation; without that, the proliferation of factions over an extended territory was just a bloomin' anarchy. James Madison, who was probably reading Hume in 1786, was not disposed to optimism as to the prospects. Speaking of the forthcoming Annapolis Convention, Madison wrote Jefferson that many wished "to make this Meeting subservient to a Plenipotentiary Convention for amending the Confederation. Tho' my wishes are in favor of such an event, yet I despair so much of its accomplishment at the present crisis that I do not extend my views beyond a Commercial Reform. To speak the truth I almost despair even of this."[45]

PART SIX
Peace Pact: The Writing and Ratification of the Constitution

24

Vices of the Critical Period

DURING THE DEBATES over the ratification of the Constitution, some Anti-Federalists would deny that the situation of the American states was critical in any respect, and they used that argument to seek a second convention. Before the meeting of the Philadelphia convention, by contrast, men who would later become Antis shared in the general feeling of crisis that increasingly pervaded the continent. Most of them saw the exigent need for a reform of their system of cooperation, for it was working (or rather not working) in a way that no one had intended at the outset. Most of the Anti-Federalists thus accepted "that our federal government *as originally formed, was defective, and wanted amendment.*"[1] They, too, were troubled by the growing irrelevance of congress in managing common concerns and resolving differences.

In these circumstances, it was inevitable that a new convention would be called. There were too many vital interests that were not getting vindicated through the federal government, and signal respects on which the Americans believed that their interests met in more points than they differed. Amendments might address these piecemeal but could not do so in a way that represented a system of equivalents. The willingness of New York to grant a federal power over imposts—a sacrifice—had to be weighed against the ability of the union to secure an execution of the peace agreement, and thus gain the evacuation of Oswego and Niagara. The willingness of Virginia to allow execution of the treaty for the recovery of debts or to vest a commercial power in the union had to be assessed in relation to what Virginia would get in return. Would it be the closure of the Mississippi? New England might acquiesce in providing support for federal military forces, but not if the result was simply to obligate New England to support the southern propensity toward Spanish and Indian wars, and not if she were deprived of the ability to make a navigation act to protect her commerce.

Beyond such interlocking considerations, there was the great and overriding sense of unfairness that surrounded the confederation. All those amendments to the Articles of Confederation that had been turned aside in 1778 and 1779 had not been forgotten. Nor had the initial charges of inequity that had arisen in the summer of 1776. The states without commercial ports—Connecticut, New Jersey, Delaware, and North Carolina—were still kegs tapped at both ends. Virginians and Pennsylvanians were still aggrieved that they counted for no more than tiny Rhode Island, who seemed to take a perverse delight in blocking their will.

Many Americans contributed their mite to assessing the nature of the situation confronted by the states in the "critical period" before the Constitution, but none gave it a keener analysis than James Madison in his paper "Vices of the Political System of the United States." If *The Federalist* is the indispensable document in understanding the Constitution, the "Vices" is of similar importance in understanding the situation the framers confronted just before they met. It is of particular interest not only because its depiction of American troubles summarizes a volume of accumulated commentary on the nature of the American malady but also because it has been relied on as a basis for radically conflicting interpretations of what the struggle for and over the Constitution was all about. In it we may find the origins of the theory developed in *Federalist* No. 10, which has long been identified by political scientists and historians, at least in the twentieth century, as the key document for understanding the nature of the system created at Philadelphia. In it, together with a few other contemporary letters of Madison, we may find the inner logic of the Virginia Plan to be proposed by Governor Edmund Randolph early in the convention. Finally, it provides a template by which to assess how far the Constitution that would be hammered out in the summer of 1787 in Philadelphia responded to the maladies that Madison identified. Let us look at it, therefore, in some detail.[2]

"1. FAILURE OF THE STATES TO COMPLY WITH THE CONSTITUTIONAL REQUISITIONS."

Madison considered this vice as "inherent in" the existing system and "fatal to the object" of it. It had been "fully experienced both during the war and since the peace." Madison's studies of the ancient and modern confederacies, completed the previous summer, had convinced him that this was a common structural flaw and had been uniformly exemplified in every confederacy similar to America's own; it resulted "naturally from the number and independent authority of the States." He explored why the requisition system could "never succeed" in a variety of places, but perhaps never so eloquently as in a letter of 1789: "Some States will be more just than others, some less just: Some will be more patriotic; others less patriotic; some will be more, some less immediately concerned in the evil to be guarded against or in the good to be obtained. The States therefore not feeling equal motives will not furnish equal aids: Those who furnish most will complain of those who furnish least. From complaints on one side will spring ill will on both sides; from ill will, quarrels; from quarrels, wars; and from wars a long catalogue of evils including the dreadful evils of disunion and a general confusion." Both reason and experience demonstrated these conclusions: "The whole history of requisitions not only during the war but since the peace stamps them with the character which I have given them."[3]

"2. ENCROACHMENTS BY THE STATES ON THE FEDERAL AUTHORITY."

Madison had numerous "examples" and "repetitions" to draw on to illustrate this point, but he mentioned only three: the separate wars and treaties of Georgia with the Indians; the "unlicensed compacts" between Virginia and Maryland, and between Pennsylvania and New Jersey; and "the troops raised and to be kept up" by Massachusetts. In "almost every case," one could foresee such encroachment when "any favorite object of a State shall present a temptation." Such encroachments were dangerous for a variety of reasons. If relations with the Indians were to be managed by the separate states, the confusion and wars that might ensue would fall not only on the individual state concerned but also on neighboring states.[4]

"3. VIOLATIONS OF THE LAW OF NATIONS AND OF TREATIES."

Not a year had passed, Madison remarked, without instances of such violations "in some one or other of the States." Of the various violations of national treaties—with Great Britain, France, and Holland—it was the violation of the Treaty of Peace that was generally considered the most serious. Jay, the secretary of foreign affairs, had conceded in 1786 that the peace treaty had been "constantly violated on our part by legislative Acts" with respect to state obstruction of the ability of British creditors to recover debts owed from before the war (Article 4) and with respect to state persecution of the loyalists (Article 6). The American violations, he also conceded, had come first in time before the British. A decade later, in the argument over the Jay Treaty of 1794, Madison would vigorously contest much of what Jay said in his 1786 report, but at this time they concurred on the larger danger such violations presented. If the United States could not ensure that "national treaties be kept and observed throughout the Union," as Jay put it, "it would be in the power of a particular State by injuries and infractions of treaties to involve the whole Confederacy in difficulties and War." John Adams, then in London seeking futilely to negotiate a commercial treaty with Great Britain, insisted that it was "vain to expect the evacuation of posts, or payment for the negroes, a treaty of commerce," or indeed any other relief so long as the United States were themselves in violation of the peace treaty. The faithlessness of the United States contributed strongly to Adams's recurring nightmare of Britain and France reaching a common understanding on the American question, a combination that would have been very dangerous indeed. Madison seems to have been not particularly alarmed by that danger, but like Jay insisted that it was wrong that "any part of the Community" might "bring on the whole" the calamities of a war.[5]

"4. TRESPASSES OF THE STATES ON THE RIGHTS OF EACH OTHER."

Madison had an abundance of examples to illustrate the "alarming symptoms" of this vice. Virginia's law "restricting foreign vessels to certain ports" and the laws of Maryland and New York in favor of vessels belonging to their own citizens showed the general tendency. So, too, did "paper money, instalments of debts, occlusion of Courts, making property a legal tender." These were not simply violations of individual property rights; they were all "aggressions on the rights of other States," and they were potential aggressions on the rights of foreign nations. The delegation to the federal authority of "the exclusive regulation of the value and alloy coin" was meant not only to "preserve uniformity in the circulating medium throughout the nation" but also "to prevent those frauds on the citizens of other States, and the subjects of foreign powers, which might disturb the tranquility at home, or involve the Union in foreign contests." Also falling into this class were the laws of "many States in restricting the commercial intercourse with other States, and putting their productions and manufactures on the same footing with those of foreign nations." The states could do this under the letter of the "federal articles," but such "vexatious" regulations, as well as their tendency "to beget" retaliations, were "adverse to the spirit of the Union" and "destructive of the general harmony."[6]

"5. WANT OF CONCERT IN MATTERS WHERE COMMON INTEREST REQUIRES IT."

This defect was most obvious with respect to "the state of our commercial affairs." There had been various attempts by congress and the states to amend this deficiency, of which the Annapolis Convention of 1786 was the most recent, but thus far experience had shown them capable of being defeated "by the perverseness of particular States whose concurrence is necessary." "Instances of inferior moment" illustrating this vice included "the want of uniformity in the laws concerning naturalization & literary property; of provision for national seminaries, for grants of incorporation for national purposes, for canals and other works of general utility."

"6. WANT OF GUARANTY TO THE STATES OF THEIR CONSTITUTIONS & LAWS AGAINST INTERNAL VIOLENCE."

The articles, Madison observed, gave no power to the federal authority to come to the aid of a state in such distress. Instead of discussing concrete examples, he was content with showing why, in three different instances, a minority might, "in an appeal to force, be an overmatch for the majority": (1) when a minority possessing military skill, and aided by "great pecuniary resources," might "conquer the remaining two-thirds; (2) when the ostensible majority excludes "those whose poverty excludes them from a right of suffrage"; and (3) "where slavery exists." Madison did not descend further into particulars, but he suspected, as did many others, that the British had not been backward in providing pecuniary sources to Daniel Shays during the recent rebellion in Massachusetts. He was clearly thinking also of the vulnerability of the southern states to slave rebellion, and indeed the inability of the federal authority to come to the aid of Massachusetts during the rebellion (which Massachusetts did not turn out to need) may have gotten him to thinking about the vulnerability of the southern states on this score. These worries, whatever their precise focus, were the origins of the clause in the Constitution guaranteeing to each state a republican form of government and permitting outside states, acting through the federal government, to come to the aid of a sister facing domestic insurrection, though how far this obliged the northern states to come to the aid of the South in the event of a slave insurrection remained in doubt.[7]

"7. WANT OF SANCTION TO THE LAWS, AND OF COERCION
IN THE GOVERNMENT OF THE CONFEDERACY."
"8. WANT OF RATIFICATION BY THE PEOPLE
OF THE ARTICLES OF CONFEDERATION."

These two vices, which summarized Madison's general indictment of the inadequacy of the articles, were intimately related. In many states, the articles had received only a legislative ratification, and in those circumstances state tribunals that were to decide the conflict of laws had a good basis for giving recognition to a state legislative act repugnant to an act of congress. That consequence, however, was but an aspect of the general feebleness of the confederation. "A sanction is essential to the idea of law, as coercion is to that of Government. The federal system being destitute of both, wants the great vital principles of a Political Constitution. Under the form of such a Constitution, it is in fact nothing more than a treaty of amity of commerce and of alliance, between so many independent and Sovereign States." The explanation for the fatal omission of a power of coercion lay in "a mistaken confidence" in the first years of the union "that the justice, the good faith, the honor, the sound policy, of the several legislative assemblies would render superfluous any appeal to the ordinary motives by which the laws secure the obedience of individuals." Madison then retraced the reasons why a system of voluntary compliance could not succeed, even if "it should be the latent disposition of all" to cooperate. Indeed, he went further: "As far as the Union of the States is to be regarded as a league of sovereign powers, and not as a political Constitution by virtue of which they are become one sovereign power"—and Madison, as we have seen, had argued that it was nothing more than that—"it seems to follow from the doctrine of compacts, that a breach of any of the articles of the confederation by any of the parties to it, absolves the other parties from their respective obligations, and gives them a right if they chuse to exert it, of dissolving the Union altogether." The essence of Madison's analysis was that the American states had tried but failed to get out of the state of nature in which they had found themselves when they renounced their allegiance to the British Empire. Their instrument of cooperation now paradoxically provided the ground—of entangling yet now broken obligations—on which, by the law of nations, they might make war against each other. Nor was it, for him, a new theme. Four years previously, he had warned that the failure to establish a general revenue would make it likely that the balances among the states would never be discharged, "even if they should be liquidated. The consequence would be a rupture of the confederacy. The Eastern States would at sea be powerful and rapacious, and the Southern opulent and weak. This would be a temptation. The demands on the southern states would be an occasion. Reprisals would be instituted. Foreign aid would be called in by first the weaker, then the stronger side; and finally both be made subservient to the wars and politics of Europe."[8]

Points 9 through 12 were devoted not to the crisis of the union but to the situation in the states. As he put it at the beginning of point 9, "In developing the evils which viciate the political system of the U.S. it is proper to include those which are found within the States individually, as well as those which directly affect the States collectively, since the former class have an indirect influence on the general malady and must not be overlooked in forming a compleat remedy." Madison complained of the multiplicity (9), the mutability (10), the injustice (11), and the impotence (12) of the laws of the states. He broke off after stating point 12, probably because he had exhausted himself in the analysis of the eleventh, but it was a theme that others would develop. The crisis of the confederation, according to one congressman, was due to this malady: whereas the states of the Netherlands were individually strong, the American states were individually weak—hence an American confederation formed on the Dutch model could scarcely work as well as the original.[9] But Madison probably would not have accepted that analysis, or at least the full implications of it, because he was convinced that the American system had structural inadequacies that would impair cooperation even had the states been stronger than they were. His focus, in any event, was on the sheer volume of legislation that the states had put forth over the past decade, making for a prolix and changeable legal code. "We daily see laws repealed or superseded, before any trial can have been made of their merits; and even before a knowledge of them can have reached the remoter districts which they were to operate." The separate commercial regulations of the states, filling the vacuum created by a want of federal power, was one instance of this, and a dangerous one because instability there "becomes a snare not only to our citizens but to foreigners also."

It was in his consideration of the injustice of state laws that Madison took flight and unfolded the gist of the argument that would later appear in *Federalist* No. 10. The most alarming feature of this unjust legislation was that it brought "into question the fundamental principle of republican Government, that the majority who rule in such Governments, are the safest Guardians both of public Good and of private rights." In legislative bodies, Madison noted how easily "base and selfish motives" could be "masked by pretexts of public good and apparent expediency." But it was not only legislative bodies that felt the lure of gratifying selfish interests; "a still more fatal if not more frequent cause lies among the people themselves." All civilized societies, Madison observed, "are divided into different interests and factions, as they happen to be creditors or debtors—Rich or poor—husbandmen, merchants or manufacturers—members of different religious sects—followers of different political leaders—inhabitants of different districts—owners of different kinds of property &c &c." Ultimately, however, the majority would rule. Madison recounted the restraints that might so bind a majority of the people—"a prudent regard for their own good as involved in the general and permanent good of the Community"; "respect for character"; and religious restraints—but had to conclude that these would often be weak and unavailing. Madison did not draw from these considerations the conclusion that republican government would have to be abandoned—that was unthinkable. Instead, he suggested an institutional remedy for these deeply rooted weaknesses—"an enlargement of the sphere"—that would afford a greater security to "private rights." Contrary to the "prevailing Theory" (most closely associated with Montesquieu), the "inconveniences of popular States . . . are in proportion not to the extent, but to the narrowness of their limits." In an extended republic, "a common interest or passion is less apt to be felt and the requisite combinations less easy to be formed by a great than by a small number." Madison's belief that "an extensive Republic meliorates the administration of a small Republic" shed new light on the great predicament of republican government: how to ensure that government will be "sufficiently neutral between the different interests and factions, to controul one part of the Society from invading the rights of another, and at the same time sufficiently controuled itself, from setting up an interest adverse to that of the whole Society."[10]

The great problems that Madison sought to resolve in the "Vices" were not novel. English critics such as Josiah Tucker had observed before the Revolution that republican governments would be incapable of forming a durable union and would also end by making citizens less free than subjects. Widely shared among proponents of constitutional reform was the chagrin that the "predictions of our Transatlantic foes" seemed so close to confirmation. But Madison's approach was distinctive in crucial respects. While the defects of the confederation summarized in the early part of the paper were well known, no one had quite drawn the conclusion that the confederation was utterly defunct and the states were again in a state of nature. So, too, the distinctive theory of the extended republic was peculiarly Madison's invention and was known as such in the convention, where he elaborated it while defending a veto by the national legislature over state legislation. That the convention rejected the veto does not necessarily mean that it also rejected the theory, but it suggests a more idiosyncratic role for the theory of the extended republic than is usually appreciated. When Madison restated the theory to Jefferson shortly after the convention was over, he used it to *critique* rather than *expound* the Constitution that had been made. Whereas he had, prepatory to the convention, envisaged a political process by which private rights were to be secured, the Constitution instead provided for a judicial process, an innovation he thought "materially defective."[11]

The distinction between what many nationalist reformers wanted to do, and what in fact was done, is an important one. Those who spoke for a national government in the early days of the convention—Madison of Virginia, James Wilson of Pennsylvania, Alexander Hamilton of New York, and Rufus King of Massachusetts—wanted a national government that was supreme, a supremacy deemed indispensably necessary both to preserve the union from dissolution and to arrest certain unjust proceedings in the states. They were truly the fathers of the Constitution, for they took the vital initiative in forming this new child of the ages. But they did not act alone. The Constitution, as it emerged from the shuttered conclave at Philadelphia—was the offspring of a mating that occurred there with a group that may be thought of (without prejudice to the eighteenth century, or to the twenty-first) as the mothers of the new child. These ladies frowned upon the advances of the nationalists, believed their claims to be quite excessive if not outrageous, and were as determined as their prospective partners to exact terms that would accord with their dignity and status. The elaborate courtship went on a whole hot summer, its consummation in doubt until the very end. Not surprisingly, the offspring they produced resembled both father and mother but was very different from what either parent had anticipated or hoped for.

25

To the Great Compromise

THE VIRGINIA PLAN that Governor Edmund Randolph presented in the early days of the Philadelphia convention proposed the institution of a national government that would provide the remedy for all these ills. It called for the establishment of a "National Legislature" of two branches, proportioned either "to the Quotas of contribution, or to the number of free inhabitants." Members of the first branch were to be elected by the people of the several states, those of the second branch were to be chosen by the first from "a proper number of persons nominated by the individual Legislatures." This legislature would "enjoy the Legislative Rights vested in Congress by the Confederation" and would be empowered "to legislate in all cases to which the separate States are incompetent, or in which the harmony of the United States may be interrupted by the exercise of individual Legislation; to negative all laws passed by the several States, contravening in the opinion of the National Legislature the articles of Union; and to call forth the force of the Union [against] any member of the Union failing to fulfill its duty under the articles thereof." The "National Executive" would be chosen by the "National Legislature." This executive, together with "a convenient number of the National Judiciary," was to "compose a council of revision with authority to examine every act of the National Legislature before it shall operate, & every act of a particular Legislature before a Negative thereon shall be final." Whether the Council of Revision's veto on the acts of congress was to be absolute or qualified was left unspecified in the Virginia Plan. A "National Judiciary" was to be established, its judges to hold their offices during good behavior but whose method of appointment was left unclear. Other aspects of the plan provided "for the admission of States lawfully arising within the limits of the United States," guaranteed a republican form of government to each state by the United States, noted the need for an amendment process that would not require the consent of the national legislature (but which was otherwise unspecified), required that officers of the state governments swear their support for the articles of union, and sketched out, in somewhat fuzzy language, a procedure for the ratification of the "amendments" it proposed to the Articles of Confederation.[1]

That this government would be "supreme" was not left in doubt, and in the early days of the convention nationalists continually recurred to the necessity of establishing a government clearly superior to the states. "[I]n all communities," said Gouverneur Morris, "there must be one supreme power, and one only." "[N]o amendment of the Confederation, leaving the States in possession of their Sovereignty," said Hamilton, "could possibly answer the purpose." None of the nationalists contended for the annihilation of the states; but they were intent on locating the power to decide the authoritative interpretation of the federal line with the national legislature. Madison's conception before the convention was as one with this view: "Conceiving that an individual independence of the states is utterly irreconcilable with their aggregate sovereignty, and that a consolidation of the whole into one simple republic would be as inexpedient as it is unattainable, I have sought for a middle ground, which may at once support a due supremacy of the national authority, and not exclude the local authorities whenever they can be subordinately useful." This "middle ground," leaving the states in a "subordinately useful" position, was very different from the middle ground the finished Constitution ultimately occupied and that Madison would defend in *The Federalist*. What Madison had in mind is well indicated by his discussion of the vital importance of the negative, extending "to all cases," that he wanted to vest in the national legislature. Borrowing an illustration "from the planetary System," he held that "[t]his prerogative of the General Govt. is the great pervading principle that must control the centrifugal tendency of the States; which, without it, will continually fly out of their proper orbits and destroy the order & harmony of the political system."[2]

Delegates from the small states, alarmed at the consolidationist thrust of the Virginia Plan, parried two weeks later with a revision, correction, and enlargement of the Articles of Confederation, presented by William Paterson of New Jersey. His plan retained two key aspects of the congress of the Confederation, for it gave each state one vote in a unicameral congress. This legislative body would have the power to levy duties on imports and certain enumerated "internal" items, like stamps. It also provided congress the power "to pass Acts for the regulation of trade & commerce," both among the American states and with foreign nations. Unlike the Virginia Plan, which assumed that the national government would have adequate sources of revenue entirely independent of the states (and which had placed no restriction on the objects of taxation), the New Jersey Plan assumed that requisitions from the states to support the national government would continue to be necessary or desirable (it is not clear which), a fact made more likely by its restriction of the national government's taxing power to imports and certain enumerated internal items. Were these requisitions not complied with, it authorized congress to "devise and pass acts directing & authorizing the same; provided that none of the powers hereby vested in the [United States in congress] shall be exercised without the consent of at least ____ States, and in that proportion if the number of Confederated States should hereafter be increased or diminished." It established a "federal Judiciary" that was to be a "supreme tribunal," to which state judicial systems were to be subordinate, and gave it authority to decide a wide range of cases. So, too, the executive was authorized to call forth the "power of the Confederated States, or so much thereof as may be necessary to enforce and compel an obedience" to federal laws and treaties. Paterson proposed a plural executive appointed by congress but left unspecified the number of such executives or the length of their term. The plan prohibited reelection for the executives, entitled them to "direct all military operations" but not to take personal command "of any troops," and made the chief executive officers liable to removal by congress "on application by a majority of the Executives of the several States."[3]

Five years previously, veterans of the Continental army, and creditors in the continental funds, would have salivated over the extensive revenues granted to the federal authority under the New Jersey Plan. Over the next seventy years, the national government basically lived off imposts; the grant of the taxing power provided in this plan, as events were to show, was ample for the funding and assumption of the revolutionary war debt, together with the regular operations of the government. The federal government, under the New Jersey Plan, would as well now have the power over commerce that the Congress of the Confederation lacked. Its judicial branch, though it did not provide for inferior federal tribunals, was given a position of supremacy and allotted a power of interpretation differing in but a few particulars from that which was ultimately provided for, and of which the confederation had been destitute. It had its own "three-fifths" clause, introduced to determine the equity of requisitions from the states rather than, as later, both direct taxes and representation. The federal government remained dependent on the states in the equality of representation it accorded them but was released from bondage in most of its essential operations. The Articles of Confederation had not been bashful in according congress a wide range of *responsibilities;* the difficulty all along was that it lacked the power to fulfill them. The New Jersey Plan acknowledged these previous responsibilities, added a few others, and provided impressive resources to fulfill them. (Thus, for example, the "full faith and credit" clause and the "privileges and immunities" clause were both in the Articles and were to be carried forward under the New Jersey Plan). There was, in this plan, an answer to nearly every vice that Madison had identified. Though the plan was silent on certain questions that the nationalists had drawn attention to—there was, for instance, no guarantee clause—the way it drew the "federal" line and allocated power to union and states was as close to the Constitution as ultimately fashioned as was the Virginia Plan. "The whole comes to this," observed Pinckney: "Give N. Jersey an equal vote, and she will dismiss her scruples, and concur in the Nati[ona]l system."[4]

Delegates from the large states, as well as delegates from the small states, objected strenuously to the plans of their rivals. The Virginia Plan sharply diminished the voice of the small states and offered them little protection. Their delegates were unalterably opposed to confederation on those principles: it would give the larger states "an enormous & monstrous influence."[5] "We would sooner submit to a foreign power than submit to be deprived of an equality of suffrage in both branches of the legislature."[6] The New Jersey Plan, however, carried over the same disjunction between representation given, and burdens exacted, that delegates from the large states had found objectionable in 1776, and which they bitterly assailed anew. The small states feared that they would be swallowed up by the Virginia Plan; the large states feared the converse. "[I]n the present mode of voting by States," as Franklin put it, "it is equally in the power of the lesser States to swallow up the greater; and this is mathematically demonstrable."[7] The colloquy between William Paterson and James Wilson on June 9 summarized the difficulty: the small states, Paterson insisted, would not confederate on the basis of the Virginia Plan; ten of them, he boldly contended, would reject it. Let the large states "unite if they please"—an answer to Wilson's threat of a separate confederacy—"but let them remember that they have no authority to compel the others to unite. N. Jersey will never confederate on the plan before the Committee. . . . He had rather submit to a monarchy, to a despot, than to such a fate." Wilson, the main object of Paterson's cutting remarks, then returned the favor: "If the small States will not confederate on this plan, [Pennsylvania] & he presumed some other States, would not confederate on any other."[8] The threat and counterthreat was a virtual replica of the colloquy that had occurred between Wilson and Witherspoon in 1776, and would be repeated in the convention over the next month.[9] Even with a rough consensus over the division of powers between the general and particular governments, the convention could make no progress. "[I]t would be impossible," Madison observed, "to say what powers could be safely and properly vested in the Government before it was known, in what manner the States were to be represented in it."[10] "Who would rule?" was a question logically and politically prior to "With what powers?" As long as this great question remained unsettled, nothing could be settled, and the deliberations meandered amid this basic stalemate.

Though the mode of representation and the extent of national powers were analytically distinct questions, it proved very difficult to separate them in debate. The more the small states sought constitutional recognition, the more the nationalists saw a revival of the slavishness to state interest that had undone the confederation. The more the nationalists hammered away at state obstruction and narrow-minded state politicians, the more the latter feared for their existence. At the same time, the initial debate showed that few among the "nationalists" were as hostile to the existence of the states as had been feared, and that few among the "State Rights party" or "federalists" denied the necessity of a general government capable of acting without the agency of the states. Hamilton's speech of June 18, which marked the ne plus ultra of centralizing tendencies in the convention, was "admired by all but supported by none." Moderates on the other side, like Dickinson, Sherman, and Ellsworth, distanced themselves from the uncompromising stand of Luther Martin, who clung to the corpse of the confederation. That mutual rejection of the antipodes foreshadowed the larger consensus over the appropriate division of power that would ultimately be registered in the Constitution, and indeed suggests that the confrontation between "nationalists" and "federalists" was not the chief point of division in the convention.[11]

The controversy between the large states and the small states was a real and not fictitious conflict. The small states had good reason for fearing that their voices would be radically diminished in the new structure raised in the Virginia plan. Within each of the three regions, which may be seen as little state systems of their own, the role of the populous states—of Massachusetts, Pennsylvania, and Virginia—had not infrequently elicited the resentment of the smaller. Maryland had long been at odds with Virginia, Delaware with Pennsylvania, New Jersey with New York and Pennsylvania, New York with Connecticut and Massachusetts. Of all the New England states, Rhode Island generally took the more independent stance and was at this time a vivid symbol of refractoriness, but conflicts were not unknown even between Massachusetts and Connecticut. While the regional blocs in congress (particularly the eastern and the southern parties) had most often found themselves in accordance on continental issues, and they voted and caucused with one another frequently, it was entirely natural that delegates from the small states could feel that their own life prospects would wither, and the vital interests of their state would suffer, if the states were not given constitutional representation in the new government. This

mixture of personal and political motives, however, operated just as powerfully on the other side, and it gave to the conflict a deep element of rancor. It also gave middling states like Connecticut a disinterested posture
that poised them to strike a middle ground.

The division between the large states and the small states was also sectional. It pit the northeast against the southwest. The small-state coalition
joined Maryland, Delaware, New Jersey, New York, and Connecticut against
Pennsylvania, Virginia, and the remainder of the southern states, all of whom
expected a continuing shift of population to the southwest. Madison, speaking the fears of the South, observed that equal state voting would provide in
"perpetuity" a "preponderance of the Northern against the Southern Scale,"
arresting the natural movement toward sectional equilibrium.[12] Equality in
the second branch, however, was vital to the northeast for precisely this reason. Ellsworth put the case plainly on June 29: "To the Eastward he was sure
Massts. was the only State that would listen to a proposition for excluding
the States as equal political Societies, from an equal voice in both branches.
The others would risk every consequence rather than part with so dear a
right. An attempt to deprive them of it, was at once cutting the body [of
America] in two, and as he supposed would be the case somewhere about this
part of it."[13] Massachusetts had done more than listen to the advocates from
Virginia and Pennsylvania over the merits of a more equitable mode of representation; her representatives, particularly Rufus King, had strongly opposed the representation of the states in the initial month of the convention.
A government with the national powers that were needed, King believed,
could not last were it provided with a defective system of representation. "A
government founded in a vicious principle of representation," he observed,
"must be as short-lived as it would be unjust."[14] As it happened, however, it
was the defection of Massachusetts from the large-state coalition, through
the division of her vote, that played a vital role in breaking the stalemate in
the convention over the acceptance of equal state voting in the upper house
on July 16, but even before that time her enthusiasm for that principle had
clearly waned. Even at the beginning, King's agreement with Madison on the
inequity of voting by states disguised deep differences of outlook over what
would constitute an equitable substitute rule—a disagreement that centered
on the rule for the admission of new states.[15]

In the course of refuting the small-state advocates, both King and Madison had attested to the fact that the "great division of interests" lay between North and South. The eastern people, King said, were "very desirous
of uniting with their Southern brethren but did not think it prudent to rely
so far on that disposition as to subject them to any gross inequality. He was

fully convinced that the question concerning a difference of interests did not lie where it had hitherto been discussed, between the great & small states; but between the Southern and Eastern."[16] Madison, too, said that the line between those states with slavery, and those without, constituted the central problem of representation that the convention had to resolve. He was, he said, "so strongly impressed with this important truth that he had been casting about in his mind for some expedient that would answer the purpose." Instead of a three-fifths rule in both houses, he suggested the possibility of computing representation in one house "according to the number of free inhabitants only," and in the other according to the number of all inhabitants. "By this arrangement the Southern Scale would have the advantage in one House, and the Northern in the other." This "expedient," however, was no sooner suggested than it was withdrawn: the proposal would not only complicate the relations between the two branches; Madison was also unwilling "to urge any diversity of interests on an occasion when it is but too apt to arise of itself."[17]

The sectional problem was indeed continually arising of itself. It had many dimensions, rooted in the existence of slavery in the South, but also reaching to all continental questions of finance, commerce, diplomacy, and western territory. From the standpoint of representation and burden-sharing, the issues separating North from South were a reiteration of those that had arisen in the First Continental Congress and in the debate in 1776 over the Articles of Confederation. In its rule for apportioning burdens among the states, congress at that time avoided a formula involving population because it could not reach agreement on how to count slaves. Instead it substituted the hopeless formula of a valuation of land. That having proved an impossible remedy, congress had in 1783, under the leadership of Wilson and Madison, proposed to the states an amendment, never successfully ratified, that counted five slaves as three men in the assessment of state quotas. During the first days of the convention, the delegates had approved that as the rule for apportioning the representation of the two houses by a nine-to-two margin, but later divisions were much closer. South Carolina wanted all her slaves counted fully. North Carolina and Virginia repudiated Carolina's extremism but considered the three-fifths ratio a sine qua non.

From Pennsylvania northward, opinion varied in intensity over how onerous a sacrifice this was for the union. If population were to be the rule, however, all the northerners would have preferred a rule making representation proportional to the number of free inhabitants. On July 11, Wilson observed that he "did not well see on what principle the admission of blacks in the proportion of three fifths could be explained. Are they admitted as Citizens? Then why are they not admitted on an equality with White Citizens? Are they admitted as property? Then why is not other property admitted into the computation?" That day, Pennsylvania voted against the three-fifths rule. The next day, Wilson proposed the solution, and Pennsylvania changed her vote: "less umbrage would perhaps be taken against an admission of the slaves into the Rule of representation, if it should be so expressed as to make them indirectly only a ingredient in the rule, by saying that they should enter into the rule of taxation: and as representation was to be according to taxation, the end would be equally attained."[18] In that form, it was adopted July 12 with the concurrence of Connecticut, Pennsylvania, Maryland, Virginia, North Carolina, and Georgia. The three-fifths rule was chosen, as Gorham suggested, because it most fairly represented the relative wealth of the states. Because any direct measure of wealth would get lost in a maze of subjective judgments, and because counting slaves either fully or not at all could never have secured the assent of the disfavored antipodes, a fractional division of the slave—a sundering of the African body—was virtually inevitable if the convention were to reach agreement. Wilson's motion conformed to Pennsylvania's longstanding insistence that a stable and just constitution had to distribute representation and taxation, or benefits and burdens, by a common rule. In other respects, however, the three-fifths compromise made a hash of accepted categories of constitutionalism, and it was disingenuous because the projectors of a national government did not intend to rely upon requisitions or state quotas to raise a national revenue. Wilson knew that but supported the compromise anyway on the conviction that the convention could not succeed without it or some close equivalent.

On July 13, the three-fifths ratio was extended to the western territory, whose future bore closely on the distribution of power among the sections. The South had been bitterly stung by the willingness of the eastern states to barter access to the Mississippi River for a paltry set of commercial concessions from Spain; that sense of aggrievement still ranked. It wanted two things: that the power of the union be exerted to gain the outlet on the Mississippi, and that the new states arising beyond the mountains be admitted on the basis of equality with the Atlantic states. It accepted as axiomatic, as indeed did everyone else at the convention, that such future development would incline the preponderance to the southern scale. If they were going to make a bargain that conceded a temporary superiority to the North, as King insisted they had to do, they would insist upon gaining their equivalent in the future. They might accept a temporary imbalance in exchange for its future correction and reversal; but the latter was a sine qua non.

The first great set-to over the admission of western states arose from the determination of the eastern states, led by Morris and King, to give the national legislature near-absolute discretion in deciding the terms on which it would allow new admissions. They were not bashful in assigning the reasons. Future population growth would give a preponderance to the western region. "It has been said," Morris noted, "that North Carolina, South Carolina and Georgia only, will in a little time have a majority of the people of America. They must in that case include the great interior country and everything is to be apprehended from their getting power into their hands."[19] The widely shared assumption that western expansion meant preponderance for the South is very significant, and there is a sense in which it was, after all, quite prescient. The next twenty-five years would demonstrate the truth of the axiom, for the North achieved, as predicted, a temporary preponderance, which then passed to the South with the Republican Revolution of 1800, leaving the northeast—as Morris and King had foreseen, and as they would both live to witness and regret—in distinct minority status. To mitigate the danger of being ruled by barbarous frontiersmen, and thinking that the haunts of the forest were not a proper school for statesmen, they contended at various times (1) for absolute discretion in the legislature over the admission of new states, using a general formula of "wealth and population" that might be easily manipulated; (2) for a two-thirds rule in the congress, and hence a qualified veto, over the admission of new states; and (3) for stipulating that the new states, however admitted, not exceed the original thirteen. None of these expedients was acceptable to the southern states, and the resistance they displayed in turn fractured the large-state coalition. The three-fifths ratio was again brought into question, and Morris said that he would be obliged to vote "for the vicious principle of equality in the 2d. Branch in order to provide some defence for the N. States."[20] Faced with a threat "to deprive the Southern States of any share of Representation for their blacks," Davie of North Carolina said he was sure that his state "would never confederate on any terms that did not rate them at least as 3/5. If the Eastern States meant therefore to exclude them altogether the business was at an end."[21]

Just as the convention was reaching the end of its rope over the question of present and future representation, one element of the western future had been clarified by the Continental Congress, then sitting in New York. Its passage of the Northwest Ordinance on July 13 brought the prospect of a new western state on the Ohio closer to reality and shed a powerful light on the whole western question. The ordinance not only satisfied a general interest in reducing the debt of the congress; it also had features that were attractive, distinctively, to North and South. While Nathan Dane of Massachusetts, who drafted the ordinance, could conclude that the new settlers in the first state created in the Northwest territory would largely hail from New England and would give its politics an eastern orientation, a new state on the Ohio also promised to add further weight to the Mississippi interest, as succeeding entrants would certainly do.[22]

While the North secured the pledge that neither slavery nor involuntary servitude would exist in the three to five states to be created north of the Ohio, the South secured the fugitive slave provision that, with nearly identical wording, was later incorporated in the Constitution. In 1784, the territorial ordinance prepared by Jefferson had proposed the abolition of slavery in all the western territories by the end of 1800, a provision that was defeated by the votes of a united South, including Virginia. The Northwest Ordinance, unlike the acts of 1784, 1785, and the first version of the 1787 measure, was for the territory of the Virginia cession rather than, as previously, for territory "ceded and to be ceded," and it indirectly confirmed that the disposition of the southeast could be established only with the voluntary consent of the South Atlantic states who still held title. In both Kentucky and Tennessee, who joined the union in 1792 and 1796, slavery was well established. In short, the line drawn in 1787 abolishing slavery north of the Ohio was also a line protecting it south of the Ohio.[23]

North and South also reached a compromise in the Ordinance of 1787 over the size of the new states. Easterners had previously supported a provision whereby new states could be admitted only after their total population reached one-thirteenth of the total population of the older thirteen at the last census before the request for statehood. This set the bar very high. The Ordinance of 1784, reaffirmed in 1785, had by contrast provided that the new states would enter the union when their population was equal to the smallest of the original thirteen states, which promised a far more rapid course for admission. (Delaware, the smallest state, was at this time estimated at only thirty-five thousand.) Jefferson's plan also provided for 14 new states in the entire western territory, of which 8 and one half were above the Ohio River. The Northwest Ordinance reduced that figure to a minimum of 3 and a maximum of 5, a salve to the North, while setting admission at sixty thousand free inhabitants, a concession to the South. The northeast could further prolong its superiority in states, while the southwest was destined to grow rapidly in whichever branch registered the majoritarian principle. That is why Virginia, the Carolinas, and Georgia—"the body of the southern interest," as Drayton had termed it in 1778—had always supported that principle on condition that it allow a fair equivalent for their slaves.[24]

Not only, then, did the "great difficulty" lie in "the affair of Represen-tation," as Madison observed.[25] The "great difficulty" was in fact many difficulties. That between large states and small states had not disappeared by the time of the crucial vote of July 16 registering the Great Compromise of the convention, but it had gotten deeply entangled in, and almost en-tirely submerged by, the larger sectional controversy. The compromise bill of July 16 that had sallied forth from a grand committee two weeks earlier had four interlocking provisions. As amended, (1) it created a first branch of sixty-five members, to sit until the completion of the first census; (2) it established the three-fifths rule for the lower house and provided that new states were to be admitted on the same basis; (3) it gave each state one vote in the second branch of the legislature; and (4) it required all bills for rais-ing or appropriating money, or fixing salaries, to originate in the lower house, forbidding alteration or amendment by the upper body.

The Northwest Ordinance was not formally part of the Great Compro-mise, but its successful passage in the congress presaged the action of the convention three days later and almost certainly helped make possible the readiness with which the July 16 vote was accepted. The eastern and south-ern delegates in congress had long been deeply divided on the territorial question; that they were able to agree on a system of equivalents for the western territory, and this by a vote of eight to zero, was a template by which the convention itself might act. Taken together, the ordinance and the compromise assured the South that its expansion would take place under the auspices of the three-fifths ratio, and gave her a basis on which she might aim for a majority in the lower house in the not too distant fu-ture. At the same time, the predominance accorded the North in the Senate by the vote of July 16 carried greater weight in light of the Northwest Or-dinance: the reduction in the number of states that could be admitted from the Northwest territory, together with the vast purchases by New England land companies in the Ohio territory, provided a good basis for thinking that the North might protract the domination of the upper house for a longer term of years.

The convention needed the clarification that the Northwest Ordinance provided if it were to resolve its fundamental problem, which was that of as-suring a balance of power among the sections. Even before the convention had begun, Madison had foreseen a bargain by which the existing populous-ness of the northern states would be counterbalanced by the expected popu-lousness of the southern states. The terms of compromise were more onerous for the South than he had expected, and he continued to wince at the com-position of the Senate, but he was resigned to building from that structure.

Other southerners, however, saw great danger therein. Mason's Anti-Federalism dated from this moment. Responding to Madison's projection in the Virginian ratifying convention of southern preponderance in the future, Mason called it "a very sound argument indeed, that we should cheerfully burn ourselves to death in hope of a joyful and happy resurrection." It also produced in the convention, over the next month and a half, a strong southern reaction in which protections were sought, and sometimes achieved, for their beleaguered position in the first years of the government.[26]

26

Commerce, Slavery, and Machiavellian Moment

THE VOTE ON July 16, and the realization by the losers that they were hopelessly divided on what was wrong with it, made the compromise the turning point of the convention. It rescued the delegates from the specter of a breakup of the convention and the emergence of separate confederacies. The question of representation had always represented the knot of the "most Gordian character," and once clarity had been brought on these terms, the framers could begin to tackle the relationship between the two branches and the composition of the executive. Those who insisted on the constitutional recognition of the states and of their agency in the government proved anxious to establish a general government adequate to the exigencies of the union. Those who had opposed this recognition began to see that an effective government capable of enforcing its decisions on individuals might successfully elude state obstruction, and that the agency of the states registered in the Senate might sustain rather than weaken the federal government's authority. The compromise, though focused on representation, effectively closed the gap between nationalist and federalist perspectives and made it possible to foresee a federal structure in which local and general authorities each hewed to their constitutionally allotted functions.[1]

Southern objections to the compromise helped secure three key concessions in the report of the Committee of Detail presented to the convention on August 6 by John Rutledge of South Carolina: it forbade any restriction on the right to import slaves; it prohibited the taxation of exports; and it required a two-thirds vote of both houses to pass a navigation act. King and Morris blasted the report and, mixing the language of moral indignation and political interest, insisted that confederation on these terms would be utterly unacceptable to the people of the North. The three-fifths rule of representation was bad enough. If slaves were men, as Morris said, they should vote; if property, why were no other types of property included in the computation? The houses in Philadelphia, Morris said, "are worth more than all the wretched slaves which cover the rice swamps of South Carolina." The provisions forbidding export taxes and allowing the indefinite importation of slaves were an insult piled on top of this injury. If the three-fifths rule were to remain in the Constitution, it had obviously to be seen as a sacrifice for which the North was entitled to compensation. What had it gotten in exchange for this sacrifice "of every principle of right, of every impulse of humanity"? Four things:

1. The northern states "are to bind themselves to march their militia for the defence of the [southern] States" in the event of an insurrection by their helots—for the defense of the South, in other words, against the very slaves of whom the North complained.
2. The North was "to supply vessels and seamen, in case of foreign Attack."
3. The restriction on export taxes meant that the burden of taxation, confined to imposts and excises, would fall disproportionately on the North: the tea "used by a Northern freeman, will pay more tax than the whole consumption of the miserable slave, which consists of nothing more than his physical subsistence and the rag that covers his nakedness."
4. The South, finally, was given a positive encouragement to import slaves, and that was certain to magnify the inequity in the future: such importations would "increase the danger of attack, and the difficulty of defence," and while increasing the representation of the southern states would make "their exports & their slaves exempt from all contributions for the public service."

Neither Morris nor King ruled out the possibility of some compromise; King was willing to accept the three-fifths ratio if compensation were given. Though he was "not sure he could assent" to the importation of slaves under any circumstances, given the sheer iniquity of the practice, he was positive that there was "so much inequality & unreasonableness" in the committee's report that the northern people would never assent to it. "[E]ither slaves should not be represented, or exports should be taxable." The South might have one or the other; it could not have both.[2]

Even at this stage in American history, opinion toward slavery divided along lines that would be characteristic of futurity. At the North, some men burned at the injustice and iniquity of the institution; Gouverneur Morris and Rufus King both gave blistering speeches at the convention to this effect. "He would never concur in upholding domestic slavery," Morris contended. "It was the curse of heaven on the States where it prevailed." In tracing its nefarious character, Morris said that "every step presents a desert increasing with the increasing proportion of these wretched beings." Few northerners at this time would have disputed the judgment that the institution was wicked, or that its perpetuation would be a fraud upon the liberty for which America stood; the northern people were well aware of

Samuel Johnson's taunt of 1775 and knew, much as they regretted it, that they shared in the hypocritical infamy that the existence of slavery cast upon the American name. But though that opinion was common, its temperature differed. The Connecticut delegates felt it much less keenly than Morris or King. The institution, after all, existed, and the typical northern man had no more idea of how to be rid of it in the southern states than the Virginians, who were, as it happened, equally emphatic on the evil of the encumbrance. No one in the North made emancipation a condition of union with the South; Morris's hints on this score—"He would never concur in upholding domestic slavery"—were nothing more than that. That policy was vulnerable to the reply that slavery would be as well fortified outside a separate northern confederation as within the American union. Confronted, on the one hand, with the evils of disunion and separate confederacies, and on the other with the fact that a refusal to confederate because of slavery would do nothing to ameliorate its curses, even northerners hostile to slavery knew they could not make emancipation a sine qua non of union, for this was identical with the proposition that there should be no union at all. At the time, as well as subsequently, northern opinion would split into two broad currents: one side held that union was possible only if the existence of slavery were recognized to be the affair of the southern states, that time would perhaps take care of the evil, that it was necessary, if any union were to be possible, to bear and forbear with the gentlemen of the South. The other view acknowledged the main premise of the conciliationists—that no union was possible without recognizing slavery—but also drew the line more closely. We will not interfere with existing institutions, they said, but we will hardly agree to encourage and extend it.

The division of opinion within the North—so characteristic of the future—had its parallel in the South. Virginians reasoned about slavery in a way very different from Carolinians and Georgians. The leading men among the Virginia gentry accepted that the institution was evil and hoped that, in some unspecified way (diffusion? colonization?), the future would bring circumstances that would allow them to be rid of it. The view in South Carolina and Georgia was far different. The politicians of the Deep South were as yet unwilling to proclaim slavery a "positive good" in a continental forum, but they accepted the institution and insisted on their right to continue a trade that, as Morris said, enabled them to go "to the Coast of Africa, and in defiance of the most sacred laws of humanity," to tear Africans away "from their dearest connections," and to damn them "to the most cruel bondages." The acknowledgment, in the Deep South, that slavery was an evil was always followed by a "but"; yes, but we depend on it;

yes, but every other great civilization has had it; yes, but we intend to per-petuate it; yes, but we require the discretion to import slaves without limi-tation and to count them fully for purposes of representation; yes, but if you bring it into question the union is at an end. The Carolinians and the Georgians were unbending on their right to import slaves; they made a con-tinuation of this practice a sine qua non and complained even of the injus-tice of the three-fifths ratio. Virginia's interest was different: it had a surplus of slaves, and its interest would actually be better secured if im-portations were prohibited, since further slave imports would decrease their value at market. The Virginia delegation, for reasons at once moral and political, and making calculations at once self-interested and idealistic, favored giving the national government the power to stop slave importa-tions altogether; it was George Mason, the defiant advocate for the inter-ests of his state and section, who gave at the convention perhaps the most effective speech urging the justice and policy of this prohibition. Yet while Virginians shed copious tears over the evils of slavery, they were far from inattentive to the interests that its existence prompted. Like the Carolini-ans, they, too, considered it their own affair, and while they would gladly pronounce a sermon on the evils that it brought, the gist of which always showed that they bore no moral responsibility for their inherited encum-brance, they reserved the right to deal with their own domestic institutions as they saw fit. They had no intention of vesting that right of determina-tion with an insolent northern majority. On this vital point, they were as one with the Carolinians.[3]

Most southerners also saw their interests vitally affected by the prospect that the general government might gain the power to impose taxes on their great staple exports. They were unmoved by the demonstration that the North also exported goods—particularly lumber and foodstuffs to the West Indies—that might also be taxed; their large exports of tobacco, rice, and indigo seemed to them highly vulnerable to sectional aggrandizement. Madison broke the common southern front on this question, holding, in one of his greatest speeches at the convention, that common equity, and the good of the union, required that the general government possess the power to tax the exports of the staple states. It was a testament to his willingness to risk his popularity in Virginia for the union that he said what he did on that occasion, but he could not carry his delegation with him.

There also existed a profound sectional disparity in what the southern and eastern states wanted from a more powerful national government, and this shaped the debate in August over the national powers. The Virginians, in particular, were convinced that the history of their commercial transactions made for a tale of inordinate oppression. The restrictions of the Acts of Trade and Navigation under the British Empire they saw as being highly injurious to them, devaluing their exports and magnifying the cost of their imports, while ensnaring them in a web of debt and dependence. They wanted out of this damnable trap, and had inveighed after the return of peace in 1783 against the larger resumption of the old pattern that saw their commerce centering in England. They thought a national power over commerce would help them break it. So far convinced was Jefferson of these points that he had toyed, a few years previously, with the idea of introducing a national power over commerce into the confederation via a treaty with France. That *projet* had failed, but he and Madison were united in their conviction that a national power over commerce was indispensably necessary. Once the new government was instituted, they planned to use it to impose discriminatory provisions in tariffs and tonnage laws to pry open the now informal but still rigid constraints that ensnared them in the British mercantile system. Their purposes were by no means narrowly sectional: they thought that the interests of the staple states, and above all of Virginia, coincided with the interests of the commercial or "Eastern" states, and they planned to use the commerce power in a way that would benefit all.[4]

These views were deeply impressed upon Madison and Jefferson; there is much in the Republican diplomacy of the next twenty-five years that is disclosed in these beliefs. Other southerners, however, were much more ambivalent about a national power over commerce, both in 1787 and later. They would be delighted, of course, to get more money for their exports, and to pay less for their imports; but they also feared the use to which this power might be put. The danger was that the "carrying states" might turn the congressional power to regulate trade to malign use and make navigation acts that would force the South to carry its products in the vessels of New England, thereby delivering themselves "bound hand and foot to the Eastern states." This exchange of masters—of New England for Old England—would be a poor return for the Revolution. To prevent it, George Mason proposed the remedy, incorporated in the August 6 report, that no navigation act could be passed without a two-thirds vote in both houses of congress. As on export taxes, Madison was at odds with dominant sentiment in his section on this question.[5]

To the North, the two-thirds provision over navigation acts, when added to the provisions concerning the slave trade and representation, rubbed salt in the wound. "If the Government," said Gorham, "is to be so fettered as to be unable to relieve the Eastern States what motive can they have to join in it, and thereby tie their own hands from measures which they could otherwise take for themselves. He deprecated the consequences of disunion, but if it should take place it was the Southern part of the Continent that had most reason to dread them."[6] New Englanders saw the uses of a national power over commerce in protecting their interest in the fisheries, in regaining the trade routes they had enjoyed under the British Empire, and breaking open the trade with French and Spanish possessions in the West Indies. They cringed at the southern demand for a veto on this legislation, for their interests, they thought, were more vitally affected by whatever dispensation might exist upon the ocean; on these matters they claimed the same *droit de regard* that the South claimed on the Mississippi question.

The adjustment of these sectional questions occurred in late August. The terms of the second compromise, the product of a committee chaired by William Livingston of New Jersey, called on the South to give up its veto over navigation acts and on the North to surrender its demand to tax exports and its right to interfere with the importation of slaves until 1800. On a subsequent vote to extend the prohibition on congressional interference with the slave trade to 1808, Massachusetts and Connecticut joined the Deep South in pushing through the measure, with Virginia, Pennsylvania, Delaware, and New Jersey voting no. South Carolina returned the favor by voting with the northern majority on the proposal to eliminate the two-thirds veto for navigation acts (with Virginia, North Carolina, Maryland, and Georgia in the minority on that question).[7] The procedure formed a model for subsequent "great compromises," like those in 1820–21, 1833, and 1850, with small numbers of conciliationists on either side willing to barter among themselves and impose a solution on their refractory colleagues. Unlike the later compromises, where the narrow margins usually came from the middle or western states, this was a compromise between the antipodes: the Deep South and New England, as different as Russia and Turkey, joined hands in a marriage of convenience.

By the end of August, the southern states had also parried various devices to deprive them of power in the future: there would be no clause restricting the number of new states, no two-thirds veto on their admission, no elastic formula for a temporary northern majority to stretch in order to preserve its faltering power. They secured, finally, a provision preventing northern states from aiding fugitives from slavery.[8] These concessions worked hard upon the future interests of the eastern states, as the next two decades would show, and they would, at a still later date, gnaw upon its conscience; but they were compensated for by equivalents in the present that might be put to good use: a temporary preponderance in both House and Senate allowing it to solve the riddle of the revolutionary war debt and to establish credit, to make navigation acts that would liberate its commerce, to form the vital precedents of the new system.

The impetus given to slavery by the Constitution raises the question whether a different arrangement might have been made. Was a compact that barred the slave trade feasible in 1787? Or is it the case, as the Deep South contended, that no confederation was possible upon these terms, and that the Carolinas and Georgia would have formed a separate confederacy rather than submit to them? These questions cannot be answered with great confidence, for the dynamic was arrested before it had the opportunity to play itself out. There is, however, little reason to doubt the credibility of the Deep South's threat to refuse confederation had the Constitution proposed an abolition of the slave trade. Morris had acknowledged as much early in the convention: "reduced to the dilemma of doing injustice to the Southern States or to human nature," he had resolved to do the injustice to the former. "For he could never agree to give such encouragement to the slave trade as would be given by allowing them a representation for their negroes, and he did not believe those States would ever confederate on terms that would deprive them of that trade."[9]

The prospects that the Deep South might make alliances in Europe were much better at this period than they were later. Cotton was not yet king—its cultivation, indeed, was hardly known in the southern states at this time—but the benefits to European powers of the transatlantic carrying trade that made the South think (delusively) its position excellent in 1860 were more highly valued in Europe at this period than they were later, when the North, besides, was far stronger and could command impressive resources of retaliation against any European power that took up the cause of the southern states. The British government, still smarting over the loss of its colonies in 1787, would certainly have been willing to entertain any fair offer that brought a reunion of the Deep South with the mother country, for these plantations would have made a perfect match for their existing possessions in the West Indies; their estimations of value might easily be seen in the southerly movement of their military operations during the war. France, too, would have listened. Vergennes had complained in 1782 that France would be poorly paid for her efforts on behalf of American independence; that the French might see an offer from the Deep South as justice delayed, but not denied, was firmly embedded in the circumstances of 1787.[10]

The imponderable concerns not so much the options of the Deep South but the calculations of Virginia. Much as Virginia would have loathed the breaking of the union, her position in the event the Deep South refused accession would have been as bad in 1787 as it was in 1860: giving the most generous interpretation to the commitment of her leaders to the progressive elimination of slavery, her role in an American union shorn of her natural allies on the other great questions of interest—of expansion and commerce and finance—would necessarily be radically diminished. Virginia was saved from the necessity of this choice by the readiness of the Massachusetts and Connecticut delegations to conciliate the Deep South. It cannot be known how she would have acted had she not enjoyed that luxury, and instead been faced with the choice of joining a confederation of the Deep South, sundered from the American union on a principle that Virginia heartily disliked, or joining a northern confederation in which her fond hopes of direction, leadership, and majority status would be blasted, and in which even her discretion over her domestic institutions, even if constitutionally affirmed, might be nibbled away by a hostile northern majority. Opinion in the state would doubtless have been sharply divided, if not paralyzed. Washington would later say that, in the event of such a sundering, he would cast his lot with the North, suggesting that Virginia herself would have been the Flanders of America. The speculation, in any event, reveals a dynamic that would prove very significant in the future. The ultras in the Deep South were frequently capable of putting Virginia in a position she did not want, of leading her in a direction she detested, but which she might be forced to follow in spite of herself. They might have done it in 1787, but for the conciliationists at the North; they would do it on many subsequent occasions in the course of federal union, but above all in 1860.[11]

The same speculation that made it dangerous to go to the wall with the Deep South applied also to the West. Secure their interests, or they will secede. Gain for them a fair representation and their rights on the Mississippi, or they will throw themselves into the arms of a foreign power. Such was the ever-recurring lament and warning. Madison and Jefferson had repeatedly recurred to this danger in their correspondence before the federal convention, and southern spokesmen made the appeal continually during the convention when arguing for the admission of the new states on the basis of equality with the old. It was a strong argument, which badly weakened the case of those in the eastern states who wanted to reduce western influence in the future. Unless the westerners were admitted on a basis of equality, said Mason, they "will either not unite with or will speedily revolt from the Union." The western states, said Randolph, "never would nor ought to accede" save on equal terms; if their claims were denied "the injustice of the government will shake it to its foundations." Spain still claimed at this time territory up to the Ohio; the "men of the western waters" had made known their willingness to make a deal with anyone—the American union, the Spanish, even the reviled British—who would make a fair deal with them. The same logic—secure the vital interests of a section, or accept disunion and foreign alliances as the inevitable consequence of your refusal—played itself out here as well. Mixed up, as it was, with diplomatic questions that the convention could not of itself resolve, it would continue to do so until a series of western political and diplomatic victories, confirming the West's position as the holder of the balance within the American union, brought the western phase of the disunion question to an end.[12]

These considerations are of crucial significance in understanding what was done at Philadelphia, just as they are of equal significance in understanding the subsequent course of American politics and diplomacy. The framers of the Constitution, and the statesmen who breathed life into the general government after its adoption, knew that their unity was more aspiration than fact; that they had the makings in North America of a state system closely resembling that which existed in Europe. There were many potential routes to this destination: every issue on which the convention bitterly divided, and where advocates on either side insisted that their mutually contradictory positions were a sine qua non, could readily serve the purpose. But they also felt and knew that the consequences of a division of the states would open the door to foreign alliances and European intervention; that the unsettled issues arising from their common war provided ample counts to justify war against one another, according to the law of nations; that unless they placed their matters of mutual interest in the hands of a general authority, constitutionally authorized to reconcile their conflicting interests and pretensions, they could not escape the whirlpool that would suck them down to the abyss. They knew, too, that the institutions of free government could not survive that perilous descent. If all this were to be arrested, they had to mutually support the vital interests of the others, even if this meant real sacrifice to each of them, and even if it meant injustice to those outside the covenant.

Injustice to African-Americans and injustice to Indian nations—a constitutional obligation to protect and even advance the slave power, and an acknowledged duty to dispossess the Indian nations of the interior—were by this powerful logic woven into the inner fabric of their beautiful union. The bargain was Machiavellian in two senses: it proposed itself as a means to maintain the stability of the "republic of many republics," as an artificial dike to arrest and channel the powerful natural forces that would otherwise produce disunion and foreign intervention; and it required a compromise with evil. The bargain over slavery was more explicit than that which was made over the West, but both were made. In defense of this contract with the devil, it may be said that the rights and interests of blacks and reds would have fared no better without the union, and may even have fared much worse. But the bargain, nevertheless, had been made; and it would be kept.

27

"A Feudal System of Republics"

IT WAS ONLY AFTER the composition of the legislature came clearly into view after July 16 that the crucial powers over war and peace, and treaties and alliances could be distributed among the president, the Senate, and the House of Representatives. Though the principle of unity in the executive had been pretty well established early in the convention, the compromises over representation probably aided that determination, as they made it less important to ensure sectional balance through the device of a plural executive. However much a tripartite executive consisting of eastern, middle, and southern tribunes appealed to those fearful of either monarchical tendencies or sectional disadvantage, the record of disunity in the executive was sufficiently woeful and so contrary to the accepted categories of constitutional thought that the advocates of unity in the executive won the day.

Some element of prerogative ended up in the office of the president, though how much is difficult to say. The concept had had a rough go of it: it had gotten trimmed in the Glorious Revolution of 1688; it was then hedged in further by jealous colonists; it subsequently got transferred to the Congress of the Confederation, where it was reduced to mimicry; and it now ended up somewhere—it has never been exactly clear where—in the interior relations of the president, the Senate, and, for some purposes, the full congress. It had clearly gotten stronger, but this was no sooner seen than it was divided.

These debates over the shape of the presidency reveal how much of the mental life of the framers was lived in the capacious house of ancient and modern history, whose lessons were digested to create an office with many precedents, and with none.[1] The executive power was given exclusively to the president, but the "federative power"—of war and peace, treaties and alliances—was to be shared. This happened in a curious way: throughout most of the convention, it was the Senate that was to be entrusted with *making* treaties. Before the composition of the Senate came clearly into view, it was virtually impossible to get to a coherent discussion and definition of the presidential function. Once it was clear that the Senate would be, as congress had been before, a committee of the states, precedents from the confederation period suggested that it would be ill suited to the exercise of a diplomatic function; its northern orientation, moreover, convinced many southern delegates, including Madison, that it needed to share its federative powers with the executive. The solution was to make the president the organ of communication with foreign states but to require that treaties be passed with the advice and consent of "two thirds of Senators present."[2]

The Senate would represent the sovereignty of the states. The composition of the Senate largely followed the formula of the confederation, though each state got two representatives with an independent vote rather than, as previously, one apiece. Allowing the state legislatures to choose their representatives and granting the states equality in the Senate might be suspected of introducing into that body the ailments of the preceding congress, and was damned as such by Wilson, Madison, and Morris. In fact, however, there was little danger on this score. The similarity in the mode of selection mattered far less than the change in function: whereas the representatives of the states had previously acted in a primarily executive capacity, they would now act in a primarily deliberative one. The Senate was neither more nor less likely to reflect the spirit of locality than the House of Representatives. It was also no more "aristocratical" than the old congress had been, or was so only in the greater duration of the senatorial term (from a minimum of three to a maximum of six years). If the similarity to the Congress of the Confederation seemed likely to mollify some potential critics, even more reassuring was the reincorporation of the two-thirds rule of the confederation for treaties. Onto the new constitution was thus engrafted the same blocking power the confederation had adopted to secure a "due Ballance." More concretely, that provision assured New England that its claim to the fisheries would not be treacherously bartered away, and it assured most southerners that no arrangement such as Jay sought with Gardoqui was now possible. The two-thirds rule was part of a larger strategy to foreclose such unequal sacrifices in the conduct of American diplomacy; that ethic of mutual support and equal sacrifice, in turn, imparted a strong expansionary impulse to it.[3]

Unlike treaties and alliances, which were given to the joint action of the executive and the Senate, the war power was shared with the House of Representatives. The consent of the whole congress—a majority of the people and a majority of the states—was required for a declaration of war. This double majority was also given the authority to raise armies and to provide and maintain a navy; the president, in turn, was made commander in chief. His mode of election—the complicated and soon to be revised electoral college—aimed for the same double majority as the congress. As Dickinson later observed, "the sovereignty of each state was *equally represented* in one legislative body, the people of each state *equally represented* in another, and the sovereignties & people of all the states *conjointly represented* in a third branch."[4] The arrangement was thus nicely symmetrical, though ungainly.

The framers imagined the electoral college as a body of wise men who would themselves exercise discretion in the choice of president, and they may have expected that the presidential canvass would often be thrown into the House of Representatives, making of the college a sort of nominating convention of the top three candidates for the House.[5] Since America had never conducted a continental election of any sort, it was difficult to imagine in 1787 what a presidential election would look like. The framers would doubtless have been alarmed to learn that the unwieldy system would soon be dominated by political parties, and they did not anticipate a system of electoral tickets. As a consequence, they failed to see how the provisions of the college would encourage the stalemates and intrigues of the 1796 and 1800 elections, thereby affording much opportunity for mischief. In this particular, their foresight was limited to the likelihood that Washington, if he could be prevailed upon, was the inevitable choice as first president. After that, who knew?

The way the convention cut through the problem of sovereignty is of special interest, both as a climax of the long disputes over its location, and as providing the ambiguous formula on which federal union would rest. It was not so much resolved as placed at a different level. Sovereignty would reside neither in the state governments nor in the general government. Instead of a national legislature clearly superior to the states, there would be a constitution superior to both, its authority resting on the consent of the people, who were to part with, or make a conditional grant of, their indissoluble sovereignty in state conventions. Each level of government was to be "equal" and "coordinate" to the other, supreme in its limited sphere, but concerned with different objects: one general, the other local.[6] To the judicial branch fell, in some measure, the task of guarding these allocations of authority; defenders of the Constitution would subsequently emphasize that if congress or the states passed beyond their authoritative jurisdictions the courts would be obliged to declare their acts null and void. The more basic check, however, lay with the distribution of power between the federal and the state governments, each of them capable of resisting the other and ensuring respect for the constitutional balance of power.

Of perhaps even greater importance than these various allocations of authority was the provision in the Constitution allowing for its formation on the ratification of nine rather than thirteen of the states. The Articles of Confederation required unanimous concurrence in the first instance, and unanimous concurrence for all subsequent amendments; nothing had hobbled the old congress more deeply than this provision. If the proponents of fundamental change were to advocate the new rule, in violation of the old rule, they needed a justification for doing so, which they found in the proposition that the old confederation had broken down. The antinationalists in the convention stoutly resisted this argument and maintained a language not too dissimilar to that of Jay and Burke in 1779, or of Lincoln in 1861: You cannot unilaterally withdraw from a constitutional process to which you have plighted your faith! You cannot build a constitution on an unconstitutional act![7] By contrast, the necessary implication for the advocates of change, probed most deeply by Madison, was that the states stood in 1787 in a state of nature toward one another, their previous obligations having dissolved by their mutual failure to abide by the reciprocities contemplated in the original instrument. Another necessary implication was that the act creating a general government would have to be a federal act, one that gave to each of the states and their people the right to come in or stay out.[8]

The Constitution omitted the clause, proposed in both the Virginia and New Jersey Plans, that authorized the general government to employ coercion against the states; it was sufficient, the framers concluded, to give the general government powers that would enable it to conduct its operations and fulfill its obligations without the intervention of the states. The reasons for the evasion of this question, so important to a later generation, were assigned by Madison early in the convention: "The more he reflected on the use of force, the more he doubted the practicability, the justice, and the efficacy of it when applied to people collectively and not individually. A Union of the States [containing such an ingredient] seemed to provide for its own destruction. The use of force against a State, would look more like a declaration of war, than an infliction of punishment, and would probably be considered by the party attacked as a dissolution of all previous compacts by which it might be bound. He hoped that such a system would be framed as might render this recourse unnecessary."[9] The omission of the provision, therefore, was assuredly not accidental. The framers, though convinced of the right, saw danger in its execution or affirmation, so they avoided the question religiously, and maintained a thoroughgoing determination to stay out of that Serbonian bog. Their reasons were a copy of those that Burke had urged in 1775; the effect of the Philadelphia convention was to make the nationalists of 1787, who had all supported the right of coercion, into the Federalists of 1788, who inveterately defended a system that would not be dependent on the exercise of that right, which they saw as equivalent to civil war, hence the dread thing they were trying to escape. Federalists, in effect, came to appreciate that if the sovereignty of the general government could not be reconciled with the liberty of the states, the opponents of a national authority would throw that sovereignty in their face. So they consigned the devilish problem of superiority and inferiority to a nether region where it need not be faced, because it could not be resolved. The framers came to understand, not without reluctance, that it was prudent to avoid direct confrontation wherever possible, to clear out a broad path for each level of government while marking out as distinctly as possible the boundaries between the two jurisdictions, and then to hope that it might be consigned to oblivion. Perhaps this was the only solution possible in circumstances where men accepted the right to use force to fulfill constitutionally specified obligations but saw also that to do so would destroy, rather than preserve, the union they wanted to make.

Ratification of the instrument was to be given by the people in their state conventions, making it a solemn covenant and constitution with an authority wholly different from a mere legislative enactment. This was a double sleight of hand: it elevated the general government by making it subordinate to the Constitution, and it incorporated both "the people" and "the states" in the formula that located the ultimate possessors of sovereignty. Though undoubtedly clever work, it left ample room for subsequent clarification and interpretation. It would also take much explaining to the suspicious minds "out of doors" who thought they knew where these matters stood. Luther Martin's lament in the convention—"the language of the States being Sovereign and independent, was once familiar and understood; though it seemed now so strange and obscure"—would be the reaction of many others when confronted with the framer's handiwork.[10]

Even the advocates of the Constitution admitted that the location of sovereignty in the new system was highly ambiguous. The framers, Madison told Jefferson shortly after the conclusion of the convention, had "generally agreed that the objects of the Union could not be secured by any system founded on the principle of a confederation of sovereign States. A *voluntary* observance of the federal law by all the members could never be hoped for. A *compulsive* one could evidently never be reduced to practice, and if it could, involved equal calamities to the innocent and the guilty, the necessity of a military force both obnoxious and dangerous, and in general, a scene resembling much more a civil war, than the administration of a regular Government." The alternative chosen escaped from both culs-de-sac by providing for a general government that would operate without the intervention of the states on the individuals composing them. Nevertheless,

Madison believed that the "most nice and difficult" question of the "partition of power" between the general and local authorities had not been given a clear adjustment. He reminded Jefferson of the importance Madison had placed on a constitutional negative vested in the national legislature. He still thought such a check was necessary "to prevent encroachments on the General authority" and "to prevent instability and injustice in the legislation of the States." That it had not been provided caused him great worry.[11]

"Without such a check in the whole over the parts," he lamented, "our system involves the evil of imperia in imperio. If a compleat supremacy some where is not necessary in every Society, a controuling power at least is so, by which the general authority may be defended against encroachments of the subordinate authorities, and by which the latter may be restrained from encroachments on each other." He ran through a variety of relevant cases in making this point. "If," he said, "the supremacy of the British Parliament is not necessary . . . for the harmony of that Empire," surely "the royal negative or some equivalent controul" was indispensable for "the unity of the system." Anticipating his subsequent reflections in the *Federalist* (Nos. 18–20), but employing them here to very different effect, he remarked that the absence of such a provision had been "mortal" to the ancient Confederacies—the Acheaean League, the Amphyctionic council— and it had been "the disease" of the modern confederacies, particularly the "United Netherlands" and the "German Empire," the latter example being particularly relevant because it had a "federal Diet with ample parchment authority" and "a regular Judiciary establishment." Still more to the point was the recent American experience under the Articles of Confederation. Had the Constitution provided a remedy for this? Was it, because founded on principles different from these other confederacies, likely to "have a different operation"? Madison thought not. The new system was admittedly materially different from these other confederacies: "It presents the aspect rather of a feudal system of republics, if such a phrase may be used, than of a Confederacy of independent States." As such, however, it could not escape "a continual struggle between the head and the inferior members," until a final victory was gained. He emphasized how even the clearest of constitutional distinctions—between raising a revenue and regulating trade, for instance, or the obvious line between spiritual and temporal powers—were perennially subject to bitter disputes, and he betrayed anxiety that "the Judicial authority under our new system will keep the States within their proper limits, and supply the place of a negative on their laws." This was, he thought, a dubious foundation for the whole system.

Not only was it "more convenient to prevent the passage of a law, than to declare it void after it is passed" but a state willing to violate "the Legislative rights of the Union"—recent experience having attested to the disposition—would be equally if not more willing to defy a judicial decree. Enforcement would then require military force, but that was "an evil which the new Constitution meant to exclude as far as possible." Candidly considered, there was no way to reason oneself out of the conclusion that the convention had brought forth an *imperia in imperio*—a plan that, in its practical operation, would prove fundamentally ambiguous in where it located the ultimate power of decision.[12]

28

Federals and Anti-Federals

IT IS SOMETIMES alleged that "republicanism" passed away with the making and ratification of the Constitution; that, in Gordon Wood's expression, "The Federalists hoped to create an entirely new and original sort of republican government—a republic which did not require a virtuous people for its sustenance." These climactic debates did not simply bring forth a more perfect union; they represented "the end of classical politics."[1] That something changed with the making of the Constitution is clear: Americans did not, at the beginning of their Revolution, appreciate how it was possible that men who wished to act together should nevertheless so bitterly divide. Experience gave their thought a much greater realism on that score, and insofar as there was a "repudiation of 1776" in 1787, it lay in that budding realism rather than in a putative antidemocratic counterrevolution. Nor was republicanism abandoned in 1787, though it had certainly been made complex and problematic by the multiple loyalties and identities that had been generated in the years since 1776. Its central concept had been the commonweal, the res publica, the country to which men gave their deepest allegiance. They still did. They knew what it meant for John Adams to have said, in reply to the British emissary who invited him to fix his price, that "I am not worth buying, but, such as I am, the treasury of England would not pay for me."[2] In a continental union of different republics, however, the affirmation of public virtue did not and could not resolve the question of where this loyalty was really owed. In a setting of diverse and multiple loyalties, such as America enjoyed in 1787, the problem of politics might as readily be seen as a conflict among competing virtues (or "patriotisms") as a conflict among competing interests. In constitutional terms, it pit squarely in contention two very different conceptions of the public good—one giving priority to the states over the union, the other giving priority to the union over the states. In political terms, it opposed the contrary visions of the American sections, each of which sought to use the national government for ends peculiar to themselves, but which also feared the domineering purposes to which this power might be put. Virtue was, in this context, identical to interest, or was problematic in the same way that interest was problematic; the question was not whether state loyalties, sectional interests, or the sisterly feelings embodied in the union were to be abandoned, but how and whether it would be possible to work out a viable relationship among them.

For the Federalists of 1788, public virtue meant a willingness to compromise; compromise, in turn, meant a willingness to sacrifice interest and even conviction for the good of the union. Far from being unimportant, republican virtue was vital in the making of the Constitution, vital in its ratification, vital for its continued existence. This quality was not written down in the Constitution, but its presence was felt in every important provision; "intra-constitutional" is a better description of its character than "extra-constitutional." Speaking for a unanimous convention, Washington gave it eloquent and oft-remembered expression in the letter, drafted by Morris, transmitting the document to the congress. He called it the "spirit of amity, and of that mutual deference and concession which the peculiarity of our political situation rendered indispensable."[3] That spirit had produced the Constitution; that spirit alone might keep it. The defenders of the Constitution allied this belief with the sentiment of virtue—a quality, they believed, that would be no less indispensable under the new system than it was under the old.[4]

Of all the appeals made by advocates for the new Constitution when it went before "the people of the states," it was Washington's invocation of the spirit of amity, and of the necessity of mutual compromise, that was clinching in a way that others were not. Franklin made much the same appeal in his speech on the final day of the convention. At eighty-one years, he could barely walk and was nearly blind. In his beautiful and simple speech, he acknowledged the imperfections of the Constitution but said that experience had taught him the fallibility and changeability of his opinions, a weakness he evoked with affecting clarity. Federalists would make the tenor of Franklin's appeal a source of formidable strength. No one who supported the Constitution admitted to being wholly pleased with the handiwork of the convention. The concessions that had been made in the convention, given so reluctantly and with such fearful apprehension of the misshapen beast that would emerge as a consequence, had seemed painful at the time; but when the Constitution went before the people, those concessions became, for its advocates, a source of great and varied pleasure. The three men who most ably expounded the meaning of the document, and who did more than any others to secure its ratification—Madison, Hamilton, and Wilson—had experienced profound doubts over what had been done; but they made their doubts into a fortress. It took no great resource in debate to show that any set of objections, even if persuasive when standing alone, made for sine qua nons that would be unacceptable to other states and sections and would run everything into the ground.[5]

Singly, the Anti-Federalists made telling objections to the new Constitution; collectively, they faced an insuperable difficulty in defeating it, if reason rather than passion were to decide the issue. For it was always possible to admit the objections and refute the argument, by invoking objections from another state or section that were their antipode. These mutually inconsistent ultimatums showed beyond doubt that no constitution was possible if everyone were to insist inflexibly on their favorite conditions. Had the Anti-Federalists disparaged the importance of union, or had they been willing to resign themselves to a system of regional confederacies, none of this would have mattered. The acute vulnerability of their position lay in the fact that they also believed that union was indispensable and that the Articles of Confederation needed correcting, while also continually objecting to the compromises that were indispensable if the federal government was to be strengthened. They willed the end, but not the means. Federalists had no difficulty in lining up these objections and showing that they were mutually incompatible: they had spent the whole previous year turning them inside out, and knew exactly where they lay.[6]

The inconsistent remedies advanced by the Anti-Federalists gave force to the Federalist contention that a second convention would simply reopen the quarrels that had almost broken apart the first. In saying this, they were quite right, but even they did not appreciate how right they were. For at the precise moment that they took common ground and made headway in their debate with the Antis, the French monarchy was tottering to its fall. Had the bitter and frenzied divisions in America later prompted by the French Revolution been present in 1788, no union would have been possible. In very short order, the leading men who made the Constitution and secured its ratification came to hate each other with righteous purity and sacred fire. Pleasing indeed is the happy amity of Hamilton and Madison as they prosecuted their joint labors on *The Federalist*. In two years they would divide sharply over the most important questions that fell to the decision of the new government. By 1793 they and their allies felt toward one another a profound suspicion and a guttural hatred. In historical memory, the founding fathers appear united in their wisdom and venerable in their concordance. Closer to the truth is the observation that, in one brief shining moment, they achieved a meeting of the minds that was deceptive, and were brought round to a concordance that was delusive. For the next decade, climaxing in 1798, there is one long descent into a witches' brew of venomous accusation, kindled by a deep conviction of mutual betrayal. It was a cauldron from which even the revered Washington was not exempt. In this climate, nothing could have been done to strengthen the union, and hardly anything might have been attempted. Had the Constitution been rejected in a sufficient number of state conventions, it is most implausible to think that a new convention would have agreed readily to terms. Given the character of the opposition, with their mutually inconsistent objections, it is hard to see how it might have been a success. The window of opportunity was indeed quite small—three or four years, at most.

Despite the divisions among the Anti-Federalists, it is nevertheless the case that the general tenor of their complaints did coalesce around one great theme that had consistency and plausibility. This was their fear of "consolidation," or "empire," or "despotic centralization." They had substantial authority and weighty arguments on their side. Most theory, and all history, showed that great size was the handmaiden of despotism, that it was impossible to erect a consolidated government over such a great extent of territory without inviting a vicious tyranny. A wrong step taken now, said Patrick Henry, "and our Republic will be lost." He meant the Commonwealth of Virginia that had been consecrated by the confederation, recognizing the equality and sovereignty of the states. So, too, did Samuel Adams stumble when he entered "the Building" erected at Philadelphia, meeting there "with a National Government, instead of a foederal Union of Sovereign States."[7] Anti-Federalists looked upon what Hamilton and Wilson had called "the amazing extent of country" and stood slack-jawed at the idea that it might be governed from a common center. "It is impossible for one code of laws to suit Georgia and Massachusetts," wrote Agrippa, yet it seemed undeniable to him that "the new system" was "a consolidation of all the states into one large mass."[8]

The debate was almost a set-piece affair, primitive in its logical structure. The Anti-Federalists charged upon the Constitution the objective of a great, consolidated government, supreme over the states, which would, sooner or later, reveal the despotic face that was already implicit in its principle. It would be the basis of a monstrous aristocracy and a bloated monarchy that would be intent on reducing all diversities to a common mass. Federalists denied every charge, patiently explaining that the general government's powers were limited to a few general objects, that everything else would remain with the states, that the Constitution, and not the general legislature, was to be supreme. Far from saving the country from a consolidated empire, argued the Federalists, the rejection of the Constitution meant the emergence of separate confederacies and the acceptance, with all its fateful consequences, of the European system of the balance of power among contending power blocs.

Anti-Federalists, as we saw earlier, viewed this specter as a "hobgoblin" of the fevered imaginations of their opponents that had no basis in reality.

The democratic character of the American states, together with the umbilical cords of commerce that connected them, made for peace, not war. Federalists countered with the argument that democratic governments were as likely to make war as despots, and they reviewed the ample sources of contention that would surely produce this result if the sections were divided and dissevered from each other. Anti-Federalists feared that the military power ostensibly generated for national purposes might be turned against their own states and sections; Federalists countered that the beauty of the plan lay in the security it provided the states for self-defense. "Through the medium of their state governments," Hamilton wrote in *Federalist* No. 28, the people would be in a situation "to take measures for their own defence with all the celerity, regularity and system of independent nations."[9] These assurances helped reconcile the Anti-Federalists to the new government, as did the likely balance of military power under the Constitution. When Hamilton and Madison argued in the convention that the coercion of the large states was "impossible" and could not be relied on for the operations of the national government, they attested to a distribution of military power that was not likely to undergo dramatic change with the inauguration of the new government. That made it easier for the suspicious to acquiesce in the Constitution and to look upon it as an experiment from which withdrawal might be practicable.[10]

The two sides also locked horns over the seriousness of the situation facing the American states. Despite the acknowledged inadequacies of the Articles of Confederation, the Anti-Federalists were driven to the contention that things, after all, were not so bad, certainly not so bad as to deny the people their sober second thought in a new convention. "Europe is engaged and we are tranquil"—there was plenty of time to address various deficiencies in the Articles of Confederation.[11] Though some Anti-Federalists acknowledged that the situation was "critical," the acknowledgment was more frequent in pamphlets than in the state ratifying conventions. In Virginia, the opponents of the Constitution often made the Federalist contention of "criticality" a source of great ridicule.[12] Anti-Federalists usually admitted that much had gone wrong in the confederation, but because they hated the remedy, they became far less willing to admit the existence of the disease. It was in the nature of the argument for the Federalists to paint the American situation in the darkest of colors, and for Anti-Federalists to minimize the dangers. If some of these rival combatants might be convicted of rhetorical exaggeration, however, it hardly follows that we should dismiss the very real fears that each entertained. Neither side thought itself to be exaggerating the dangers: the fears, on both sides, were compelling, immediate, and formidable.

Federalists saw with utter clarity the alternative of a system of regional confederacies, verily believed it would make a Europe of America, and saw that outcome as fated in events were the work of the convention to fail. Their dread of it was primordial. Anti-Federalists saw consolidation and centralization in a similar light. At the core of their position was the belief that centralized rule and consolidated government were, given America's diversity, impossible. Reasoning on the basis of its impossibility, they rapidly deduced that the motivation underlying it was sinister. It was against nature, but nature would have its revenge. If it could only be held together by force, the remedy would produce the very thing—anarchy, rebellion, and war—that it was ostensibly combating.[13]

Rather than the conflict between aristocracy and democracy, it is the contrast between universal empire and international anarchy (usually rendered as the conflict between centralization and decentralization) that lay at the heart of the ratification debates. Many Anti-Federalists, to be sure, denounced the Constitution as an aristocratic document and saw its supporters as having "the dictatorial air, the magisterial voice, the imperious tone, the haughty countenance, the lofty look, the majestic mien."[14] Many Federalists, by contrast, saw the opposition to it proceeding from men with no regard for the rights of property. When the Constitution was presented to the state conventions, the lines of political division largely followed the political divide that had previously opened up in the larger northern states. In Massachusetts, the Berkshires, the unhappy scene of Shays's Rebellion, were hostile. In New York, all classes in the city, mechanics and the monied aristocracy alike, were resolutely in favor; opposition came from the up-state counties. In Pennsylvania, the split followed the bitter dispute that had opened up, in 1776, between "Constitutionalists" and "Anti-Constitutionalists," which was a religious, ethnic, and ideological division that pit the city against the country, and East versus West. In Pennsylvania more than anywhere else did the dispute have the tenor of a class conflict between aristocrats and democrats, but elsewhere the division followed no such lines. In South Carolina, opposition (as well as support) came from large slaveholders who feared northern domination. Nor is the debate in Virginia intelligible in class terms: the great men in the state who opposed the Constitution—old stalwarts like Patrick Henry and George Mason, and up-and-comers like James Monroe—were of the same class as those who opposed it, and there was an undeterminable number of indebted grandees who saw peril in the clauses relating to contracts and treaties. In Virginia, too, the western counties, symbolically holding the balance in the most critical state in the ratification struggle, provided the votes that secured the narrow passage. Much of the denunciation of the Constitution for its aristocratical features, finally, was clearly rooted in sectional fears. Northern Anti-Federalists worried about being subjected to an aristocracy of slaveholders, and southern Anti-Federalists worried about being subjected to a "commercial aristocracy" managed by the northern states.[15]

These considerations cast doubt on the thesis that the struggle over the Constitution turned on an issue of democracy versus aristocracy. The diplomatic plenipotentiaries who met in Philadelphia, true, were a distinguished lot, and the wealth and learning of the union centered in them. But the instrument they designed did not deny the democratic impulse so much as it directed and balanced it. The states, with few exceptions, were to be left with control over the vast mass of internal legislation that affected life and liberty. As modified by the "federal ratio" and by state equality in the Senate, the popular voice was also given strong expression in the congress; such modifications as did exist stemmed not from an aristocratical impulse but from the exigencies and necessities of sectional compromise. Given the life tenure of justices and the restrictions relating to paper money and contracts in Article 1, Section 10, the more fulsome expressions of the Constitution's democratic character might be viewed with some skepticism, but it is important not to exaggerate the power seen as inhering in the judicial branch. Madison himself was a great skeptic on this point, believing after the convention adjourned that the convention's effective substitute for the national legislative veto would be weak and ineffective. Restrictions on paper money also had a strong "federal" aspect. State issues of paper money, like those in Rhode Island, had not only allowed debtors to defraud creditors but also permitted the citizens of one state to defraud the citizens of another. Recognition that thirteen separate experiments in monetary policy would be disruptive to the development of commercial intercourse and good faith among the states would not seem to be an intrinsically antidemocratic sentiment, nor the belief that a leading principle of civil government—as Thomas Paine, one of the foremost democrats of the age, had it—is "to compel the exact performance of engagements entered into between man and man."[16]

First in Massachusetts and then in other state ratifying conventions, supporters of the Constitution mollified opponents by promising a bill of rights, an expedient they had initially opposed. When the new government did go into operation, Madison introduced in the House of Representatives the seventeen amendments that, whittled down to twelve by the Senate, were submitted to the states as a bill of rights. Though the ten amendments adopted altered the character of the document in no basic respect, Madison was surely correct to believe that good faith on this question would help reconcile opponents of the Constitution to its authority. The amendments in effect wrote down the construction that the Federalists had placed upon the Constitution in the state ratifying conventions, above all the doctrine that everything not given to the federal government was reserved to the states, but it left ample room for argument over the line of partition. The main question that would be important to posterity was whether the general language used in most of these amendments applied to the states as well as to the national government. It was a question that would become important after the Civil War, when over the course of the century after 1865 prohibitions initially held to apply against the general government were held to apply, via the Fourteenth Amendment, against the states. Before the Civil War, however, it was "universally understood," as John Marshall said in 1835, that the first ten amendments had been proposed as "security against the apprehended encroachments of the general government—not against those of the local governments."[17] They left the state constitutions exactly where they stood. They were, as such, a Magna Carta for state rather than individual rights, or rather for the proposition that individual rights to life and liberty would be secured under the umbrella of state authority in the new system.[18]

Since the Bill of Rights simply declared a construction that had been previously expounded by the Federalists themselves, it might be thought that the hostility toward centralization represented by the Anti-Federalists played only a minor role in the making of the Constitution. But the inference is a mistake. The Anti-Federalists were not so much defeated as preempted: half their case was written into the Constitution. In the decision of the convention to grant equality to the states in the Senate, in its elimination of the constitutional negative, in the transfer of sovereignty from the national legislature to the Constitution—in all the ways, in sum, by which the Virginia Plan had been substantially altered in the course of the convention's deliberations—the influence and power of the antifederal disposition may be seen. Anti-Federalists wanted the whole loaf, of course, and not just half of it, so they denied the significance of these concessions and saw, in 1788, a consolidated government instead of a federal union. Once the Constitution was ratified, however, they found ample grounds in its provisions and its justification to give to it the construction they had previously denied. By these means, the antifederal attitude was carried forward into the new system, and observers were left to wonder whether it was more true that the federal constitution had settled everything, or settled nothing.

29

Conclusion

We have been seeking to understand the making of the union as an experiment in international cooperation, one that took place against the background of a menacing crisis of internal dissolution and that prompted a systematic investigation of the possibilities and limits of joint action among independent sovereigns. At the core of the scheme of thought that produced this peculiar and unprecedented scheme of federal government were two opposing fears—that of a centralized despotic empire, and of a system of regional confederacies—that found themselves in dialectical antagonism in the late 1780s. Historical reflection might be used to reinforce either side in the great debate: the experience of Greece and Rome provided object lessons for both sides, as did the whole experience of modern Europe, with its contending demons of universal monarchy and the balance of power. These historical analogies seemed compelling to the Americans of 1787, but they would not have occupied so prominent a place in their minds had their own experience not brought them face-to-face with the predicament they espied in history. They had revolted from an empire whose pretensions they had found despotic, and had seen the meaning of liberty first in the autonomy, and then in the independence, of their little commonwealths. Expecting that voluntary concordance and republican virtue would carry them through the travails of war, they had become alarmed, and then disgusted, at the inadequacies of the instrument by which their cooperation was to be expressed. On the eve of the Philadelphia convention, they had fallen back into the state of nature from which the Articles of Confederation had attempted to lift them. This was not yet a state of war, but the conviction that the American states were tending in that direction pointed to the overriding problem the convention would have to resolve. That deeply held conviction is why the Federalists so consistently and overwhelmingly posed the choice over the Constitution as one between peace and war, and it is why we have styled it as a peace pact.

When Americans began their Revolution, they were far from constituting a unified nation. The terms of the colonial dispute with the mother country had made each colony hostile to central control and intoxicated with the idea of their sovereignty, and the colonies launched their experiment less as one people than as free and independent states, with all the rights and powers thereunto pertaining. The exigencies, oaths, and necessities of the war did produce in many Americans a distinctive and compelling vision of national greatness, but this was more the stuff of anticipation and vision than fact. The war also confirmed the separate identities and conflicting interests of rival states and sections, just as it created a set of grievances and fears that were of the character that had traditionally disrupted past confederacies and produced war among erstwhile allies. Americans emerged from the revolutionary war as "neither the same nation nor different Nations," and they seemed disinclined "to pursue the one or the other of these ideas too closely."[1] Faced with the breakdown of the instrument by which their conflicts were to be peacefully resolved, Americans concluded that they were in desperate need of a new arrangement. The oddity is that the enmities they had developed were just as important as, if not more important than, their friendships, in prompting their felt need for a new system, and largely forgotten is the sense in which the Constitution emerged as a focus of loyalty not because it expressed a common nationalism but because it provided the framework for the peaceful reconciliation of difference. Over two hundred years on, it is difficult to recapture the sense of artificiality that surrounded its creation, and the nation seems like an inevitable force of nature rather than one among a variety of historical possibilities. But the latter is all it was or could be at the time.

In keeping with this anomalous situation, the Constitution created a republic of different republics and a nation of many nations; the resulting system was sui generis in establishing a continental order that partook of the character of both a state and a state system.[2] Like the federal idea itself, the Constitution stood at a juncture between the worlds of constitutionalism and diplomacy, and this in ways both abstract and very practical. The inability of the old congress to execute the treaty of peace was a compelling motivation to strengthen the federal authority, as was the more general danger that individual state action could implicate the others in postures that might lead to war. So, too, the class of powers given to the general government were largely "federative" in character, concerning the matters of war and peace, treaties and alliances, and external commerce. Those were the things they were obliged to decide in common. In their continental constitutionalism as well as their foreign diplomacy, the founders typically found themselves working not "on the natural rights of men not yet gathered into society, but upon those rights, modified by society, and interwoven with what we call the rights of states."[3] That habitual attention gave their thought a strongly internationalist flavor.

In fact and in form, as James Brown Scott once emphasized, the federal convention was an international conference, conducted in secrecy among diplomatic plenipotentiaries of the states.[4] The rival theories of international politics put forward in the debate over the Constitution—opposing the structural realism of the Federalists to the liberal democratic peace theory of the Anti-Federalists—also underline the internationalist character of the founding, as do the borrowings in debate from the writers on the law of nature and of nations. The proposed settlement constitutionalized a set of doctrines—of comity, nonintervention in internal affairs, state equality, and good faith—that had taken root among the publicists, and its advocates put themselves in the "peace plan" tradition associated with the grand design of Henry IV, who had sketched "but the picture in miniature of the great portrait to be exhibited."[5] The Constitution also incorporated, while domesticating, the hoary doctrine of the balance of power, and indeed projected it into the interior of federal government. This operation was most strikingly revealed in the compromises of the Constitution over representation, but the division of power between the state and federal government, with each a sentinel against the encroachments of the other, was also expressive of the balancing doctrine, as was the requirement that treaties receive the consent of two-thirds of the senators present.[6] The struggle over the Constitution may have been a "contest for dominion—for empire," as William Grayson called it[7]—but the governing charter also reflected an artful attempt to contain and regulate this competition. It was more than an arms control treaty, but it was in part just that. It was more than an alliance that parceled out spheres of influence and nicely adjusted the continental balance of power, but it was in part just that. Above all, it was the reasoned response to a serious security problem that espied a sequence in which internal division and the intervention of external powers would create the same whirlwind in America that had undone Europe.

The complex of thought that arose in response to the dual specters of international anarchy and universal empire is of keen historical importance, and I have sought to demonstrate that the making of the Constitution cannot be understood without it. At the same time, the cluster of ideas associated with the unionist paradigm has a certain timeless quality and bears a striking family resemblance to the ideas that have swirled around the construction of world order in the twentieth century and that promise to be of continuing importance in the future.

In the waning years of the twentieth century, we Americans and our friends abroad were befuddled by the diffuse locations and sharings of sovereignty that came increasingly to characterize the contemporary world system; we struggled to discover the key to that delicate balance between representation and burden-sharing that is an elixir to states-unions that find it, and a poison to those that do not; we searched for the proper purpose of the array of functional supranational institutions that increasingly assumed important responsibilities in the domains of security, trade, and finance (the same spheres of authority allocated to the general government under the Constitution); we were still working on a tenable relationship between the rights of individuals and the liberties of states, and wondered whether "the national state [had] become too small for the big problems in life, and too big for the small problems." Those polarities and antinomies are often thought of as new, but they are not so novel after all: very similar problems entered deeply into the domain of thought I have sought to explicate.[8]

At the beginning of the twenty-first century, and particularly after the events of September 11, 2001, the political and intellectual climate suddenly altered, and the whole question of international cooperation underwent a startling change in aspect. Despite this sea change, the old polarities of the unionist paradigm—of international anarchy and universal empire, of independence and union—retained their salience in thought and practice. It belongs to the living to pursue these intimations—to decide, for instance, whether the specter of international anarchy or universal empire is most repellent, or whether the hope of independence or the dream of union is most attractive. Whatever our nation's choice, it is striking that the founders' discourse on federalism anticipates in crucial respects our own discourse on nationalism, internationalism, and imperialism, with the structure of the argument continuing to revolve around similar theories, predicaments, and aspirations. Like the cluster of ideas associated with liberalism and republicanism, the values and theorems embraced in the unionist paradigm continue to find expression in the contemporary world, and it appears not simply likely but inevitable that this should continue to be the case. Obligated to think not only about the relation of the individual to the state but also of states in their relation to one another, and forced not only to weigh the contending claims of individual liberty and communal attachment but also to find some basis of peace and power in a system of states prone to collective violence and unilateral action, we are borne back ceaselessly against the tide to an argument announced at the founding of the American experiment.[9]

A NOTE ON CAPITALIZATION, STYLE, AND BIBLIOGRAPHY

IN MY QUOTATION from primary sources, I have sought to render the quote exactly as given, with all the various particularities of spelling, capitalization, and grammar (and without the use of "sic"). Only in a few instances have I taken the liberty of adjusting the punctuation and spelling.

The correct system of capitalization has posed something of a quandary. If "naming is the first act of theorizing," as has been well said, then capitalization is the first act of naming. Usages then were different from the standardized usages now prevailing, and the differences can be revealing. The usage "united States" occurs, according to my unscientific survey, about as often as "United States" in the *Letters of Delegates,* especially in the early years of the war. Even in the two official copies of the Declaration of Independence (one "authenticated" and for distribution, the other the "engrossed" original parchment), we find "United States" in one and "united States" in the other (see Leonard W. Levy and Dennis J. Mahoney, *The Framing and Ratification of the Constitution* [New York, 1987], 57). In either case, the United States were invariably treated as a plural noun, a usage I have followed. "Congress" was usually capitalized, but the "State" or "the States" were so elevated just as often. While I employ the term "United States," it seems unreasonable and misleading to capitalize "Congress" without capitalizing the "States," though it would be contrary to modern stylistic conventions to do the latter. Faced with this delicate quandary, I decided to take a leaf from Thomas Jefferson and lowercase the whole damn thing. The states, congress, the union, the king—all exist in democratic lowercase equality, save as they are elevated into uppercasedom by my quotations from the original sources.

States and countries are referred to with the feminine pronoun, as contemporaries did. That usage is important because it helps recall an idea— once prevalent, now forgotten—that the states had personality. They could be quirky and unpredictable, true, but they also displayed a certain deep consistency that gave them a distinct character, as when one delegate to congress said that Maryland had always been a "froward Hussy." States were also objects of love and affection, and such sentiments seem more appropriate for a "she" than an "it." An outstanding evocation of the distinctive character of the states, though from a later period of American history, is Frederika Bremer's of 1853: "That which struck me most in the [Senate] was the mode of representation. . . . This mode of representation brings forth much nationality, and much that is picturesque in the living, peculiar life of each state. The Granite State and the Palmetto State, 'Old Virginny' and new Wisconsin, Minnesota and Louisiana, stand forth in Congress as individuals, and take part in the treatment of public questions, which are interesting to the whole human race, according to characteristics which are peculiar to themselves and common to all" (cited in Hans Kohn, *American Nationalism* [New York, 1957], 91).

The bibliographical essay that follows the appendix is limited to the historiography of the Constitution—a vast subject that I have only imperfectly surrounded. For other topics considered in the work, the endnotes are themselves often bibliographical in character, and thus I have dispensed with a formal bibliography of secondary titles. The list of short titles consists mainly of primary sources cited more than once. All students of the founding must feel a profound debt to those historians, dead and living, who labored hard to bring to life these superbly edited projects of the founders' papers. That list of short titles may therefore be considered as something of an honor roll.

APPENDIX:
THE ARGUMENT DIAGRAMED

FIGURE 1. ASSOCIATIONS OF STATES:
COMPARATIVE STATE SYSTEMS AND EMPIRES

This diagram seeks to locate federal union within a larger set of possible relationships or associations among states. It is considered here as a distinct species of the genus "federative system."

The diagram displays a continuum with three principal ideal types: international anarchy, the federative system, and universal empire, embodying principles of conflict, cooperation, or dominance among distinct peoples. The continuum is bounded on one side by a raging state system (international anarchy or the state of war) and on the other by the most extreme form of concentrated power (universal empire). The federative system, in the middle, represents states in various stages of cooperation or concert. The eighteenth-century "grand alliance" and the nineteenth-century concert of Europe are historical exemplifications of the type, as was America's federal union. Reared on the basis of fidelity to basic norms in the society of states, each expressed a cooperative impulse that fell short of full-fledged statehood. System of states, confederate republic, *Stattenbund,* and even some forms of "extended and detached empire" also fall within the box.[1]

The outer edge of the continuum, on both sides, represents states of extreme enmity. This should obviously be the case with regard to the state of war, with the terms cold war, détente, and entente indicating a cooling of enmity that may ripen into something approaching friendship, but it is also arguably so with regard to universal empire. Universal empire refers not literally to dominance over the entire earth—a feat not as yet accomplished by any state—but to dominance and mastery over a wide swath of peoples (who should otherwise, by virtue of proximity or interaction, form a system of states). The loss of liberty and independence is invariably a source of extreme enmity among conquered peoples, and hence the continuum shows a movement to lesser degrees of enmity from its right side as well.

The same logic applies to the degree of centralization at various points of the continuum. If the right side of the continuum represents extreme centralization of power, it might seem to follow that the state of anarchy should be identified with extreme decentralization. In fact, however, the state of war notoriously breeds centralized arrangements among the combatants, an eighteenth-century theorem that the twentieth century rather spectacularly reaffirmed. The converse proposition—that despotism would lead to anarchy—was also widely believed in the eighteenth century, and the claim and counterclaim actually did battle in the argument over the federal constitution.

Hegemonies and suzerain state systems approach universal empire insofar as they suggest centralization of command or leadership, but the former particularly may also display elements of common purpose and mutual acceptance that bring them closer to the middle part of the continuum. Since the Renaissance, universal empire and the international anarchy (or synonymous expressions) have been key concepts in the theory and practice of international relations, and they remain so today.[2] They were, as is shown in figure 3, also of fundamental salience in American political thought.

Attempts to find a middle ground between anarchy and empire through cooperative ventures among states distinguish the federative system from other forms of state association. The experiment of 1787 stands by itself in certain respects—it was a unique and exceptional accomplishment—but it is only one of several other cases that fall within the genus. The classic conception of the *societas* of independent states, with its norms of sovereignty, nonintervention, *cujus regio ejus religio,* and the balance of power, is normatively quite similar to early conceptions of America's federal union, as are various periods of the European Concert in the nineteenth century.[3] Any security union based on the precept of "one for all and all for one" is a version of the federative system, usually studied under the labels of "collective defense" or "collective security."[4] Present-day variations on the theme of the federative system include the European Union, or the larger web of transatlantic and Western institutions in which the EU and the United States are embedded. The term "federative system" is still in use among some specialists, but the thing being signified would more commonly appear today as "international regime" or "security community."[5]

Two further points about this typology. Political speculation is seldom in accord in describing and assessing these various associations. In later years, for instance, the American union could be denounced as "a league with death and a covenant with hell" or as "a most unequal alliance by which the south has always been the loser and the north always the gainer." What to some seemed to be a "Universal Empire in the western world" could to others appear on the precipice of breakdown, little better than a disorganized anarchy. These contrary depictions must be accounted for if the nature and character of any political association are to be made intelligible, and the examples constitute a cautionary flag to political scientists who want to classify such associations in a definitive way for purposes of their models and typologies.[6]

Note, too, that it is possible and even characteristic for a state or an association of states to be in a variety of postures or relations to others—to be, that is, simultaneously at various points on the spectrum. In 1820, for instance, the United States had gone from cold war to war to détente with Great Britain in the previous decade, and there were various expressions of an Anglo-American alliance, entente, or concert in the decade to follow. In 1820, the federal government had entered into some two hundred treaties with Indian nations, and that web of relations may be classified as a suzerain state system (though the treaties between the states and the federal government, which the latter had also to accommodate, made it unclear whether there was one or many suzerains).[7] At the same time, the union itself constituted a federative system or system of states; facing east, it stood counterpoised with a developing federative system or concert among the great powers of Europe. In keeping with the emerging American doctrine of the "two hemispheres," it was the policy of the United States government to ensure a political separation between the two spheres. Thus, in response to a British effort to mediate the dispute between the United States and Spain over Florida, Secretary of State John Quincy Adams declined the offer, appealing to "the policy, both of Europe and of the United States, to keep aloof from the general federative system, of each other."[8]

Lest the reader conclude that all is well in the cozy middle of this continuum, it must be emphasized that relations among the states making up these federative systems are frequently by no means cordial, and they may resemble troubled marriages that cohere not from mutual affection but from reflection on the unacceptable consequences of a divorce. But in this characteristic, too, they are of the same type. Historically, each of these particular instances of the federative system has represented an attempt to navigate between the rival dangers of international anarchy and universal empire, and the parties to them have frequently understood their intention as one of "coming together to stay apart." Inevitably, they are forced to grapple with the characteristic problems of states acting in concert: ensuring a fair representation (or "voice") within the system; arriving at an equitable sharing of the burdens; attending to the balance of power among the confederates and with outsiders; adjusting clashing sovereignties; above all, devising a stable system of cooperation in a domain where the actors are prone to unilateral action.

FIGURE 2. CONSTITUTIONAL INTERPRETATION: VARIETIES OF FEDERAL UNION, 1763–1787

This figure suggests that federal union is a better descriptor than nation-state for the four associations represented in the diagram. The British Empire is not usually thought of in those terms, but it was alleged to be a federal union by American theorists of the imperial constitution, who in their own estimation went from one federal union to another in 1776. As an extended polity with both centralized and decentralized institutions, and beset with centripetal and centrifugal forces, the British Empire generated an argument over its character that strongly prefigures the disputes over the successive phases of American union. The making of the Constitution cannot be fully understood without bringing these prior associations and experiences into clear view—hence the lavish attention given to them in parts three and four of this book.

Of these four experiments in federal union, the one created by the federal constitution most resembles a nation-state. As Madison said, it was "partly national and partly federal." It created a republic of many republics and a nation of many nations; the resulting system was sui generis in partaking of the character of both a state and a state system. It was, in short, an entirely new form of federal government, but it was, withal, a federal government.

FIGURE 3. AMERICAN POLITICAL THOUGHT: THE UNIONIST PARADIGM, C. 1776

The historiography of early American political thought has been dominated by the clash between liberal perspectives and "the republican paradigm." I posit the existence of a third approach—"the unionist paradigm"—that seems to me to better characterize the architecture of American political thought during the founding period. Both liberal ideas of consent and individual rights, on the one hand, and republican ideas of civic virtue and community, on the other, were immensely complicated by the existence in America of different conceptions of the commonwealth—centering on state, section, and nation—to which the idea of consent, the vindication of individual rights, or the sentiment of virtue was appropriate. Neither inherited tradition provided any clear guidance on the construction of a federative system.

This figure shows Americans arriving at independence armed with a valuable legacy (the ideas associated with liberalism and republicanism) but still having to figure out the problem of cooperation among the "several states in the union of the empire," as one observer described the American confederation in 1779.[9] The diagram indicates some (but by no means all) of the theoretical and practical questions that contemporaries began raising when confronted with this great question. The relationship of the unionist paradigm to liberalism and republicanism is developed further in chapters 3, 15, 16, and 28.

FIGURE 4. THEORIES OF AMERICAN POLITICS

By theories of American politics, I mean those explanations that offer the clearest view of the motive forces in history, that do the best job of explaining why the big things happened. Of an empirical theory of politics, we ask how powerful it is, how much it explains. This diagram gives, in shorthand fashion, the leading contenders. The right side is based on Huntington's depiction of the main interpretive schools, which he neatly classifies as "the one, the two, and the many," corresponding to the consensus, Progressive, and pluralist interpretations of American politics.[10] (See the further discussion in the bibliographical essay that follows.) Counterpoised to these three interpretations is the view advanced in this book, arguing that more explanatory power is given by attention to the exigencies of the union, the potency of sectional rivalries, and the existence of a multiplicity of sovereignties (and distinct loyalties to states) in the American political system.

The terms "unipolarity," "bipolarity," and "multipolarity" are drawn from the lexicon of theorists of international relations, but they closely correspond to the division into one, two, and many. The great dividing line in continental politics set apart slaveholding and non-slaveholding, planting and commercial, southern and eastern states, and was thus bipolar in character. At the same time, the political division into thirteen states gave the system a striking multipolar aspect. Depending on circumstances, state loyalties and identities might either further or disrupt a bipolar alignment based on the sections, and the rule of the confederation requiring unanimous consent for the revision of its terms gave a blocking power to individual states that often was of critical importance. During and after the constitutional era, the middle states often found themselves mediating the rival and clashing objectives entertained by the southern and eastern states. They "held the balance" in the union, as the western states would later do. At the same time, there were sometimes collaborations that overleaped the great sectional divide, the two most important of which were the great concert between

Massachusetts and Virginia at the outset of independence and the infamous
deal between New England and South Carolina over the slave trade at the
Constitutional Convention. These themes are developed at various points
in the book, but see particularly chapters 22, 25, and 26 for further discussion of "the significance of the section."[11]

FIGURE 5. AMERICAN DIPLOMACY AND THEORIES OF INTERNATIONAL RELATIONS

This diagram places the founding fathers in an "international society" approach to international relations, counterpoised to realist and revolutionist
perspectives. It also speaks to the controversy among American historians
over the strains of "utopian idealism" and "realism" in early American
thought concerning foreign policy. It is based on the typology devised by
Martin Wight and further elaborated by Hedley Bull and Robert Jackson.[12]

The founders' larger identification with the internationalist tradition, together with their encounter with realism and Machiavelli, is considered in
chapters 8 and 21. Their encounter with "revolutionism," though given
some attention in those chapters, comes into sharpest focus after the period
considered in this book, during the wars and upheavals inaugurated by the
French Revolution. Both sides in the developing American debate over the
Revolution convicted the rival belligerents of fundamental offenses against
the law of nations. Hamilton's detestation of French conduct in the 1790s
arose mainly from his conviction that the French had deeply offended
against cardinal principles in the law of nations. The French offer of fra-
ternal assistance "to all peoples who shall wish to recover their liberty"
was "little short of a declaration of War against all Nations, having princes
and privileged classes," equally repugnant "to the general rights of Nations, to the true principles of liberty, [and] to the freedom of opinion of
mankind." Jefferson was far more sympathetic to the French Revolution,
and through most of the 1790s felt a profound kinship with its fortunes,
but he also acknowledged that "the French have been guilty of great errors
in their conduct towards other nations, not only in insulting uselessly all
crowned heads, but endeavouring to force liberty on their neighbours in
their own form." Jefferson was convinced that "the confederacy of kings"
was the aggressor in the European war, and he detested the allied powers
because he believed them intent on denying to the French nation its fundamental right under the law of nations to choose its own government. Much
as the perspectives of Hamilton and Jefferson differed in their assignment

of guilt to the warring parties and in their prescriptions for American conduct, their normative assessment of the European war was deeply embedded in the framework of the law of nations.[13]

Among the most important disputes fostered by Wight's typology was whether Kant belonged more in the revolutionist or the international society category.[14] That question cannot be seriously examined here, but a few comments are in order regarding the founders' relationship to Kant's statement of the peace problem. As did the founders, Kant held before him the twin specters of an international anarchy and a "soulless" universal empire, and sought a via media between them. Because he emphasized the terrors of the former—as much, indeed, as the most hard-bitten realist—it followed for him that states, like individuals in a state of nature, needed to "give up their savage (lawless) freedom, adjust themselves to public coercive laws, and thus build a (of course continuously growing) state of nations *(civitas gentium),* which will ultimately include all the nations of the world." Existing states, Kant acknowledged, would not accept this because they prized the independence accorded them by the existing law of nations, and hence he replaced "the positive idea of a *world-republic [Weltrepublik]* . . . with the negative surrogate of a lasting, always widening, *league [Bund]* to prevent war, thus checking the current of the lawless, antagonistic inclination—though with the constant danger of its breaking out."[15] Recalling John Witherspoon's distinction between balance of power and federal union, Kant distinguished between a peace treaty *(pactum pacis)* ending a particular war and a pacific federation or peace pact *(foedus pacificum)* that "would seek to end *all* wars for good." By the latter expression, Kant meant in institutional terms something akin to that which was formed under the Articles of Confederation—a federative republic or *Stattenbund* whose confederating states need not "submit to public laws and to a coercive power which enforces them, as do men in a state of nature." By a world-republic or *civitas gentium* he meant a universal state with powers akin to (but probably surpassing) those accorded to the federal government formed by the Constitution. The *Bund* was an alliance of republican states that cooperated to maintain the peace among themselves and to repel foreign enemies, the *Weltrepublik* a federal state "with teeth" that preserved to the contracting parties their independence in internal affairs but that placed their external relations in the hands of a common authority. Kant believed that the latter alternative would be impossible for many ages but still constituted the ultimate logic of human history, whereas he treated the prospects of the former with an inconsistent mélange of optimism and pessimism as to its prospects. The wolf would still howl at the door of this new federal system among republics; nevertheless, "it can be shown that this idea of *federalism,* extending gradually to encompass all states and thus leading to perpetual peace, is practicable and has objective reality. For if by good fortune one powerful and enlightened nation can form a republic (which is by its nature inclined to seek perpetual peace), this will provide a focal point for federal association among other states. These will join up with the first one, thus securing the freedom of each state in accordance with the idea of international right, and the whole will gradually spread further and further by a series of alliances of this kind."[16]

Though Kant's statement of the peace problem has clear affinities with the larger American debate over federal union, there are also pointed contrasts. Kant's treatment of the internal relations among cooperating republics most resembles the assumption of near-automatic cooperation that infused many Americans at the outset of independence, and it certainly recalls Paine's confident assertion in *Common Sense* of the democratic peace hypothesis. Kant, like the Americans of that era, did not believe it inconsistent for the confederating states of the *foedus pacificum* to pledge cooperation while not submitting, "as men do in a state of nature," to a coercive power which enforces public laws. Experience, however, profoundly affected the tenor of American thinking on this great question. Well before Hamilton's full-throated refutation of the democratic peace hypothesis in *The Federalist,* Americans came to understand how problematic cooperation was in a system that left it to each state to decide the extent of its obligations. Kant was aware of that inadequacy when he reflected on the peace problem more generally, but it did not enter into his assessment of the relations among the liberal republics that constituted the *foedus pacificum.* For Americans of that generation, such was the unavoidable centerpiece of their reflections, and they took up with considerable intensity the range of questions bearing on it, including among others the bases of representation and burden-sharing, the division of sovereignty, the distribution and control of military power, and the relationship between expansion or "imperial distances" and cohesion. The richness and density of the founders' consideration of these problems form a striking contrast with Kant's total neglect of them, and one suspects that *Perpetual Peace* would have fallen coldly from the founders' hands had they read it.[17] (There is no evidence that any of them did.) No American of that era projected, as Kant did, the universal instantiation of federal union. Aware of the problematic effects of expansion on the internal balance of power, and conscious that what cohesion they enjoyed had arisen in the first instance from the pressure of a great external adversary, Kant's projection—or at least the manner in which he made it—would doubtless have seemed strange and inexplicable from the vantage point of 1787.[18]

The refutation of the democratic peace hypothesis sets the Federalists apart from the "Kantians" and lends support to contemporary criticisms of that theory, but their strong commitment to the law of nations and to devising a federative system that would instantiate a democratic peace sets them far apart from "hard realists" or "offensive realists."[19] As is suggested in chapter 26, the framers faced a "Machiavellian moment" at the convention, and they resolved it in a fashion inconsistent with an ethic of Kantian cosmopolitanism. The injustice of the compromises, indeed, is most apparent from a Kantian perspective, and their necessity is most apparent from a Machiavellian one. That analysis demonstrates a key teaching of the "English school" or "international society" approach—that a full understanding of the world of states cannot dispense with the insights offered by any of the three traditions.

FIGURE 6. OBJECTIVES, DOCTRINES, AND PRINCIPLES OF EARLY AMERICAN DIPLOMACY

This diagram counterpoises two conventional depictions of early American diplomacy—as "isolationist" or "unilateralist"—with the understanding developed in this book, particularly in part five. "Union and Independence," in my interpretation, were the *Staatsräson* of this states-union, each of them mutually affecting the other. Independence meant freedom from foreign domination and avoidance of dependence on the wars and politics of Europe; union meant the reconciliation of difference so as to achieve the classic aims of the federative system—peace among the American states and protection against foreign powers. The bargaining and sectional deals associated with the maintenance of the partnership—what contemporaries called "the exigencies of the union"—suggest a pattern of interaction readily identifiable with what would now be called "multilateralism." The two bedrock principles of union and independence profoundly shaped the most important objectives, doctrines, and principles of American diplomacy. These are set against a shaded background or milieu identified with the law of nations, indicating that these objectives, doctrines, and principles were generally pursued within the framework dictated by that law.[20]

As an objective of American statecraft, "isolationism" seems to me to be not a particularly good descriptor. The desire to knock off the shackles of commercial restriction or the belief in the radiating power of the American example, for instance, are not well summarized by that term. Nor is the doctrine of neutrality, which required for its preservation a punctilious adherence to the law of nations. But the principal objection to the term is the misleading image it fosters of a United States cut off from the larger currents of the Atlantic world. Americans wanted, certainly, to have their own independent system and not be subject to the whims of the European powers; the impulse to be separate from the European system predates Washington's Farewell Address and is coterminous with the Revolution. From 1776 to 1787, however (and indeed for well beyond), the relative strength of the European powers as compared with the fledgling United States made that a long-term hope rather than an immediate reality. For better or ill, the United States could not be isolated from the larger currents of the Atlantic state system at the tail end of the eighteenth century; they were in it.

If "isolationism" is but a half-truth, the attribution of "unilateralism" to early American diplomacy and statecraft seems to me to be entirely off base, though that has become the predominant interpretation in the last generation among "realists" and "revisionists" alike.[21] Not only does subscription to the law of nations—a multilateral norm—not figure in this analysis. There is also complete neglect of how "the federal system and many of the goals of the Founding Fathers emerged within the context of ideas about international order."[22] Most striking of all is that the features of American foreign policy that are characteristically seen as unilateralist actually grew out of the multilateral imperatives associated with the creation and maintenance of federal union. It was the imperious needs associated with the construction of an American system based on internationalist ideals that, more than any other factor, dictated separation and "no entangling alliances" with the European system. Internationalism was, in this sense, a potent auxiliary and abettor to traits normally seen as either "unilateralist" or "isolationist."

This diagram is limited to American diplomatic objectives, doctrines, and principles, but it is important to note that many of these ideas were also registered in the emerging order of American constitutionalism. Freedom of commerce, for example, was an objective sought both among the American states and with foreign countries. The principles of balance of power and nonintervention (in the domestic affairs of other states) were also applicable to both spheres, as were associated doctrines of comity, good faith, and the peaceful settlement of disputes.[23]

Missing from this figure is any mention of religious toleration, a precept that played little role in American diplomacy at this time but which did figure in the emerging American constitutional order. Though interest in the broad principles of religious toleration was sparked and advanced by the American Revolution, the rule of the American constitutional order both before and after 1789 rather closely resembled the old rule of Augsburg (1555) and Westphalia (1648): *cujus regio ejus religio.* This rule allowed each prince or potentate to declare which brand of Christianity would be established in his territories.[24] In the First Amendment to the Constitution, only congress was prevented from making any law respecting an establishment of religion; the states were left free to regulate religious matters and to provide state support in keeping with their own distinctive constitutions and inclinations. Recognition of this point should not understate the vital contributions that Americans of this generation—and particularly the Virginians—made to advancing the cause of religious toleration; it is, however, to insist that the rule of the eighteenth-century Constitution on this score is closer to the rule of Westphalia or Augsburg than it is to contemporary understandings of the protection accorded by the First Amendment.

FIGURE 7. GENERAL MAP OF THE INTERPRETATION

I have designated the general interpretation as "internationalist." Of the various contenders, that seems to be the best rubric under which to group these various interpretations. In smaller type is "federalist," a designation that would do just as handily if eighteenth-century usage were taken as the guide. As noted in chapter 3, however, "federal" now means something approaching the opposite of what it once did. Whereas it once found states bound in treaty, compact, or alliance, it now largely connotes the devolution of power within a single state, and its formerly close association with diplomacy and international order has been almost altogether lost from view. So "internationalist" edges out "federalist," albeit by a thin margin. From an eighteenth-century vantage point, as I have tried to demonstrate, the two traditions are really one tradition, which is, at the same time, multifaceted and Janus-faced; for on those simple themes of unity amid diversity, of "empires of liberty," of civic unions and republican alliances among independent states and distinct peoples, an array of complex variations may be, and has been, played.

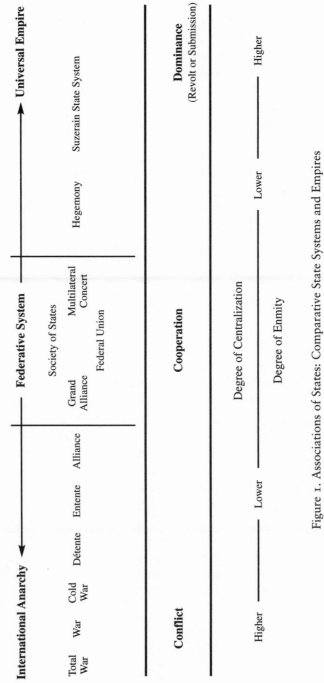

Figure 1. Associations of States: Comparative State Systems and Empires

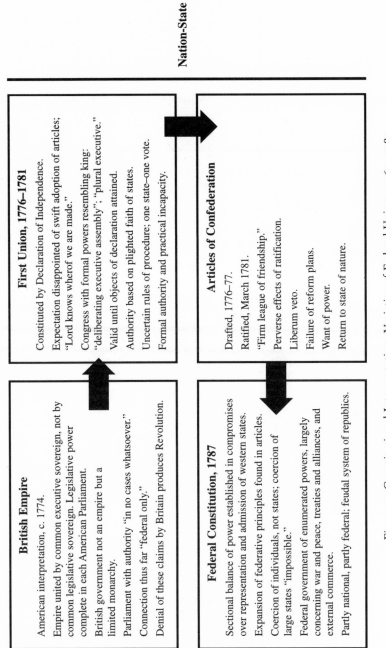

Nation-State

British Empire

American interpretation, c. 1774.

Empire united by common executive sovereign, not by common legislative sovereign. Legislative power complete in each American Parliament.

British government not an empire but a limited monarchy.

Parliament with authority "in no cases whatsoever."

Connection thus far "federal only."

Denial of these claims by Britain produces Revolution.

First Union, 1776–1781

Constituted by Declaration of Independence.

Expectation disappointed of swift adoption of articles; "Lord knows wherof we are made."

Congress with formal powers resembling king: "deliberating executive assembly"; "plural executive."

Valid until objects of declaration attained.

Authority based on plighted faith of states.

Uncertain rules of procedure; one state–one vote.

Formal authority and practical incapacity.

Federal Constitution, 1787

Sectional balance of power established in compromises over representation and admission of western states.

Expansion of federative principles found in articles.

Coercion of individuals, not states; coercion of large states "impossible."

Federal government of enumerated powers, largely concerning war and peace, treaties and alliances, and external commerce.

Partly national, partly federal: feudal system of republics.

Articles of Confederation

Drafted, 1776–77.

Ratified, March 1781.

"Firm league of friendship."

Perverse effects of ratification.

Liberum veto.

Failure of reform plans.

Want of power.

Return to state of nature.

Figure 2. Constitutional Interpretation: Varieties of Federal Union, 1763–1787

Colonial Inheritance

Liberalism

Individual Liberty
Limited Government
Religious Toleration

Republicanism

Loyalty to Commonwealth
Public Virtue
Suspiciousness of Power

Representative Government
Constitutionalism
13 sacred compacts
Internal Autonomy
Requisition System

Independence →

The Several States in the
Union of the Empire:
The Problem of Cooperation

Union will dissolve if
made on unjust basis

American theory
of British Empire
a template of legitimacy
for American union

Unionist Paradigm

Multiple Loyalties,
Identities, Interests:
States & Sections
almost as different
as distinct nations

Security problem:
Ambitions of
foreign powers;
Internal dissolution

Peace Pact:
From Balance of Power
to Federal Union

Consolidation

Universal Empire
Loss of Independence
Imperial Rome
A Victorious Britain

Disunion

International Anarchy
Europeanization of
American Politics
Greece & Italy

Dreaded Specters

Questions: Theory

Are democracies
pacific?
Can republics cooperate
successfully?
Are neighboring nations
natural enemies?
Does commerce promote
peace or war?
Are covenants made
without the sword,
but words?
What is a body politic?
What is sovereignty?
Why do empires rise
and fall?

Questions: Practice

What is a fair method of
voting in Congress? By
states, people, property?
Are the states in a
state of nature toward
one another?
Is the independence of
the states best secured
through a weaker or
stronger federal
government?
Why do my confederates
seek unfair advantages?
Why are they trying to
do me in?
What belongs to
Congress, what to
the states?

What is a fair system
for allocating burdens
of the common cause?
Where is my
allegiance owed?
Is there a right
(or effective power)
of withdrawal from
the union, or of
compulsion by it?
Where is sovereignty
located?
Can you imagine the
consequences of a
disunion?

Figure 3. American Political Thought: The Unionist Paradigm, c. 1776

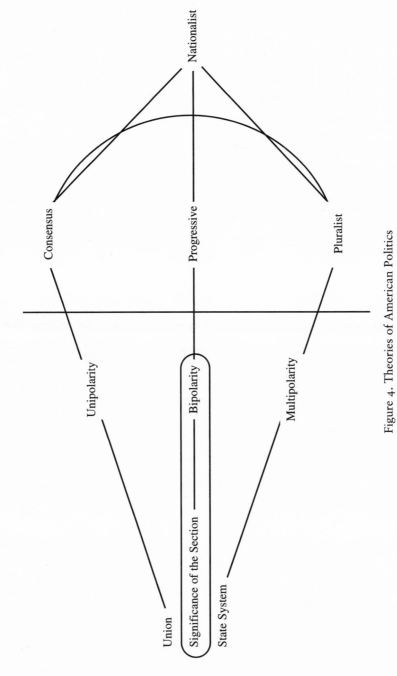

Figure 4. Theories of American Politics

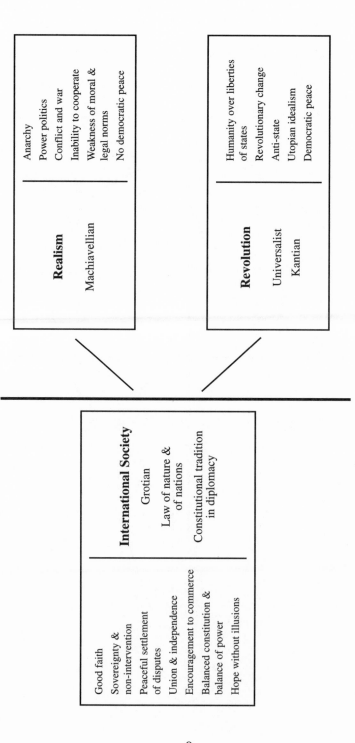

Realism

Machiavellian

Anarchy
Power politics
Conflict and war
Inability to cooperate
Weakness of moral &
legal norms
No democratic peace

Revolution

Universalist
Kantian

Humanity over liberties
of states
Revolutionary change
Anti-state
Utopian idealism
Democratic peace

International Society

Grotian
Law of nature &
of nations
Constitutional tradition
in diplomacy

Good faith
Sovereignty &
non-intervention
Peaceful settlement
of disputes
Union & independence
Encouragement to commerce
Balanced constitution &
balance of power
Hope without illusions

Figure 5. American Diplomacy and Theories of International Relations

Unilateralism

Isolationism

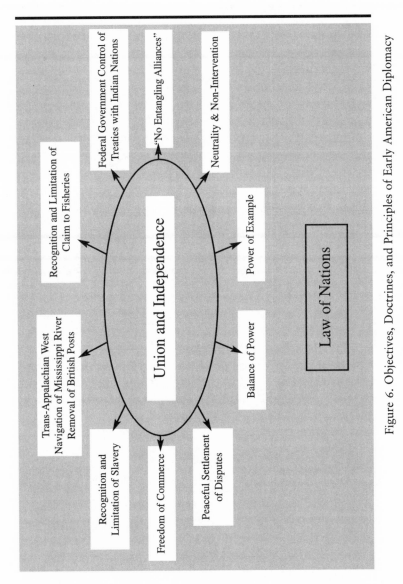

Trans-Appalachian West
Navigation of Mississippi River
Removal of British Posts

Recognition and Limitation of
Claim to Fisheries

Federal Government Control of
Treaties with Indian Nations

"No Entangling Alliances"

Neutrality & Non-Intervention

Recognition and
Limitation of Slavery

Union and Independence

Power of Example

Freedom of Commerce

Peaceful Settlement
of Disputes

Balance of Power

Law of Nations

Figure 6. Objectives, Doctrines, and Principles of Early American Diplomacy

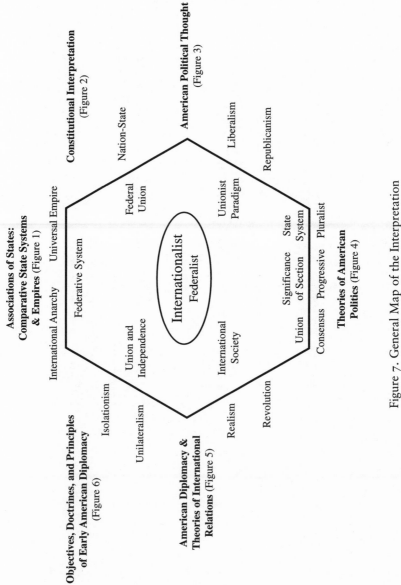

Figure 7. General Map of the Interpretation

THE CONSTITUTION
IN HISTORY:
A BIBLIOGRAPHICAL ESSAY

THE STORY OF THE writing and ratification of the federal constitution is the oldest set piece in American history. The drama of the four months of deliberation in Philadelphia, the high intellectual caliber of the debates during and after the convention, the closeness of the votes in many of the states—the concentration, in short, of so much in so little time—has justified many a study concentrating on a year or less. The focus on a short period, of course, brings many advantages—not least of which is a manageable topic—and a substantial number of historians, both scholarly and popular, have found it irresistible.[1]

Good things, however, do tend to come at a price, and this strategy of attacking the problem of founding is no exception. Seldom brought into view in these accounts is the bitter sectional strife that had pitted easterners against southerners in the preceding decade. Nor do we see the estrangement among the supporters of the Constitution that occurred immediately with the institution of the new government in 1789. When the story is focused on 1787 and 1788, the denouement tends to be some later epic act of the United States—Lincoln's victory in the Civil War, or the march of America to world power, or even the New Deal—for which the work of the convention laid the foundation and which it foreshadows. To know it as it was in the 1790s, however, is to see it in a fragile and experimental state. Before 1789 was out, Madison declared in the House of Representatives that had "a prophet appeared in the Virginia ratifying convention and brought the declarations and proceedings of this day into their view, . . . Virginia might not have been a part of the Union at this moment." In the Virginia convention, Henry Lee had given the most eloquent appeal to his identity as both a Virginian and an American, and he had scorned the narrow patriotism that animated the opposition. A year later he was complaining to Madison that "the government which we both admired so much [would] prove ruinous in its operation to our native state." Lee pronounced himself ready to "submit to all the hazards of war and risk the loss of everything dear to me in life" rather than "to live under the rule of a fixed insolent northern majority." The seeming consensus among supporters of the Constitution concealed deep fissures of outlook, and these were immediately brought to the fore with the inauguration of the new government.[2]

The mutual sense of betrayal that arose between Hamilton and Madison—and both men felt it very keenly—raises the question of whether the consensus of 1788 was as sturdy as it is usually portrayed. It also reinforces our characterization of the Constitution as a peace pact, albeit a peace pact that was dogged in its initial years with strong intimations of its potential mortality. Americans are not accustomed to understanding their Constitution in these terms, yet there was a time when they did so. If one considers not simply the latest generation of interpreters but goes back into the nineteenth century, this understanding of the Constitution as the alternative to war is deeply etched in the interpretive apparatus of nearly all accounts. Students of the Constitution might disagree on who the parties to it were and whether it was properly styled as a compact, but they were perfectly united in thinking of the Constitution as the alternative to war. The most distinguished early interpreters—John Marshall, St. George Tucker, William Rawle, and Joseph Story—all affirmed this view, though they otherwise differed in vital respects. It was routine in congressional debate: the magisterial eloquence of Daniel Webster, the daring and impassioned oratory of Henry Clay, and the finely chiseled dissertations of John C. Calhoun seldom strayed far from the doctrine that without the Constitution and the union the descent into war would be altogether probable.[3]

When adherents of the "State rights" and "National supremacy" schools looked back to the founding records, however, what they found was often most disagreeable to their intention. Oddly, both sides discovered their allies from the past—the men who thought and reasoned just as they did—giving a construction of the Constitution that was in serious tension with, if not flatly contradictory to, their own views. Were it not for the fact that the issue of interpretation formed a title page "to a great tragic volume," the result might be found highly amusing. Imagine Calhoun rummaging through these records, noting that so many of the sentiments expressed by the opposers of the Constitution corresponded exactly with his own, heartily approving the ideas of those, like Patrick Henry, who held the same priority as he did—"Our federal union, next to our liberty the most dear."[4] Imagine, then, his mortification on discovering that the Anti-Federalists affirmed everything he wished to deny in their construction of the Constitution: that the "tyranny of Philadelphia" was to be the act of a single consolidated people, and not of equal sovereign states; that it formed a supreme, consolidated government whose manifest intention was to extinguish the rights of the states; that it was perpetual and would be maintained by force, and was nothing better than a tyrannical despotism! The Anti-Federal construction was ample authority for the war that Lincoln would wage to keep Calhoun's beloved South within the union, just as it was ample authority for Jackson's Force Bill. Of that latter measure, called by its advocates "a measure of peace," Calhoun said: "Yes, such peace as the wolf gives to the lamb—the kite to the dove! Such peace as Russia gives to Poland, or death to its victims!"[5] According to the Anti-Federal construction, alas, such odious measures were plainly authorized by the Constitution. Every construction that Calhoun wished to deny, in short, the Anti-Federalists had affirmed.

Had it not been for the fact that his adversaries suffered the same mortification in their review of the evidence, this would have severely damaged Calhoun's interpretation, already deficient in the rigor of its syllogisms. But the nationalists suffered the same embarrassment. For it was the Federalists of 1788 who insisted, in their construction, that "the people of the states" and not the people of a consolidated nation, were to make the Constitution; that the government, in its foundation, was therefore federal, and not national; that it was to be a government of laws, and not of force, substituting reason and deliberation for the sword; that the federal government could not begin to make laws on every subject, having no implied powers, but only those expressly given; and that its perpetuity could not be answered for, but that it was an experiment that had to be run. Nothing was more inconvenient to Calhoun than the proposition, maintained by large numbers of Anti-Federalists, that secession from a covenant, even if violated by both sides, is impermissible; nothing was more inconvenient to nationalists than the proposition, maintained by Madison, that the obligations of an instrument must cease when its reciprocities were no longer observed. The Federalists certainly hoped that the union would be perpetual, but there was almost nothing in their public utterances that explicitly affirmed the right of the general government to use force to bar a state from secession, and they were in any case impressed that the use of force against a large state would be virtually impossible. That an explicit right of coercion had not been provided for was not fatal to the nationalist case, for it was equally true that an explicit right of withdrawal had not been granted either. As subsequent generations scrambled for evidence within the interstellar void marked out by these double silences, each side found a few scraps from their natural allies to bolster their case, but there was also considerable mortification and embarrassment over the inconvenient evidence these diligent researches produced. That made the debate in 1788 a satire on the subsequent debate over states' rights and national supremacy.[6]

The historians who first had access to Madison's notes, only published in 1840, wrote in the shadow of an impending war, and they emphasized "slavery questions" and sectionalism in their treatment of the federal convention. As Max Farrand later complained, one-third of Richard Hildreth's chapter on the formation of the Constitution, published in 1849, "is taken up with slavery debates." The conflict between large and small states, which Farrand thought decisive in 1904, was considered by Hildreth to be "less radical and vital than that between slaveholding and non-slaveholding, planting and commercial, Atlantic and western states." The abolitionists, of which Hildreth was one, focused their fire on the sectional compromises over slavery and denounced the Constitution for its fatal betrayal of the liberty promised in the Declaration of Independence. Others, like George Ticknor Curtis's *History of the Constitution,* defended the framers for their choice. Neither critics nor defenders of the fathers, however, doubted the centrality of those compromises in evaluating the birth of the Constitution.[7]

When the oft-prophesied great war finally came, exigent need made northerners receptive to the view that the prospect of disunion had been without real precedent and had arisen suddenly in the 1850s among an unrepresentative band of southern traitors—a view reinforced by the results of the conflict, which made disunion no longer thinkable. Historians subsequently emphasized the indissoluble sovereignty established by the Constitution and the judicial protection it accorded to the rights of property. The Anti-Federalists were doubly disfavored in the late nineteenth century and might be lampooned as either secessionists or paper money enthusiasts, but in either case "theorizing fanatics and demagogues," as Hermann von Holst called them.[8] Von Holst, "immutably convinced that the Union cause was written in the stars," gave a strong brief for national sovereignty but also acknowledged that it was "a historical representation made in the interests of party" to argue "that during the first years of the existence of the republic the thought of separation was never seriously entertained." "Until the first part of the nineteenth century, the dissolution of the Union was a standing element in political speculation; and both previous to and after that period, it was repeatedly considered possible and even probable in moments of excitement, by either party, that it would be necessary to resort to this radical remedy."[9]

The specter of disunion also haunted John Fiske. In the most popular and widely read account of the late nineteenth century, Fiske highlighted incipient international anarchy as the demon against which the Constitution was directed. Though Fiske never received the Harvard professorship for which he yearned, he was "perhaps the most popular lecturer on history America has ever known." In his most successful historical study, *The*

Critical Period of American History, 1783–1789, Fiske sought to determine "the causes which determined a century ago that the continent of North America should be dominated by a single powerful and pacific federal nation instead of being parceled out among forty or fifty small communities, wasting their strength and lowering their moral tone by perpetual warfare, like the states of ancient Greece, or by perpetual preparation for war, like the nations of modern Europe." Like the Federalists of 1788, Fiske thought the situation facing the American states was critical in the four years after the conclusion of the Treaty of Paris. In that robust and valorous style so characteristic of the late nineteenth century, Fiske painted a dramatic picture of the weakness and "imbecilities" of the confederation, but he heralded from the unpromising soil of incipient dissolution a "series of causes" that prepared the way "for the foundation of a national sovereignty." Fiske was keen to emphasize that "a state which had once ratified was in the federal bond forever. . . . There could be no such thing as a constitutional right of secession." America had gone from international anarchy to indissoluble national sovereignty in one fell swoop.[10]

A generation later, the making of the Constitution was also placed in an internationalist setting by James Brown Scott, the distinguished scholar and authority on international law. Whereas von Holst and Fiske wrote in the shadow of the Civil War, Scott wrote in the shadow of World War I. In 1918 he published a little book called *James Madison's Notes of Debates in the Federal Convention of 1787 and Their Relation to a More Perfect Society of Nations.* "For some years past," Scott observed in his preface, he had "been of the opinion that the Federal Constitution of the United States was in fact as well as in form an international conference." Two years later he followed with *The United States of America: A Study in International Organization.* Unlike Fiske, who emphasized the national sovereignty established by the Constitution, Scott accentuated the limited character of the allocation of powers given to the federal government: "The delegates in Federal Convention did not merge the States in a union, but formed a union of the States." Neither the legislative nor the executive branch possessed any powers "save those specified in the instrument," and any attempt by either branch "to exercise powers in excess of the grant contained in the Constitution is declared null and void and of no effect by the judicial branch of the Union. . . . This is accomplished without the use of force against the Union on the part of a State or combination of States. Only the individual is coerced." Scott knew the force of the American reluctance to enter into binding commitments with foreign nations, and he acknowledged that the "Society of Nations may not be willing, and indeed even with good will may not be able, to go so far now or at any time as have the States forming the American Union. But however many steps they may take or however few toward the closer Union, the experience of the framers of the Constitution who traversed the entire path should be as a lamp to their feet."[11]

In the era shadowed by World War I, Scott was by no means unique in thinking that the work of the federal convention shed a fascinating light on the question of how to establish international order in the present. Ten years previously, Hamilton Holt had propounded the same view, and he returned to the charge on the outbreak of European war: The headlong plunge into war demonstrated the need, Holt argued, for "a great Confederation or League of Peace." He acknowledged that the "Federation of the World must still be a dream for many years to come" and would have to develop slowly, "step by step." But the immediate establishment of a League of Peace would constitute a "first step toward world federation" and did not, Holt thought, present "insuperable difficulties." It was the "manifest destiny of the United States to lead in the establishment of such a League." "The United States is the world in miniature. The United States is the greatest league of peace known to history. The United States is a demonstration to the world that all the races and peoples of the earth can live in peace under one form of government, and its chief value to civilization is a demonstration of what this form of government is." While few writers were quite as fulsome as Holt, the assumption that the making of the Constitution cast a fascinating light on the question of international order in their own day was widely shared. Woodrow Wilson, Theodore Roosevelt, and William Howard Taft—the three contenders for the 1912 presidential nomination—would all at various times acknowledge a certain parallelism of circumstances between the task the framers confronted in 1787 and the task they confronted in their own day. They all knew and respected Scott, who published in 1918 a collection of President Wilson's addresses on the war, many of them touching on the coming problems of international organization.[12]

The idea of the American Constitution as a template to assess the contemporary tasks of international order entered broadly into American reflection from 1914 to 1920. Complaining of the part played by Roosevelt and Henry Cabot Lodge in the presidential campaign of 1916, the *New Republic* found it absurd that they should join William Borah and Albert Cummins in defense of American isolation:

From every platform and editorial desk [the Republican party] has been telling the country that it was the party of national responsibility and international purpose. The Democrats were negative, irresponsible, without policy, and blind to the facts of the modern world. Yet today it is a Democratic President who grasps the truth that isolation is over and strives to guide our entrance into world politics towards stability and safety. It is the Republican party which proposes to crouch at its own fireside, build a high tariff wall, arm against the whole world, cultivate no friendships, take no steps to forestall another great war, and then let things rip. The party which was inspired by the idea of American union is becoming a party of secession and states' rights as against world union.

Throughout the epoch of World War I, innumerable variations were played upon this theme: the parallel did exist, was fruitful, and multiplied. In thinking about the problems of international order, many Americans found for themselves a usable past in the making and ratification of the Constitution.[13]

The larger significance of this parallel between the American founding and problems of world order in the twentieth century is that it was one of the primary means by which the unionist paradigm was restated in the course of that century. International anarchy and universal empire remained, as before, the primordial fears. Some kind of union as the means toward the avoidance of international anarchy and universal empire was the recurring refrain of internationalists, though they were sharply divided among themselves regarding the geographic reach and institutional characteristics of the sought-for American commitment. The recurring refrain of isolationists, by contrast, was that any such project would lead not only to the sacrifice of national independence but also to the establishment of centralized and militarized institutions at home, imperiling freedom and the constitutional order. Neither position was without serious vulnerabilities: isolationists had to reckon on the possibility that universal empire might rise out of the ashes of a European system no longer capable of maintaining its historic balance, forcing America to become a garrison state. Internationalists, by contrast, realized that any federative system among the democracies would fall short even of the Articles of Confederation, and why such a thing should work when the previous instrument had dissolved raised a question for which they did not have a ready answer. One point seems clear: despite vastly differing circumstances, the quarrel over foreign policy bore a close resemblance to the great debate between the Federalists and Anti-Federalists: the essential terms of the unionist paradigm had gotten restated in relation to the potentialities and dangers of America's world role.[14]

While this parallel, in the dramatic circumstances of World War I, assumed a new shape as the question of international order acquired a new urgency, it was in one sense not new at all. That America's federal union might form a model for the peaceful organization of Europe had been propounded by a large number of other writers in the course of the nineteenth century. Fiske himself, a few years before composing *The Critical Period,* had wondered whether Europe "will find it worth while to adopt the lesson of federalism in order to do away with the chances of useless warfare which remain so long as its different states own no allegiance to any common authority." War between civilized nations was an absurdity, Fiske thought. The questions that had in the past led to war "will have to be settled by discussion in some sort of federal council or parliament if Europe would keep pace with America in the advance toward universal law and order." Before 1914, few Americans thought that their country would play any role, save as an inspired example, in the construction of a new federative system for Europe. The cataclysm of 1914 brought that question to the fore. Isolationists from 1914 on were happy to reiterate Fiske's advice and give the remedy of federal union their most solemn endorsement. They just wanted nothing to do with its establishment. Internationalists, by contrast, saw the need for a new federative system but disagreed about its proper contours.[15]

Perhaps the most remarkable feature of these various appeals to the past to vindicate a course for the future is that virtually none of them was made by professional historians. Fiske was read out of the historical fraternity at a fairly early date. Scott was an international lawyer, of signal influence within the State Department and the foreign policy community, but generally ignored by historians. The one historian who did pursue the themes of Fiske and Scott, though from a different vantage point, was Frederick Jackson Turner. Unlike Fiske and Scott, who minimized the influence of sectionalism, Turner thought that sectionalism had been unjustly neglected as a factor in American history. Turner's ideas on the significance of the section germinated in the internationalist ferment of World War I, and in a sparkling series of essays he laid them bare in the 1920s. In the most famous of these, in 1925, Turner argued that "we have furnished to Europe the example of a continental federation of sections over an area equal to Europe itself, and by substituting discussion and concession and compromised legislation for peace, we have shown the possibility of international political parties, international legislative bodies, and international peace." Turner not only held up federal union as a model; he also intimated that the European state system was a mirror by which to understand the course of American political development, arguing that "the significance of the section in

American history is that it is the faint image of a European nation and that we need to examine our history in the light of this fact." Turner's plea did not fall entirely on deaf ears, and it helped inaugurate and sustain the study of regionalism in history and literature in the interwar period. Generally speaking, however, it was Turner's early work on the significance of the frontier that commanded the attention—and more often than not the denunciation—of historians. For every one historian fascinated by Turner's dissection of the significance of sectionalism, there were twenty others determined to overthrow the frontier thesis. The sectional thesis invited a view of the making and ratification of the Constitution as a peace pact among the sections, but Turner's expertise lay in the middle period between the Constitution and the Civil War, which he died trying to comprehend, and none of his small but devoted band of followers undertook that project. His view of sectionalism, moreover, was one that highlighted the disparity between East and West—that between North and South was old hat when he made his breakthrough—and the persistent tendency in his thought was to assimilate the southern plantation to the agrarian frontier.[16]

Despite the great reentry from 1914 to 1920 of the unionist paradigm into a larger American intellectual discourse, it never found favor, Turner apart, in the American historical profession. Even as publicists and politicians were holding the parallel up before their eyes and asking themselves what it meant, historians seemed to find the whole exercise somewhat idiotic. Beard had no regard for Fiske, and his own outlook on the American role in the world—which was Anti-Federalist in orientation—did not dispose him to grant any purchase in the parallel. Beard and Parrington were convinced instead that the conflict between socioeconomic classes provided the key to understanding American history, including most particularly the epoch of the Constitution. "From the first," wrote Parrington,

> we have been divided into two main parties. Names and battle cries and strategies have often changed repeatedly, but the broad party division has remained. On one side has been the party of the current aristocracy—of church, of gentry, of merchant, of slave holder, or manufacturer—and on the other the party of the commonality—of farmer, villager, small tradesman, mechanic, proletariat. The one has persistently sought to check and limit the popular power, to keep the control of the government in the hands of the few in order to serve special interests, whereas the other has sought to augment the popular power, to make government more responsive to the will of the majority, to further the democratic rather than the republican ideal.

For the Progressives, the story of the Constitution could be understood only in this framework, and those who saw it as an escape from international anarchy or an experiment in international cooperation missed fundamentally what was really going on. What the Federalists said they wanted to do was not really what they wanted to do. It covered other intentions—above all the intention to check the democracy ostensibly running riot in the states.[17]

The Progressive interpretation was worlds apart from the line of inquiry suggested by the work of Fiske and Scott. Whereas both these figures—together with various other journalists and politicians—had placed the founding in the context of a problem of international peace, the Progressives saw it as an episode in the class struggle. The conflict between the two perspectives reached a sort of climax with the publication of Merrill Jensen's *The New Nation* in 1950. Jensen dismissed Fiske as a hack and said that his interpretation showed "almost no evidence of first hand acquaintance with the sources." He also took aim at Clarence Streit, who had become famous in 1939 with the publication of *Union Now: A Proposal for a Federal Union of the Democracies of the North Atlantic,* and who continued to propagandize for this project in the aftermath of World War II. Streit, like Fiske, saw a critical period before the making of the Constitution, believed it to be nearly identical with the great problem of his own day, and thought the remedy of federal union the only proper medicine for the ailments of the world's democracies. To all this Jensen administered the classic rebuke of the professional historian: "[E]ven if it can be granted that most appeals to the history of the Confederation have been sincere, they have seldom been infused with any knowledge of the period or its problems." There was no critical period, Jensen insisted. American commerce was looking up by the time of the Convention, the states were steadily retiring the national debt; with a few modifications to the Articles of Confederation, the future would be bright. Jensen was sufficiently cynical about men and motives to affect a sneaking admiration for the way the Federalists had bamboozled the public through artful propaganda, but he could not stomach the way their silly rhetoric had been confused with the historical reality. Jensen emphasized that the Anti-Federalists were patriots, too; indeed, they were the real federalists. Rectifying the names used in the struggle over the ratification, Jensen insisted that those who styled themselves "Federalists" were really "nationalists"; the true federalists lay with those who opposed a national government. It was high time, Jensen said, to get rid of this false caricature of the opposition to the Constitution. The issue between the two parties was not "whether there was a 'nation' before the adoption of the Constitution of 1787. That was not the question at all during the 1780's. There was a new nation, as the men of the time agreed: they disagreed as to whether the new nation should have a federal or a national government." So far as historians were concerned, these damning judgments were the last rites for an internationalist interpretation of the founding.[18]

From the 1950s to the bicentennial celebrations of 1987, scholarship on the Constitution fell into one of three broad classes: the "consensus," "Progressive," or "pluralist" interpretations that have represented the three main paradigms for the understanding of American politics in the twentieth century. The one emphasizes a great and commanding consensus in American society, sustained by its middle-class character, over the great liberal principles of representative government, individual liberty, and indissoluble union—a consensus that marked not only the making of the Constitution but also American society and government throughout nearly all our history. The pluralist view emphasizes the separation and balancing of distinct powers in a national government that presides over an extended territory riven into clashing interest groups, none of which can achieve dominance. Its gloss on the founding emphasizes the centrality of *Federalist* Nos. 10 and 51. The consensus and pluralist views are both nationalist in orientation and are by no means mutually incompatible; indeed, they are mutually supportive if the competition of interest groups over an extended nation is seen as describing a leading element of the American consensus or a vital factor explaining the stability of its political institutions.[19]

The Progressive interpretation achieved its greatest influence in the interwar period; the righteous character of World War II, together with the revival of a working capitalism after 1945, helped ensure that it would be sharply challenged. In the two decades after World War II, historians were generally impressed not with the class divisions of American society but with its (then resurgent) middle-class character. The fearsome deconstructions of Beard performed by Robert E. Brown and Forrest McDonald in the 1950s were part of a larger reaction against the Progressive approach. Brown, a consensus historian, scored Beard for his misuse of evidence, while McDonald, a pluralist then in the grip of a severe case of economism, demolished Beard's primitive binary framework between "personalty" and "realty" and emphasized the large number of distinct economic interests the framers had to accommodate. It was a clever stratagem to challenge Beard on his own ground, but already the Progressive emphasis on material factors was beginning to seem narrowly restrictive and misleading by numerous historians, and the way was clear for the revival of interest in ideas and political culture sparked by Douglass Adair, Bernard Bailyn, Gordon Wood, and J. G. A. Pocock in the 1960s.[20]

Despite wounding criticism, however, the Progressive interpretation by no means disappeared, and even critics who challenged its materialist biases and who saw the Constitution as the fulfillment rather than the betrayal of the democratic promise of the Declaration of Independence could also accept Jensen's denial of a "critical period" and the Progressive belief that American nationalism had won a resounding victory in 1787 and 1788. The central thrust of the Progressive interpretation, moreover, continued to find adherents, including Gordon Wood's influential *Creation of the American Republic*. "It seems obvious by now," wrote Wood, "that Beard's notion that men's property holdings, particularly personalty holdings, determined their ideas and their behavior was so crude that no further time should be spent on it." Yet while Wood found Beard's interpretation "in the narrow sense" to be "undeniably dead," he still thought the Progressive interpretation "to be the most helpful framework for understanding the politics and ideology surrounding the Constitution." It sprang from men whose focus "was not so much on the politics of the congress as it was on the politics of the states," and it "was in some sense an aristocratic document designed to curb the democratic excesses of the Revolution." Wood did much more than simply restate the Progressive interpretation. He gave it, as it were, an intellectual home by a full-scale examination of the debates that had arisen within the states over the character of their new republican constitutions (which the Progressives, distrustful of the importance of ideas, had never really tried to do). He also tried to account for the putative shift in American discourse from "republicanism" to interest-group liberalism, and in effect provided a synthesis of all three paradigms. The extended republic of *Federalist* No. 10 was a response to the class conflict that defined American politics, and it represented the new liberal consensus that displaced republicanism and made for "the end of classical politics."[21]

While the scholarship produced on the occasion of the bicentennial largely fell within the grooves of the three paradigms,[22] there were stirrings that suggested a return to many of the themes that had preoccupied Fiske, Scott, and Turner. This work does not by any means represent a new orthodoxy, but it is striking that the dissenters have emerged in a variety of fields and come at the problem from a multiplicity of disciplinary perspectives. David Hackett Fischer's *Albion's Seed: Four British Folkways in America* has underlined the vital importance of America's regional societies and has seen the Constitution of 1787 as "an attempt to write the rules of engagement among these regional 'republics' of British America." The monumental series of D. W. Meinig, a historical geographer, has also cast into question the adequacy of a nationalist framework, seeing the America of the founding era as "a precarious patchwork of regions." "Whereas nation and federation were tentative and to a large degree contrived and intangible, these regions were deep rooted and distinctive, cumulative creations of several generations." What Meinig does, better than anyone else, is to locate identity and loyalty in a sense of place, but he also has a lively sense of the "geopolitical alternatives" and structures that existed in North America not just in 1787 but throughout early American history. In this respect, Meinig's work runs in parallel with that of John Murrin, whose essays on the framework of early American history also display an inventive grasp of the alternative possibilities that were latent in events. Though different from Turner (and from one another) in key respects, all these writers may fairly be described as neo-Turnerians. They have all given fresh answers to the great problem Turner posed: What is the significance of the section in American history?[23]

If these writers recall Turner in basic respects, the work of Peter Onuf and Daniel Deudney suggests a certain revival of Fiske, Scott, and the internationalist orientation that prevailed among commentators in the World War I era. Both Onuf and Deudney place the founding in the context of a problem of international peace and see it as an inventive refashioning of the "peace plan" tradition and an escape from the potential Europeanization of American politics. Both, too, give key importance to the structure of fears and hopes I have identified with the unionist paradigm—with international anarchy and consolidated empire as the things most feared, and union and independence as the key values that statecraft must vindicate. Onuf came to his mature perspective in a roundabout way. In his first book, *The Origins of the Federal Republic*, he was still operating under Jensen's assumption "that the 'critical period' was largely a creation of contemporary rhetoric" and was more impressed by the mythic character it lent the Federalist achievement than with the actual dangers it presented. By the time of the bicentennial celebrations, however, that assumption had been cast aside. To reduce Federalist fears to disingenuous rhetoric did not make sense; you could not hang an era on an insincerity. That had been at the root of Bernard Bailyn's conceptual breakthrough in writing *The Ideological Origins of the American Revolution*. Those hot-tempered and fiery whigs had meant what they said! Onuf applied the insight to the founding and was now prepared to see Federalist fears of international anarchy as a deeply felt response to the problems of the confederation. This was, however, no narrow revival of Fiske, who had portrayed the Anti-Federalists in a highly unflattering light.

Whatever their other weaknesses, the signal achievement of the Progressive historians was to insist that the Anti-Federalists be taken seriously—amazingly, no previous school had done so. By the time that Onuf was rethinking the Federalist case, the Antis had already achieved a certain status as cofounders, as Wood called them. New collections of their writings—above all the seven volumes of Herbert Storing—increased the interest of historians in their outlook. Bringing both perspectives into the examination of the founding era led Onuf to a full statement of the essentials of the unionist paradigm. The debate over the Constitution was no longer a controversy between aristocrats and democrats but a structured discourse among states and sections on how best to organize the peace.[24]

Though Onuf called the regime created by the American Constitution a "new world order," in echo of the ascendant American worldview of the early 1990s, there seemed little in the way of presentist concern in his work.[25] He never really looked over his shoulder, as Scott had done, at the organization of the peace in the contemporary era. Daniel Deudney, by contrast, has placed the founding in that context. As a theorist of international relations, he wants to understand how power is structured and organized in systems of states so as to facilitate peace and prevent war. What he calls "The Philadelphian System, c. 1787–1861," represented a distinctive way of doing this, all the more remarkable in that many of its presuppositions had somehow migrated into the agenda of American liberal internationalism in the second half of the twentieth century. Conceived in this way, the Philadelphian system was a type of state system or international order, one that came to an end with what Deudney called "The War of Southern Secession." So far as his interpretation of the founding was concerned, Deudney had simply swept up Fiske, Scott, and Turner in a striking new synthesis, but to put it this way would be to altogether miss the significance of the essay within American political science, where such a view was virtually unknown. Despite the occurrence of a great war in 1861, political scientists had never considered the epoch from 1789 to 1861 as an episode in international history or as fodder for the science of international politics. The great war of sections was a brief and soon-repaired interruption of a national existence that had begun in 1776 or 1787. It belonged to the class of conflicts called civil wars, certainly outside the domain of the specialist in international relations. None of postwar realists in international relations—figures such as Hans Morgenthau, Kenneth Waltz, Henry Kissinger, Samuel P. Huntington, or Robert W. Tucker—considered the early American experience as representing a "states-union," as Deudney called it. The political association to which the Declaration or the Constitution gave birth was, in the view of this generation of realist scholars, a unit in a competitive world of nation-states; to think of it as a state system would have seemed bizarre and incomprehensible to them. When a liberal-institutionalist challenge to realism arose in the 1970s (reviving in certain particulars the outlook of Scott), it took the form of a critique of the realist depiction of the post–World War II world system and never looked back to the long peace from 1789 to 1861. Unlike the scholars of international relations, students of American politics had to take account of the founding, but they worked almost exclusively within some variation of the consensus-pluralist paradigm. Over large reaches of this scholarship what Deudney called "the security analysis cumulatively addressed in Federalists 1–14" (and brought to a dramatic pitch in Nos. 6–8) was nowhere to be found.[26]

Surveying the entire historiography of the founding, it is remarkable how deep an imprint has always been made by the epoch in which the historian or political scientist lives. It is not only Fiske and Scott who bear out this generalization—the one seeking intelligibility and legitimacy for the northern victory in the Civil War, the other seeking guidance to the perplexing problems of international order in his own day. The Progressives, too, fall clearly within the pattern: their heyday was the long period of intensified class consciousness that arose in the 1890s and that came to a bitter climax in the 1930s. When Beard composed the *Economic Interpretation*, the Supreme Court had for a generation struck down a wide range of state legislation that sought to improve the conditions of labor. Dissenting justices like Oliver Wendell Holmes and Louis Brandeis objected to the incorporation of Herbert Spencer's *Social Statics* into the Constitution and took the view that the Court had sharply departed from the original understanding of both the contract clause and the Fourteenth Amendment. Working in a different medium, Beard in effect overthrew this judgment: it was a shock to historical consciousness because it made the founding fathers into plutocrats, bankers, and spoilsmen and drew a direct line between the judicially enforced plutocracy of his day and the intentions of the framers. The "discovery that struck home like a submarine tornado," in Parrington's words, was "that the drift toward plutocracy was not a drift away from the spirit of the Constitution, but an inevitable unfolding from its premises."[27]

It also seems difficult to understand the rise of the consensus and pluralist schools to dominance in the 1950s and 1960s save against the background of the cold war and the larger racial, social, and economic challenges facing American society. Sophisticated defenders of Western pluralism did not deny that liberal democratic polities had a tendency to fracture into classes. The saving grace of the system, in the expression of

Raymond Aron, was that it allowed for "a plurality of ruling minorities." Defenders of the American system looked to those elements of the *Federalist* that stressed the competition of multifarious interest groups over an extended territory and the distribution and balancing of powers within the government. To the pluralists, Madison had refuted Marx before he had written a line, and they naturally elevated in their interpretation of the founding those elements in *Federalist* Nos. 10 and 51 where the core of the refutation was concentrated. The founders' desire to so contrive "the interior structure of the government as that its several constituent parts may, by their mutual relations, be the means of keeping each other in their proper places" may not have worked out precisely as intended, but it had proved far more workable and less subject to the abuse of power than the dictatorship of the proletariat.[28]

The challenge of securing civil rights for African-Americans, and doing so through national power, also strongly influenced the interpretation of the founding in the post–World War II period. The liberal-pluralists of the 1950s and 1960s, in other words, not only had a battle on their hands with Marxists; they were also fighting the South's resistance, in the name of states' rights, to equal rights for black citizens. Any interpretation of the Constitution that questioned the supremacy of the national idea at the moment of founding ran the risk of giving aid and comfort to segregationists and racists.[29] It also might threaten national control of the economy, an aspiration that in the early post–World War II years was not yet fully secure.[30] The nationalism of the liberal-pluralists was in one sense the diametric opposite of Progressive decentralists, but in another sense they were as one: both camps saw the triumph of nationalism in the Constitution. In Parrington's words, "The history of the rise of the coercive state in America, with the ultimate arrest of all the centrifugal tendencies, was implicit in [the] momentous counter movement" that had arisen in the aftermath of the Revolutionary War. Whereas Parrington saw tragedy in the unfolding drama, with slavery fatally compromising the moral and political integrity of localist and democratic resistance to the homogenizing tendencies of the centralist state, liberal-pluralists saw the founders as having laid the basis in practice for an indissoluble nation and in theory for the abolition of slavery.[31]

Both schools, too, generally accepted the minimization of sectional factors and slavery at the convention.[32] For the first three-quarters of the twentieth century, slavery as a factor in the making of the Constitution was considered a mistaken emphasis of nineteenth-century historians obsessed with the Civil War. Max Farrand set the tone for this view in his essay "Compromises of the Constitution" (1904), in which he sharply challenged the interpretation of the Constitutional Convention that had prevailed for a generation in the North, one strand of which found a compact with the devil in the making of the Constitution, but which in most of its varieties recognized the potency of the antagonism between North and South in 1787. When Staughton Lynd revived "The Abolitionist Critique of the United States Constitution" in the late 1960s, in the midst of the civil rights revolution, he struck a note that sounded anachronistic to Gordon Wood, and indeed Lynd's argument was antithetical and threatening to the three main paradigms of interpretation. In the past thirty years, however, recognition of the importance of slavery and its role in the two great compromises of the convention has been well established by a number of historians, thus reviving the characteristic view of the middle to late nineteenth century.[33]

Historians may seek to stand outside of time and achieve a sort of immortal detachment from contemporary needs and aspirations, but that is a very difficult thing to do. Thirty or forty years after a book is published, and sometimes well before, the imprint of the historian's own era is usually unmistakable. Since we cannot know in the present those features of the contemporary period that will seem most distinctive about us to future observers, I shall forbear any attempt to historicize contemporary scholarship on the Constitution, which would unavoidably terminate in a historicization of myself. Let us instead conclude this survey by noting the reemergence of a vein of inquiry on the founding that several generations ago intrigued scholars and other men of letters, but which then passed out of scholarly consciousness in both history and political science. The present work runs in its argument and emphases in parallel lines with this new scholarship, and it seems to me to constitute a distinct school of interpretation, which might be described as unionist, federalist, neo-Turnerian, or internationalist. The existence of such a school of opinion does not mean that the conclusions reached in this body of scholarship are the same. There are wide variations in the way in which each scholar conceptualizes his research agenda, and wide variations, too, in how the problem of multiple identities is understood and solved. None of them adds up the relationship among state, section, union, nation, and frontier in precisely the same way. The unity of the school consists perhaps above all in their attention to the same vein of historical material (different flowers, same soil). It is more attentive to the elements of heterogeneity that existed in North America, and less prone to see a unified future as immanent in the discordant past. Above all, it questions whether the national idea, at least as that is conventionally understood, had before or after the writing of the Constitution the hegemonic status that it subsequently attained both in fact and in thought.

SHORT TITLES

Adams Diary	*Diary and Autobiography of John Adams.* Edited by L. H. Butterfield, Leonard C. Faber, and Wendell D. Garrett. 4 vols. Cambridge, Mass., 1961.
Adams Family Correspondence	*Adams Family Correspondence.* Edited by L. H. Butterfield. Cambridge, Mass., 1963–.
Adams Papers	*Papers of John Adams.* Edited by Robert J. Taylor, Gregg L. Lint, Celeste Walker, and Richard Alan Ryerson. Cambridge, Mass., 1977–.
Adams Works	*The Works of John Adams.* Edited by Charles Francis Adams. 10 vols. Boston, 1850–56.
American Colonial Documents	*English Historical Documents.* Vol. 9, *American Colonial Documents to 1776.* Edited by Merrill Jensen. New York, 1964.
Ames Works	*Works of Fisher Ames, As Published by Seth Ames.* Edited by W. B. Allen. 2 vols. Indianapolis [1854] 1983.
Annals of Congress	*The Debates and Proceedings in the Congress of the United States . . . , 1789–1824.* 42 vols. Washington, D.C., 1834–56.
Bailyn, *Debate*	Bailyn, Bernard, ed. *The Debate on the Constitution: Federalist and Antifederalist Speeches, Articles, and Letters During the Struggle over Ratification.* 2 vols. New York, 1993.
Bailyn, *Pamphlets*	Bailyn, Bernard, ed. *Pamphlets of the American Revolution: 1750–1776.* Vol. 1, 1750–1765. Cambridge, 1965.

Bolingbroke Works   *The Works of Lord Bolingbroke.* 4
                             vols. New York, [1844] 1967.

Burke, *American Revolution*   Burke, Edmund. *Selections. 1972: On
                             the American Revolution, Selected
                             Speeches and Letters.* Edited by Elliot
                             Robert Barkan. 2d ed. Gloucester,
                             Mass., 1972.

Cappon, *Adams-Jefferson*   *The Adams-Jefferson Letters: The
                             Complete Correspondence Between
                             Thomas Jefferson and Abigail and
                             John Adams.* Edited by Lester J. Cap-
                             pon. 2 vols. Chapel Hill, 1959.

Choate Works   *The Works of Rufus Choate, with
                             Memoir of His Life.* Edited by
                             Samuel Gilman Brown. 2 vols.
                             Boston, 1862.

Cooke, *Federalist*   Hamilton, Alexander, James Madi-
                             son, and John Jay. *The Federalist.*
                             Edited by Jacob E. Cooke. Middle-
                             town, Conn., 1961.

Deane Papers   *The Deane Papers: Correspondence
                             Between Silas Deane, His Brothers
                             and Their Business and Political As-
                             sociates, 1771–1795.* Collections of
                             the New York Historical Society.
                             New York, 1887–91.

DHRC   *Documentary History of the Ratifica-
                             tion of the Constitution.* Edited by
                             Merrill Jensen and John P. Kaminski.
                             Madison, Wis., 1976–.

Dickinson Writings   *The Writings of John Dickinson.* Vol.
                             1, *Political Writings: 1764–1774.*
                             Edited by Paul Leicester Ford.
                             Philadelphia, 1895.

Elliot, *Debates*   Elliot, Jonathan, ed. *The Debates in
                             the Several State Conventions on the
                             Adoption of the Federal Constitution
                             as Recommended by the General
                             Convention at Philadelphia in
                             1787 . . . 5 vols. Philadelphia, 1859.*

Farrand, *Records*	Farrand, Max, ed. *The Records of the Federal Convention of 1787.* Rev. ed. 4 vols. New Haven, Conn., 1937.
Ford, *Essays*	Ford, Paul Leicester, ed. *Essays on the Constitution of the United States, Published During Its Discussion by the People, 1787–1788.* Brooklyn, 1892.
Ford, *Pamphlets*	Ford, Paul Leicester, ed. *Pamphlets on the Constitution of the United States, Published During Its Discussion by the People, 1787–1788.* Brooklyn, 1888.
Founders' Constitution	*The Founders' Constitution.* Edited by Philip B. Kurland and Ralph Lerner. 5 vols. Indianapolis, 1987.
Franklin Papers	*The Papers of Benjamin Franklin.* Edited by Leonard W. Labaree, Whitfield J. Bell Jr., and William B. Willcox. New Haven, Conn., 1959–.
Franklin Works	*The Works of Benjamin Franklin.* Edited by Jared Sparks. 10 vols. Boston, 1840.
Franklin Writings	*The Writings of Benjamin Franklin.* Edited by Albert Henry Smyth. 10 vols. New York, 1905–7.
Gipson, *British Empire*	Gipson, Lawrence Henry. *The British Empire Before the American Revolution.* 15 vols. New York, 1936–70.
Giunta, *Documents*	Mary A. Giunta et al., eds. *Documents of the Emerging Nation: U.S. Foreign Relations, 1775–1789.* Wilmington, Del., 1998.
Giunta, *Emerging Nation*	Mary A. Giunta et al., eds. *The Emerging Nation: A Documentary History of the Foreign Relations of the United States Under the Articles of Confederation, 1780–1789.* 3 vols. Washington, D.C., 1996–.

Hamilton Papers	*The Papers of Alexander Hamilton.* Edited by Harold C. Syrett and Jacob E. Cooke. 26 vols. New York, 1961–79.
Hume, *Essays*	*Essays: Moral, Political and Literary.* Edited by Eugene F. Miller. Indianapolis, [1777] 1985.
Hutson, *Supplement*	Hutson, James, ed. *Supplement to Max Farrand's the Records of the Federal Convention of 1787.* New Haven, Conn., 1987.
Iredell Papers	*The Papers of James Iredell.* Edited by Don Higginbotham. Raleigh, N.C., 1976–.
Jay Correspondence	*The Correspondence and Public Papers of John Jay.* Edited by Henry P. Johnston. 4 vols. New York, 1890–93.
Jay Papers	*John Jay: The Making of a Revolutionary: Unpublished Papers.* New York, 1975 (vol. 1). *John Jay: The Winning of the Peace: Unpublished Papers, 1780–1784.* New York, 1980 (vol. 2). Edited by Richard B. Morris.
Jefferson Papers	*The Papers of Thomas Jefferson.* Edited by Julian P. Boyd et al. Princeton, N.J., 1950–.
Jefferson Writings	*The Writings of Thomas Jefferson.* Edited by Andrew A. Lipscomb and Albert Ellery Bergh. 20 vols. Washington, D.C., 1905.
JCC	*Journals of the Continental Congress, 1774–1789.* Edited by Worthington C. Ford et al. 34 vols. Washington, D.C., 1904–37.
King Correspondence	*The Life and Correspondence of Rufus King.* Edited by Charles R. King. 6 vols. New York, 1894–1900.
Koch, *Writings of Adams*	Koch, Adrienne, ed. *Selected Writings of John and John Quincy Adams.* New York, 1946.

Lee Letters	*The Letters of Richard Henry Lee.* Edited by James Curtis Ballagh. 2 vols. New York, 1911–14.
Lemay, *Franklin Writings*	Lemay, J. A. Leo, ed. *Benjamin Franklin: Writings.* New York, 1987.
Letters of Delegates	*Letters of Delegates to Congress, 1774–1789.* Edited by Paul H. Smith. Washington, D.C., 1976–.
LMCC	Burnett, Edmund C., ed. *Letters of Members of the Continental Congress.* Edited by Edmund C. Burnett. 8 vols. Washington, D.C., 1921–36.
Locke, *Two Treatises*	Locke, John. *Two Treatises on Government.* Edited by Peter Laslett. Cambridge, 1988.
Madison Letters	*Letters and Other Writings of James Madison.* Published by order of Congress. 4 vols. Philadelphia, 1865.
Madison Papers	*The Papers of James Madison.* Edited by William T. Hutchinson et al. Chicago, 1962–77 (vols. 1–10); Charlottesville, Va., 1977– (vols. 11–).
Madison Writings	*James Madison: Writings.* Edited by Jack N. Rakove. New York, 1999.
Mason Papers	*The Papers of George Mason, 1725–1792.* Edited by Robert A. Rutland. 3 vols. Chapel Hill, N.C., 1970.
Meng, *Despatches of Gérard*	Meng, John J., ed. *Despatches and Instructions of Conrad Alexandre Gérard, 1778–1780: Correspondence of the First French Minister to the United States with the Comte de Vergennes.* Baltimore, 1939.
Montesquieu, *Spirit of the Laws*	Montesquieu, Charles de Secondat, baron de. *The Spirit of the Laws.* Edited and translated by Anne M. Cohler, Basia Carolyn Miller, and Harold Samuel Stone. Cambridge, 1989.

Morison, *Sources* — *Sources and Documents Illustrating the American Revolution and the Formation of the Federal Constitution 1764–1788.* Edited by Samuel Eliot Morison. New York, 1965.

Morris Papers — *The Papers of Robert Morris, 1781–1784.* Edited by E. James Ferguson et al. 9 vols. Pittsburgh, 1973.

Niles, *Principles* — Niles, Hezekiah. *Principles and Acts of the Revolution in America.* New York, 1876.

Paine Writings — *Thomas Paine: Collected Writings.* Edited by Eric Foner. New York, 1995.

Parliamentary History — *Parliamentary History of England from the Earliest Period to 1803.* Edited by William Cobbett and T. C. Hansard. 36 vols. London, 1806–20.

Peterson, *Jefferson Writings* — *Thomas Jefferson: Writings.* Edited by Merrill D. Peterson. New York, 1984.

Potter, *Nationalism* — *Nationalism and Sectionalism in America, 1775–1877.* Edited by David M. Potter and Thomas G. Manning. New York, 1949.

Pownall, *Administration* — Pownall, Thomas. *Administration of the Colonies (1768).* Edited by Daniel A. Baugh and Alison Gilbert Olson. Delmar, N.Y., 1993.

Pownall, *Memorial* — *Memorial to the Sovereigns of Europe, on the Present State of Affairs Between the Old and New World.* 2d ed. London, 1780.

Price Political Writings — *Richard Price: Political Writings.* Edited by D. O. Thomas. Cambridge, 1991.

Ramsay, *History* — Ramsay, David. *The History of the American Revolution.* Edited by Lester H. Cohen. 2 vols. Indianapolis, 1990.

Robertson, *History of Charles V*	Robertson, William. *The History of the Reign of the Emperior Charles the Fifth, with a View of the Progress of Society in Europe, from the Subversion of the Roman Empire to the Beginning of the Sixteenth Century . . .* Edited by William H. Prescott. 4 vols. Philadelphia, [1769] 1884.
Rousseau, *International Relations*	*Rousseau on International Relations.* Edited by Stanley Hoffmann and David P. Fidler. New York, 1991.
Rush Letters	*Letters of Benjamin Rush.* Edited by L. H. Butterfield. 2 vols. Princeton, N.J., 1951.
Rush Selected Writings	*The Selected Writings of Benjamin Rush.* Edited by Dagobert D. Runes. New York, 1947.
Schuyler, *Josiah Tucker*	Schuyler, Robert Livingston, ed. *Josiah Tucker: A Selection from His Economic and Political Writings.* New York, 1931.
Sheehan, *Friends*	*Friends of the Constitution: Writings of the "Other" Federalists, 1787–1788.* Edited by Colleen A. Sheehan and Gary L. McDowell. Indianapolis, 1998.
Smith, *Republic of Letters*	Smith, James Morton, ed. *The Republic of Letters: Correspondence Between Thomas Jefferson and James Madison, 1776–1826.* 3 vols. New York, 1995.
Smith, *Wealth of Nations*	Smith, Adam. *An Inquiry into the Nature and Causes of the Wealth of Nations.* Edited by Edwin Cannan. New York, [1776] 1937.
Storing, *Anti-Federalist*	Storing, Herbert J., with Murray Dry, eds. *The Complete Anti-Federalist.* 7 vols. Chicago, 1981.

Story, *Commentaries*

Story, Joseph. *Commentaries on the Constitution of the United States.* 3 vols. Boston, 1833.

Tucker, *View of the Constitution*

Tucker, St. George. *View of the Constitution of the United States with Selected Writings.* Indianapolis, [1803] 1999.

Vattel, *Law of Nations*

Vattel, Emmerich de. *The Law of Nations or the Principles of Natural Law applied to the Conduct and to the Affairs of Nations and of Sovereigns.* Edited by Charles G. Fenwick. 3 vols. Washington, D.C., [1758] 1916.

Washington Writings

The Writings of George Washington from the Original Manuscript Sources, 1745–1799. Edited by John C. Fitzpatrick. 39 vols. Washington, D.C., 1931–44.

Wharton, *Diplomatic Correspondence*

Wharton, Francis, ed. *The Revolutionary Diplomatic Correspondence of the United States.* 6 vols. Washington, D.C., 1889.

Wheaton, *Elements*

Wheaton, Henry. *Elements of International Law.* Edited by George Grafton Wilson. Oxford, 1936.

Wilson Works

The Works of James Wilson. Edited by Robert Green McCloskey. 2 vols. Cambridge, Mass., 1967.

Wright, *Balance of Power*

Wright, Moorhead, ed. *Theory and Practice of the Balance of Power, 1486–1914.* Towata, N.J., 1975.

NOTES

PREFACE

1. "Official Letter Accompanying Act of Confederation," November 17, 1777, Elliot, *Debates,* 1: 69–70.

2. Arnold H. L. Heeren, *A Manual of the History of the Political System of Europe and Its Colonies from Its Formation at the Close of the Fifteenth Century to Its Re-establishment upon the Fall of Napoleon* (Freeport, N.Y., 1971 [1833]), vii.

3. Friedrich von Gentz, *Fragments upon the Balance of Power in Europe* (London, 1806), xiii, 61.

4. See Hedley Bull, "Society and Anarchy in International Relations," in *Diplomatic Investigations: Essays in the Theory of International Politics,* ed. Martin Wright and Herbert Butterfield (Cambridge, Mass., 1966).

CHAPTER 1

1. John Francis Mercer to James Madison, March 28, 1786, *Madison Papers,* 8: 511; Madison to Edmund Pendleton, February 24, 1787, ibid., 9: 294–95.

2. Josiah Tucker, *Cui Bono?* (London, 1781), cited in Potter, *Nationalism,* 23–24.

3. September 17, 1787, Lemay, *Franklin Writings,* 1140.

4. Fabius [John Dickinson], Letter 1, Sheehan, *Friends,* 58.

5. James Madison to Martin Van Buren, May 13, 1828, *Madison Letters,* 3: 634.

6. Speech of June 28, Farrand, *Records,* 1: 449.

7. November 26, 1787, Elliot, *Debates,* 2: 427.

8. As noted by Bruce D. Porter, *War and the Rise of the State: The Military Foundations of Modern Politics* (New York, 1994), 243, the authors of *The Federalist* "coined sundry names for the political system envisioned by the constitution—it was a federal government, a union, a national government, an administration, republic, federation, and federal republic—but not once did they refer to it as a state."

9. Speech of Fisher Ames, Massachusetts Ratifying Convention, Elliot, *Debates,* 2: 158–59. Federalists spoke, incongruously, of both the preservation and the creation of the nation. While some argued that the federal constitution was indispensable to the preservation of the nation, others said, like Wilson, that "we become a NATION" with the adoption of the federal constitution; "at present we are not one" (Bailyn, *Debate,* 1: 864).

10. Cooke, *Federalist,* No. 45.

11. Herbert J. Storing, "The 'Other' Federalist Papers: A Preliminary Sketch,"

Sheehan, *Friends,* xxvii. The "federal liberty" view, Storing remarks, "was very widespread among Federalist writers." See also Cooke, *Federalist,* No. 39: 257, where Madison says that the proposed Constitution "is in strictness neither a national nor a federal constitution; but a composition of both. In its foundation, it is federal, not national; in the sources from which the ordinary powers of Government are drawn, it is partly federal, and partly national; in the operation of these powers, it is national, not federal: In the extent of them again, it is federal, not national: And finally, in the authoritative mode of introducing amendments, it is neither wholly federal, nor wholly national."

12. James McHenry before the Maryland House of Delegates, Nov. 29, 1787, Farrand, *Records,* 3: 146.

13. Eliot, *Debates,* 3: 603.

14. Edmund Randolph, *Letter on the Federal Constitution,* October 16, 1787, Ford, *Pamphlets,* 269.

15. For Washington, see Charles Warren, *The Making of the Constitution* (Boston, 1937), 717, citing report in *Pennsylvania Journal* of November 14, 1787: "Should the States reject this excellent Constitution, the probability is that an opportunity will never again offer to cancel another in peace—the next will be drawn in blood." To similar effect, see Charles Cotesworth Pinckney, South Carolina Ratifying Convention, May 14, 1788, Bailyn, *Debate,* 2: 590–91; Farrand, *Records,* 1: 26 (Randolph): "Are we not on the eve of war, which is only prevented by the hopes from this convention?" For further elaboration and sources, see Peter S. Onuf, "Anarchy and the Crisis of the Union," in *To Form a More Perfect Union: The Critical Ideas of the Constitution,* ed. Herman Belz, Ronald Hoffman, and Peter J. Albert (Charlottesville, Va., 1992). A broader treatment of this anxiety, which survives the making of the Constitution, may be found in Paul C. Nagel, *One Nation Indivisible: The Union in American Thought, 1776–1861* (New York, 1964); Peter B. Knupfer, *The Union As It Is: Constitutional Unionism and Sectional Compromise, 1787–1861* (Chapel Hill, N.C., 1991); and Robert V. Bruce, "The Shadow of a Coming War," in *Lincoln, the War President,* ed. Gabor S. Boritt (New York, 1992), 1–28.

CHAPTER 2

1. James Barbour, *Eulogium upon the Life and Character of James Madison* (Washington, D.C., 1836), 16.

2. Cooke, *Federalist,* No. 14: 83.

3. Ibid., No. 8: 45, 49; ibid., No. 41: 272. For these themes in the convention, see Farrand, *Records,* 1: 464–65 (Madison).

4. Cooke, *Federalist,* No. 13: 80.

5. Ibid., No. 8: 50. See also Farrand, *Records,* 1: 168, 448–49 (Madison); 462 (Gorham).

6. Cooke, *Federalist,* No. 13: 81–82.

7. Ibid., No. 7: 38.

8. Ibid., No. 13: 80.

9. Ibid., No. 6: 28; ibid., No. 7: 43. See also Farrand, *Records,* 1: 466–67 (Hamilton).

10. The classic modern statement of "structural realism" is Kenneth N. Waltz, *Theory of International Politics* (New York, 1979). See also by Waltz, *Man, the State, and War: A Theoretical Analysis* (New York, 1959), and the discussion in the bibliographical essay.

11. *Notes on the State of Virginia,* Peterson, *Jefferson Writings,* Query XXII, 301.

12. This passage from Tocqueville is cited as the epigraph in Louis Hartz, *The Liberal Tradition in America* (New York, 1955).

13. John De Witt III, Storing, *Anti-Federalist,* 4: 25, 31; Agrippa IV [James Winthrop], December 4, 1787, Bailyn, *Debate,* 1: 449. See further Cecelia Kenyon, *The Antifederalists* (Boston, 1985), ixl–xlvii; Herbert J. Storing, *What the Anti-Federalists Were For* (Chicago, 1981).

14. Elliot, *Debates,* 3: 53.

15. Centinel XI, January 12, 1788, Storing, *Anti-Federalist,* 2: 186.

16. Elliot, *Debates,* 3: 277, 212, 209. See also the speeches of Melancton Smith and Thomas Tredwell in the New York ratifying convention, ibid., 2: 223–24, 396–97. On the pacific effects of commercial intercourse among the American states, see Agrippa VIII [James Winthrop of Massachusetts], December 25, 1787, Storing, *Anti-Federalist,* 4: 84.

17. For present-day theories of the liberal or democratic peace, see Michael Doyle, "Kant, Liberal Legacies, and Foreign Affairs," parts 1 and 2, *Philosophy and Public Affairs* 12 (1983): 205–35, 323–53; Doyle, "Liberalism and World Politics," *American Political Science Review* 80 (1986): 1151–69; Bruce Russett, with collaboration of William Antholis, Carol R. Ember, Melvin Ember, and Zeev Maoz, *Grasping the Democratic Peace: Principles for a Post-Cold War World* (Princeton, N.J., 1993), esp. 16–17; James Lee Ray, *Democracy and International Conflict: An Evaluation of the Democratic Peace Proposition* (Columbia, S.C., 1995); John M. Owen IV, *Liberal Peace, Liberal War: American Politics and International Security* (Ithaca, N.Y., 1997); and Michael E. Brown, Sean M. Lynn-Jones, and Steven E. Miller, *Debating the Democratic Peace: An International Security Reader* (Cambridge, 1996). For an earlier statement of the democratic peace hypothesis, see "Common Sense Addressed to the Inhabitants of America," February 14, 1776, *Paine Writings,* 32. See also by Paine, *Rights of Man, Being an Answer to Mr. Burke's Attack on the French Revolution,* 1791; and *Rights of Man, Part the Second, Combining Principle and Practice,* 1792, in *Paine Writings,* 538–40, 650–57.

18. "A Freeman III" [Tench Coxe], Sheehan, *Friends,* 98. See also Elliot, *Debates,* 2: 427 (Wilson).

19. Oliver Ellsworth in the Connecticut Convention, January 7, 1788, Farrand, *Records,* 3: 241.

20. "A Freeman I" [Tench Coxe], Sheehan, *Friends,* 91. "Had the foederal convention meant to exclude the idea of *"union,"* that is, of *several and separate* sovereignties joining in a confederacy, they would have said, we *the people of America.*" See also *Federalist,* No. 39.

21. Cooke, *Federalist,* No. 6: 31–32.

CHAPTER 3

1. The definition of a paradigm closely follows Samuel P. Huntington, *The Clash of Civilizations and the Remaking of World Order* (New York, 1996), 30. On the significance of the normative order, see Kai Alderson and Andrew Hurrell, eds., *Hedley Bull on International Society* (New York, 2000); and Robert Jackson, *The Global Covenant: Human Conduct in a World of States* (New York, 2000).

2. The historian who has most fully and brilliantly explicated the complex of thought I have identified with the unionist paradigm is Peter Onuf. See, in particular, Onuf, "Anarchy and the Crisis of the Union," in *To Form a More Perfect Union: The Critical Ideas of the Constitution*, ed. Herman Belz, Ronald Hoffman, and Peter J. Albert (Charlottesville, Va., 1992); idem, "Constitutional Politics: States, Sections, and the National Interest," in *Toward a More Perfect Union: Six Essays on the Constitution*, ed. Neil. L. York (Provo, Utah, 1988); idem, *Statehood and Union: A History of the Northwest Ordinance* (Bloomington, Ind., 1987); idem, "State Sovereignty and the Making of the Constitution," in *Conceptual Change and the Constitution*, ed. Terence Ball and J. G. A. Pocock (Lawrence, Kans., 1988), 78–98; idem, "The Expanding Union," in *Devising Liberty: Preserving and Creating Freedom in the New American Republic*, ed. David Thomas Konig (Stanford, Calif., 1995); idem (with Cathy D. Matson), *A Union of Interests: Political and Economic Thought in Revolutionary America* (Lawrence, Kans., 1990); and idem (with Nicholas Onuf), *Federal Union, Modern World: The Law of Nations in an Age of Revolutions, 1776–1814* (Madison, Wis., 1993). For further assessment of Onuf's contribution, see the bibliographical essay. For a lucid exposition of key elements in the unionist paradigm, see also James E. Lewis, *The American Union and the Problem of Neighborhood: The United States and the Collapse of the Spanish Empire, 1783–1829* (Chapel Hill, N.C., 1998). Lewis calls it "the logic of unionism."

3. Richard Falk, review of *The Domestic Analogy and World Order*, by Hidemi Suganami (Cambridge, 1989), *American Political Science Review* 84 (1990): 1460.

4. "The government of the Union," as Hamilton explained, "like that of each State, must be able to address itself immediately to the hopes and fears of individuals; and to attract to its support those passions which have the strongest influence upon the human heart. It must, in short, possess all the means, and have a right to resort to all the methods, of executing the powers with which it is intrusted, that are possessed and exercised by the governments of the particular States." Cooke, *Federalist*, No. 16: 102–3.

5. The greater penetration of Publius as compared with Kant is well shown in Daniel Deudney, "Publius Before Kant: Federal Republican Security vs. Democratic Peace," *European Journal of International Relations* (forthcoming). See also the discussion in appendix, figure 5. The founders' contributions to a science of international politics are further explored in idem, "The Philadelphian System: Sovereignty, Arms Control, and Balance of Power in the American States-Union, Circa 1787–1861," *International Organization* 49 (1995): 191–228; and idem, "Binding Sovereigns: Authorities, Structures, and Geopolitics in Philadelphian Systems," in *State Sovereignty as Social Construct*, ed. Thomas J. Biersteker and Cynthia Weber (Cambridge, 1996), 190–239. See also the neglected studies of Gottfried Dietze,

The Federalist: A Classic on Federalism and Free Government (Baltimore, 1960), pt. 2; and Gerald Stourzh, *Alexander Hamilton and the Idea of Republican Government* (Stanford, Calif., 1970).

6. James Madison to Daniel Webster, May 27, 1830, *Madison Letters*, 4: 85.

7. Rufus Choate, "A Discourse Commemorative of Daniel Webster," July 27, 1853, *Choate Works*, 1: 537. The literature on liberalism and republicanism is vast. On liberalism, see particularly Louis Hartz, *The Liberal Tradition in America* (New York, 1955). On republicanism, see Robert E. Shalhope, "Toward a Republican Synthesis: The Emergence of an Understanding of Republicanism in American Historiography," *William and Mary Quarterly* 29 (1972): 49–80; idem, "Republicanism and Early American Historiography," *William and Mary Quarterly* 39 (1982): 334–56; and the remarkable essay of Daniel T. Rodgers, "Republicanism: The Career of a Concept," *Journal of American History* 79 (1992): 11–38. The canonical works in the republican tradition are Bernard Bailyn, *Ideological Origins of the American Revolution* (Cambridge, Mass., 1967); Gordon Wood, *The Creation of the American Republic, 1776–1787* (Chapel Hill, N.C., 1969); and J. G. A. Pocock, *The Machiavellian Moment: Florentine Political Thought and the Atlantic Republican Tradition* (Princeton, N.J., 1975). Critics of the republican paradigm include Joyce Appleby, *Liberalism and Republicanism in the Historical Imagination* (Cambridge, Mass., 1992); and Isaac Kramnick, *Republicanism and Bourgeois Radicalism: Political Ideology in Late Eighteenth-Century England and America* (Ithaca, N.Y., 1990) The most effective synthesis of contending views may be found in Lance Banning, "Some Second Thoughts on Virtue and the Course of Revolutionary Thinking," in Ball and Pocock, *Conceptual Change*, 194–212; and idem, "The Republican Interpretation: Retrospect and Prospect," in *The Republican Synthesis Revisited: Essays in Honor of George Athan Billias*, ed. Milton M. Klein, Richard D. Brown, and John B. Hench (Worcester, Mass., 1992). Banning suggests that "Revolutionary thought—in 1787 as in 1776—is best conceived as an early modern *blend* of liberal and neoclassical ideas, that a coherent mixture of the two traditions was in fact its most distinctive feature" (108–9). He persuasively styles the founders as "liberal republicans." See also by Banning, *The Sacred Fire of Liberty: James Madison and the Founding of the Federal Republic* (Ithaca, N.Y., 1994), where he notes, "None of the republicans of revolutionary times envisioned anything except a representative, contractual, and limited regime" (84). For the founders' rejection of much of what passed for "the liberty of the ancients," see also Paul A. Rahe, *Republics Ancient and Modern: Classical Republicanism and the American Revolution* (Chapel Hill, N.C., 1992), and idem, "Antiquity Surpassed: The Repudiation of Classical Republicanism," in *Republicanism, Liberty, and Commercial Society, 1649–1776*, ed. David Wootton (Stanford, Calif., 1994), 233–69.

8. R. W. B. Lewis, *The American Adam: Innocence, Tragedy, and Tradition in the Nineteenth Century* (Chicago, 1955), 2. Intellectual historians have used a variety of terms to describe the object of their study: "ideologies," "paradigms," "clusters of ideas," "traditions of thought." Ideology was not particularly favored in the 1950s and 1960s because the term was associated with Marxism and because it also carried the connotation of ideas that were out of touch with reality; the historiographical mainstream, as Daniel Rodgers has suggested, "ran toward looser,

suppler, more figurative categories: currents of ideas, persuasions, myths, mind" (Rodgers, "Republicanism," 21). With the publication of Clifford Geertz's "Ideology as a Cultural System" in 1964 and of Bernard Bailyn's *The Ideological Origins of the American Revolution* in 1967, ideology made something of a comeback, though it was now dissevered from its Marxist connotations. *The Structure of Scientific Revolutions* by Thomas Kuhn had meanwhile introduced another concept—the "paradigm"—the usage of which spread rapidly among intellectual historians, while also undergoing a shift in meaning. Among the more fruitful adaptations of this usage was that of J. G. A. Pocock and associated historians (the "Cambridge school"), who gave renewed attention to the historical context within which canonical works in the Western tradition got produced, and who drew attention to other distinctive traditions that had not been registered in the prevailing Hartzian consensus. These historians spoke of "paradigmatic structures" and "language systems" as they reconceptualized the activity of historians of political thought. I differ in usage from some others in emphasizing, like Lewis, the need to embrace the *argument* over key ideas, albeit within an ideological framework that displays both consensus and conflict. Hence it seems to me more revealing to situate Federalist and Anti-Federalist thought within a single "unionist paradigm" rather than to separate them out into two opposing ones—a strategy in keeping with Gordon Wood's observation that Federalists and Anti-Federalists need to be considered as "co-Founders." In effect, Banning's argument, summarized in the previous note, follows the same strategy in its explication of liberal-republicanism.

9. [WilliamVans Murray], *Political Sketches . . .* (London, 1787); and discussion in Alexander DeConde, "William Vans Murray's *Political Sketches:* A Defense of the American Experiment," *Mississippi Valley Historical Review* 41 (1955): 623–40, esp. 638.

10. Minutes of the Board of Visitors, March 4, 1825, Peterson, *Jefferson Writings,* 479.

11. Cooke, *Federalist,* No. 22.

12. Ibid., No. 45: 314; ibid., No. 40: 262.

13. Speech of John Jay, Elliot, *Debates,* 2: 283.

14. On the "Whig or constitutional tradition in diplomacy," see Martin Wight, "Western Values in International Relations," in *Diplomatic Investigations: Essays in the Theory of International Politics,* ed. Martin Wight and Herbert Butterfield (Cambridge, Mass., 1966). In lectures delivered in the 1950s, but not published until 1992, Wight identified a realist, a rationalist, and a revolutionist approach to international relations. Martin Wight, *International Theory: The Three Traditions* (New York, 1992); a similar framework was developed by Hedley Bull, *The Anarchical Society: A Study of Order in World Politics* (New York, 1977). As Bull comments, the choice of rationalist to describe "the broad middle tradition" was unfortunate ("Martin Wight and the Theory of International Relations," Wight, *International Theory,* xiv). The importance that experience, "settled practice," and customary law played in elaborations of the law of nations, even in the heyday of natural law theory, makes "rationalism" an inapt terminology. The inadequacies of rationalism as a descriptive term for the international society tradition are also apparent from Terry Nardin, *Law and Morality in the Relations of States* (Princeton, N.J., 1983), though Nardin's insistence on excluding instrumental reasoning and

cooperative endeavor from the classic conception of international society appears unduly restrictive. Bull's substitute terms—the Grotian or internationalist tradition—are useful labels that will be employed in this work, but they need to be understood as closely related to what Wight called "the Whig or constitutional tradition in diplomacy." That tradition was distinguished by its consciousness of law, "its explicit connection with the political philosophy of constitutional government," by its search for the "*juste milieu* between definable extremes," and by its "disciplined skepticism." Wight, "Western Values," 90–91.

There is no general agreement among scholars on how best to classify the various schools of thought on international relations, though scholarly interest in the subject has certainly quickened. See Michael W. Doyle, *Ways of War and Peace: Realism, Liberalism, and Socialism* (New York, 1997), where Wight's framework is criticized; Terry Nardin and David Mapel, eds., *Traditions of International Ethics* (Cambridge, 1992); Richard Tuck, *The Rights of War and Peace: Political Thought and the International Order from Grotius to Kant* (Oxford, 1999); Thomas L. Pangle and Peter J. Ahrensdorf, *Justice Among Nations: On the Moral Basis of Power and Peace* (Lawrence, Kans., 1999); and the works cited in chapter 4, note 3. Wight's framework is ably defended and elaborated in Robert Jackson and Georg Sørensen, *Introduction to International Relations* (New York, 1999). This work is an excellent primer on theoretical approaches to international relations and offers a succinct and lucid depiction of the "English school" or "international society" approach, with which I closely identify on both methodological and conceptual grounds. Of the major treatises in international relations of the last half century, Raymond Aron's *Peace and War* (New York, 1967) comes closest to a Grotian or internationalist framework. Despite certain Kantian proclivities, Stanley Hoffmann's work is also describable in these terms. See Hoffmann, *Janus and Minerva: Essays in the Theory and Practice of International Politics* (Boulder, Colo., 1987); and idem, *World Disorders: Troubled Peace in the Post–Cold War Era* (Lanham, Md., 1998), esp. chaps. 2 and 4. Hans J. Morgenthau, *Politics Among Nations* (New York, [1948] 1967), is a self-described realist, but there are internationalist elements in Morgenthau's thought that most interpreters, intent on debunking a primitive version of realism, have ignored. Internationalist characteristics are even more pronounced in the thought of George Kennan and Reinhold Niebuhr. Robert Jackson, *The Global Covenant,* is an outstanding recent statement in the Grotian or international society approach. See further Tim Dunne, *Inventing International Society: A History of the English School* (New York, 1998); and Ian Clark and Iver B. Neumann, *Classical Theories of International Relations* (New York, 1996).

15. John Adams to Abigail Adams, March 17, 1797, cited in Stanley Elkins and Eric McKitrick, *The Age of Federalism* (New York, 1993), 549.

16. Edmund Randolph, Draft Sketch of Constitution, July 26, 1787, Hutson, *Supplement,* 183.

17. Locke, *Two Treatises,* 2nd Treatise, 12: para. 146: 365; Nicholas Greenwood Onuf, *The Republican Legacy in International Thought* (Cambridge, 1998), 233; J. G. A. Pocock, "States, Republics, and Empires: The American Founding in Early Modern Perspective," in Ball and Pocock, *Conceptual Change,* 55–77; Frederick Gentz, *On the State of Europe Before and After the French Revolution; Being an Answer to L'Etat de la France à la Fin de l' An 8* (London, 1802); Martin Diamond,

"What the Framers Meant by Federalism," in _A Nation of States: Essays on the American Federal System,_ ed. Robert A. Goldwin (Chicago, 1961), 27–30.

18. "Smith's Thoughts on the State of the Contest with America, February 1778," in _The Correspondence of Adam Smith,_ ed. Ernest Campbell Mossner (Oxford, 1987), 377–85. See also Edmund Burke, _Thoughts on French Affairs,_ December 1791, in _Further Reflections on the Revolution in France,_ ed. Daniel E. Ritchie (Indianapolis, 1992), 205. Speaking of the treatment of France by the other powers of Europe, Burke remarked that "monarchy was considered in all the external relations of that kingdom . . . as it's legal and constitutional Government, and that in which alone it's federal capacity was vested."

19. S. Rufus Davis, _The Federal Principle: A Journey Through Time in Quest of a Meaning_ (Berkeley, 1978), 38, 3, 215–16. See also Daniel J. Elazar, _Exploring Federalism_ (University, Ala., 1987).

CHAPTER 4

1. "John Witherspoon's Speech in Congress," July 30, 1776, _Letters of Delegates,_ 4: 586–87.

2. James Wilson's Summation and Final Rebuttal, December 11, 1787, Bailyn, _Debate,_ 1: 832–68, at 866; Franklin to Ferdinand Grand, October 22, 1787, _Franklin Writings,_ 9: 619. For other contemporaneous references to the plan of Henry IV, see Ezra Stiles, _The United States Elevated to Glory and Honour_ (Worcester, Mass., [1783] 1785), 31; and "Aristides" [Alexander Contee Hanson], _Remarks on the Proposed Plan_ (Annapolis, Md., 1788), Ford, _Pamphlets,_ 248. Explorations of federal union as an alternative to and remedy for the evils of the European system include Richard Price, _Two Tracts_ (1778), _Price Political Writings,_ 24–25; idem, _Observations on the Importance of the American Revolution_ (1785), _Price Political Writings,_ 143–44; and Thomas Paine, _Rights of Man_ (Part One), _Paine Writings,_ 540. For an incisive analysis of these and other thinkers, including Joel Barlow and Allan Bowie Magruder, see Peter S. Onuf and Nicholas G. Onuf, _Federal Union, Modern World: The Law of Nations in an Age of Revolutions, 1776–1814_ (Madison, Wis., 1993); and the discussion in Gerald Stourzh, _Benjamin Franklin and American Foreign Policy_ (Chicago, 1954), 222–24. For the consideration of this theme in 1787, see Peter S. Onuf, _Origins of the Federal Republic: Jurisdictional Controversies in the United States, 1775–1787_ (Philadelphia, 1983), 203–5. For Madison's later musings on this point, see Ralph Ketchum, _James Madison: A Biography_ (Charlottesville, Va., 1990), 632, 735 n. 21. Found interleaved in the third filling of Madison's notes of the federal convention was the reflection, evidently prepared during his retirement, that "were it possible by human contrivance so to accelerate the intercourse between every part of the globe that all its inhabitants could be united under the superintending authority of an ecumenical Council, how great a portion of human evils would be avoided. Wars, famines, with pestilence as far as the fruit of either, could not exist; taxes to pay for wars, or to provide against them, would be needless, and the expense and perplexities of local fetters on interchange beneficial to all would no longer oppress the social state."

3. See, e.g., M. S. Anderson, _The Rise of Modern Diplomacy, 1450–1919_ (Lon-

don, 1993), esp. chaps. 4 and 5; F. H. Hinsley, *Power and the Pursuit of Peace: Theory and Practice in the History of Relations Between States* (Cambridge, 1967); James Turner Johnson, *The Quest for Peace: Three Moral Traditions in Western Cultural History* (Princeton, N.J., 1987); Michael Doyle, *Ways of War and Peace: Realism, Liberalism, and Socialism* (New York, 1997); Hidemi Suganami, *The Domestic Analogy and World Order Proposals* (Cambridge, 1989); Walter Schiffer, *The Legal Community of Mankind: A Critical Analysis of the Modern Concept of World Organization* (New York, 1954) (but cf. 107–8); Sylvester John Hamleben, *Plans for World Peace Through Six Centuries* (Chicago, 1938); F. Melian Stawell, *The Growth of International Thought* (London, 1929); Elizabeth V. Souleyman, *The Vision of World Peace in Seventeenth- and Eighteenth-Century France* (New York, 1941) (but cf. 176); Carl Joachim Friedrich, *Inevitable Peace* (Cambridge, Mass., 1948). There is brief mention of but no development of the theme in the classic study of Warren Kuehl, *Seeking World Order: The United States and International Organization to 1920* (Nashville, Tenn., 1969). For a brief antidote to this Eurocentric myopia, see Peter S. Onuf and Nicholas G. Onuf, "American Constitutionalism and the Emergence of a Liberal World Order," in *American Constitutionalism Abroad: Selected Essays in Comparative Constitutional History*, ed. George Athan Billias (New York, 1990), 65–89.

4. For the nationalist interpretation of the Declaration of Independence, see Richard Morris, *The Forging of the Union, 1781–1789* (New York, 1987), 55–63; Joseph Story, *Commentaries on the Constitution of the United States* (New York, [1833] 1970); Samuel H. Beer, *To Make a Nation: The Rediscovery of American Federalism* (Cambridge, Mass., 1993), 200–202; idem, "Federalism, Nationalism, and Democracy in America," *American Political Science Review* 72 (1978): 9–21; Curtis P. Nettels, "The Origin of the Union and of the States," *Proceedings of the Massachusetts Historical Society* 72 (1957–60): 68–83; and Jack N. Rakove, *The Beginnings of National Politics: An Interpretive History of the Continental Congress* (Baltimore, [1979] 1982). Rakove's presentation is more moderate than those of other historians, but he nevertheless finds the nationalist case to be essentially accurate (see Rakove, *Beginnings,* 173–74 n). Jack P. Greene calls this view "the new orthodoxy" in "The Problematic Character of the American Union: The Background of the Articles of Confederation," in *Understanding the American Revolution: Issues and Actors* (Charlottesville, Va., 1995), 128–63.

5. Gordon Wood, *The Creation of the American Republic, 1776–1787* (New York, [1969] 1972), 475, 465–67; and idem, "Interests and Disinterestedness in the Making of the Constitution," in *Beyond Confederation: Origins of the Constitution and American National Identity,* ed. Richard Beeman, Stephen Botein, and Edward C. Carter II (Chapel Hill, N.C., 1987), 72. For endorsement of Wood's view, see, e.g., Stanley Elkins and Eric McKitrick, *The Age of Federalism* (New York, 1993), 702; and Joyce Appleby, "The American Heritage—The Heirs and the Disinherited," in *Liberalism and Republicanism in the Historical Imagination* (Cambridge, Mass., 1992), 210–31.

6. See especially Merrill Jensen, *The New Nation: A History of the United States During the Confederation, 1781–1789* (Boston, [1950] 1981); and the discussion in the bibliographical essay. Renewed appreciation of the significance of the section, however, is notable in D. W. Meinig, *Atlantic America, 1492–1800* (vol. 1 in

his series *The Shaping of America: A Geographical Perspective on 500 Years of History*) (New Haven, Conn., 1986, 3 vols. to date); David Hackett Fischer, *Albion's Seed: Four British Pathways in America* (New York, 1989); and Kevin Phillips, *The Cousins' Wars: Religion, Politics, and the Triumph of Anglo-America* (New York, 1999).

7. For signs that this common assumption of twentieth-century historiography is changing, see the discussion and sources in the bibliographical essay and the excellent discussion in Joseph J. Ellis, *Founding Brothers: The Revolutionary Generation* (New York, 2000). See also the questioning of this framework in Gordon Wood, "Ideology and the Origins of Liberal America," *William and Mary Quarterly* 44 (1987): 633. On the nineteenth-century perspective, see Richard C. Vitzthum, *The American Compromise: Theme and Method in the Histories of Bancroft, Parkman, and Adams* (Norman, Okla., 1974). George Bancroft, Francis Parkman, and Henry Adams, as Vitzthum observes, interpreted "American history as an intensely dramatic journey along a narrow path of moderation between abysses of excess yawning on either side. Though they establish many polarities in their works, the one they all see as fundamental consists of anarchy, or complete diffusion and decentralization, at one extreme and tyranny—complete subordination and centralization—at the other. Between anarchy and tyranny, they argue, America has charted and must continue to chart a wary middle course. . . . The works of all three hum with the conviction that America drifted, almost unconsciously, into nationality: the pressures that forced it to unify are often shown as being external rather than internal, providing barely enough momentum, usually in the nick of time, to nudge it out of danger" (7–8). For an assessment of centripetal and centrifugal forces during the era of revolution and constitution-making, see Jack P. Greene, *Peripheries and Center: Constitutional Development in the Extended Polities of the British Empire and the United States, 1607–1788* (Athens, Ga., 1986).

8. The phrase is from Edmund Morgan's famous essay on the causes of the American Revolution, "Revisions in Need of Revising" (1950), reprinted in *The Challenge of the American Revolution* (New York, 1976).

9. John Adams's Notes of Debates, September 6, 1774, *Letters of Delegates,* 1: 28.

10. John Adams to Hezekiah Niles, February 13, 1818, *Adams Works,* 10: 283. For other expressions identifying each state with a sentiment of nationality, see Allan Nevins, *The American States During and After the Revolution, 1775–1789* (New York, 1927), 544–605; Thomas Burke to Richard Caswell, March 11, 1777, *Letters of Delegates,* 6: 427–29; Speech to Jean Baptiste Ducoigne, [ca. 1] June 1781, *Jefferson Papers,* 6: 61; Koch, *Writings of Adams,* 81.

11. Fisher Ames to George Richards Minot, February 16, 1792, *Ames Works,* 2: 912; New York Ratifying Convention, Remarks, June 27, 1788, *Hamilton Papers,* 5: 102; and Hamilton to George Washington, March 24, 1783, where Hamilton observes that "the centrifugal is much stronger than the centripetal force in these states—the seeds of disunion much more numerous than those of union" (ibid., 3: 304). See also Gerald Stourzh, *Alexander Hamilton and the Idea of Republican Government* (Stanford, Calif., 1970); Raoul Berger, *Federalism: The Founders' Design* (Norman, Okla., 1987), 55–56; and the perceptive essay of John Murrin, "A

Roof Without Walls: The Dilemma of American National Identity," in Beeman, *Beyond Confederation,* 344. I agree with Murrin that American national identity was "an unexpected, impromptu, artificial, and therefore extremely fragile creation of the Revolution." For a critique of Murrin, see Peter S. Onuf, "Federalism, Republicanism, and the Origins of American Sectionalism," in Edward L. Ayers, Patricia Nelson Limerick, Stephen Nissenbaum, and Peter S. Onuf, *All Over the Map: Rethinking American Regions* (Baltimore, 1996), 11–37; and also by Onuf, *Jefferson's Empire: The Language of American Nationhood* (Charlottesville, Va., 2000). While emphasizing that "Jefferson's republican empire could only be said to exist, much less to grow and prosper, if Americans constituted a single nation," Onuf also stresses the Jeffersonian understanding that there was a world of difference "between an extended polity held in place by consolidated, coercive power and a consensual union of free republican states in a regime of reciprocal benefits and perpetual peace. This notion of a republican imperium enlisted the modernizing discourses of Enlightenment political economy, social theory, and jurisprudence to envision a post-monarchical future in which power would be domesticated, diffused, and decentered." Other works in the rich literature on American nationalism that deal in some depth with the early period include Liah Greenfeld, *Nationalism: Five Roads to Modernity* (Cambridge, Mass., 1992), pt. 5; David Waldstreicher, *In the Midst of Perpetual Fetes: The Making of American Nationalism, 1776–1820* (Chapel Hill, N.C., 1997); Paul C. Nagel, *One Nation Indivisible: The Union in American Thought, 1776–1861* (New York, 1964); idem, *This Sacred Trust: American Nationality, 1798–1898* (New York, 1971); Merle Curti, *The Roots of American Loyalty* (New York, 1946); and Yehoshua Arieli, *Individualism and Nationalism in American Ideology* (Cambridge, Mass., 1964). The most accessible introduction remains Hans Kohn, *American Nationalism: An Interpretive Essay* (New York, 1957).

12. See M. J. C. Vile, *Constitutionalism and the Separation of Powers,* 2d ed. (Indianapolis, [1967] 1998); Paul A. Rahe, *Republics Ancient and Modern: Classical Republicanism and the American Revolution* (Chapel Hill, N.C., 1992), 582, 598–99. "In most of our American constitutions," as Noah Webster observed, "we have all the advantages of checks and balance, without the danger which may arise from a superior and independent order of men." "A Citizen of America," *An Examination into the Leading Principles of the Federal Constitution,* October 17, 1787, Sheehan, *Friends,* 378.

CHAPTER 5

1. Gordon Wood, *The Creation of the American Republic, 1776–1787* (New York, [1969] 1972), 7.

2. Hutson, *Supplement* (Lansing Notes), 112. "When," Wilson said, "he considered the amazing extent of country—the immense population which is to fill it, the influence which the Government we are to form will have, not only on the present generation of our people & their multiplied posterity, but on the whole Globe, he was lost in the magnitude of the object." Farrand, *Records,* 1: 405 (Madison Notes, June 25).

3. Quoted in Arthur M. Schlesinger Jr., *The Cycles of American History* (New York, 1986).

4. John Adams to Secretary Livingston, February 5, 1783, *Adams Works,* 8: 38.

5. George Bancroft, *Memorial Address on the Life and Character of Abraham Lincoln* (Washington, D.C., 1866), 4–5. The spirit that Bancroft evoked in 1866 entered broadly into American speculation and had earlier been given a fine expression by James Russell Lowell. "Let us not tolerate in our criticism," Lowell said, "a principle which would operate as a prohibitory tariff of ideas. . . . It detracts nothing from Chaucer that we can trace in him the influence of Dante and Boccaccio; . . . nothing from Milton that he brought fire from Hebrew and Greek altars. There is no degradation in such indebtedness. Venerable rather is this apostolic succession, and inspiring to see *vitae lampada* passed thus consecrated from hand to hand." Cited in Hans Kohn, *American Nationalism: An Interpretive Essay* (New York, 1957), 71. John Adams wrote in this spirit when he justified his examination of the history of Florence in his *Defence of the Constitution of Government of the United States of America* (1787): "[W]e shall not . . . find it tedious to consider minutely" the affairs of a people whose history is "full of lessons of wisdom, extremely to our purpose." *Adams Works,* 5: 9. The classic study, though focused on the period leading up to the Revolution, is H. Trevor Colbourn, *The Lamp of Experience: Whig History and the Intellectual Origins of the American Revolution* (Chapel Hill, N.C., 1965). For intellectual influences more generally, see Bernard Bailyn, *The Ideological Origins of the American Revolution* (Cambridge, Mass., 1967); Donald S. Lutz, "The Relative Influence of European Writers on Late Eighteenth-Century American Political Thought," *American Political Science Review* 78 (1984): 189–97; and Peter S. Onuf, ed., *The New American Nation, 1775–1820,* Vol. 1, *The Revolution in American Thought* (New York, 1991).

6. G. Huehns, ed., *Clarendon: Selections from* The History of the Rebellion . . . (London, 1955), 81. On "ordered liberty," see further Michael Kammen, *Spheres of Liberty: Changing Perceptions of Liberty in American Culture* (Ithaca, N.Y., 1986).

CHAPTER 6

1. See D. W. Meinig, *Atlantic America, 1492–1800* (New Haven, Conn., 1986), 435; Douglas Adair, "'Experience Must Be Our Only Guide': History, Democratic Theory, and the United States Constitution," and "A Note on Certain of Hamilton's Pseudonyms," in *Fame and the Founding Fathers,* ed. Trevor Colbourn (Indianapolis, [1974] 1998), 152–75, 385–405; Richard M. Gummere, "The Classical Ancestry of the United States Constitution," *American Quarterly* 14 (1962): 3–18. The most authoritative study is Carl J. Richard, *The Founders and the Classics: Greece, Rome, and the American Enlightenment* (Cambridge, Mass., 1994).

2. Cooke, *Federalist,* No. 9: 50.

3. Herodotus, *The Histories,* ed. Aubrey de Selincourt (New York, 1996), 375, 423.

4. Madison to Jefferson, March 18, 1786, *Madison Papers,* 8: 503; Cooke, *Federalist,* No. 9: 52–53. See also the numerous examples discussed in Richard, *Founders and the Classics,* 85–122.

5. Speech of Richard Henry Lee, in Congress, June 8, 1776, Niles, *Principles,* 397.

6. Alexander Hamilton, Continentalist No. 1, July 12, 1781, *Hamilton Papers,* 1: 651–52. See also Hamilton to James Duane, September 3, 1780: Of "the leagues among the old Grecian republics," he wrote that "[t]hey were continually at war with each other, and for want of union fell a prey to their neighbours. They frequently held general councils, but their resolutions were no further observed than as they suited the interests and inclinations of all the parties and at length, they sunk intirely into contempt." *Hamilton Papers,* 2: 403. Jefferson later recorded the movement toward the Philadelphia convention in the following terms: "The alliance between the states under the old articles of confederation, for the purpose of joint defence against the aggression of Great Britain, was found insufficient, as treaties of alliance generally are, to enforce compliance with their mutual stipulations: and these, once fulfilled, that bond was to expire of itself, & each state to become sovereign and independant in all things. Yet it could not but occur to every one that these separate independencies, like the petty States of Greece, would be eternally at war with each other, & would become at length the mere partisans & satellites of the leading powers of Europe. All then must have looked forward to some further bond of union, which would ensure internal peace, and a political system of our own, independant of that of Europe." "The Anas. 1791–1806," February 4, 1818, Peterson, *Jefferson Writings,* 663. See also John Dickinson, *The Letters of Fabius,* Ford, *Pamphlets,* 166–67, 191–94, 201–2, 215; Charles Pinckney's Speech to the New Jersey Assembly, [March 13, 1786], *Letters of Delegates,* 23: 192–93; Thomas Dawes Jr., Oration Delivered at Boston, March 5, 1781, Niles, *Principles,* 67–72, at 69; and "Notes on Ancient and Modern Confederacies," April–June, 1786," *Madison Papers,* 9: 6–7. The founders, in the later summary of Rufus Choate, discerned "perfectly that unless the doom of man was to be reversed for them, there was no alternative but to become dearest friends or bitterest enemies,—so much Thucydides and the historians of the beautiful and miserable Italian republics of the Middle Age had taught them" ("On Nationality").

7. John Witherspoon's Speech in Congress, *Letters of Delegates,* 4: 585. See also *The Farmer Refuted, &c.,* [February 23,] 1775, *Hamilton Papers,* 1: 100 n, in which Hamilton cites Hume's "That Politics May Be Reduced to a Science": "though free governments have been commonly the most happy, for those who partake of their freedom, yet are they the most ruinous and oppressive to *their provinces.*" See discussion in Karl-Friedrich Walling, *Republican Empire: Alexander Hamilton on War and Free Government* (Lawrence, Kans., 1999).

8. Brutus I, October 18, 1787, *DHRC,* 13: 417; Centinel III, *DHRC,* 14: 58. Brutus and other writers are cited in M. N. S. Sellers, *American Republicanism: Roman Ideology in the United States Constitution* (New York, 1994), 156.

9. *Annals of Congress,* 16th Cong., 1st sess., Sen., February 1, 1820.

CHAPTER 7

1. Cooke, *Federalist,* No. 41: 270–71.

2. The continuing salience of these two themes is well brought out in Michael J. Hogan, *A Cross of Iron: Harry S. Truman and the Origins of the National Security State, 1945–1954* (Cambridge, 1998), esp. chap. 1.

3. For a modern account showing how medieval constitutionalism (as reflected in parliaments, local autonomy, the rule of law, and personal freedoms) was subverted by the "military revolution," see Brian M. Downing, *The Military Revolution and Political Change: Origins of Democracy and Autocracy in Early Modern Europe* (Princeton, N.J., 1992).

4. Robertson, *History of Charles V,* 1: 100–104.

5. Ibid., 1: 116–21. See also 1: 458, 3: 264–65; and Smith, *Wealth of Nations,* 199.

6. See Anthony Pagden, *Lords of All the World: Ideologies of Empire in Spain, Britain and France c. 1500–1800* (New Haven, Conn., 1995).

7. Vattel, *Law of Nations,* 249–51. This permissive view was not shared by Hugo Grotius or Christian Wolff, as noted by Alfred Vagts and Detlev F. Vagts, "The Balance of Power in International Law: A History of an Idea," *American Journal of International Law* 73 (1979): 555–80, at 560–62.

8. Wright, *Balance of Power,* 41.

9. Edward Gibbon, *The History of the Decline and Fall of the Roman Empire,* 7 vols., ed. J. B. Bury (London, 1930), 1: 111.

10. Hume, *Essays,* 333; Montesquieu, *Spirit of the Laws,* bk. 9, chap. 7, 136.

11. Quoted in George F. Kennan, *Memoirs: 1925–1950* (Boston, 1967), 130.

12. Hume, *Essays,* 341. Writing in the aftermath of the Napoleonic Wars, Benjamin Constant made a very similar observation. Constant distinguished between the spirit of conquest in ancient and modern times. In the latter, he stressed, the conqueror insisted upon uniformity: "[I]t pursues the vanquished into the most intimate aspects of their existence. It mutilates them in order to reduce them to uniform proportions. In the past conquerors expected the deputies of conquered nations to appear on their knees before them. Today it is man's morale that they wish to prostrate." Like Montesquieu and Hume before him, however, Constant insisted that this "obsession with uniformity"—what the twentieth century would call "totalitarianism"—would recoil upon the conquerors: "[O]nly the excess of despotism can in fact prolong a combination that tends to dissolve itself and retain under the same domination states that everything conspires to separate. The prompt establishment of limitless power, says Montesquieu, is the only remedy that can prevent dissolution in these cases: yet another evil, he adds, on top of that of the state's aggrandizement. Even this remedy, though worse than the evil itself, is of no lasting efficacy. The natural order of things takes revenge on the outrages that men attempt against it, and the more violent the suppression, the more terrible will be the reaction to it." *The Spirit of Conquest and Usurpation and Their Relation to European Civilization,* in *Benjamin Constant: Political Writings,* ed. Biancamaria Fontana (Cambridge, 1988), 78. Constant had Napoleon in mind when he wrote this passage; but the passage might also form an instructive epitaph on the disintegration of the Soviet Union, where the zeal for centralization and uniformity recoiled upon its authors, producing dismemberment.

13. *Abstract and Judgement of Saint-Pierre's Project for Perpetual Peace* [1756], Rousseau, *International Relations,* 62–64.

14. See Edward Vose Gulick, *Europe's Classical Balance of Power* (New York, [1955] 1967), for the identification of the balance of power with public law; and Peter Onuf and Nicholas Onuf, *Federal Union, Modern World: The Law of Na-*

tions in an Age of Revolutions, 1776–1814 (Madison, Wis., 1993), for its status as a progressive principle.

15. Montesquieu, *Spirit of the Laws,* bk. 13, chap. 17, 224.

16. Rousseau, *International Relations,* 65.

17. Cooke, *Federalist,* No. 8: 45.

18. Alexander Pope, *The Balance of Europe* (1715), cited in H. L. Mencken, ed., *A New Dictionary of Quotations on Historical Principles from Ancient and Modern Sources* (New York, 1989), 952.

19. Farrand, *Records,* 1: 448.

20. *Annual Register* for 1760, 2–3, cited in Herbert Butterfield, "The Balance of Power," in *Diplomatic Investigations: Essays in the Theory of International Politics,* ed. Herbert Butterfield and Martin Wight (Cambridge, Mass., 1966), 132–148, at 144.

21. Jean-Jacques Rousseau, Abstract, in Wright, *Balance of Power,* 75.

CHAPTER 8

1. John Adams to John Quincy Adams, July 27, 1777, *Letters of Delegates,* 7: 384–86.

2. John Adams to Abigail Adams, July 21, 1777, ibid., 7: 356–57.

3. John Dickinson's Speech, July 22, 1779, ibid., 13: 279. See also An American [Gouverneur Morris] to George Johnstone, March 4, 1779, ibid., 12: 149, for another tribute to a Dutch leader. Instancing the "unalterable resolution" of "the GREAT NASSAU . . . *to die in the last ditch,*" Morris said that "in the mouth of a hero contending for freedom after the loss of many battles, against superior force and almost exhaustless resources, it hath a dignity and elevation which description cannot reach." He was ridiculing its invocation by Johnstone in the latter's November 27, 1778, speech to Parliament explaining the failure of the Carlisle Peace Commission.

4. December 28, 1774, ibid., 1: 275–76. For Madison, see Cooke, *Federalist,* No. 18. On the Dutch experience, see Geoffrey Parker, *The Dutch Revolt* (Ithaca, N.Y., 1977); Jonathan Israel, *The Dutch Republic: Its Rise, Greatness, and Fall: 1477–1806* (Oxford, 1995); Herbert H. Rowen, "The Dutch Republic and the Idea of Freedom," in *Republicanism, Liberty, and Commercial Society, 1649–1776,* ed. David Wootton (Stanford, Calif., 1994); Jonathan R. Dull, "Two Republics in a Hostile World: The United States and the Netherlands in the 1780s," and Don Higginbotham, "The American Republic in a Wider World," both in *American Revolution: Its Character and Limits,* ed. Jack P. Greene (New York, 1987), 149–170. A sour but pertinent survey, emphasizing American ignorance and misreading of Dutch history and institutions, may be found in William H. Riker, "Dutch and American Federalism," *Journal of the History of Ideas* 18 (1957): 495–521. On Adams's judgment of the abortive Dutch Revolution of 1787—which strongly sympathized with the democratic desire to rein in the powers of the House of Orange—see Edward Handler, *America and Europe in the Political Thought of John Adams* (Cambridge, 1964), 108–16. The Prussian intervention of 1787 suppressing this democratic movement caused Adams to

"tremble and agonize for the suffering Patriots in Holland," and reinforced the equation drawn in America between the related dangers of internal division and foreign domination. See also Farrand, *Debates,* 1: 89 (Butler arguing that Dutch experience showed folly of a "plurality of military heads"); 1: 103 (Franklin praising "the original" government of the United Netherlands but deploring its advance toward monarchy over time and denouncing the present stadtholder's willingness to "wade thro' a bloody civil war to the establishment of a monarchy").

5. Koch, *Writings of Adams,* 81.

6. *Adams Works,* 5: 37; 4: 579. In his *Thoughts on Government . . .* (1776), Adams had said that "the very definition of a republic is 'an empire of laws, and not of men'" and that "that form of government which is best contrived to secure an impartial and exact execution of the laws, is the best of republics." *Adams Works,* 4: 194. See also Lance Banning, *Sacred Fire of Liberty: James Madison and the Founding of the Federal Republic* (Ithaca, N.Y., 1995); Paul Rahe, *Republics, Ancient and Modern* (Chapel Hill, N.C., 1994); and the provocative discussion in Scott Gordon, *Controlling the State: Constitutionalism from Ancient Athens to Today* (Cambridge, Mass., 1999).

7. Adams, *Defence of the Constitutions,* in *Adams Works,* 5: 179.

8. Francesco Guicciardini, *The History of Italy,* ed. Sidney Alexander (Princeton, N.J., 1984), 4, 7, 32, 48–49. For the same view of the humiliations and disgraces entailed by foreign submission, see the final chapter of Niccolò Machiavelli, *The Prince,* ed. Robert M. Adams (New York, 1977), chap. 26. Events had left Italy "more enslaved than the Hebrews, more abject than the Persians, more widely dispersed than the Athenians; headless, orderless, beaten, stripped, scarred, overrun, and plagued by every sort of disaster." Almost lifeless, it awaited the leader "who will heal her wounds, stop the ravaging of Lombardy, end the looting of the Kingdom and of Tuscany, and minister to those sores of hers that have been festering so long" (*The Prince,* 73). Cf. Hamilton's similar depiction of the American situation in Cooke, *Federalist,* No. 15.

9. John Hale, *The Civilization of Europe in the Renaissance* (New York, 1994), 132–33.

10. Quentin Skinner, *The Foundations of Modern Political Thought,* Vol. 1, *The Renaissance* (Cambridge, 1978), 113; Guicciardini, *History of Italy,* 86. On the character of the Italian system, see also the lucid study of Felix Gilbert, *Machiavelli and Guicciardini: Politics and History in Sixteenth-Century Florence* (Princeton, N.J., 1965); Cecilia M. Ady, "The Invasions of Italy," *The New Cambridge Modern History,* Vol. 1, *The Renaissance, 1493–1520,* ed. G. R. Potter and Denys Hay (Cambridge, 1957), 343–67; and the classic volume of Garrett Mattingly, *Renaissance Diplomacy* (Boston, 1971). Mattingly calls the forty-year period after the Peace of Lodi the "Concert of Italy."

11. See Cooke, *Federalist,* Nos. 18–20; and "Notes on Ancient and Modern Confederacies," April–June 1786, *Madison Papers,* 9: 3–24. The "tendency of fœderal bodies, rather to anarchy among the members, than to tyranny in the head," was Madison's primary lesson from his examination of these confederacies (Cooke, *Federalist,* No. 18: 117). The result had fallen little short of *bellum omnium contra omnia:* "The history of Germany is a history of wars between the Emperor and the Princes and States; of wars among the Princes and States themselves; of the licen-

ciousness of the strong, and the oppression of the weak; of requisitions of men and money, disregarded, or partially complied with; of attempts to enforce them, altogether abortive, or attended with slaughter and desolation, involving the innocent with the guilty; of general imbecility, confusion, and misery." Cooke, *Federalist,* No. 19: 119–20. For discussion to similar effect in the federal convention, see Farrand, *Records,* 1: 285–86 (Hamilton); ibid., 530 (Morris); ibid., 3: 115 (Pinckney).

Madison's study of the ancient and modern confederacies was the fullest examination of the "monitory" lessons they held for America. Adams had called for such a study in his *Defence* but did not himself actually pursue the subject in that work. It would be a "useful work," he noted, "to collect together the ancient and modern leagues,—the Amphictyonic, the Olynthian, the Argive, the Arcadian, and the Achæan confederacies, among the Greeks; the general diet of the Swiss cantons, and the states-general of the United Netherlands; the union of the Hanse-towns, &c" for the purpose of determining whether additional powers ought to be given to the American congress (*Adams Works,* 4: 580–81). But it was a generally recognized deficiency of *The Defence* that it gave almost no attention to that subject but instead lavished its attention on the internal constitutions of the ancient and modern republics and how they compared with the constitutions of the American states. Adams prided himself on the idea that the first volume of *The Defence,* which landed in Philadelphia coincident with the opening of the federal convention, had exerted a salutary and important influence on those deliberations; but Adams's insistence that the separated powers of a government reflect the different "orders" of the society was generally rejected, and his inattention to the federal problem in that work made it otherwise irrelevant to the proceedings. Adams soon emerged as a strong supporter of the federal constitution, but that was not apparent from the first volume of *The Defence.* His son John Quincy told one correspondent that his father "does not say" that a plan of government embracing the "three orders" would be "practicable, for the whole continent. He does not even canvass the subject, but from what he says, I think it may easily be inferred that he would think such a government fatal to our liberties." To William Cranch, December 8, 1787, *DHRC,* 14: 227.

Madison's researches into past confederacies bore the ripest fruit. His inability to satisfy his curiosity regarding "the process, the principles, the reasons, & the anticipations, which prevailed in the formation of . . . the most distinguished Confederacies, particularly those of antiquity," made him determined to preserve "an exact account of what might pass in the Convention." "A Sketch Never Finished Nor Applied," ca. 1830, *Madison Writings,* 840.

12. *Adams Works,* 4: 287–88.

13. See the discussion in Frederick W. Marks III, *Independence on Trial: Foreign Affairs and the Making of the Constitution,* 2d ed. (Wilmington, Del., 1986), 103–5, 130; Peter S. Onuf, *Origins of the Federal Republic: Jurisdictional Controversies in the United States, 1775–1787* (Philadelphia, 1983), 37, 174–78, 182–85; Max Mintz, *Gouverneur Morris and the American Revolution* (Norman, Okla., 1970), 157, 184, 186; Louise B. Dunbar, *A Study of "Monarchical" Tendencies in the United States, from 1776 to 1801* (Urbana, Ill., 1922).

14. Rufus King to Jonathan Jackson, September 3, 1786, *Letters of Delegates,* 23: 543. King mentions a range of examples in which clashes among "small, and

unequal, Sovereignties" terminated with the establishment of monarchy. Though reprobating that remedy, he thought this experience showed that without proper remedies "the causes which changed the Governments alluded to may, and probably will, change those of America." See further Peter S. Onuf and Cathy D. Matson, *A Union of Interests: Political and Economic Thought in Revolutionary America* (Lawrence, Kans., 1990), 86–90.

15. J. G. A. Pocock, *The Machiavellian Moment: Florentine Political Thought and the Atlantic Republican Tradition* (Princeton, N.J., 1975), viii; John Adams to John Jay, May 8, 1787, Giunta, *The Emerging Nation*, 3: 494.

16. Pocock, *Machiavellian Moment*, viii, went on to define the moment as one in which the republic attempted "to remain morally and politically stable in a stream of irrational events conceived as essentially destructive of all systems of secular stability." Pocock demonstrated in this work that "the English speaking political tradition has been a bearer of republican and Machiavellian, as well as constitutionalist, Lockean, and Burkean, concepts and values." Though I am much indebted to this book and to Pocock's larger corpus, two reservations may be entered with regard to his treatment of the republican theme in American history. Though rightly emphasizing the passage from republic to empire as a central aspect of America's Machiavellian moment, he paid little attention to the sequence of ideas that lay at the heart of the unionist paradigm—that which traced the movement from foreign intervention and intestine division to war and despotism. This specter, we shall be arguing, was the alpha and omega of American thought, and if it may accurately be characterized as "republican and Machiavellian," as Skinner's account of the Italian wars strongly suggests, it plays little role in Pocock's treatment of the passage of the republican paradigm through time. It seems to me, in the second place, that the use of the term "Machiavellian moment" must be seen as raising the question whether unethical or unlawful means are necessary for the preservation of the republic; to be in that moment is to confront the prospect that the survival or stability of the commonwealth may require a compromise with evil. For an exploration of the Machiavellian tradition emphasizing this dilemma, see the great work of Friedrich Meinecke, *Machiavellism: The Doctrine of Raison d'Etat and Its Place in Modern History*, trans. Douglas Scott (New Haven, Conn., 1957). See also chapter 26. There is a judicious appraisal of Machiavelli's outlook in Quentin Skinner, *The Foundations of Modern Political Thought*, 2 vols. (New York, 1978), 1: 128–38; and an engaging sketch of his sphere of influence, if such an expression may be used, in Albert O. Hirschman, *The Passions and the Interests: Political Arguments for Capitalism Before Its Triumph* (Princeton, N.J., 1977). In Pocock's most recent work, *Barbarism and Religion* (Cambridge, 2000), he sees the eighteenth-century version of the Machiavellian moment as signifying "the need Enlightenment was under to show itself superior to the ancient virtue of the Romans, which it recognized as its principal moral and philosophical challenger the more it moved away from the values of ecclesiastical Christianity" (2: 376). For Gibbon (as, indeed, for many Americans), this particularly entailed commitment to "a civilization of commerce rather than slavery or feudalism, of polite manners rather than warrior virtue or religious faith, of trade and treaties between a system of states rather than a universal empire or an anarchy of contending theocracies" (2: 371). See further the bibliographical essay, note 24.

17. "Crotona," *Adams Works,* 4: 559.

18. See Adams Diary, September 1, 1774 (characterizing the "Machiavelian dissimulation" of the court party in Massachusetts), *Adams Works,* 2: 362.

19. That the last refuge of Machiavellism was the denunciation of Machiavelli is well shown in the career of Frederick of Prussia. See particularly the text and commentary in Frederick of Prussia, *The Refutation of Machiavelli's Prince or ANTI-MACHIAVEL,* ed. Paul Sonnino (Athens, Ohio, [1740] 1981).

20. Jefferson to Madison, August 28, 1789, Smith, *Republic of Letters,* 1: 629.

21. Wheaton, *Elements,* xv.

22. Jefferson to John B. Colvin, September 20, 1810, Peterson, *Jefferson Writings,* 1231. Machiavelli taught that when the safety of one's country was in question, "no considerations of justice or injustice, humanity or cruelty, nor of glory or of shame, should be allowed to prevail." Niccolò Machiavelli, *Discourses on the First Ten Books of Titus Livius,* bk. 3, Max Lerner, ed., *The Prince and the Discourses* (New York, 1940), 528. Bolingbroke would write in a similar vein. Though Bolingbroke castigated Machiavelli for urging the appearance, rather than reality, of virtue in the prince, he accepted that "there is a law in behalf of the public, more sacred and more ancient too, for it is as ancient as political society." Dictated by "nature and reason," it declared "the preservation of the commonwealth to be superior to all other laws." *Present State of the Nation, Bolingbroke Works,* 2: 458. For Bolingbroke's estimate of "Machiavel," see *Idea of a Patriot King,* ibid., 2: 389–90. In his discussion of Burke, David Armitage, "Edmund Burke and Reason of State," *Journal of the History of Ideas* 61 (2000): 617–34, distinguishes between a Grotian or Ciceronian and a Machiavellian understanding of reason of state, necessity, and expediency, a distinction also relevant in understanding the outlook of those on this side of the water. See also the earlier discussion of Carl Joachim Friedrich, *Constitutional Reason of State* (Providence, R.I., 1957).

23. Montesquieu, *Spirit of the Laws,* 3, 7; Alexander Hamilton, The Defense No. 20, October 23 and 24, 1795, *Hamilton Papers,* 19: 341, with accompanying citations. Henry is cited in Wheaton, *Elements.* The founders' debt to Vattel is well developed in Daniel G. Lang, *Foreign Policy in the New Republic: The Law of Nations and the Balance of Power* (Baton Rouge, La., 1985). As Karl-Friedrich Walling shrewdly observes in *Republican Empire: Alexander Hamilton on War and Free Government* (Lawrence, Kans., 1999): "[T]he essential yet paradoxical truth is that Hamilton was much more like Machiavelli than commonly believed and was at the same time fundamentally opposed to a kind of politics that we usually call Machiavellian" (15). See also James Wilson, "Of the Law of Nations," in *Selected Political Essays of James Wilson,* ed. Randolph G. Adams (New York, 1930), 302–3. "It is of the highest, and, in free states, it is of the most general importance, that the sacred obligation of the law of nations should be accurately known and deeply felt." On the status of the law of nations in the American constitutional order, see Chief Justice Marshall's holding in *The Nereide* (9 Cranch 388, 423 [1815]), that if congress desired to ignore or violate the tenets of international law, it must expressly do so by legislation, and "till such an act be passed the Court is bound by the law of nations, which is part of the law of the land." Quoted in Benjamin Munn Zeigler, *The International Law of John Marshall* (Chapel Hill, N.C., 1939), 5.

24. For valuable explorations of the conflict between Grotius and Machiavelli, see Martin Wight, *International Theory: The Three Traditions* (New York, 1992); Hedley Bull, *The Anarchical Society: A Study of Order in World Politics* (New York, 1977); Hedley Bull, Benedict Kingsbury, and Adam Roberts, *Hugo Grotius and International Relations* (Oxford, 1990); Gerald Stourzh, *Alexander Hamilton and the Idea of Republican Government* (Stanford, Calif., 1970); and Meinecke, *Machiavellism*. See also figure 5 in the appendix.

CHAPTER 9

1. J. G. A. Pocock, *The Politics of Extent and the Problems of Freedom* (Colorado Springs, Colo., 1988), 8. See further Eliga H. Gould, *The Persistence of Empire: British Political Culture in the Age of the American Revolution* (Chapel Hill, N.C., 2000); and David Armitage, *The Ideological Origins of the British Empire* (Cambridge, 2000).

2. For examinations of the eighteenth-century debate over foreign policy, see Richard Pares, "American Versus Continental Warfare, 1739–1763," *English Historical Review* 51 (1936): 429–65; Felix Gilbert, *To the Farewell Address: Ideas of Early American Foreign Policy* (Princeton, N.J., 1961); Paul Langford, *Modern British Foreign Policy: The Eighteenth Century* (New York, 1976); Jeremy Black, *America or Europe? British Foreign Policy, 1739–63* (London, 1998); Robert W. Tucker and David C. Hendrickson, *Fall of the First British Empire* (Baltimore, 1982), 29–37; Gould, *Persistence of Empire*; and Armitage, *Ideological Origins of the British Empire*.

3. Charles Jenkinson, First Earl of Liverpool, ed., *A Collection of Treaties Between Great Britain and Other Powers* (London, 1785; reprint, New York, 1969), 66–67. This passage occurs in the treaty of peace and friendship between Britain and Spain but not in the treaty concluded between Britain and France.

4. Henry St. John, Viscount Bolingbroke, *The Idea of a Patriot King, Bolingbroke Works*, 2: 416–18.

5. Vattel, *Law of Nations*, 1: bk. 3, chap. 3, § 50: 253.

6. *A Review of the State of the English Nation* (1706), excerpted in Wright, *Balance of Power*, 48.

7. For the same comparison, see Simeon Baldwin's Oration at New Haven, Conn., July 4, 1788, Bailyn, *Debate*, 2: 522: "The checks and balances of different orders, have the same effect in the regularity of government, as the political balance of power in the peace and happiness of nations." In his fight against the peerage bill, Walpole had argued that too much independence in the branches of the government would create "a state of war, instead of a civil state." Quoted in M. J. C. Vile, *Constitutionalism and the Separation of Powers* (Oxford, 1967), 73. See also the insightful essay of M. S. Anderson, "Eighteenth-Century Theories of the Balance of Power," in *Studies in Diplomatic History: Essays in Memory of David Bayne Horn*, ed. Ragnhild Hatton and M. S. Anderson (London, 1970), 183–98, who cites this and other illustrations but remarks that the term "balance of power" was seldom, if at all, used to describe the mixed or balanced constitution of England after 1720. This seems unlikely to me. A keen student of the British constitution, John Adams, wrote in such terms in 1776. "A Legislative, an Executive, and a judicial Power, comprehend the whole of what is

meant and understood by Government. It is by balancing each of these Powers against the other two, that the Effort in humane Nature towards Tyranny, can alone be checked and restrained and any degree of Freedom preserved in the Constitution." John Adams to Richard Henry Lee, November 15, 1775, *Adams Papers,* 3: 307.

8. "The Occasional Writer. Number II," *Bolingbroke Works,* 1: 215, 222; *Some Reflections on the Present State of the Nation, Principally with Regard to her Taxes and her Debts . . .* , ibid., 2: 442–43, 460; "A Plan for a General History of Europe. Letter I," ibid., 2: 337.

9. Jefferson to Thomas Gates, May 30, 1797, *Jefferson Writings,* 7: 130.

10. "On the Study and Use of History," *Bolingbroke Works,* 2: 312–13. The comparison with the "military-industrial complex" is suggested by J. G. A. Pocock, *The Machiavellian Moment: Florentine Political Thought and the Atlantic Republican Tradition* (Princeton, N.J., 1975), 543. See also Isaac Kramnick, *Bolingbroke and His Circle: The Politics of Nostalgia in the Age of Walpole* (Ithaca, N.Y., 1968); Lance Banning, *The Jeffersonian Persuasion: Evolution of a Party Ideology* (Ithaca, N.Y., 1978); and Stanley Elkins and Eric McKitrick, *The Age of Federalism* (New York, 1993).

11. "The Occasional Writer. Number II," *Bolingbroke Works,* 1: 221.

12. Cited in Pares, "American Versus Continental Warfare," 436.

13. Bolingbroke, *Idea of a Patriot King, Bolingbroke Works,* 2: 418.

14. *Some Reflections on the Present State of the Nation, Bolingbroke Works,* 2: 452.

15. Israel Mauduit, *Considerations on the Present German War* (London, 1760), 7, 47.

16. David Hume, "Of the Balance of Power," Hume, *Essays,* 332–41. See also "Of Public Credit," ibid., and J. G. A. Pocock, "Hume and the American Revolution: The Dying Thoughts of a North Briton," in *Virtue, Commerce, and History* (Cambridge, 1985), 125–41.

17. Smith, *Wealth of Nations,* 863, 878, 872; Henry St. John, Viscount, Lord Bolingbroke, *Some Reflections on the Present State of the Nation . . . , Bolingbroke Works,* 2: 439–61; Richard Price, *Observations on the Importance of the American Revolution* (1785), *Price Political Writings,* 149. On the financial revolution more generally, see P. G. M. Dickson, *The Financial Revolution in England: A Study of the Development of Public Credit, 1688–1756* (London, 1967); and John Brewer, *The Sinews of Power: War, Money, and the English State, 1688–1783* (New York, 1990).

Paul Kennedy, *The Rise and Fall of the Great Powers* (New York, 1987), examines the eighteenth-century financial revolution in detail. Strangely, however, his accent is on the enormous resources this gave to the British, and not to the enormous encumbrances, à la Hume and Smith, that it laid upon them. The fact is strange because Kennedy's critique of the contemporary American empire and its decline is predicated on a theory of "imperial overstretch" that is very close to that which Hume and Smith articulated in the eighteenth century.

18. "Universal Peace," *Madison Writings,* 6: 88–91.

19. Adams to James McHenry, July 29, 1799, *Adams Works,* 9: 4–5; and discussion in Jacob E. Cooke, "Country Above Party: John Adams and the 1799 Mission to France," in *Fame and the Founding Fathers,* ed. Edmund P. Willis (Bethlehem, Pa., 1967), 53–77.

20. For Adams's praise of Bolingbroke, see Adams to Edmé Jacques Genet, April 29, 1780, *Adams Papers*, 9: 249–50. Jefferson is cited in Merrill Peterson, *Thomas Jefferson and the New Nation: A Biography* (New York, 1970), 314. For discussions of Bolingbroke's influence, though from a variety of perspectives, see Bernard Bailyn, *The Ideological Origins of the American Revolution* (Cambridge, 1967); Joseph J. Ellis, *The Passionate Sage: The Character and Legacy of John Adams* (New York, 1993); James H. Hutson, *John Adams and the Diplomacy of the American Revolution* (Lexington, Ky., 1980); Ralph Ketchum, *Presidents Above Party: The First American Presidency: 1789–1829* (Chapel Hill, N.C., 1984).

21. "Farewell Address," September 19, 1796, *Washington Writings*, 35: 233–35. The classic essay investigating the influence of eighteenth-century British writings on the development of an American attitude toward the external world is Felix Gilbert, *To the Farewell Address: Ideas of Early American Foreign Policy* (Princeton, N.J., 1961).

22. Rufus Choate, "A Discourse Commemorative of Daniel Webster," July 27, 1853, *Choate Works*, 1: 537.

CHAPTER 10

1. See Franklin's claim to this effect in "Examination Before the Committee of the Whole of the House of Commons," *Franklin Papers*, 13: 150–51.

2. On the "experience and outcome" of the Great War for the Empire, see Jack P. Greene, "The Seven Years' War and the American Revolution: The Causal Relationship Reconsidered," in *The British Atlantic Empire Before the American Revolution*, ed. Peter Marshall and Glyn Williams (London, 1980); on the "sacred moral order," see also by Greene, "An Uneasy Connection: An Analysis of the Preconditions of the American Revolution," in *Essays on the American Revolution*, ed. Steven G. Kurtz and James H. Hutson (Chapel Hill, N.C., 1973). See also the essay of Lawrence Henry Gipson, "The American Revolution as an Aftermath of the Great War for the Empire," *Political Science Quarterly* 65 (1950): 86–104, for the classic analysis of this relationship, as well as for the justification in employing this term in preference to the Seven Years' War or the French and Indian War.

3. *Tract II. The Case of Going to War . . .* (1763), Schuyler, *Josiah Tucker*, 291. In this tract, Tucker showed, with proofs from ancient and modern history, that "of all Absurdities, that of going to War for the Sake of getting Trade is the most absurd" (295). For the broader recognition of this point among Tucker, Hume, Smith, and Turgot, see Anthony Pagden, *Lords of All the World: Ideologies of Empire in Spain, Britain, and France c. 1500–c. 1800* (New Haven, Conn., 1995), 109–10, 191–94; for Hume, see J. G. A. Pocock, "Hume and the American Revolution: The Dying Thoughts of a North Briton," in *Virtue, Commerce, and History* (Cambridge, 1985), 125–41.

CHAPTER 11

1. *Considerations on the Nature and Extent of the Legislative Authority of the British Parliament*, *Wilson Works*, 2: 721.

2. *Novanglus* No. VII, *Adams Papers,* 2: 314, 320. The theory of the imperial constitution to which Americans were committed in 1774 was later well summarized by James Madison: "The fundamental principle of the Revolution was, that the colonies were co-ordinate members with each other and with Great Britain, of an empire united by a common executive sovereign, but not united by a common legislative sovereign. The legislative power was maintained to be as complete in each American Parliament, as in the British Parliament. And the royal prerogative was in force in each colony by the virtue of its acknowledging the King for its executive magistrate, as it was in Great Britain by virtue of a like acknowledgment there. A denial of these principles by Great Britain, and the assertion of them by America, produced the Revolution." *Madison Writings,* 6: 373.

3. Notes of Proceedings, June 8, 1776, *Jefferson Papers,* 1: 311.

4. See the discussion in J. G. A. Pocock, "States, Republics, and Empires: The American Founding in Early Modern Perspective," in *Conceptual Change and the Constitution,* ed. Terence Ball and J. G. A. Pocock (Lawrence, Kans., 1988).

5. Richard Bland, *An Enquiry into the Rights of the British Colonies* (1766), quoted in Ian R. Christie and Benjamin W. Labaree, *Empire or Independence: A British-American Dialogue on the Coming of the American Revolution* (New York, 1976), 88.

6. Franklin to Galloway, January 9, 1769, *Franklin Papers,* 16: 17.

7. *JCC,* 1: 89.

8. Thomas Whately, *The Regulations Lately Made with Respect to the Colonies Considered* (London, 1765), 109–13.

9. For a classic statement of this theme, see Charles Andrews, *The Colonial Period of American History* (New Haven, Conn., 1938), 4: 410 ff. On regional differentiation more generally, see Jack P. Greene, *Imperatives, Behaviors, and Identities: Essays in Early American Cultural History* (Charlottesville, Va., 1992); D. W. Meinig, *Atlantic America, 1792–1800* (New Haven, Conn., 1986); David Hackett Fischer, *Albion's Seed: Four British Folkways in America* (New York, 1989); and Richard Hofstadter, *America at 1750: A Social Portrait* (New York, 1971).

10. The Declaration of the Stamp Act Congress, October 19, 1765, *American Colonial Documents,* 672–73.

11. On the Whig-Tory distinction, see Lewis B. Namier, *England in the Age of the American Revolution,* 2d ed. (New York, 1961); J. G. A. Pocock, "The Varieties of Whiggism from Exclusion to Reform," in *Virtue, Commerce, and History* (Cambridge, 1985), 215–310; and H. T. Dickinson, *Liberty and Property: Political Ideologies in Eighteenth-Century Britain* (London, 1977). Grenville and Bedford were of the great Whig families but were Tories in the new political context of the 1760s.

12. Burke defined a party as "a body of men united, for promoting by their joint endeavours the national interest, upon some particular principle in which they are all agreed."

13. Gipson, *British Empire,* 7: 12.

14. John Adams to Dr. J. Morse, December 22, 1815, *Adams Works,* 10: 3.

CHAPTER 12

1. Smith, *Wealth of Nations,* 591.

2. "On the instructions given to the first delegation of Virginia to Congress," August 1774, *Jefferson Writings,* 1: 190–91. On Virginia's peculiar geography and political economy, see the incisive treatment in D. W. Meinig, *Atlantic America, 1492–1800* (New Haven, Conn., 1986).

3. For Jefferson's classic depiction of the web of dependency, see *Jefferson Papers,* 10: 27.

4. Smith, *Wealth of Nations,* 571.

5. Ramsay, *History,* 1: 74–75.

6. North cited in "Letters of William Samuel Johnson to the Governors of Connecticut [1766–71]," Trumball Papers, *Massachusetts Historical Society Collections,* 5th ser., 9 (1855): 337.

7. Benjamin Franklin, Reasons and Motives for the Albany Plan of Union, *Franklin Papers,* 5: 399.

8. Speech on American Taxation, Burke, *American Revolution,* 68. On the Grenville program, see John L. Bullion, *A Great and Necessary Measure: George Grenville and the Genesis of the Stamp Act: 1763–1765* (Columbia, Mo., 1982); and P. D. G. Thomas, *British Politics and the Stamp Act Crisis* (Oxford, 1975). On the American reaction to the British army, see John Shy, *Toward Lexington: The Role of the British Army in the Coming of the American Revolution* (Princeton, N.J., 1965).

9. "The free men of America," as James Madison characterized the colonial position in his Memorial and Remonstrance Against Religious Assessments, "did not wait till usurped power had strengthened itself by exercise and entangled the question in precedents. They saw all the consequences in the principle, and they avoided the consequences by denying the principle." June 20, 1785, *Madison Papers,* 8: 300.

10. The Declarations of the Stamp Act Congress, October 19, 1765, *American Colonial Documents,* 672.

11. Robert M. Calhoon, "William Smith Jr.'s Alternative to the American Revolution," *William and Mary Quarterly* 22 (1965): 113.

12. See Charles McIlwain, *The American Revolution: A Constitutional Interpretation* (New York, 1923), 169–70: "The whole theory of virtual representation was as empty in law as it was unjust in policy. Of all the arguments urged in England against the American claims it was the least weighty," and this primarily because of its "fatal confusion of under-representation and non-representation." On the role of the colonial agents, see Jack M. Sosin, *Agents and Merchants: British Colonial Policy and the Origins of the American Revolution, 1763–1775* (Lincoln, Nebr., 1965); and Michael G. Kammen, *A Rope of Sand: The Colonial Agents, British Politics, and the American Revolution* (Ithaca, N.Y., 1968).

13. Both Benjamin Franklin and James Otis argued at various times the desirability of a colonial representation in Parliament, but they also attached onerous conditions to it. See the discussion in Randolph G. Adams, *Political Ideas of the American Revolution: Britannic-American Contributions to the Problem of Imperial Organization, 1765 to 1775,* 3d ed., with commentary by Merrill Jensen (New York, 1958), 56.

14. Smith, *Wealth of Nations,* 587–88. James H. Hutson, *John Adams and the Diplomacy of the American Revolution* (Lexington, Ky., 1980), 6–7, shows that such prophecies were widely propounded in the colonies as well.

CHAPTER 13

1. The Albany Plan of Union is reprinted, together with valuable editorial commentary, in *Franklin Papers,* 5: 374–92. A good account of the congress and its aftermath may be found in Gipson, *British Empire,* 5: 113–66. See also Fred Anderson, *Crucible of War: The Seven Years' War and the Fate of Empire in British North America, 1754–1766* (New York, 2000), 77–85; and Robert C. Newbold, *The Albany Congress and the Plan of Union of 1754* (New York, 1955). The most important precedents for the Albany Plan are reprinted in Frederick D. Stone, ed., "Plans for the Union of the British Colonies of North America, 1643–1776," in *History of the Celebration of the One Hundredth Anniversary . . . of the Constitution . . . ,* ed. Hampton L. Carson, 2 vols. (Philadelphia, 1889), 2: 439–503; and Albert B. Hart and Edward Channing, "Plans of Union, 1696–1780," *American History Leaflets,* no. 14 (1894). See also Jack P. Greene, "Martin Bladen's Blueprint for a Colonial Union," *William and Mary Quarterly,* 3d ser., 17 (1960): 516–30; and Charles M. Andrews, *The Colonial Period of American History* (New Haven, Conn., 1938), 4: 408–19.

2. Lawrence C. Wroth, "The Indian Treaty as Literature," *Yale Review* 17 (1928): 749–66, at 752; Gipson, *British Empire,* 5: 64–112.

3. Reasons and Motives for the Albany Plan of Union, *Franklin Papers,* 5: 400–402; Franklin to William Shirley, December 4, 1754, ibid., 5: 443–47. For the evolution of Franklin's thinking on intercolonial union, see Gerald Stourzh, *Benjamin Franklin and American Foreign Policy* (Chicago, 1954), 48–82.

4. Secretary Willard to William Bollan, December 31, 1754, Gipson, *British Empire,* 5: 155, 157; William Shirley to Secretary of State Robinson, December 24, 1754, ibid., 160–61; Speaker of House of Commons (September 9, 1754) cited in Alison Gilbert Olson, "The British Government and Colonial Union, 1754," *William and Mary Quarterly* 17 (1960): 22–34, at 31. See also George Louis Beer, *British Colonial Policy, 1754–1765* (New York, 1907); and Max Savelle, *Seeds of Liberty: The Genesis of the American Mind* (Seattle, 1965), 333. As Savelle suggests, the Albany Plan "ran counter to the deepest trend in the thought and practice of the assemblies' struggle, the trend toward complete, particularistic, provincial autonomy for each separate colony, with the greatest possible degree of freedom from interference, either by the mother country, the other colonies, or a combination of them." Cf. Franklin's similar analysis in his pamphlet *The Interest of Great Britain Considered* 1760 (1760), *Franklin Papers,* 9: 90.

5. Joseph Galloway's Proposed Resolution & Plan of Union, September 28, 1774, *Letters of Delegates,* 1: 112, 117, 118, and editorial note at 112–17. Galloway on authorship in *Pennsylvania Gazette,* April 26, 1775; John Dickinson and Charles Thomson, *Pennsylvania Journal,* March 8, 1775; Galloway to Thomas McKean, March 7, 1793, all in Julian P. Boyd, *Anglo-American Union: Joseph Galloway's Plans to Preserve the British Empire 1774–1788* (Philadelphia, 1941), 37.

See also Robert M. Calhoon, "'I Have Deduced Your Rights': Joseph Galloway's Concept of His Role, 1774–1775," *Pennsylvania History* 35 (1968): 372–73. In John Adams's Notes of Debates he cites Galloway thusly: "Burlamaqui, Grotius, Pufendorf, Hooker.—There must be an Union of Wills and Strength. Distinction between a State and a Multitude. A State is animated by one Soul." *Adams Diary*, 2: 142.

6. Dickinson and Thomson characterizing sentiment in congress, March 8, 1775, *Letters of Delegates*, 1: 116; *Novanglus* III, February 6, 1775; *Adams Papers*, 2: 250–51; Gipson, *British Empire*, 12: 166.

7. Dartmouth to Colden, January 7, 1775, Gipson, *British Empire*, 12: 250; Benjamin Franklin to Joseph Galloway, February 25, 1775, Morison, *Sources*, 137.

8. Gipson says this depiction of the congress was "doubtless" furnished by William Smith, attorney general of New York; *British Empire*, 5: 138–39; Benjamin Franklin, Remark, February 9, 1789, *Franklin Papers*, 5: 417.

9. "Equal force" is from Thomas Pownall, cited in G. H. Guttridge, "Thomas Pownall's *The Administration of the Colonies*: The Six Editions," *William and Mary Quarterly*, 3d ser., 26 (1969): 31–46. On the evolution of Pownall's thinking, see further Pownall, *Administration*, 9–46; and John W. Shy, "Thomas Pownall, Henry Ellis, and the Spectrum of Possibilities, 1763–1775," in *A People Numerous and Armed* (Oxford, 1976). In 1742, James Logan of Pennsylvania pointed to the dilemma later espied by Pownall and "saw the very multiplicity of colonial governments as a product of Britain's 'Natural Policy to keep the several Colonies under distinct and independant Commands, the more effectually to Secure them from a Revolt from the Crown.'" In 1755, Mitchell explained the failure of Parliament to unite the colonies in an effective union as the result of a long-standing policy of *divide et impera* intended to obviate "the danger, in a united state, of their throwing off dependence and setting up for themselves." *State of the British and French Colonies* (London, 1755), 57–58. For this and other examples, see J. M. Bumsted, "'Things in the Womb of Time': Ideas of American Independence, 1633–1763," *William and Mary Quarterly* 31 (1974): 533–64, at 542, 550–51.

CHAPTER 14

1. Speech on Conciliation [1], March 22, 1775, Burke, *American Revolution*, 88–89.

2. Speech on American Taxation, April 19, 1774, ibid., 66.

3. April 19, 1774, ibid., 65.

4. Speech on Conciliation [1], March 22, 1775, ibid., 95–95. Burke's reference is to Milton, *Paradise Lost*, bk. II, l. 592. Despite my wishes, the "Serbonian bog betwixt Damiata and Mount Cassius old" was in Lake Serbonis in ancient Egypt; the reader, however, will indulge the author's fancy in locating this bog in the neighborhood of Bosnia and Kosovo.

5. Speech on American Taxation, Burke, *American Revolution*, 67.

6. Andrew C. McLaughlin, "The Background of American Federalism," *American Political Science Review* 12 (1918): 215–17; Bernard Bailyn, *The Ideological Origins of the American Revolution* (Cambridge, 1967), 223–24. The positions ad-

vanced by McLaughlin and Bailyn are among the more moderate statements of this point of view.

7. "All questions concerning sovereign rights," as Burke had commented on the margins of Pownall's *Administration of the Colonies,* "end at last in this—Who is to be the Judge?" Cited in G. H. Guttridge, "Thomas Pownall's *The Administration of the Colonies:* The Six Editions," *William and Mary Quarterly* 26 (1969): 43.

8. *Letters of a Farmer in Pennsylvania,* No. 6, *Dickinson Writings,* 349. Emphasizing change rather than continuity in the colonial position is the classic essay of Carl L. Becker, *The Declaration of Independence: A Study in the History of Political Ideas* (New York, 1942).

CHAPTER 15

1. On the imperial school, largely identified with Herbert Osgood, George Louis Beer, Charles Andrews, and Lawrence Henry Gipson, see Jack P. Greene, ed., *The Reinterpretation of the American Revolution, 1763–1789* (New York, 1968); Lawrence Henry Gipson "The Imperial Approach to Early American History," in *The Reinterpretation of Early American History: Essays in Honor of John Edwin Pomfret,* ed. Ray Allen Billington (New York, 1968); Richard B. Morris, "The Spacious Empire of Lawrence Henry Gipson," in *Perspectives on Early American History: Essays in Honor of Richard B. Morris,* ed. Alden T. Vaughan and George Athan Billias (New York, 1973); and the discussion in Bernard Bailyn, "The Central Themes of the American Revolution: An Interpretation," in *Essays on the American Revolution,* ed. Stephen G. Kurtz and James H. Hutson (Chapel Hill, N.C., 1973). Of these four historians, Andrews's views were distinctly whig in attributing the Revolution to a change in British policy. See Charles Andrews, *The Colonial Background of the American Revolution* (New Haven, Conn., 1924). The persistence of a morally charged framework in assessing British policy is well illustrated in T. H. Breen, "Ideology and Nationalism on the Eve of the American Revolution: Revisions Once More in Need of Revising," *Journal of American History* 84 (1997): 13–39. Recent entries in the imperial tradition include Thomas Barrow, *Trade and Empire: The British Customs Service in Colonial America, 1660–1775* (Cambridge, Mass., 1967); Robert W. Tucker and David C. Hendrickson, *Fall of the First British Empire* (Baltimore, 1982); and Theodore Draper, *A Struggle for Power: The American Revolution* (New York, 1996).

2. Speech on Conciliation [1], March 22, 1775, Burke, *American Revolution,* 81–82.

3. Pitt (1766), *Parliamentary History,* 16: 107.

4. Cf. Edmund Morgan, *The Challenge of the American Revolution* (New York, 1976), 55–56: "All the objectives of the Americans before 1776 could have been attained within the empire and would have cost the mother country little or nothing."

5. On Hutchinson, see the prizewinning portrait in Bernard Bailyn, *The Ordeal of Thomas Hutchinson* (Cambridge, Mass., 1974). On the "swollen claims and shrunken powers" of the royal governors, see Bailyn's *The Origin of American Politics* (New York, 1967).

6. Josiah Tucker, *True Interest of Great-Britain,* Schuyler, *Josiah Tucker,* 355–57. See also the discussions of Tucker in J. G. A. Pocock, "Josiah Tucker on Burke, Locke, and Price: A Study in the Varieties of Eighteenth-Century Conservatism," in *Virtue, Commerce, and History* (Cambridge, 1985), 157–91; and George Shelton, *Dean Tucker and Eighteenth-Century Economic and Political Thought* (New York, 1981).

7. Tucker, True Interest of Great-Britain, 347–49.

8. Ibid., 358–59.

9. Ibid., 363–64.

10. Ibid., 366. See further Charles Royster, "Founding a Nation in Blood: Military Conflict and American Nationality," in *Arms and Independence: The Military Character of the American Revolution,* ed. Ronald Hoffman and Peter J. Albert (Charlottesville, Va., 1984), 25–49; Max Savelle, "Nationalism and Other Loyalties in the American Revolution," *American Historical Review* 67 (1962): 901–23; Higginbotham, *War of American Independence,* 263–64. Thinking along similar lines in 1776 was Benjamin Rush. "The States of America," he wrote Patrick Henry, "cannot be a Nation without War. They will have Wars in Europe. Canada may be reserved to the Crown of Britain as a nursery of enemies to the States on purpose to keep alive their martial virtue. If this be the case, it becomes us to reconcile ourselves to the Loss of Canada, and to resolve it into the goodness of that being with whom 'all partial evil is universal good.'" July 16, 1776, *Letters of Delegates,* 4: 494. See also George Mason to Richard Henry Lee, July 21, 1778, *Mason Papers,* 1: 430. Unlike Rush, Mason wanted the British out of Canada but otherwise saw the happy effect of British hostility. Commenting on the death of Chatham, Mason thought it a "favorable Event to America; there was nothing I dreaded so much as his taking the Helm, & nothing I more heartily wish than the Continuance of the present Ministry. After 'his Most Christian Majesty, & Happiness & Prosperity to the French Nation,' my next Toast shall be 'long Life & Continuance in Office to the present British Ministry' in the first Bottle of good Claret I get; & I expect some by the first Ships from France."

11. Speech on Conciliation [1], March 22, 1775, Burke, *American Revolution,* 84–85; Josiah Tucker, *Letter to Edmund Burke,* Schuyler, *Josiah Tucker,* 377, 381–82. The Puritans of Massachusetts, wrote Tucker, were "universally Calvinists of the most inflexible Sort" and professed enemies to popery and Arminianism, yet they were "no Enemies to religious Establishments." On the contrary, "their great Aim was, to establish the *solemn League and Covenant,* as the only System which ought to be admitted into a Christian State. Nor would they have suffered any other religious Persuasion to have existed, if they could have prevented it." Though all in favor of "pulling down proud and lordly Prelacy," they were "most indefatigable" in erecting "Classes, and Synods, and Elderships, in the genuine Spirit of High-Church, Presbyterian Hierarchy, and armed with the Terrors and Powers of an Inquisition. In short, their Aim was to establish a republican Form of Government built on republican Principles both in Church and State. But, like all other Republicans ancient and modern, they were extremely averse from granting any Portion of that Liberty to others, which they claimed to themselves as their unalienable Birth-Right" (Tucker, *Letter to Edmund Burke,* 381–82). Tucker thought that justice and policy required "[t]hat each Religious Persuasion ought to have a full Tol-

eration from the State to worship Almighty God, according to the Dictates of their own Consciences," but he did not think that the Episcopal Church would suffer in the colonies in the event of independence. Noting the "Persecution which the Church of *England* daily suffers in *America,* by being denied those Rights which every other Sect of Christians so amply enjoys," Tucker attributed it to the fact that "[t]he *Americans* have taken it into their Heads to believe, that an Episcopate would operate as some further Tie upon them" and would be "used as an Engine, under the Masque of Religion, to rivet those Chains, which they imagine we are forging for them." Were the mother country to surrender its authority, "all their Fears will vanish away, and their Panics be at an End." And so it did indeed prove to be (Tucker, True Interest of Great-Britain, 368). For these fears, see Carl Brindenbaugh, *Mitre and Sceptre: Transatlantic Faiths, Ideas, Personalities, and Politics, 1689–1775* (New York, 1962); and J. C. D. Clark, *The Language of Liberty: 1660–1832: Political Discourse and Social Dynamics in the Anglo-American World* (Cambridge, 1994). For a survey of religious freedom in America that broadly confirms Tucker's account, see Forrest Mcdonald, *Novus Ordo Seclorum: The Intellectual Origins of the Constitution* (Lawrence, Kans., 1985), 42–45. Rhode Island was unique in its charter provision guaranteeing that no person "shall be any wise molested, punished, disquieted, or called in question for any differences in opinion in matters of religion." As Joseph Story commented, however, it is lamentable "how little a similar spirit of toleration was encouraged either by the precepts or example of any other of the New-England colonies." Story, *Commentaries,* 1: 85.

12. Tucker, *Letter to Edmund Burke,* 382–84.

13. Tucker, *True Interest of Great-Britain,* 338. Jefferson's depiction of the effect of slavery on the masters differs little from those of Tucker and Burke. See *Notes on the State of Virginia,* Peterson, *Jefferson Writings,* Query XVIII; and Peter S. Onuf, *Jefferson's Empire: The Language of American Nationhood* (Charlottesville, Va., 2000). On the familial images pervasively employed in the decades leading up to the Revolution, see Gordon Wood, *The Radicalism of the American Revolution* (New York, 1991), 165. All knew the observation in James Harrington's *Oceana*—cited, for example, in Adams's *Novanglus*—that the American colonies were "babes that cannot live without sucking the breast of their mother-cities." Since they would "wean themselves" when they came of age, Harrington wondered "at princes that delight to be exhausted in this way." *Novanglus* VII, *Adams Papers,* 2: 313.

14. Tucker, *Letter to Edmund Burke,* 394.

15. Smith, *Wealth of Nations,* 899–900.

16. Smith, *Wealth of Nations,* 429–31; "Smith's Thoughts on the State of the Contest with America, February 1778," *The Correspondence of Adam Smith,* ed. Ernest Campbell Mossner and Ian Simpson Rose (Oxford, 1987), 377–85, at 381, 384–85. In this memorandum, written two years after war had broken out, Smith also made a striking comparison with the experience of Holland. After having shown that a complete military victory would not be a paying proposition—"[w]hatever could be extorted from them, and probably much more than could be extorted from them, would be spent in maintaining that military force which would be requisite to command their obedience"—he went on to show that a partial conquest would be even more destructive, for it would throw the remainder of the colonies "into the alliance

of the enemies of Great Britain." The Spanish attempt under Philip II to prevent the emancipation of the Netherlands, in the long eighty-year war that ended in 1648, taught an important lesson in this respect. "If all the seventeen provinces of the Netherlands had completely emancipated themselves from the dominion of Spain, their situation, as soon as their independency was acknowledged, would have rendered them the natural enemies of France and consequently the natural enemies of Spain." Spain's subsequent decline was due "more to the recovery of the ten, than to the loss of the seven united provinces." The ten provinces recovered "never paid the tenth part of the expence of the armies which Spain was obliged to maintain in them," and the dominion over them forfeited the "solid advantage of a powerful, and probably a faithful alliance, against the most formidable of all her enemies."

17. Smith, *Wealth of Nations*, 587–88, 899–900. In his 1778 memorandum, Smith called this a plan of "constitutional union" by which "both parts of the empire" would enjoy "the same freedom of trade" and would share "in their proper proportion both in the burden of taxation and in the benefit of representation." He commented, however, that this plan, though it "would certainly tend most to the prosperity, to the splendour, and to the duration of the empire," had no advocates in Britain save a few "solitary philosophers" like himself. There remained, then, a plan of "federal union with America." This would entail the "complete emancipation of America from all dependency upon Great Britain," and Smith believed with Tucker that its advantages were great. If paired with the restoration of Canada to the French, and of the two Floridas to Spain, "we would certainly revive old enmities, and probably old friendships." Even if Canada, Nova Scotia, and the Floridas were given up or fell by conquest to the Americans, the basis would be laid for a lasting friendship. Once they were assured "that we meant to claim no dominion over them," ancient affections would revive, and "the similarity of language and manners would in most cases dispose the Americans to prefer our alliance to that of any other nation." "Smith's Thoughts," *Correspondence*, 381–83.

18. *Parliamentary History*, 18: 739. Smith, of course, knew well the power of this reasoning. Of his plan for "federal union," he remarked that it would not appear "honourable" to Great Britain and would substantially weaken, in the eyes of Europe, "her power and dignity." Of even greater importance was that "it could scarce fail to discredit the Government in the eyes of our own people." In that eventuality, the ministers "would have every thing to fear from their rage and indignation at the public disgrace and calamity, for such they would suppose it to be, of thus dismembering the empire." "Smith's Thoughts," *Correspondence*, 382–83.

19. Burke, Speech on Conciliation [1], Burke, *American Revolution*, 93.

20. "The immutable Condition! The eternal Law! Extensive and detached empire!" wrote Tucker: "Pray, Sir," he asked Burke, "on which Side of the Question were you retained? And whose Cause are you now pleading? I have heard of Lawyers in great Practice, who, thro' Hurry and Inattention, mistook one Brief for another, and then, pleading on a contrary Side to that on which they were retained, did not perceive their Error, 'till their Clients had lost their Cause. Whether any Thing of the like Kind has happened to you, is more than I can say. But it is Matter of Astonishment to all, to your own Friends and Admirers, as well as to others, that you should bring such Arguments as these, to prove the Necessity of continuing an Union of Empire between *Great-Britain* and the detached continental Pow-

ers of *North-America*. You instance the case of *Spain:* But to what End or Purpose have you brought it into the present Argument? For if it be, to display the Benefit and Advantage of distant and extensive Colonies, you surely are the most unfortunate of all Men living in the Nature of your Proofs: *Spain* being a striking Example, and a full Illustration of the direct contrary. *Spain,* Sir, as you well know, was, before it was seized with an epidemic Madness of settling Colonies in *America,* one of the richest, the best peopled, the best cultivated, and the most flourishing Country in *Europe*. . . . But now alas! how fallen!" (Tucker, *Letter to Edmund Burke,* 391–92). For other eighteenth-century variations on the theme of the effect of distance on power, see Anthony Pagden, *Lords of All the World: Ideologies of Empire in Spain, Britain, and France c. 1500–c. 1800* (New Haven, Conn., 1995); and D. W. Meinig, *Atlantic America, 1492–1800* (New Haven, Conn., 1986), 374.

21. As John Campbell had observed in 1755, the colonies had "in many cases acted as if they thought themselves so many independent states, under their respective charters, rather than as provinces of the same empire." Quoted in Pagden, *Lords of All the World,* 135.

22. For classic statements of this theme, see Report on Address to the States by Congress, April 25, 1783, *Madison Papers,* 6: 494; John Adams, *A Defence of the Constitutions of Government of the United States of America . . . , Adams Works,* 4: 290; Alexander Hamilton, "Second Letter from Phocion," April 1784, *Hamilton Papers,* 3: 557–58; and Abraham Lincoln, "Address Before the Young Men's Lyceum of Springfield, Illinois," January 27, 1838, *Collected Works of Abraham Lincoln,* 9 vols., ed. Roy P. Basler (New Brunswick, N.J., 1953–55), 1: 113.

CHAPTER 16

1. David Ramsay, "An Oration on the Advantages of American Independence . . . , July 4, 1778," Niles, *Principles,* 381. Cf. John Adams, *Novanglus* III, February 6, 1775, *Adams Papers,* 2: 249.

2. John Adams's Notes of Debates, September 6, 1774, *Letters of Delegates,* 1: 28–29; James Duane's Notes of Debates, ibid., 30–31. For this interpretation of Henry's motives, see also Edmund Cody Burnett, *The Continental Congress* (New York, 1941), 37.

3. *Letters of Delegates,* 1: 31.

4. *LMCC,* 1: 42–43.

5. Carter Braxton to Landon Carter, *LMCC,* 1: 420–21.

6. John Adams to Abigail Adams, October 29, 1775, *Adams Family Correspondence,* 1: 318–19. Those Englishmen, Adams noted, had left Europe "in purer Times than the present." His four other reasons were (1) "The Institutions in New England for the Support of Religion, Morals and Decency, . . . obliging every Parish to have a Minister, and every Person to go to Meeting &c.; (2) "The Public Institutions . . . for the Education of Youth"; (3) "The Division of . . . our Counties into Townships," which "gives every Man an opportunity of shewing and improving that Education," and which "makes Knowledge and Dexterity at public Business common"; and (4) "Our Laws for the Distribution of Intestate Estates," which ensured "a frequent Division of landed Property."

7. "Journal of Josiah Quincy, Junior," *Proceedings of the Massachusetts Historical Society* 49 (1916): 454–57, cited in Potter, *Nationalism*, 20–21. John Adams described the manners of Maryland thusly: "They are chiefly Planters and Farmers. The Planters are those who raise Tobacco and the Farmers such as raise Wheat &c. The Lands are cultivated, and all Sorts of Trades are exercised by Negroes, or by transported Convicts, which has occasioned the Planters and Farmers to assume the Title of Gentlemen, and they hold their Negroes and Convicts, that is all labouring People and Tradesmen, in such Contempt, that they think themselves a distinct order of Beings. Hence they never will suffer their Sons to labour or to learn any Trade, but they bring them up in Idleness or what is worse in Horse Racing, Cock fighting, and Card Playing." February 23, 1777, *Adams Diary*, 2: 261.

8. Joseph L. Davis, *Sectionalism in American Politics, 1774–1787* (Madison, Wis., 1977); John Adams's Notes of Debates, September 6, 1774, *Letters of Delegates*, 1: 28.

9. Cf. Daniel Webster, Speech on Panama Mission, April 14, 1826, *Works of Daniel Webster*, 6 vols. (Boston, [1851] 1858), 3: 195–96: "A congress, by the law of nations, is but an appointed meeting for the settlement of affairs between different nations, in which the representatives or agents of each treat and negotiate as they are instructed by their own government. . . . No nation is a party to any thing done in such assemblies, to which it does not expressly make itself a party. No one's rights are put at the disposition of any of the rest, or of all the rest. . . . Every thing is settled by the use of the word Plenipotentiary. That proves the meeting to be diplomatic, and nothing else. Who ever heard of a plenipotentiary member of the legislature? a plenipotentiary burgess of a city? or a plenipotentiary knight of the shire?"

10. John Adams to Abigail Adams, June 17, 1775, *LMCC*, 1: 130. To similar effect, see Samuel Adams to Benjamin Kent, July 27, 1776, *Letters of Delegates*, 4: 552.

11. John Adams to James Warren, July 24, 1775, *Adams Papers*, 3: 89; J. Gregory Rossie, *Politics of Command* (Syracuse, 1975), 9; John Adams to James Warren, July 6, 1775, *Adams Papers*, 3: 62; ibid., 93 n.

12. John Adams to Abigail Adams, June 17, 1775, *Letters of Delegates*, 1: 497; *Adams Diary*, 3: 321–22; Rossie, *Politics of Command*, 11–12. On sectional compromise, see Don Higginbotham, *The War of American Independence: Military Attitudes, Policies, and Practice, 1763–1789* (New York, 1971), 83. The Massachusetts Provincial Congress, insisting that "the sword should, in all free States, be subservient to the civil powers," had previously (May 16, 1775) urged congress to take "the regulation and general direction of it" (ibid., 83). Adams later remarked, referring to this episode, that "We owe no thanks to Virginia for Washington. Virginia is indebted to Massachusetts for Washington, not Massachusetts to Virginia. Massachusetts made him a general against the inclinations of Virginia. Virginia never made him more than a colonel." To James Lloyd, April 24, 1815, *Adams Works*, 10: 165.

13. George Washington to Richard Henry Lee, August 29, 1775, cited in Rossie, *Politics of Command*, 28; John Adams to Henry Knox, September 29, 1776, *Letters of Delegates*, 5: 260; John Thomas to John Adams, October 24, 1775, *Adams Papers*, 3: 241; John Witherspoon, *The Dominion of Providence over the Passions*

of Men . . . (Philadelphia, 1776), 47, cited in H. James Henderson, *Party Politics in the Continental Congress* (New York, 1974), 71.

14. John Dickinson to William Pitt, December 21, 1765, Edmund S. Morgan, *Prologue to Revolution: Sources and Documents on the Stamp Act Crisis, 1764–1766* (New York, 1973), 119; John Dickinson, Letters to the Inhabitants of the British Colonies, May 1774, Letter IV, *Dickinson Writings*, 494; James H. Hutson, *John Adams and Diplomacy of the American Revolution* (Lexington, Ky., 1980), 14–15; John Dickinson's Notes for a Speech in Congress, July 1, 1776, *Letters of Delegates*, 4: 354.

15. Leonard and Inglis cited in Hutson, *John Adams*, 13; Andrew Burnaby, *Travels Through the Middle Settlements in North America* (Ithaca, N.Y., [1775] 1960), 113–14, and discussion in Merrill Jensen, "The Sovereign States: Their Antagonisms and Rivalries and Some Consequences," in *Sovereign States in an Age of Uncertainty*, ed. Ronald Hoffman and Peter J. Albert (Charlottesville, Va., 1981), 227.

16. See Proclamation of Lord Dunmore Offering Freedom to the Slaves Belonging to the British in Virginia, November 7, 1775; Lord Dunmore to General Howe, November 30, 1775, and "Proceedings in the Convention of Virginia Relating to the Proclamation of Lord Dunmore," Niles, *Principles*, 286–90; and the imaginative treatment in Woody Holton, *Forced Founders: Indians, Debtors, Slaves, and the Making of the American Revolution in Virginia* (Chapel Hill, N.C., 1999). This consideration was also decisive for Edward Rutledge, who had formed a close relationship with those in the congress—Dickinson, Wilson, Duane—who urged caution and restraint on those pushing for independence. On South Carolina, see Robert A. Olwell, "'Domestic Enemies': Slavery and Political Independence in South Carolina, May 1775–March 1776," *Journal of Southern History* 55 (1989): 21–48.

17. John Dickinson's Notes, July 1, 1776, *Letters of Delegates*, 1: 355.

18. *LMCC*, 2: 32.

CHAPTER 17

1. Henry Laurens to John Lewis Gervais, October 16, 1777, *Letters of Delegates*, 8: 124.

2. Thomas Burke to Richard Caswell, March 11, 1777, ibid., 6: 427.

3. "Government is dissolved," said Patrick Henry in one of the first meetings of the Continental Congress. "Fleets and Armies and the present State of Things shew that Government is dissolved. . . . We are in a State of Nature, Sir." John Adams's Notes of Debates, September 6, 1774, ibid., 1: 28.

4. Congress was at York Town, Pennsylvania, when on November 15, 1777, it sent the Articles of Confederation to the states. Four years later, on October 19, 1781, General Cornwallis surrendered his eight thousand men to General Washington at Yorktown, Virginia.

5. Proposed Articles of Confederation, May 10 or July 21, 1775 (both dates are attached to the document), Lemay, *Franklin Writings*, 730–33.

6. *Thoughts on Government* (1776), *Adams Papers*, 4: 87, 90, 92. For the few other plans of union discussed in newspapers in 1776, see Jack N. Rakove, *The*

Beginnings of National Politics: An Interpretive History of the Continental Congress (Baltimore, [1979] 1982).

7. John Adams to Patrick Henry, June 3, 1776, *Adams Papers,* 4: 234–35. For a similar enumeration, see Adams to William Cushing, June 9, 1776, ibid., 4: 244–45. "Every Colony must be induced to institute a perfect Government. All the Colonies must confederate together in some solemn Compact. The Colonies must be declared free and independent states, and Embassadors, must be Sent abroad to foreign Courts, to solicit their Acknowledgment of Us, as Sovereign States, and to form with them, at least with some of them commercial Treaties of Friendship and Alliance." Charles Francis Adams, *Adams Works,* 9: 390, renders "Compact" as "band of union" in this passage. Since Americans, at the time he published his grandfather's works (1854), had been for decades poring over the records from the founding to justify the respective claims of the "national sovereignty" and "compact" schools, this alteration represents a remarkable attempt to fudge the evidence on the part of Charles Francis.

8. "Previous to Independence," Braxton held, "all disputes must be healed and Harmony prevail. A grand Continental league must be formed and a superintending Power." Without that bond of union, "[t]he Continent would be torn in pieces by Intestine Wars and Convulsions. . . . It is a true saying of a Wit—We must hang together or separately." Carter Braxton to Landon Carter, April 14, 1776, *LMCC,* 1: 420–21.

9. Jefferson, Notes of Proceedings in the Continental Congress, June 8, 1776, *Jefferson Papers,* 1: 309–13.

10. Adams's resolution to this effect was offered June 10.

11. See John Adams to Richard Henry Lee, June 4, 1776, *Adams Papers,* 4: 239. "Is it not a little remarkable that this Congress and your Convention should come to Resolutions so nearly Similar, on the Same Day? . . ."

12. John Adams to Hezekiah Niles, February 13, 1818, *Adams Works,* 10: 283.

13. The Declaration of Independence, Peterson, *Jefferson Writings,* 19, 23–24.

14. On the nationalist interpretation, see chapter 4, note 4. On Jefferson's characteristic mode of constitutional reasoning, see David N. Mayer, *The Constitutional Thought of Thomas Jefferson* (Charlottesville, Va., 1994).

15. Resolution on Required Texts, Minutes of the Board of Visitors of the University of Virginia, March 4, 1825, Peterson, *Jefferson Writings,* 479.

CHAPTER 18

1. Editorial note, *Letters of Delegates,* 4: 251–52. See also William Elery to Ezra Stiles? July 20, 1776, on Dickinson's whereabouts, ibid., 4: 497–98.

2. *Adams Diary,* 3: 410–11; Paul H. Smith et al., eds., *Letters of Delegates to Congress, 1774–1789,* is an outstanding work of editorial scholarship, but it sheds little more light than Edmund C. Burnett's pioneering collection on the making of the confederation, *Letters of Members of the Continental Congress,* 8 vols. (Washington, D.C., 1921–36). Most valuable in the *Letters of Delegates* is its printing of the "Dickinson draft" and the redating of Witherspoon's important address on the

articles, discussed later. On Thomson, see the sketch in Richard B. Morris, *The Forging of the Union, 1781–1789* (New York, 1987).

3. See, e.g., Jack N. Rakove, *The Beginnings of National Politics: An Interpretive History of the Continental Congress* (Baltimore, [1979] 1982); Merrill Jensen, *The Articles of Confederation: An Interpretation of the Social-Constitutional History of the American Revolution, 1774–1781* (Madison, Wis., 1959); Edmund Cody Burnett, *The Continental Congress* (New York, 1941).

4. Edward Rutledge to John Jay, *Letters of Delegates*, 4: 338. One instance of extraordinary prolixity is the article on religious toleration that Dickinson drew but the committee deleted in its submission of July 12. See the analysis of this provision in Rakove, *Beginnings*. Another is Article 2, analyzed later. Josiah Bartlett noted on July 1 that the committee had worked on the articles "for about a fortnight at all opportunities." Bartlett emphasized the great importance of the measure—"the future happiness of America will depend on it in great measure"—as well as the evident difficulty of framing it "so as to be agreable to the Delegates of all the Different Colonies & of the Colonial Legislatures also; for without the unanimous Consent of all it Cannot be Established." To Nathaniel Folsom, *Letters of Delegates*, 4: 349.

5. John Adams to Abigail Adams, July 10, 1776, *Letters of Delegates*, 4: 423.

6. Samuel Chase to John Adams, July 5, 1776, ibid., 4; 415; John Dickinson to Charles Thomson, August 7, 1776, *Collections of the New York Historical Society for the Year 1878* (New York, 1879), 29. In a letter written on August 10 to Thomson, Dickinson showed, despite his protestations of liberation, that the hurt ran deep: "The enemy are moving—and an attack on New York is quickly expected. As for myself I can form no Idea of a more noble fate than after being the constant advocate for, and Promoter of every measure that could possibly lead to peace or prevent her return from being barred up; after cheerfully & deliberately sacrificing my popularity and all the emoluments I might so certainly have derived from it to Principles; after suffering all the indignities that my Countrymen now bearing Rule are inclined if they could so plentifully to shower down upon my innocent Head willingly to resign my life if divine providence shall please so to dispose of me, even for the defence and happiness of those unkind Countrymen whom I cannot forbear to esteem as fellow Citizens amidst their Fury against me." Dickinson seemed momentarily embarrassed by this sincere and effusive declaration, or at least that his correspondent might infer a suicidal intention, and he immediately assured Thomson that he did not covet "the Glory of such an exit from the Stage of life" but rather longed for a return to "my books and my fields." That, after all, was far more agreeable than plunging after the martyred fame of the Roman Curtius, whom Dickinson in the preceding passage had imagined himself to be (ibid., 31). That the assumption of this role could provide deep satisfactions is attested by John Adams's lament to Abigail: "Oh that I was a Soldier!" he exclaimed to her one day as he responded to the developing martial enthusiasm in Philadelphia in the late spring of 1775. May 29, 1775, *Letters of Delegates*, 1: 417.

7. John Dickinson's Draft Articles of Confederation [June 17–July 1?, 1776], *Letters of Delegates*, 4: 233–55, at 233.

8. On the articles as being formed "on the Dutch model," see William Grayson

to Richard Henry Lee, *Letters of Delegates,* 23: 205. See also John Adams, "To the Boston Committee of Correspondence," [September? 1774], *Adams Papers,* 2: 178. The Union of Utrecht, January 23, 1579, is reprinted in A. P. Newton, *Federal and Unified Constitutions: A Collection of Constitutional Documents . . .* (New York, 1923), 43–50. That Dickinson knew well the constitution of the United Provinces seems certain, though there is no direct evidence on the point. As we saw earlier, Dickinson looked to Dutch history for many of his illustrious heroes, on whom he modeled his conduct (see chapter 8, note 3). The debates in congress in 1776, discussed below, also presumed among the delegates a knowledge of these institutions. In a letter of June 24, 1777, to Joseph Trumball, James Lovell referred to congress as "the States General of the United American Colonies." June 24, 1777, *Letters of Delegates,* 7: 247.

9. Murray Forsyth, *Unions of States: The Theory and Practice of Confederation* (New York, 1981), 33.

10. Dickinson draft, *Letters of Delegates,* 4: 236–38.

11. Ibid., 4: 237–38.

12. Ibid., 4: 238–39.

13. Ibid., 4: 242–45.

14. Thomas Burke, for example, iconoclastically objected to the restraints placed on the states in regard to foreign treaties. "The various affairs of a free Commercial People will require them often to enter into Conferences and agreements with foreign States." Each of the states "should be at liberty to increase its wealth and strength as much as possible," and commercial treaties were one legitimate means of doing this. It would be sufficient to simply restrain the states from using those powers "to the Injury of their Neighbors," and to oblige them "to Contribute in Just proportion to the Common defence." Even Burke's declaration that "the United States ought to be as One Sovereign with respect to foreign Powers" was qualified by him in several particulars. "A private Citizen who embarques a part of his fortune in a Co-partnership would be deemed very unwise should he suffer the members of that partnership to possess a power that might restrain him from [improving] the remaining part of his Fortune to what extent he pleased consistent with the Common Interest." In commercial matters, therefore, he wished to reserve each state's entire discretion. Even in war he thought it reasonable that if war were declared before any invasion, or in close expectation thereof, "any State ought to be at Liberty to renounce the War and become a Neutral power." In defensive wars, therefore, they were to serve the common cause, but in all offensive wars they would each retain the right of remaining neutral "whether the united States be principles or allies in it." Thomas Burke's Notes on the Articles of Confederation, [ca. December 18, 1777], ibid., 8: 436–37. Burke's idea that states might maintain separate embassies to foreign countries was doubtless considered objectionable because it would present too ready an opportunity for succumbing to temptation; nor was it really possible to separate the claim of precedence to treaties made by congress from its ability to make war or peace. The power to treat over commerce was indispensably necessary in negotiation with foreign powers; a reservation by the states in this particular would have seriously weakened the position of American emissaries in Europe. Burke perhaps most departed from the larger consensus in his belief that the war was not the time to sort out the complexities of confederation,

and that the whole subject ought to be deferred to a time of "peace and tranquillity." As he observed, he differed "very widely" on that point "with a majority in Congress," the consensus being that a temporary arrangement would lead others (France among them) to suspect the durability of their federal tie. Most other delegates in 1776 and 1777 felt congress badly in need of an assurance of perpetuity. Thomas Burke to Richard Caswell, November 4, 1777, ibid., 8: 227.

15. Ibid., 8: 242–43.

16. Dickinson draft, ibid., 4: 242–43; *JCC,* 5: 548.

17. Rufus S. Davis, *The Federal Principle: A Journey Through Time in Quest of a Meaning* (Berkeley, 1978), 75.

18. *DHRC,* 1: 86.

19. *American Colonial Documents,* 137; Morris, *Forging of the Union,* 88. Rakove's nuanced and imaginative treatment still gives a greater importance to this amendment than in my judgment it deserves. Rakove, *Beginnings,* 171.

20. *Thoughts on Government* (1776), *Adams Papers,* 4: 92. The same understanding informed his reaction to Pennsylvania's new constitution of 1776. When Benjamin Rush cited the *Thoughts* and first identified its author, Adams said his enlistment in the bitter contest over the new constitution was much against his will, "for altho I am no Admirer of the Form of this Government, yet I think it is agreable to the Body of the People, and if they please themselves they will please me." John Adams to Abigail Adams, June 4, 1777, *Letters of Delegates,* 7: 167.

21. "A number of sovereign and independent states," as Vattel put it, "may unite to form a perpetual confederation, without individually ceasing to be perfect States. Together they will form a confederate republic. Their joint resolutions will not impair the sovereignty of the individual members, although its exercise may be somewhat restrained by reason of voluntary agreements. The obligation to fulfill agreements one has voluntarily made does not detract from one's liberty and independence." Vattel, *Law of Nations,* chap. 1, no. 10: 12. See also the discussion of Burlamaqui, Pufendorf, and Montesquieu in Tucker, *View of the Constitution,* 75–88; and, more generally, the analysis in S. Rufus Davis, *The Federal Principle* (Berkeley, 1978); and Peter Onuf and Nicholas Onuf, *Federal Union, Modern World: The Law of Nations in an Age of Revolutions, 1776–1814* (Madison, Wis., 1993).

22. Thomas Burke's Notes on the Articles of Confederation, [ca. December 18, 1777], *Letters of Delegates,* 8: 435; and Jack N. Rakove, "The Articles of Confederation, 1775–1783," in *The Blackwell Encyclopedia of the American Revolution,* ed. Jack P. Greene and J. R. Pole (Cambridge, Mass., 1994), 292. In offering his amendment, Burke evidently feared that, since the original article "expressed only a reservation of the power of regulating internal police," it had "consequently resigned every other power." It appeared to Burke, as he informed the governor of North Carolina, "that this was not what the States expected, and, I thought, it left it in the power of the future Congress or General Council to explain away every right belonging to the States, and to make their own power as unlimited as they please." The amendment, Burke observed, "was at first so little understood that it was some time before it was seconded." Once South Carolina had done so, however, the amendment was carried by a vote of eleven states in favor. The opposition was made by James Wilson of Pennsylvania and Richard Henry Lee of Virginia,

though only Virginia voted no (with New Hampshire divided). Burke was delighted "to find the opinion of accumulating powers to Congress so little supported." Thomas Burke to Richard Caswell, April 29, 1777, *Letters of Delegates,* 6: 672. For the interpretation of Jensen and Morris to be sustained, we must suppose that congress at first did not understand that Burke proposed a complete transformation in the instrument they had before them, but once they had done so, they found that this revolutionary change corresponded exactly with their prevailing sentiments, and they adopted it with near unanimity! The more natural interpretation is that the delegates were initially puzzled by the amendment because they did not understand the need or purpose of it. Once it was understood that the amendment simply expressed their previously manifested intention with respect to the distribution of powers to the union and the states, they readily adopted it.

23. For a similar analysis, see Jerrilyn Greene Marston, *King and Congress: The Transfer of Political Legitimacy, 1774–76* (Princeton, N.J., 1987); Peter S. Onuf, "The First Federal Constitution: The Articles of Confederation," in *The Framing and Ratification of the Constitution,* ed. Leonard W. Levy and Dennis J. Mahoney (New York, 1987), 82–97; John M. Murrin, "1787: The Invention of American Federalism," in *Essays on Liberty and Federalism: The Shaping of the U.S. Constitution,* ed. John M. Murrin et al. (College Station, Tex., 1988), 32.

24. On the continuities between 1777 and 1787 in the authority allocated to congress and the states, see Andrew C. McLaughlin, *The Constitutional History of the United States* (New York, 1935), 125; and Alexander Hamilton Stephens, *A Constitutional View of the Late War Between the States,* 2 vols. (Philadelphia, [1868–70]), 1: 84–87. On congress as a "theoretical anomaly," see Rakove, *Beginnings.* If congress is not considered as a "national government" but as the arena in which the states proposed to concert their measures, the anomalous character of the congress appears far less striking. Objecting to the characterization of congress as a "weak legislature," Murrin suggests that "we probably ought to abandon this conceptualization entirely, at least for the early years of the Revolutionary War. Congress was not a legislature. It was a plural executive." Murrin, "Invention of American Federalism," 32.

25. William Henry Drayton, January 20, 1778, South Carolina General Assembly, in Niles, *Principles,* 357–74. "Neither the northern nor southern interest should be affected," according to Drayton, "but by the consent of at least half the states in such interests respectively" (363). In a letter of May 16, 1777, to John Adams, Jefferson asked Adams to revive "the proposition I formerly made you in private," which was "that any proposition might be negatived by the representatives of a majority of the people of America, or of a majority of the colonies of America" (*Jefferson Papers,* 2: 19). Jefferson did not propose a division of the congress into two bodies, and he probably was thinking of a separate taking of voices within the congress as then conceived. Adams thought well of the idea and promised to get it introduced if the "perfect" and more equitable rule of voting by numbers were rejected. John Adams to Thomas Jefferson, May 26, 1777, ibid., 2: 21. At some point in the deliberations, Burke offered an amendment that would have provided for a bicameral congress, divided into a General Council and a Council of State. It is reprinted in *JCC,* 7: 328–29. The latter was to consist of one delegate from every state, but the former would be chosen by the states in proportions that

Burke did not specify in his amendment. It made a majority of both bodies necessary to pass every "act Edict and ordinance" save in case of war, in which a three-fourths rule would apply. This seems to have been rejected, in the first place, because it mistook the character congress was to have under the articles; it was not a legislature, like Parliament, but an "Executive Body resembling King &c." Others sniffed an aristocratic purpose and objected to the "Idea of Distinctions resembling British Constitution." See H. James Henderson, *Party Politics in the Continental Congress* (New York, 1974), 145. Sam Adams suggested that it would perhaps "be more easy for a disinterested Foreigner to see, than for the united States to fix upon the Principles" by which this "weighty Subject" might get resolved. A proper resolution was crucial, for on it "depends the Union of the States and the Security of the Liberty of the whole." The resolution that Adams then thought congress would settle upon the next day was "that each State shall have one Vote, but that certain great and very interesting Questions shall have the concurrent Votes of nine States for a decision." He asked his correspondent, James Warren, to consider "whether this Composition will go near towards the Preservation of a due Ballance." June 30, 1777, *Letters of Delegates*, 7: 271–72.

CHAPTER 19

1. Notes of Proceedings, July 30–August 1, 1776, *Jefferson Papers*, 1: 323.

2. Ibid., 1: 325; *Adams Diary*, 2: 245.

3. *Jefferson Papers*, 1: 324–25.

4. Ibid., 1: 322–26; *Adams Diary*, 2: 245–46.

5. August 2, 1776, *Adams Diary*, 2: 249–50. South Carolina had no extensive western claims, but Carolinians were speculating heavily in their Georgian hinterland; they had a common interest with the other southern states (excepting Maryland) on the disposition of the western domain.

6. *Adams Diary*, 2: 241–42. For the claim that the dispute really concerned "a contest between certain States claiming Western lands for themselves, on one side, and those claiming it in the interest of certain land companies, on the other, the middle group of States being controlled largely by members of the great land companies," see Thomas Perkins Abernethy, *Western Lands and the American Revolution* (New York, 1937), 172.

7. John Witherspoon's Speech in Congress, [July 30, 1776], *Letters of Delegates*, 4: 584–87. To similar effect, see Cornelius Harnett to Richard Caswell: "unless the States Confederate a door will be left open for Continual Contention & Bloodshed, and *that*, very soon after we are at peace with Europe." March 20, 1778, *Letters of Delegates*, 9: 317; John Adams to William Lee, November 19, 1780, *Adams Papers*, 10: 359–60. "A Zeal for the Union of the 13 States" Adams thought "one of the first Duties of every American Citizen." Though Adams thought that all thirteen "would maintain their Independancy, if they were rent into two or three Divisions—yet there would be too much Hazard of Britains prevailing over some—and if she should not prevail over any, yet the different divisions of the continent, would soon be at War, with each other."

8. *Jefferson Papers*, 1: 324–27; *Adams Diary*, 2: 247–48.

9. Benjamin Rush's Notes for a Speech in Congress, August 1, 1776, *Letters of Delegates,* 4: 598–602.

10. Thomas Burke to Richard Caswell, March 11, 1777, ibid., 6: 427.

11. See, e.g., Drayton, Niles, *Principles,* 360–63; and Edward Rutledge to John Jay, June 29, 1776, *Letters of Delegates,* 4: 338.

12. On the imperial constitution as a "template" for federal union, see Peter S. Onuf, *Jefferson's Empire: The Language of American Nationhood* (Charlottesville, Va., 2000).

13. *DHRC,* 1: 90. On the legal case of the respective states, see Peter S. Onuf, *Origins of the Federal Republic: Jurisdictional Controversies in the United States, 1775–1787* (Philadelphia, 1983).

14. Roger Sherman to Richard Henry Lee, November 3, 1777, *Letters of Delegates,* 8: 320–21 n.

15. See James Madison's Notes of Debates, March 27, 1783, ibid., 20: 117, for James Wilson's later recollection of this point.

16. For the unanimous opposition of the New England delegates to Witherspoon's amendment, see Nathaniel Folsom to Meshech Weare, October 27, 1777, ibid., 8: 198. See also Folson to Weare, November 21, 1777, on the injustice of the rule for apportioning the charges of the war. "In the first place it appears to me that one third part of the [wealth] of the Southern States which consists in negroes, is entirely left out and no Notice taken of them, in determining their ability to pay taxes, notwithstanding it is by them that they procure their wealth. Neither are we to have any advantage of them in proportioning the Number of men to be drawn from the Several States to Carry on the war, that being fixed on the Number of white inhabitants in each state, so that by their negroes being left at home, they Can till their lands and git Bread & Riches, while some other States may be greatly distressed." Southern perspectives differed sharply. The "Eastern people," as Cornelius Harnett noted, "were for settling the Quota by the Number of Inhabitants including Slaves," which he thought "would have ruined Poor No. Carolina," who "has as many Inhabitants as Connecticut (almost) Tho the Land in that State wuld sell for five times as Much as the Lands in ours" (Harnett to William Wilkinson, November 30, 1777, ibid., 8: 349). Southerners like Drayton, who feared putting the South under the domination of the North, also saw the mischievous character of the formula apportioning charges to the value of lands. "Shall we, with our reason in full vigor, wish to extend to an immense circle, a principle that we are sensible fails us even in a small one? . . . Is there any certain criterion of value? Does not value altogether depend on opinion, imagination, caprice?" (Niles, *Principles,* 360). From the beginning, the dispute over the rule that would fairly apportion contributions became entangled with the numerous controversies over what counted as a state or federal expenditure. In seeking a settlement of accounts, the delegates went round and round in a circle that would never be squared under the old congress. "The only point on which Congress are generally agreed," as Madison fairly summarized "this complication of embarrassments," "is that something ought to be attempted, but what that something ought to be, is a theorem not solved alike by scarcely any two members." He doubted strongly "whether a sufficient number of States will be found in favor for any plan that can be devised" (*Madison Papers,* 6: 215–16). Congress finally gave up the principle of land valuation in 1783, agreeing

to a compromise amendment to the articles (never ratified) to count population for purposes of assessing contributions, by which slaves were counted as three-fifths of a person. See Madison's Notes of Debates, March 28 and April 1, 1783, *Letters of Delegates,* 20: 121, 128.

17. Richard Henry Lee to Roger Sherman, November 24, 1777, ibid., 8: 319–20.

18. John Henry noted of Maryland's efforts to revise the articles that "the bare mentioning of the Subject rouses Virginia, and conscious of her own importance, she views her vast Dominion with the surest expectations of holding it unimpaired." To Nicholas Thomas, March 17, 1778, ibid., 9: 305. Despite, or because of, this reservation, Virginia had shown herself "ever desirous of taking the lead in this great Contest." By being first to offer a ratification of the confederation, "She stood, single, and enjoyed a secret pride in having laid the corner stone of a confederated world."

19. Official Letter Accompanying Act of Confederation, November 17, 1777, Elliot, *Debates,* 1: 69–70. Charles Carroll noted in June 1777 that "a very considerable, nay a very great majority of Congress," saw the necessity of a confederacy. Though Carroll feared that "the confederacy will not be formed on principles so mutually advantageous as it ought & might be, . . . an imperfect & somewhat unequal Confederacy is better than none." Charles Carroll of Carrollton to Charles Carroll, Sr., June 26, 1777, *Letters of Delegates,* 7: 251. For other expressions of urgency, see Cornelius Harnett to Richard Caswell, October 10, 1777, ibid., 8: 98; Harnett to Thomas Burke, November 13, 1777, ibid., 8: 254. Many delegates, Harnett noted, believed that "Our Affairs must be ruined" without confederation, and he later called it "the most difficult piece of Business that ever was undertaken by any Public Body." Harnett to William Wilkinson, November 30, 1777, ibid., 8: 348.

20. Nathaniel Folsom to Meshech Weare, November 21, 1777, ibid., 8: 299; James Duane to John Jay, December 23, 1777, *Jay Papers,* 1: 459.

21. *Common Sense,* February 14, 1776, *Paine Writings,* 21. The amendments proposed by the states are contained in *DHRC,* 1: 96–137. It is notable, as Madison observed in *Federalist* No. 38, "that among the numerous objections and amendments suggested by the several States, when these articles were submitted for their ratification, not one is found which alludes to the great and radical error, which on actual trial has discovered itself." Cooke, *Federalist,* No. 38: 242.

CHAPTER 20

1. Editorial Note, *Letters of Delegates,* 9: 263; St. George L. Sioussat, "The Chevalier de la Luzerne and the Ratification of the Articles of Confederation by Maryland, 1780–1781," *Pennsylvania Magazine of History and Biography* 60 (1936): 391–418.

2. Cooke, *Federalist,* No. 22: 140.

3. On the difficulties of maintaining a quorum of nine states during the war, see Thomas Burke's Proposed Statement to Congress, April 13, 1778, *Letters of Delegates,* 9: 404–7; Laurens to John Rutledge, ibid., 8: 692–94; John Harvie to Jefferson, December 29, 1777, ibid., 9: 493–95; Lovell to Samuel Adams, January 13,

1778, ibid., 8: 579–82. Some delegates were in favor of a "partial Confederacy" if Maryland refused to sign, but this posed severe complications. The General Assembly of North Carolina had declared its willingness to join a confederation of fewer than thirteen states if unanimous ratification could not be obtained, but Burke thought it "[e]vident that the Confederacy, formed for thirteen, will not fit a smaller number, and that if a partial Confederacy be found Necessary, the articles thereof must be previously adjusted." Writing in the midst of the bitter controversy over war aims in 1779, Burke intimated that the loss of Maryland's vote would unbalance the confederacy. He also thought it important to avoid "even an appearance of divided councils; a partial Confederacy must be followed by confusion, the states so confederated, and such as are now so Confederated, could no longer form one Common Council; and separately they could not form or Execute any Common resolutions; in a word, it would destroy the old union." October 31, 1779, ibid., 14: 119–20 n.

4. Thomas Burke's Remarks on the Articles of Confederation [ante December 16, 1777], ibid., 8: 420.

5. Thomas Burke to the North Carolina Assembly, October 25, 1779, ibid., 14: 109.

6. See, e.g., Lovell to Unknown, February 10, 1779, ibid., 12: 44–45.

7. For this expression, by Jacob Read of South Carolina, see Charles Thomson to Richard Peters, January 19, 1784, ibid., 11: 294.

8. Gouverneur Morris to John Dunlap, April 22, 1779, ibid., 12: 374.

9. The Remonstrance of the General Assembly of Virginia to the Delegates of the United American States in Congress Assembled, December 10, 1779, *Mason Papers,* 2: 596–97.

10. Alexander Hamilton to James Duane, September 3, 1780, *Hamilton Papers,* 2: 401.

11. North Carolina Delegates to Richard Caswell, May 20, 1779, *Letters of Delegates,* 12: 499.

12. Thomas Burke to the Assembly of the State of North Carolina, October 31, 1779, ibid., 14: 119 n.

13. Circular-Letter from Congress to their Constituents, September 13, 1779, *Jay Correspondence,* 1: 218–26, at 229–30.

14. Richard B. Morris, *The Forging of the Union, 1781–1789* (New York, 1987), 68–69.

15. Observations on the Article Etats-Unis Prepared for the Encyclopedie, June 22, 1786, Peterson, *Jefferson Writings,* 578.

16. James Madison to Mathew Carey, July 31, 1831, *Madison Writings,* 858. See also Drew R. McCoy, *The Last of the Fathers: James Madison and the Republican Legacy* (Cambridge, 1989), 119–70.

17. Alexander Hamilton to James Duane, September 3, 1780, *Hamilton Papers,* 2: 401.

18. Meng, *Despatches of Gérard,* 763–67. Daniel of St. Thomas Jennifer's Notes on Franco-American Alliance, [July 4? 1779], *Letters of Delegates,* 13: 145–48 n.

19. As John Witherspoon observed, in the context of the convention of Saratoga, "the simplest man in the world knows, that a mutual onerous contract is always conditional; and that if the condition fails on one side, whether from necessity or

fraud, the other is free." John Witherspoon's Speech in Congress, January 8, 1778, *Letters of Delegates,* 8: 554–55.

20. Andrew C. McLaughlin, *The Confederation and the Constitution, 1783–1789* (New York, [1905] 1962), 45–46.

21. See the discussion in Lance Banning, *The Sacred Fire of Liberty: James Madison and the Founding of the Federal Republic* (Ithaca, N.Y., 1995); and the consideration of this issue in Cooke, *Federalist,* No. 22.

22. David Ramsay to Nicholas Van Dyke, April 1, 1786, *Letters of Delegates,* 23: 214.

23. Speech to Jean Baptiste Ducoigne, [ca. 1] June 1781, *Jefferson Papers,* 6: 61.

24. John Harvie to Thomas Jefferson, October 18, 1777, *Letters of Delegates,* 8: 139.

CHAPTER 21

1. *Common Sense,* February 14, 1776, *Paine Writings,* 22, 24–25, 40–41.

2. Ibid., 31–32.

3. John Adams to James Warren, October 7, 1775, *Letters of Delegates,* 2: 137.

4. John Adams to John Winthrop, June 23, 1776, *Adams Papers,* 4: 332. A year later, Adams was still insisting on the wisdom of avoiding entanglement in the quarrels of Europe: "I don't wish to be under Obligations to any of them, and I am very unwilling they should rob Us of the Glory of vindicating our own Liberties." He was "ashamed" that so many whigs were "groaning and Sighing . . . that We must be Subdued unless France should step in. Are We to be beholden to France for our Liberties?" John Adams to James Warren, May 3, 1777, *Letters of Delegates,* 7: 21.

5. Robert Morris to Silas Deane, December 20, 1776, *Letters of Delegates,* 5: 53. Choiseul and other sources to the same effect are cited in James H. Hutson, *John Adams and the Diplomacy of the American Revolution* (Lexington, Ky., 1980), 1–7. Adams's initial draft of the Model Treaty, the committee report (August 27), and the plan of treaties as adopted (September 17) are reprinted, with valuable editorial commentary, in *Adams Papers,* 4: 260–302. See also Gregg L. Lint, "John Adams on the Drafting of the Treaty Plan of 1776," *Diplomatic History* 2 (1978): 313–20; and William C. Stinchcombe, "John Adams and the Model Treaty," in *The American Revolution and "A Candid World,"* ed. Lawrence S. Kaplan (Kent, Ohio, 1977), 69. The controversy over whether the plan of treaties was alien to the diplomatic spirit of the time—a thesis maintained by Felix Gilbert, *To the Farewell Address: Ideas of Early American Foreign Policy* (Princeton, N.J., 1961), 50–54—may be followed in Hutson, *John Adams;* Hutson, "Early American Diplomacy: A Reappraisal," in Kaplan, *American Revolution,* 40–68, at 50; and Jonathan R. Dull, *A Diplomatic History of the American Revolution* (New Haven, Conn., 1985). On the historic sources of the aspiration to be separate from Europe's wars, see Max Savelle, with Margaret Anne Fisher, *The Origins of American Diplomacy: The International History of Angloamerica, 1492–1763* (New York, 1967), esp. 511–54. Adams displayed considerable pride of authorship in his system of avoiding treaties of alliance and separating America "as far as possible and as long as possible from all European politics and wars." Jefferson and Hamilton, he wrote in

1805, "ought not to steal from me my good name and rob me of the reputation of a system which I was born to introduce, 'refin'd it first and show'd its use,' as really as Dean Swift did irony." Adams to Benjamin Rush, September 30, 1805, *The Spur of Fame: Dialogues of John Adams and Benjamin Rush, 1805–1813,* ed. John A Schutz and Douglass Adair (San Marino, Calif., 1966), 38–39.

6. Address of Congress, May 8, 1778, *JCC,* 11: 481; David Ramsay, "An Oration on the Advantage of American Independence . . . ," July 4, 1778, Charleston, S.C., Niles, *Principles,* 374–83, at 378. For a contrary interpretation, stressing the "mercantilist" character of early American thinking, see Hutson, *John Adams;* and John E. Crowley, *The Privileges of Independence: Neomercantilism and the American Revolution* (Baltimore, 1993).

7. John Adams to John M. Jackson, December 30, 1817, *Adams Works,* 10: 269.

8. Benjamin Franklin to David Hartley, February 12, 1778, Wharton, *Diplomatic Correspondence,* 2: 493; Franklin to William Pulteney, March 30, 1778, ibid., 2: 527; both cited in Gerald Stourzh, *Benjamin Franklin and American Foreign Policy* (Chicago, 1954), 148. For Adams's claim in 1780, see "Letters from a Distinguished American," No. 5, *Adams Papers,* 9: 534. The standard works on the making of the alliance are Edward S. Corwin, *French Policy and the American Alliance of 1778* (Hamden, Conn., [1916] 1962) (where the treaty is reprinted at 385–91); William C. Stinchcombe, *The American Revolution and the French Alliance* (Syracuse, N.Y., 1969); and Ronald Hoffman and Peter J. Albert, eds., *Diplomacy and Revolution: The Franco-American Alliance of 1778* (Charlottesville, Va., 1981).

9. For an instance of such threats, see the congressional instructions to the American commissioners in Giunta, *Documents,* 1: 13. On French motives, see Dull, *Diplomatic History;* Corwin, *French Alliance.*

10. John Adams to Samuel Adams, July 28, 1778, *Adams Papers,* 6: 325–27; John Adams to James Warren, August 4, 1778, ibid., 6: 346–49.

11. "Letters from a Distinguished American," [ante 14–22 July] 1780, ibid., No. 1: 541–44; No. 6: 562.

12. Pownall, *Memorial,* 5, 9, 85, 103–4, 107–9. See also Benjamin Franklin to James Lovell, July 22, 1778, *Franklin Papers,* 27: 137. "Commerce among Nations," wrote Franklin, "as well as between Private Persons should be fair and equitable, by *Equivalent* Exchanges, and mutual Supplies." See also Stourzh, *Benjamin Franklin,* 108–10.

13. John Adams to James Warren, *Adams Papers,* 6: 348. See Editorial Note, *Adams Papers,* 9: 157–64, for the circumstances of the various versions of the "translation."

14. Pownall, *Memorial,* 87; David Ramsay, "An Oration on the Advantage of American Independence . . . ," July 4, 1778, Charleston, S.C., Niles, *Principles,* 374–83, at 377–78. The strong pressures in favor of emigration before the outbreak of war and the deep concern of British officials over that situation are detailed in Bernard Bailyn, with the assistance of Barbara DeWolfe, *Voyagers to the West: A Passage in the Peopling of America on the Eve of the Revolution* (New York, 1986). See also George Frost to Josiah Bartlett, August 18, 1777, *Letters of Delegates,* 7: 510. Frost found it "a very general Opinion" in both Europe and America "that if

we succeed in establishing our liberties we shall as soon as peace is restored receive an immence addition of numbers and wealth from Europe." The liberalizing effects of the capacity to emigrate were also a key element in the defense of capitalism in the eighteenth century, as is shown in Albert Hirschman, *The Passions and the Interests: Political Arguments for Capitalism Before Its Triumph* (Princeton, N.J., 1977). Pownall drew the connection thusly: exchange had taught statesmen "that they cannot confine money: and the state of the Empire of these European states must fall back to an old feudal community, in which its own people are locked up, and from which all others are excluded, or *commerce will open the door to Emigration*" (88). Ramsay's insistence that large empires were not favorable to true philosophy was borrowed from David Hume, "The Rise of Arts and Sciences," Hume, *Essays,* 119–23. To the same effect, see Robertson, *Reign of Charles V,* 1: 502–5. According to him, the cause of Protestantism was virtually identical to the cause of learning: both were protected by the emergence of a system of independent states, tied together by commerce, whose independence was maintained by a salutary balance among them. See further J. G. A. Pocock, *Barbarism and Religion,* 2 vols. (Cambridge, 1999), 2: 289–299.

15. Gilbert, *Farewell Address,* 17.

16. Hutson, "Early American Diplomacy," 50; and idem, *John Adams,* passim.

17. Gilbert, *Farewell Address,* emphasizes that Americans marched, at the beginning, to the strains of "idealism" and "internationalism," whereas Hutson, *John Adams,* emphasizes their political realism. Whereas Gilbert emphasizes the turn to realism as a consequence of a reaction, in the 1780s, to misguided idealism, Hutson insists that the realist strain was present and dominant at the very beginning. Gilbert sees the 1776 Model Treaty as marking, in the American estimation, the beginnings of a new diplomacy that was to usher in an age of universal peace—that is what he appears to mean by "internationalism"—whereas Hutson sees its purpose as providing "for American security by using American commerce to maintain the European balance of power" (Hutson, *Adams and Diplomacy,* 28). Whereas Gilbert pushes early American thought in the direction of an "idealistic internationalism" that was also rather woolly-minded, Hutson pushes it in the direction of a bleak and unsparing realism. There are perceptive reviews of this debate in Jonathan R. Dull, "Benjamin Franklin and the Nature of American Diplomacy," *International History Review* 3 (1983): 346–63; and David M. Fitzsimons, "Tom Paine's New World Order: Idealistic Internationalism in the Ideology of Early American Foreign Relations," *Diplomatic History* 19 (1995): 569–82. The best guide to these questions for the Revolutionary era remains Stourzh, *Benjamin Franklin.* To generally the same effect on the role of realism and idealism, though for later periods of American history, see Robert E. Osgood, *Ideals and Self-Interest in America's Foreign Relations: The Great Transformation of the Twentieth Century* (Chicago, 1953); Walter A. McDougall, *Promised Land, Crusader State: The American Encounter with the World Since 1776* (Boston, 1997); and Robert W. Tucker and David C. Hendrickson, *Empire of Liberty: The Statecraft of Thomas Jefferson* (New York, 1990).

18. What Martin Wight called "the Whig or constitutional tradition in diplomacy" is essentially identical in content to what he and his "school" have elsewhere identified as the Grotian, internationalist, or rationalist traditions. See Martin

Wight, "Western Values in International Relations," in *Diplomatic Investigations: Essays in the Theory of International Politics,* ed. Martin Wight and Herbert Butterfield (Cambridge, Mass., 1966); idem, *International Theory: The Three Traditions* (New York, 1992); Hedley Bull, *The Anarchical Society: A Study of Order in World Politics* (New York, 1977), 23–52; and the discussion in chapter 3, note 14, and figure 5 of the appendix. In Wight's view, the whig or constitutional tradition was exemplified "in different ways by Suarez, Grotius, Locke, Halifax, Callières, Montesquieu, Burke, Gentz, Coleridge, Castlereagh, Tocqueville, Lincoln, Gladstone, Cecil of Chelwod, Ferrero, Brierly, Harold Nicolson, Churchill, [and] Spaak" (Wight, "Western Values," 90). So far as the earlier writers are concerned, Wight's list might be supplemented by the names that one constitutional whig, Thomas Pownall, identified as inspirational in 1780: Sully, Fleury, Clarendon, Somers, and De Witt (Pownall, *Memorial,* iv).

19. Franklin to President of Congress, July 22, 1783, Giunta, *Emerging Nation,* 1: 896.

20. On this point, see the discussion in Peter Onuf and Nicholas Onuf, *Federal Union, Modern World: The Law of Nations in an Age of Revolutions, 1776–1814* (Madison, Wis., 1993), 103–8. In support of his critique minimizing the importance of the liberation of commerce as a goal of the Revolution, Hutson draws attention to the "republican" fear that commerce and its concomitant luxury would prove a source of corruption. As Fitzsimons notes, the republican critique was focused more on the national debts and stock exchanges associated with finance capitalism than on commerce as such. But even if commerce itself might be denounced as a source of corruption, as it on occasion was, American leaders believed that a "Chinese" policy of commercial isolation was "theory only," as even Hutson readily acknowledges (Hutson, *John Adams,* 148–50). "If all Intercourse between Europe and America," Adams wrote, "could be cutt off, forever, if every ship We have were burnt, and the Keel of another never to be laid, We might still be the happiest People upon earth and in fifty years the most powerfull." Given the "Character of our people," however, it was vain "to amuse ourselves, with the Thoughts of annihilating Commerce unless as philosophical Speculations." Considering "Men and Things as practical Statesmen, and . . . who our Constituents are and what they expect of Us," the thing was impossible: "They are as Aquatic as the Sea Fowl, and the Love of Commerce with its Conveniences and Pleasures are habits, in them as unalterable as their Natures." John Adams to John Jay, December 6, 1785, Giunta, *Emerging Nation,* 2: 943. Jefferson's famous speculations to similar effect are contained in Thomas Jefferson to G. K. van Hogendorp, October 13, 1785, Peterson, *Jefferson Writings,* 836–37. Jefferson mused that, were he to indulge his "own theory," he would wish America "to practice neither commerce nor navigation, but to stand with respect to Europe precisely on the footing of China. We should thus avoid wars, and all our citizens would be husbandmen." Jefferson quickly added that it was "theory only, & a theory which the servants of America are not at liberty to follow. Our people have a decided taste for navigation & commerce. They take this from their mother country: & their servants are in duty bound to calculate all their measures on this datum: we wish to do it by throwing open all the doors of commerce & knocking off its shackles."

21. *Adams Diary,* 4: 38–39.

22. Edward Rutledge to John Adams, July 16, 1778, *Adams Papers,* 6: 294–95.

23. John Adams to James Warren, August 4, 1778, ibid., 6: 348. One might identify this as evidence of a "conservative" as opposed to "liberal" internationalism, looking to the preservation rather than the reform of the international system. Hutson draws attention frequently to Adams's invocation of the balance of power and believes that it affords evidence of his consistent "realism." But insofar as the "balance of power" is considered not as a synonym for realpolitik but as pointing to the necessary underpinning of international society, without which the law of nations would be incapable of securing the liberty and independence of states, it surely qualifies as an internationalist norm. Vattel and other eighteenth-century writers, as we saw earlier in chapter 7, had understood the balance of power in those terms and had placed it in opposition to the dreaded specter of universal monarchy. So did Adams and other Americans. See, e.g., Robert Morris to John Jay, July 4, 1781, speaking of Britain's pursuit of "those Schemes of universal Empire which the Virtue and Fortitude of America first checked, and which it is the Object of the present War to frustrate." *Morris Papers,* 1: 230.

24. James Duane's Draft Manifesto Respecting Henry Laurens, [April 3–May 9?, 1781], *Letters of Delegates,* 17: 120.

25. See the citations from Fénelon, Callières, Montesquieu, Voltaire, Gibbon, and Burke in Terry Nardin, *Law, Morality, and the Relations of States* (Princeton, N.J., 1983), 61–62. On "union and independence" as a theme of the law of nations, see Edward Vose Gulick, *Europe's Classical Balance of Power: A Case History of the Theory and Practice of One of the Great Concepts of European Statecraft* (Ithaca, N.Y., 1955).

26. Benjamin Franklin to Edmund Burke, October 15, 1781, *Franklin Writings,* 9: 84.

27. John Adams to Baron De Thulemeier, February 13, 1785, *Adams Works,* 8: 225. For Franklin's proposition, see Benjamin Franklin to Richard Oswald, January 14, 1783, with enclosure, "Propositions relative to privateering, &c. communicated to Mr. Oswald," Giunta, *Emerging Nation,* 1: 750–52.

28. John Adams to Abigail Adams, June 2, 1777, *Letters of Delegates,* 7: 160. Earlier he had written to Abigail that "In a Time of Warr, and especially a war like this, one may see the Necessity and Utility, of the divine Prohibitions of Revenge." If men were not restrained in some degree by the "benevolent laws" found "in the Christian Religion," they "would be Devils, at such a Time as this." March 14, 1777, ibid., 6: 442. Fifteen years later, Benjamin Rush attributed the "material change for the better" in the world over the "the last two hundred years" to "the influence of Christianity upon the hearts of men," but he believed this influence to be unacknowledged. Six salient changes marked "the influence of Christianity upon the modes of war." "1st. In rescuing women and children from being the objects of the desolutions of war in common with men. 2dly. In preventing the destruction of captives taken in battle, in cold blood. 3dly. In protecting the peaceable husbandman from sharing in the carnage of war. 4thly. In producing an exchange of prisoners, instead of dooming them to perpetual slavery. 5thly. In avoiding the invasion or destruction, in certain cases, of private property. 6thly. In declaring all wars to be unlawful but such as are purely *defensive.*" "On Punishing Murder by Death" [1792], *Rush Selected Writings,* 51.

29. Henry Laurens to John Lewis Gervais, August 5, 1777, *Letters of Delegates,* 7: 419; Richard Henry Lee to Patrick Henry, May 13, 1777, ibid., 7: 75. See also Lee to Henry, May 6, 1777, ibid., 7: 33 n. Retaliation against Indians and territorial cupidity were closely linked, as is evident in James Duane to George Clinton, March 21, 1779, ibid., 12: 214. Duane unfolded a plan for punitive expeditions against the Six Nations, whose "violation of the great treaty at Albany with the United States was perfidious beyond example." "If they are suffered to remain on this side of Niagara, I mean the perfidious tribes, they at least must make a full compensation for all the injuries they have done to our State; not in words, but according to the South Carolina plan, by a large cession of territory." See also Jefferson to John Page, August 5, 1776. Jefferson was sorry to hear from Page "that the Indians have commenced war" but pleased that the governor of Virginia had been decisive in countering them. Recommending that the war be pushed into the heart of their country, Jefferson added that "I would not stop there. I would never cease pursuing them while one of them remained on this side of the Misisippi. So unprovoked an attack and so treacherous a one should never be forgiven while one of them remains near enough to do us injury." This was said not in reference to all Indians, for Jefferson next recounted the threat that congress, where he was sitting, had made to the Six Nations: "if they chuse to go to war with us, they should be at liberty to remove their families out of our settlements, but to remember that they should not only never more return to their dwellings on any terms but that we would never cease pursuing them with war while one remained on the face of the earth." Momentarily, at least, "this decisive declaration" produced the intended effect, and pacific gestures from the Six Nations followed; *Jefferson Papers,* 1: 485–86. Jefferson's unwillingness to "stop there," though employing the form of an argument from retaliation, went well beyond the limits that the law of nations allowed. See further Jack M. Sosin, "The Use of Indians in the War of the American Revolution: A Reassessment of Responsibility," *Canadian Historical Review* 46 (1965): 101–21; Reginald C. Stuart, *The Half-Way Pacifist: Thomas Jefferson's View of War* (Toronto, 1978), 7–10; and Harold E. Selesky, "Colonial America," in *The Laws of War: Constraints on Warfare in the Western World,* ed. Michael Howard, George J. Andreopoulos, and Mark R. Shulman (New Haven, Conn., 1994), 59–85.

30. There are many such debates recorded in the congress. The issue, for example, arose in pointed form in the context of whether the United States should observe the convention of Saratoga, concluded after Burgoyne's defeat in 1777 by New England troops under the command of General Horatio Gates. The issue was invariably framed in blended strains of realism and idealism. "It is unfortunately too true," wrote Richard Henry Lee, "that our enemies pay little regard to good faith, or any obligations of justice and humanity, which renders the convention of Saratoga a matter of great moment, and . . . of infinite delicacy. The undoubted advantage they will take, even of the appearance of infraction on our part, and the American Character, which is concerned in preserving its faith inviolate, cover this affair with difficulties, and prove the disadvantage we are under in conducting war against an old, corrupt, and powerful people, who having much credit and influence in the world will venture on things that would totally ruin the reputation of young and rising communities like ours" (Richard Henry Lee to George Washington, November 20, 1777, *Letters of Delegates,* 8: 293). Witherspoon framed the

moral and political issue in a similar fashion: the "preservation of faith and honor in solemn contracts," he noted, was of great moment to private persons as well as "every incorporated society," and "it is especially so to us, as representing the United States of America, associated so lately." Witherspoon thought it obligatory to "detest" any idea of measures that were "mean, captious, or insidious, whatever advantage may seem to arise from it." At the same time, "the interest of this continent" was committed to congress, and it had to ensure "that the public suffer no injury by deception, or abuse and insult, on the part of our enemies." Thinking that the latter danger did indeed exist, he urged the repudiation of the convention until such time as the congress might gain sufficient proof that the British would carry out its terms. A similar conclusion was reached by James Lovell of Massachusetts, who told Samuel Adams that the debate was likely to unfold on the following lines: "Those who have been chiefly theoretic students will shake their hands and cry nay. These will be joined by some timorous christians who are always doubting even when they say they have *sure* hope. On the other hand practical Politicians joined by all such good Folk as, supposing themselves past the days of miraculous Exhibition, look upon natural vigorous exertions as somewhat connected with the essence of Hope; these I suppose, will cry aloud aye." Lovell put himself in the latter class (James Lovell to Samuel Adams, January 13, 1778, ibid., 8: 580). Witherspoon and Lovell defended a similar point of view in March 1777, which Thomas Burke described as "tending to the Doctrine that we were bound by no such agreements no longer than we found them convenient." North Carolina "vehemently opposed" that doctrine, holding that "it was good policy even abstracted from all Moral Consideration, to keep inviolate the Faith of Nations, because on that alone was founded all compact between them, that to a young Country the reputation of Fidelity was as Essential as that of Immaculate Chastity to a Young Beauty, the Smallest blot in either must sink the Subject forever in the Estimation of mankind." Thomas Burke's Notes of Debates, March 14, 1777, ibid., 6: 443.

31. John Adams to Secretary Jay, August 10, 1785, *Adams Works,* 8: 298–99. Faced with such resistance, Adams was happy to "venture upon monopolies and exclusions, if they were found to be the only arms of defence against monopolies and exclusions, without fear of offending Dean Tucker or the ghost of Doctor Quesnay."

32. John Emerich Edward Dalberg-Acton, *Lectures on the French Revolution* (Indianapolis, 2000), 17–32; R. R. Palmer, *The Age of Democratic Revolutions: A Political History of Europe and America 1760–1800.* 2 vols. (Princeton, N.J., 1959, 1964).

33. Friedrich Gentz, trans. John Quincy Adams, *The French and American Revolutions Compared,* in Stefan T. Possony, *Three Revolutions* (Chicago, 1959).

34. Immanuel Kant, *Perpetual Peace: A Philosophical Sketch* (1795), ed. Hans Reiss (Cambridge, 1970), 103.

CHAPTER 22

1. On the state of the parties in 1779, see H. James Henderson, *Party Politics in the Continental Congress* (New York, [1974]); Jack N. Rakove, *The Beginnings of*

National Politics: An Interpretive History of the Continental Congress (Baltimore, [1979] 1982). On "English" and "French" parties, see Meng, *Despatches of Gérard.*

2. John Dickinson to Caesar Rodney, May 10, 1779, *Letters of Delegates,* 12: 447–48.

3. Thomas Burke to Richard Caswell, March 11, 1777, ibid., 6: 427–29.

4. Ibid.

5. North Carolina Delegates to Richard Caswell, May 20, 1779, ibid., 12: 500.

6. D. W. Meinig, *Atlantic America, 1492–1800* (New Haven, Conn., 1986); Drayton in Niles, *Principles,* 363.

7. Meinig, *Atlantic America.*

8. Autobiography, Peterson, *Jefferson Writings,* 18.

9. See Meinig, *Atlantic America;* Drew R. McCoy, *The Elusive Republic: Political Economy in Jeffersonian America* (New York, [1980] 1982); Joyce Oldham Appleby, *Capitalism and a New Social Order: The Republican Vision of the 1790s* (New York, 1984).

10. Autobiography, Peterson, *Jefferson Writings,* 18.

11. James Warren to John Adams, June 22, 1777, *Letters of Delegates,* 7: 309 n; John Adams to James Warren, July 7, 1777, ibid., 7: 308; Donald L. Robinson, *Slavery in the Structure of American Politics, 1765–1820* (New York, 1971).

12. William Duer, a New Yorker, noted in 1777 that one New Jersey delegate (Jonathan Dickinson Sergeant) had a "political Line of Conduct" that lay "to the Eastward of Biram's River." William Duer to Robert R. Livingston, May 28, 1777, *Letters of Delegates,* 7: 141.

13. See Meinig, *Atlantic America;* and Daniel H. Deudney, "The Philadelphian System: Sovereignty, Arms Control, and Balance of Power in the American States-Union, Circa 1787–1861," *International Organization* 49 (1995): 191–228.

14. Max M. Mintz, *Gouverneur Morris and the American Revolution* (Norman, Okla., 1970). For conflicts over military policy during the war, see J. Gregory Rossie, *The Politics of Command in the American Revolution* (Syracuse, N.Y., 1975). On Morris's role, see also William Duer to Robert R. Livingston, July 9, 1777, *Letters of Delegates,* 7: 328. On New York's larger political orientation in the early years of the war, see also James Duane to Robert R. Livingston, June 28, 1777, ibid., 7: 261–62.

15. Samuel Adams to Arthur Lee, July 4, 1777, ibid., 7: 289.

16. All these explanations were proferred by congressmen to account for the "langour of the most alarming Nature" prevailing in Philadelphia and Pennsylvania. See William Duer to Robert R. Livingston, May 28, 1777, ibid., 7: 141; William Duer to John Jay, May 28, 1777, ibid., 7: 138: "In this State Toryism (or rather Treason) stalks triumphant . . ."; James Duane to George Clinton, November 9, 1777, ibid., 8: 247: "her military Exertions are so feeble, the Body of her Inhabitants so dissatisfied, or so intent upon Gain, that she in effect contributes next to nothing to the Common Cause." In late 1777, Richard Henry Lee thought it would be "no great matter of surprize if we were to find a total revolution in Pennsylvania and Delaware" favoring loyalism. "You well know, Sir, how weak and divided the people of this State [Pennsylvania] are from various causes. Those of Delaware are still worse." Richard Henry Lee to George Washington, November 20, 1777, ibid., 8: 293.

17. Richard Henry Lee to Patrick Henry, May 26, 1777, ibid., 7: 123–24.

18. Thomas Jefferson to William Fleming, June 8, 1779, *Jefferson Papers*, 2: 288. Cf. Jefferson to Richard Henry Lee, August 30, 1778, on the importance of the fisheries as a nursery for seamen. *Jefferson Papers*, 2: 210.

19. This was said of the later instructions of 1781. See James H. Hutson, *John Adams and the Diplomacy of the American Revolution* (Lexington, Ky., 1980), 123. The 1779 instructions allowed the American plenipotentiary (Adams) a bit more leeway. His propensity to see a power of discretion *in* the 1779 instructions was what made Vergennes determined to squeeze the discretion *out* of the instructions in 1781.

20. See Gerry's remarks in Congress, June 19, 1779, *Letters of Delegates*, 13: 84 n; and George A. Billias, *Elbridge Gerry: Founding Father and Republican Statesman* (New York, 1976), 92–95.

21. On this reorientation, see Piers Mackesy, *The War for America, 1775–1783* (Lincoln, Nebr., [1964] 1993), esp. 157–59.

22. James Lovell to John Adams, June 13, 1779, *Adams Papers*, 8: 87.

23. North Carolina Delegates to the South Carolina Delegates, April 2, 1779, *Letters of Delegates*, 12: 277. See the further exchanges among Laurens, William Henry Drayton, Richard Henry Lee, and various North Carolinians in ibid., 12: 282–83, 285, 288–94, 310–14, 326–27.

24. Christopher Gadsen to Samuel Adams, April 4, 1779, in *The Writings of Christopher Gadsen, 1746–1805*, ed. Richard Walsh (Columbia, S.C., 1966), 161–64. James Lovell to Richard Henry Lee, August 17, 1779, *Letters of Delegates*, 13: 381, mentions William Henry Drayton's "invidious motion" requesting the eastern states to send *"their* Fleet to relieve" South Carolina and Georgia.

25. "If the People, in Pensylvania, Maryland, Delaware and Jersy had the Feelings and the Spirit of some People that I know, Howe would be soon ensnared in a Trap, more fatal than that in which, as it is said, Burgoigne was taken." John Adams to Abigail Adams, October 28, 1777, *Adams Family Correspondence*, 2: 361–62. "I was greatly surprizd when I heard that the Enemy were in possession of Philadelphia without any engagement upon our part. If Men will not fight and defend their own perticuliar spot, if they will not drive the Enemy from their Doors, they deserve the slavery and subjection which awaits them." Abigail Adams to John Adams, October 20, 1777, ibid., 2: 354.

26. James Warren to John Adams, June 13, 1777, *Adams Papers*, 8: 93–94; and Joseph L. Davis, *Sectionalism in American Politics, 1774–1787* (Madison, Wis., 1977), 19–20.

27. John Adams to James Warren, April 29, 1777, *Letters of Delegates*, 6: 670: "Every Man of the Massachusetts Quota ought to have been ready last December. And not one Man has yet arrived in the Field. . . . If Ticonderoga is not lost it will be because it is not attacked—and if It should be New England will bear all the shame and all the Blame of it. In plain English I beg to be supported or recalled." For Adams's conception of Massachusetts's role, see Adams to Warren, June 19, 1777, ibid., 7: 220. On the competitive emulation of the states, and the jealousies attendant on that contest, see also Henry Marchant to Nicholas Cooke, July 13, 1777, ibid., 7: 340–41; Charles Thomson's Notes of Debates, July 28, 1777, ibid., 7: 388–90; Thomas Burke to Richard Caswell, July 30, 1777, ibid., 7: 395–96;

Samuel Adams to James Warren, February 11, 1779, ibid. 12: 50. Reporting Virginia's "glorious Example to the Southern States, & indeed to every State in the Union" by her vigorous military measures, Cornelius Harnett lamented that "Alass! We have few Virginias in the Union. As for Pensylvania, she is rotten to the very heart, if she is saved, it will not be by her own exertions." Cornelius Harnett to Thomas Burke, December 8, 1777, ibid., 8: 389; Harnett to William Wilkinson, December 8, 1777, ibid., 8: 391.

28. Samuel Adams to Samuel P. Savage, October 26, 1777, ibid., 8: 188.

29. Massachusetts Delegates to the Massachusetts Assembly, May 21, 1777, ibid., 7: 100.

30. John Adams to Abigail Adams, May 17, 1777, ibid., 7: 88–89.

31. For various expressions of this discontent, see Daniel of St. Thomas Jenifer to Thomas Johnson, May 24, 1779, ibid., 12: 522–23: "I see very plainly, that the Southern States will be obliged to shift for themselves." The standard account of congressional finances, E. James Ferguson, *The Power of the Purse: A History of American Public Finance, 1776–1790* (Chapel Hill, N.C., 1961), neglects this sectional dynamic.

32. Piers Mackesy, *The War for America, 1775–1783* (Lincoln, Nebr., 1992 [1964], 157–59.

33. In the 1779 peace instructions, congress agreed to help Spain obtain the Floridas if she entered the war.

34. Address to the People of Great Britain, October 21, 1774, *JCC*, 1: 88.

35. A Letter to the Inhabitants of the Province of Quebec, October 26, 1774, ibid., 1: 112.

36. George Mason to Richard Henry Lee, July 21, 1778, *Mason Papers*, 1: 430.

37. Reginald C. Stuart, *United States Expansionism and British North America, 1775–1871* (Chapel Hill, N.C., 1988), 11–20.

38. Luzerne to Vergennes, August 26, 1780, Giunta, *Emerging Nation*, 1: 103; Samuel Adams to Samuel Cooper, April 29, 1779, *Letters of Delegates*, 12: 401–3 n; William Whipple to Josiah Bartlett, February 7, 1779, ibid., 12: 29. In late 1777, Lovell wrote to John Adams that he was "altogether averse from strong sollicitations to that People to become immediately active. They will fall to us of Course. I wish to have them acquainted with the nature of our union. But I would not wish to be bound to carry an Expedition into their Country till their Friendship was certain and quite General." December 1, 1777, ibid., 8: 362–63.

39. Luzerne to Vergennes, February 11, 1780, Giunta, *Emerging Nation*, 1: 27–33. Luzerne noted that some delegates "from the Eastern States have announced the same opinion as those from the South, with the difference, however, that they are inclined to think that if Spain were to seize a part of these same countries while they were still in the hands of the English, the right of the Southern States deprived of possession would become difficult to exercise, and that this might result in awkward situations" (29). See also Charles Thomson's Notes of Debates, August 8, 1782, *Letters of Delegates*, 19: 45–46, where Witherspoon "observed that the happiness of the people on this side of the Alleghany Mountains was a sufficient object to induce them to enter into the war; that some of the States had their boundaries fixed and determined; that the State he had the honor to represent was one of them; that it had not entered into the war nor would it he believed be willing to continue

it for the sake of boundless claims of wild uncultivated country; more especially as it was a matter of dispute & will undoubtedly occasion much contention among the States to whom that country if ceded will of right belong."

40. Pennsylvania voted with the northern states in 1786 in favor of Jay's proposal to surrender the navigation of the Mississippi for twenty-five years in return for commercial concessions from Spain, but this came as an alarming surprise to most southern delegates.

41. James Duane to George Clinton, March 21, 1779, *Letters of Delegates,* 12: 214. This letter contains an extended description of New York's glittering prospects after the war, her expectations of a large emigration from both Europe and "the settled states," and unfolds a plan for punitive expeditions against the Six Nations. See chapter 21, note 29, and New York Delegates to George Clinton, February 3, 1779, ibid., 12: 18. On the decision to give up Vermont, see Peter S. Onuf, *Origins of the Federal Republic: Jurisdictional Controversies in the United States, 1775–1787* (Philadelphia, 1983). For a map of the various northern lines proposed during the war, see Samuel Flagg Bemis, *A Diplomatic History of the United States,* 4th ed. (New York, 1955), 60–61. For an imaginative but unpersuasive criticism of the peace negotiators in accepting the line of the lakes in 1782, see Bradford Perkins, "The Peace of Paris: Patterns and Legacies," in *Peace and the Peacemakers: The Treaty of 1783,* ed. Ronald Hoffman and Peter J. Albert (Charlottesville, Va., 1986), 190–229, at 212–14; and the discussion in Samuel Flagg Bemis, *The Diplomacy of the American Revolution* (Bloomington, Ind., [1957]); and Richard B. Morris, *The Peacemakers: The Great Powers and American Independence* (New York, 1965), 361. On Jay's sensitivity to the need "to do Justice to Virginia and the Western Country near the Mississippi," see John Jay's Instructions to William Carmichael, January 27, 1780, Giunta, *Emerging Nation,* 1: 18. Even when others had given it up, Benjamin Franklin retained his attachment to the incorporation of Canada until the end of the peace negotiations in 1782, but his thinking on that question owed less to territorial cupidity than to his fear that if the British kept it they would settle the loyalists there. Franklin wanted them an ocean away. He appreciated, however, that all the states to the southward, Pennsylvania included, saw their future development beyond the western mountains and accounted their claim to it a vital interest, as indeed he did as well.

42. Instructions for a Treaty of Peace with Great Britain, and John Jay, President of Congress, to Franklin, August 14, 1779, Wharton, *Diplomatic Correspondence,* 3: 300–305. While not making the fisheries a sine qua non of a peace treaty, congress pledged that if Great Britain, after such a peace, disturbed Americans in the exercise of the fishery, "we will make it a common cause to obtain redress for the parties injured." Jay asked Franklin to secure the assent of the French court to an additional article of guaranty providing that France would also consider it a *casus foederis* were Britain, after the peace, to molest or disturb Americans "in taking fish on the banks, seas, and places formerly used and frequented by them." The French court declined the offer.

43. *JCC,* 20: 651; *Adams Diary,* 3: 39 n.

44. Chevalier de la Luzerne to Comte de Vergennes, June 23, 1781, Giunta, *Emerging Nation,* 1: 203–4.

45. Comte de Vergennes to Chevalier de la Luzerne, June 30, 1781, ibid., 1: 205.

For concurrent speculations in Europe, see Morris, *Peacemakers;* and, idem, "The Diplomats and the Mythmakers," in *The American Revolution Reconsidered* (New York, 1967), 123: "everybody but America," Morris notes, wanted "a partition of the American continent."

46. James Madison to Edmund Pendleton, October 30, 1781, *Letters of Delegates,* 18: 169.

47. See the detailed account in Onuf, *Origins,* particularly the discussion on p. 118: "Some New York politicians," Onuf writes, "believed that these territorial controversies created artificial alliances and enmities among the states and that if the Vermont question could be laid to rest, then their state would become aligned with the eastern (northern) states."

48. Observations Relating to the Influence of Vermont and the Territorial Claims on the Politics of Congress, May 1, 1782, *Madison Papers,* 4: 201–2. See Henderson, *Party Politics,* 308, and Onuf, *Origins,* for further analysis of the politics of the Vermont claim.

49. Richard Henry Lee to R. Wormley Carter, June 3, 1783, *Lee Letters,* 2: 282.

50. Pierce Butler to James Iredell, April 5, 1782, cited in Henderson, *Party Politics,* 309. A few years earlier, Daniel of St. Thomas Jenifer had speculated that if New England succeeded in her desire to gain another vote in congress, "I suppose another State must be erected out of Virga., as a Counterbalance." To Thomas Johnson, June 8, 1779, *Letters of Delegates,* 13: 37. Both Henderson, *Party Politics,* and Davis, *Sectionalism,* note the salience of sectional factors throughout the confederation but also emphasize the deepening of sectional alignments in 1779 and after. See also by Henderson, "The Structure of Politics in the Continental Congress," in *Essays on the American Revolution,* ed. Stanley G. Kurtz and James H. Hutson (Chapel Hill, N.C., [1974]), 157–96; and Calvin Jillson and Rick K. Wilson, *Congressional Dynamics: Structure, Coordination, and Choice in the First American Congress, 1774–1789* (Stanford, Calif., 1994).

CHAPTER 23

1. Alexander Hamilton to John Jay, July 25, 1783, *Hamilton Papers,* 3: 416.

2. Preliminary Articles of Peace between the United States and Great Britain, Giunta, *Emerging Nation,* 1: 697.

3. Jay to Livingston, November 17, 1782, ibid., 1: 668.

4. Shelburne to Oswald, July 27, 1782, ibid., 1: 480.

5. David Hartley to Benjamin Franklin, October 4, 1783, ibid., 1: 948.

6. Jay to Congress, November 17, 1782, ibid., 1: 668. On Shelburne's motivations, see Vincent Harlow, *The Founding of the Second British Empire,* 2 vols. (New York, 1952–64). Benjamin Vaughan, a confidant of Shelburne's and a peace negotiator in 1782, later explained to James Monroe the "systems of this statesman." They "go to the abolition of wars, the promotion of agriculture, the unlimited freedom of trade, and the just freedom of man. He is in short against governing too much, and for reconciling the happiness of nations with that of their rulers." September 18, 1795, *Jay Papers,* 2: 3.

7. Vergennes to Reyneval, December 4, 1782, Giunta, *Emerging Nation,* 1: 706.

8. See Jonathan R. Dull, *A Diplomatic History of the American Revolution* (New Haven, Conn., 1985).

9. Vergennes to Franklin, December 15, 1782, Giunta, *Emerging Nation,* 1: 720.

10. Vergennes to Luzerne, July 21, 1783, ibid., 1: 889–93.

11. November 5, 1782, *Adams Diary,* 3: 47.

12. Adams to Livingston, November 18, 1782, *Adams Works,* 8: 11–12.

13. Giunta, *Emerging Nation,* 1: 674

14. Adams to Livingston, July 9, 1783, *Adams Works,* 8: 88.

15. Alleyne Fitzherbert to Henry Strachey, December 19, 1782, Giunta, *Emerging Nation,* 1: 726.

16. Franklin to Vergennes, December 17, 1782, *Franklin Works,* 9: 450–52.

17. Franklin to President of Congress, December 25, 1783, Giunta, *Emerging Nation,* 1: 959.

18. See, e.g., Madison to Jefferson, February 11, 1783, *Madison Papers,* 6: 21. Henry Laurens of South Carolina, who had always treasured a role independent of narrow state particularisms, and who had fought for the fisheries in 1779 against the pressure of France, was also in 1782 much closer to Franklin than Adams on the critical importance of the French alliance. Laurens joined the negotiations in its final days. His sole contribution to the treaty was the insistence on a stipulation "that the British Troops should carry off no Negroes or other American Property." November 30, 1782, *Adams Diary,* 3:82.

19. Franklin to Robert R. Livingston, July 22, 1783, Giunta, *Emerging Nation,* 1: 894–95.

20. John Adams to James Warren, March 20, 1783, cited in James H. Hutson, *John Adams and the Diplomacy of the American Revolution* (Lexington, Ky., 1980), 28–29.

21. Adams to Secretary Livingston, February 5, 1783, *Adams Works,* 8: 35–36.

22. Adams to Secretary Livingston, November 11, 1782, ibid., 8: 9. Adams did not totally deny the claim of gratitude to France. On July 10, he wrote to congress that to talk of confidence in the French court was "to use a general language which may mean almost any thing or almost nothing." If by confidence was meant a belief that the French court would support American claims in the peace talks, Adams said, "I own I have no such confidence, and never had. Seeing and hearing what I have seen and heard, I must have been an idiot to have entertained such confidence; I should be more of a Machiavelian, or a Jesuit, than I ever was or will be, to counterfeit it to you or to congress" (ibid., 8: 89). After going on in this vein for some considerable time, Adams seems to have thought better of it the next day. Ingratitude, he then told congress, was indeed "an odious vice, & ought to be held in detestation by every American Citizen." Though Americans ought not to feel gratitude for the great points gained in the settlement regarding the fisheries, the boundaries, and the tories—that was no doing of France—they did owe a debt of gratitude to France "for making the treaty when they did; for those sums of money which they have generously given us, and for those even which they have lent us, which I hope we shall punctually pay, and be thankful still for the loan; for the fleet and army they sent to America, and for all the important services they did." Besides, he said, with Britain in possession of Canada and Nova Scotia, "a continuance of the friendship

and alliance of France is of importance to our tranquillity, and even to our safety" (July 11, 1783, ibid., 8: 94).

23. November 30, 1782, *Adams Diary*, 3: 82.

24. Hamilton to Jay, July 25, 1783, *Hamilton Papers*, 3: 416.

25. See Luzerne to Vergennes, September 26, 1783, Giunta, *Emerging Nation*, 1: 942–45. Of Franklin, Luzerne noted that "he is thought extremely attached to France, but . . . no one does him the injury of thinking that he has sold himself to us." Luzerne convicted Adams of the charge of anti-Gallicanism but acquited Jay: "I do not think he has any gratitude to us, but he is incapable of preferring England to us; he prides himself on being independent, and his desire to show his attachment to his Country renders him sometimes unjust, but we should not fear from him any premeditated act capable of being prejudicial to the alliance."

26. On the reorientation of British policy, see Charles R. Ritcheson, *Aftermath of Revolution: British Policy Toward the United States, 1783–95* (New York, 1971); and Harlow, *Founding of Second British Empire*. See also Merrill D. Peterson, *Thomas Jefferson and the New Nation* (New York, 1970); Drew R. McCoy, *The Elusive Republic: Political Economy in Jeffersonian America* (New York, [1980] 1982); Frederick W. Marks III, *Independence on Trial: Foreign Affairs and the Making of the Constitution*, 2d ed. (Wilmington, Del., 1986).

27. "I am much mistaken," wrote Charles Thomson to his wife, Hannah, "if at this moment we are not puppets in the hands of the juggling politicians of Europe." October 17, 1783, *Letters of Delegates*, 21: 73. See also John Adams to Secretary Livingston, November 11, 1782, *Adams Works*, 8: 9, where Adams says that America "has been a football between contending nations from the beginning." A similar imagery occurs frequently in Hamilton's correspondence.

28. American Peace Commissioners to Livingston, July 18, 1783, Giunta, *Emerging Nation*, 1: 884.

29. On French emoluments during the war, see William C. Stinchcombe, *American Revolution and the French Alliance* (Syracuse, N.Y., 1969). The vulnerability of the American president to such inducements was also stressed by many observers during and after the federal convention. See Jefferson to Madison, December 20, 1787, Smith, *Republic of Letters*, 1: 513. On susceptibility of republics to foreign corruption, see Farrand, *Records*, 1: 319 (Madison); Cooke, *Federalist*, No. 22: 142–43.

30. Adams to Jay, August 13, 1782, *Adams Works*, 7: 610.

31. John Adams to Secretary Livingston, ibid., 8: 27.

32. This was the comment of John Mercer of Virginia in response to news of the peace preliminaries. James Madison's Notes of Debates, March 19, 1783, *Letters of Delegates*, 20: 57. The contrast between the paper provisions of the Treaty of Paris and the actual implementation of the agreement is not taken up in the two classic accounts of peacemaking, Samuel Flagg Bemis, *The Diplomacy of the American Revolution* (Bloomington, Ind., [1935] 1957), and Richard B. Morris, *The Peacemakers: The Great Powers and American Independence* (New York, 1965). Both works are very similar in basic argument, highly celebratory of the role of Jay and Adams in the negotiations, and very nationalistic in tone and outlook. Since what Americans expected from the settlement turned out to be a lot less than they actually got, Bemis's concluding judgment—the Peace of Paris was "the greatest vic-

tory in the annals of American diplomacy"—seems excessive. The treaties that actually settled the status of the eastern Mississippi Valley—Jay's Treaty of 1794 with Great Britain, and Pinckney's Treaty of 1795 with Spain—would seem more significant. Both Bemis and Morris also write as if a peace that confined the Americans to the mountains would have been an unmitigated disaster and would have severely compromised "our national destiny." In fact, though, it is difficult to see why it would have resulted in a constellation of forces different in any essential respects from what occurred over the next ten years. Had the United States accepted a settlement in 1783 that left the western boundaries to future negotiation (a more likely response to tough British terms than a formal renunciation of the western claims), that resolution would not have lasted forever, nor would it have stopped emigration westward from the Atlantic states. The crucial question was not whether the states and peoples of America would expand westward; it was whether they would do it together, and with more or less bloodshed. The peace treaty did not resolve that question. Nor, in the final analysis, was the question of national destiny something, after 1781, that it was in the power of Europe to either bestow or withhold. The European powers might complicate the achievement thereof, but the resolution of it depended on the Americans themselves. They had to decide whether they wanted a national destiny, and they had not yet decided it. These considerations suggest that some other peace treaty—I nominate the Constitution of the United States—deserves our plaudits as "the greatest victory in the annals of American diplomacy."

33. Charles Thomson to Hannah Thomson, October 17, 1783, *Letters of Delegates,* 21: 73.

34. Charles Thomson to Hannah Thomson, October 14, 1783, ibid., 21: 57.

35. Silas Deane to Beauharnais, *Deane Papers,* 5: 286–87.

36. Benjamin Franklin to David Hartley, October 22, 1783, *Franklin Works,* 10: 27; Franklin to President of Congress, December 25, 1783, Giunta, *Emerging Nation,* 1: 960.

37. American peace commissioners to Congress, September 10, 1783, Giunta, *Emerging Nation,* 1: 938.

38. Samuel Osgood to John Adams, January 14, 1784, *Letters of Delegates,* 21: 277.

39. William Gordon to John Adams, September 7, 1782, quoted in Joseph L. Davis, *Sectionalism in American Politics, 1774–1787.* (Madison, Wis., 1977), 59–60.

40. Samuel Osgood to Stephen Higginson, February 2, 1784, *Letters of Delegates,* 21: 326–27.

41. Richard Dobbs Spaight to Alexander Martin, October 16, 1784, ibid., 21: 813.

42. James Monroe to Patrick Henry, August 12, 1786, *Letters of Delegates,* 23: 462–66; James Monroe to James Madison, September 12, 1786, *Madison Papers,* 9: 123; James Monroe to Madison, September 3, 1786, ibid., 9: 113–14, and discussion in Lance Banning, *Sacred Fire of Liberty: James Madison and the Founding of the Federal Republic* (Ithaca, N.Y., 1995), 66–71. "The general voice of the western community" in response to news of Jay's negotiation was "EQUAL LIBERTY with the thirteen states, or a *breach of peace,* and a *new alliance.*"

43. Madison to Monroe, June 21, 1786, *Madison Papers,* 9: 82–83.

44. For discussion of separate confederacies, Peter S. Onuf and Cathy Matson, *A Union of Interests: Political and Economic Thought in Revolutionary America* (Lawrence, Kans., 1990), 82–86.

45. James Madison to Thomas Jefferson, August 12, 1786, *Madison Papers,* 9: 96.

CHAPTER 24

1. Luther Martin, "The Genuine Information . . . ," Farrand, *Records,* 3: 197; George Mason: Memorandum, June 1787, Hutson, *Supplement,* 140; Speech of Elbridge Gerry, Farrand, *Records,* 1: 519: "If we do nothing, it appears to me we must have war and confusion—for the old confederation would be at an end." See further Herbert Storing, *What the Anti-Federalists Were For* (Chicago, 1981), 26.

2. "Vices of the Political System of the United States," April 1787, *Madison Papers,* 9: 345–58.

3. Ibid., 9: 348; Madison to George Thompson, January 29, 1789, ibid., 11: 433–34. See also Cooke, *Federalist,* No. 15, for Hamilton's statement of the same theme, and chapter 3 for Franklin's almost identical analysis in 1754. See also Speech of R.R. Livingston, New York Ratifying Convention, Elliot, *Debates,* 2: 342. "Sir, what are these requisitions? what are these pompous petitions for public charity, which have made so much noise, and brought so little cash into the treasury?"

4. "Vices," *Madison Papers,* 9: 348–49. Pennsylvania, as noted in chapter 20, had disputed the right of congress to review the judgment of state juries. At the time of writing (April 1787), New York was conducting a separate negotiation with the Iroquois that fell into the same class as Georgia's separate negotiations with the Creeks and Cherokee.

5. Ibid., 9: 349; John Jay's Report on State Laws Contrary to the Treaty of Peace, Giunta, *Emerging Nation,* 3: 333–49, at 346; John Adams to Secretary Jay, May 25, 1786, *Adams Works,* 8: 394–95. To the same effect, see Adams to James Bowdoin, June 2, 1786, ibid., 8: 397–98; John Adams to John Jay, October 27, 1786, Giunta, *Emerging Nation,* 3: 359–60. These "melancholy forebodings" of "a Combination of England and the House of Bourbon, against the United States," said Adams earnestly, were "no chimeras." He felt them "not in gloomy Moments only, but in the utmost Gaiety of Heart."

6. "Vices," *Madison Papers,* 9: 349–50.

7. Ibid., 9: 350–51. In *Federalist,* No. 43, Madison referred "with exquisite circumlocution" to "an unhappy species of population abounding in some of the States, who during the calm of regular government are sunk below the level of men; but who in the tempestuous scenes of civil violence may emerge into the human character, and give a superiority of strength to any party with which they may associate themselves." William M. Wiecek, "Slavery and Constitution's Origins," in *The Framing and Ratification of the Constitution,* ed. Leonard W. Levy and Dennis J. Mahoney (New York, 1987), 182.

8. "Vices," *Madison Papers,* 9: 351–353; "Notes on Debates," February 21, 1783, ibid., 6: 272 n. To similar effect, see James Madison to Edmund Randolph, February 25, 1783, ibid., 6: 287.

9. Jack N. Rakove, in *The Beginnings of National Politics: An Interpretative History of the Continental Congress* (Baltimore, [1979] 1982), develops this theme also at considerable length.

10. "Vices," *Madison Papers,* 9: 353–57.

11. James Madison to Thomas Jefferson, October 24 and November 1, 1787, Smith, *Republic of Letters,* 1: 500.

CHAPTER 25

1. Farrand, *Records,* 1: 20–23.

2. Ibid., 1: 34 (Morris); Hamilton, ibid., 1: 283; Madison to Edmund Randolph, April 8, 1787, *Madison Papers,* 9: 369; Farrand, *Records,* 1: 165 (Madison). See also Charles F. Hobson, "The Negative on State Laws: James Madison, the Constitution, and the Crisis of Republican Government," *William and Mary Quarterly* 36 (1979): 215–35, at 218.

3. Farrand, *Records,* 1: 242–45.

4. Ibid., 1: 255.

5. June 8, ibid., 1: 167 (Bedford).

6. Ibid., 1: 242 n (Dickinson).

7. Ibid., 1: 198. Wilson read the prepared remarks of the aged statesmen to the convention.

8. June 9, ibid., 1: 179–80.

9. "If the minority of the people of America refuse to coalesce with the majority on just and proper principles," Wilson warned, "a separation . . . could never happen on better grounds." The reply of Gunning Bedford, delegate from Delaware, said it all: "I do not, gentlemen, trust you." If the larger states allowed a disunion to take place, "the small ones will find some foreign ally . . . who will take them by the hand." Ibid., 1: 500 (Yates), 492. Bedford later apologized for this remark, but his indiscretion had been no greater than Wilson's, who made no apology. By indirection, both sides were threatening war, and knew it, because both sides threatened the disunion they believed would produce foreign alliances and war.

10. July 7, ibid., 1: 551. See also ibid., 2: 9, for Madison's remark that "the people of the large states would in some way or other secure to themselves a weight proportioned to the importance accruing from their superior numbers. If they could not effect it by a proportional representation in the Govt. they would probably accede to no Govt. which did not in great measure depend for its efficacy on their voluntary cooperation."

11. Hamilton's plan gave the national legislature the power to veto state legislation in all cases whatsoever, provided life terms to the Senate and the executive; and vested the power of appointing the governors of the states in the national executive. Hamilton explained later that he did not wish for the annihilation of the states, but he was firm in his conviction that the convention needed to specify the constitutional supremacy of the general government. Not a man for *imperia in imperio,* Hamilton suggested a plan that had undoubted coherence on the point of national supremacy and was therefore profoundly objectionable to a majority of the convention. It was, of course, utterly unacceptable to the small states, who would not acquiesce in their

constitutional annihilation, but its centralizing thrust also went beyond what most delegates from the large states wanted. The supremacy of the general government also meant that it could dictate whatever terms of admission it wished for new states, and hence was unacceptable to the South and West. Despite Hamilton's silence on the question of how to count slaves, the plan would have established a northern preponderance that was able to maintain itself over time, and it seems rather unlikely that this feature of the plan, albeit implicit, escaped the attention of either its author or his critics.

12. Farrand, *Records*, 2: 9–10.

13. Ibid., 2: 469.

14. Ibid., 1: 490.

15. Gorham, who voted with King against "the Connecticut Compromise" on July 16, had earlier signaled the appropriateness of equal state voting in the Senate.

16. Farrand, *Records*, 1: 566.

17. June 30, ibid., 1: 486–87. On July 9, Madison spoke more positively of this expedient, holding it forth as "proper ground of compromise." Ibid., 1: 562.

18. Ibid., 1: 587; ibid., 1: 595.

19. Ibid., 1: 604–5.

20. Ibid., 1: 604.

21. Ibid., 1: 593. On the identity of interests between South and West, see Drew R. McCoy, "James Madison and Visions of American Nationality in the Confederation Period," in *Beyond Confederation: Origins of the Constitution and American National Identity*, ed. Richard Beeman, Stephen Botein, and Edward C. Carter II (Chapel Hill, N.C., 1987), 26–58; and Lance Banning, *Sacred Fire of Liberty: James Madison and the Founding of the Federal Republic* (Ithaca, N.Y., 1995), 67–68. For another prediction of southern dominance in the future, see David Ramsay, *An Address to the Freemen of South Carolina on the Subject of the Federal Constitution*, May, 1788, Ford, *Pamphlets*, 375: "In fifty years, it is probable that the Southern states will have a great ascendency over the Eastern." The committee report that fixed the initial representation of the states gave the legislature the power to alter this ratio in the future "upon the principles of their wealth and number of inhabitants." This was, as William Paterson observed, a very vague criterion, but that, of course, was precisely the point. According to Gorham of Massachusetts, it was put in to respond to the fear that the western states would grow in population and come to outvote the Atlantic states: "[T]he Atlantic states having the government in their own hands, may take care of their own interest, by dealing out the right of Representation in safe proportions to the Western States." Morris, too, "dwelt much on the danger of throwing such a preponderancy into the Western Scale, suggesting that in time the Western people would outnumber the Atlantic States. He wished therefore to put it in the power of the latter to keep a majority of votes in their own hands." July 10, Farrand, *Records*, 1: 571. "The Busy haunts of men not the remote wilderness," he said the next day, "was the proper School of political Talents. If the Western people get the power into their hands they will ruin the Atlantic interests. The Back members are always most averse to the best measures (July 11, ibid., 1: 583). When Morris said "Atlantic," he bid for the concurrence of the whole seaboard. With the exception of a few Carolinians, how-

ever, the representatives of the South Atlantic states did not accept this pretended similitude of interest.

22. On the connection between the Ordinance and the Great Compromise, the best study is Staughton Lynd, "The Compromise of 1787," in *Class Conflict, Slavery, and the United States Constitution* (Indianapolis, 1967), 185–213. See further Peter S. Onuf, *Statehood and Union: A History of the Northwest Ordinance* (Bloomington, Ind., 1987); Frederick D. Williams, ed., *The Northwest Ordinance: Essays on Its Formulation, Provisions, and Legacy* (East Lansing, Mich., 1988); and John Porter Bloom, ed., *The American Territorial System* (Athens, Ohio, 1973).

23. Lynd, "Compromise of 1787," 189–90. See also William Grayson to James Monroe, August 8, 1787, *LMCC*, 8: 632; and extract from Edward Coles, "History of the Ordinance of 1787," in Hutson, *Supplement*, 321.

24. Lynd, "Compromise of 1787," 195, 209–10.

25. Farrand, *Records*, 1: 321.

26. Mason cited in Banning, *Sacred Fire*, 255. The compromises of the Constitution over representation also demonstrate the irrelevance of the categories of English constitutionalism to the constitutional predicament of the American states. John Adams, in his *Defence* of the American constitutions, took as his point of departure the proposition that the division between the few and the many—between patricians and plebeians, the well-born and the middling—was a feature of every society, including the America of his day. Though America had no formal "distinctions of ranks" and lacked "legal distinctions, titles, powers, and privileges" that were hereditary, there was still, Adams insisted, a rage for distinction "as earnestly desired and sought, as titles, garters and ribbons are in any nation of Europe" (*Defence of the Constitutions, Adams Works*, 5: 488). From this Adams deduced the need to divide the few and the many into separate branches, with a strong executive necessary to mediate the inevitable class struggle. In suggesting the need to approximate the American constitutions to the British constitution, Adams made himself unpopular, and he earned the implicit rebuke of James Wilson in the convention: "The British Government cannot be our model. We have no materials for a similar one. Our manners, our laws, the abolition of entails and of primogeniture, the whole genius of the people, are opposed to it" (Farrand, *Records*, 1: 153). So far as the continental problem was concerned, however, Adams's approach was not so much wrong as irrelevant. The great problem concerning representation was the adjustment of the competing pretensions of states and sections, not the adjustment of the clashing pretensions of antagonistic social classes. The age-old struggle between democracy and aristocracy, which Adams thought so fundamental, had little to do with it, or was so far transformed by the federal problem as to offer no guidance to the convention's perplexity.

John Adams prided himself on his knowledge of history, which indeed was deep and comprehensive. He once objected (famously) to Condorcet's observation that the American Constitution "had not grown, but was planned," that it had taken no weight from the centuries but was put together mechanically in a few years, with the penciled margin: "Fool! Fool!" It is, accordingly, with pleasure that we see Adams getting hoisted on his own petard, as the theory of the British constitution got clobbered in its encounter with the American state system. See further on

Adams the discussion in Gordon S. Wood, "The Relevance and Irrelevance of John Adams," in *The Creation of the American Republic, 1776–1787* (New York, 1972), 567–92; and C. Bradley Thompson, *John Adams and the Spirit of Liberty* (Lawrence, Kans., 1998).

CHAPTER 26

1. A minor instance of this closing of perspectives, though significant in its broader implications, was King's argument, on August 7, against fixing a time for the national legislature to meet every year. He thought it unnecessary: "A great vice in our system was that of legislating too much. The most numerous objects of legislation belong to the States. Those of the Natl. Legislature were but few. The chief of them were commerce & revenue. When these should be once settled, alterations would be rarely necessary & easily made." Farrand, *Records*, 2: 198.

2. Ibid., 2: 220 (King); August 8, ibid., 2: 221–23 (Morris).

3. See Elliot, *Debates*, 269–70 (Mason); ibid., 452–54 (colloquy between Mason and Madison). Mason said that the Constitution was defective not only because it failed to stop slave importations but also because it did not explicitly rule out emancipation. Madison and Randolph said that it did guarantee slavery where it existed. "[T]here was no member of the Virginia delegation," said Randolph, "who had *the smallest suspicion of the abolition of slavery*" (ibid., 599). See also the illuminating discussion in Joseph Ellis, *Founding Brothers: The Revolutionary Generation* (New York, 2000), 81–119. As Ellis recounts, Madison succeeded in confirming his interpretation in the First Congress.

4. Madison and Jefferson thought they had an ally in Hamilton for this project, but they would discover soon enough that they were mistaken. Hamilton's apparent concordance was stated in *Federalist* No. 11. The Virginia project, however, required commercial war against Great Britain; once Hamilton's financial system had been made, crucially dependent on revenue from imposts and therefore on stability in Anglo-American commerce, he became an inveterate opponent of these ideas. Their dispute on this point then got embedded in the larger controversies over ideology and foreign policy that arose as a consequence of the Wars of the French Revolution.

5. Farrand, *Records*, 2: 451–52.

6. August 29, 1787, ibid., 2: 453. See also ibid., 2: 374.

7. Ibid., 2: 453.

8. "No Person held to Service or Labour in one State, under the Laws thereof, escaping into another, shall, in Consequence of any Law or Regulation therein, be discharged from such Service or Labour, but shall be delivered up on Claim of the Party to whom such Service or Labour may be due" (Article 4, Sec. 3).

9. July 11, Farrand, *Records*, 1: 588.

10. In his subsequent defense of the Constitution, Charles Pinckney ("A Steady Open Republican") noted that the "three Southern states, particularly, . . . had for several years past, good grounds to think Great Britain wishes to separate them from the rest, and to have reverted to her if possible." Quoted in John Richard Alden, *The First South* (Baton Rouge, La., 1961), 106. On slavery as a sine qua non

for the South Carolinians and Georgians, see Robert M. Weir, "South Carolina," in *Ratifying the Constitution,* ed. Michael Allen Gillespie and Michael Lienesch (Lawrence, Kans., 1989), 209; and *Annals of Congress,* February 12, 1790, 1244, H.R. (Smith): "the States would never have entered into the Confederation, unless their property had been guaranteed to Them, for such is the state of agriculture in that country, that without slaves it must be abandoned."

11. On Washington, see James Thomas Flexner, *Washington: The Indispensable Man* (New York, 1984), 384. Madison said in the Virginia ratifying convention that the slave trade clause was "impolitic" but that it was one of those things that could not be "excluded without encountering greater evils. The Southern States would not have entered into the Union of America without the temporary permission of that trade; and if they were excluded from the Union, the consequences might be dreadful to them and to us." Elliott, *Debates,* 3: 453. On the later dilemma, see D. W. Meinig, *Continental America, 1800–1867* (New Haven, Conn., 1993), 494, citing the *Richard Enquirer* in 1858, wondering whether to be "the South of the Northern confederacy would not be more preferable . . . than [being] the North of a Southern confederacy."

12. Cf. also a speech of 1789 by Madison: "It is impossible to reflect a moment on the possible severance of that branch of the Union without seeing the mischiefs which such an event must create. . . .We shall speedily behold an astonishing mass of people on the western waters. Whether this great mass shall form a permanent part of the confederacy or whether it shall be separated into an alien, a jealous, and a hostile people, may depend on the system of measures that is shortly to be taken. The difference, he observed, between considering them in the light of fellow citizens, bound to us by a common affection, obeying common laws, pursuing a common good, and considering them in the other light, presents one of the most interesting questions that can occupy an American mind: Instead of peace and friendship, we shall have rivalship and enmity; instead of being a great people, invulnerable on all sides, and without the necessity of those military establishments which other nations require, we shall be driven into the same expensive and dangerous means of defense: We shall be obliged to lay burdens on the people to support establishments which, sooner or later, may prove fatal to their liberties." September 4, 1789, *Madison Papers,* 12: 377. See also Madison to Lafayette, 1785, warning of the danger if the future states "on the waters of the Mississippi were to be viewed in the same relation to the Atlantic States as exists between the heterogeneous and hostile Societies of Europe." Ibid., 8: 250–51.

CHAPTER 27

1. See Forrest McDonald, *The American Presidency: An Intellectual History* (Lawrence, Kans., 1994); Harvey Mansfield, *Taming the Prince: The Ambivalence of Modern Executive Power* (New York, 1989); Thomas E. Cronin, ed., *Inventing the American Presidency* (Lawrence, Kans., 1989).

2. See Jack N. Rakove, "Solving a Constitutional Puzzle: The Treaty-making Clause as a Case Study," *Perspectives in American History,* n.s., 1 (1984): 233–81.

3. See R. Earl McClendon, "The Origins of the Two-Thirds Rule in Senate

Action upon Treaties," in *The Shaping of American Diplomacy,* ed. William A. Williams (Chicago, 1956), 53–56. On the importance of the two-thirds rule for the making of treaties, see David Ramsay, *An Address to the Freemen of South Carolina,* May 1787, Ford, *Pamphlets,* 376.

4. "Fabius" VIII, April 29, 1788, Bailyn, *Debate,* 2: 425.

5. See Jack Rakove, *Original Meanings: Politics and Ideas in the Making of the Constitution* (New York, 1996), 264–66.

6. Cooke, *Federalist,* No. 40; Raoul Berger, *Federalism: The Framers' Design* (Norman, Okla., 1987), passim. Davis remarks that a true consensus existed on only one principle, that of "duality articulated in a single constitutional system of two distinct governments, national and state, each acting in its own right, each acting directly on individuals, and each qualified master of a limited domain of action. . . . All else was controversial presumption, inference and supposition." Rufus S. Davis, *The Federal Principle: A Journey Through Time in Quest of a Meaning* (Berkeley, 1978), 114.

7. Farrand, *Records,* 1: 250 (Patterson); ibid., 1: 324 , 455 (Martin); ibid., 1: 485 (Ellsworth). See also Luther Martin, "The Genuine Information . . . ," ibid., 3: 189, 228–30; John Dickinson, Notes for a Speech (II), June 30, 1787, Hutson, *Supplement,* 136; Elliot, *Debates,* 2: 134 (Nason); "A Columbian Patriot" [Mercy Otis Warren], Observations on the Constitution, Bailyn, *Debate,* 2: 295; "Portius," *American Herald,* November 12, 1787, DHRC, 4: 218–19; John Quincy Adams to William Cranch, December 8, 1787, ibid., 4: 402; Cornelius, *Hampshire Chronicle,* December 11, 1787, ibid., 4: 410–11; speech of Thomas Tredwell, New York ratifying convention, Elliot, *Debates,* 2: 401–2; and Dissent of the Minority of the Pennsylvania Convention, DHRC, 2: 639.

8. Farrand, *Records,* 1: 314–15. See also Elliot, *Debates,* 4: 228–29 (Iredell); ibid., 4: 308 (Pinckney); Cooke, *Federalist,* No. 39.

9. Farrand, *Records,* 1: 54.

10. Ibid., 1: 468.

11. James Madison to Thomas Jefferson, October 24 and November 1, 1787, Smith, *Republic of Letters,* 1: 496, 498.

12. Ibid., 1: 498–500. Madison's expression of *imperia in imperio* is preferable to the customary usage of *imperium in imperio* because it highlights the tension between a plurality of states and the union. See also Speech of Alexander Hamilton, New York ratifying convention, Elliot, *Debates,* 2: 305. Responding to predictions that the general government would swallow up the state governments, Hamilton said that the "probable evil is, that the general government will be too dependent on the state legislatures, too much governed by their prejudices, and too obsequious to their humors; that the states, with every power in their hands, will make encroachments on the national authority, till the Union is weakened and dissolved." To similar effect, see "America" [Noah Webster], Reply to the Dissenting Members of the late Convention of Pennsylvania, December 31, 1787, 176. Recent works stressing the ambiguous character of the Constitution include Kenneth M. Stampp, "Concept of Perpetual Union," *Journal of American History* 65 (1978): 5–33; Murray Forsyth, *Unions of States: The Theory and Practice of Confederation* (New York, 1981); Davis, *Federal Principle;* Alfred H. Kelly and Winfred A. Harbison, *The American Constitution: Its Origins and Development,* 5th ed. (New York,

1976), esp. 134; and Forrest McDonald, *States' Rights and the Union: Imperium in Imperio* (Lawrence, Kans., 2000). For the standard view that the Constitution did make a decisive determination of the locus of sovereignty, see Edward S. Corwin, "National Power and State Interposition, 1787–1861," *Michigan Law Review* 10 (1912): 535–51; Andrew C. McLaughlin, *A Constitutional History of the United States* (New York, 1935), 214–19; and Clinton Rossiter, *1787: The Grand Convention* (New York, 1966).

CHAPTER 28

1. Gordon Wood, *The Creation of the American Republic, 1776–1787* (New York, [1969] 1972), 606–15. In later essays, Wood qualified his argument in various ways, stressing that the debate over which was "the more dominant tradition, republicanism or liberalism, . . . assumes a sharp dichotomy between two clearly identifiable traditions that eighteenth-century reality will not support" (Wood, "Ideology and the Origins of Liberal America," *William and Mary Quarterly* 44 (1987): 628–40, at 634). Elsewhere, he identifies the Anti-Federalists rather than the Federalists with "the emerging world of egalitarian democracy and the private pursuit of happiness" (Wood, "Interests and Disinterestedness in the Making of the Constitution," in *Beyond Confederation: Origins of the Constitution and American National Identity*, ed. Richard Breeman, Stephen Botein, and Edward C. Carter II (Chapel Hill, N.C., 1987), 69–109, at 109). The most striking formulation of the "new world" of interest-group politics that entailed a displacement of the republican emphasis on civic virtue is Martin Diamond's: "The Madisonian solution involved a fundamental reliance on ceaseless striving after immediate interest. . . . [I]t is a system that has no necessary place and makes no provision for men of the founding kind . . . a durable regime whose perpetuation requires nothing like the wisdom and virtue necessary for its creation." "Democracy and *The Federalist*: A Reconsideration of the Framers' Intent," in *As Far As Republican Principles Will Admit: Essays by Martin Diamond*, ed. William A. Schambra (Washington, D.C., 1992), 34–36. For further consideration, see Lance Banning, *Sacred Fire of Liberty: James Madison and the Founding of the Federal Republic* (Ithaca, N.Y., 1995), esp. 202–19.

2. Cited in Alexander Hill Everett, *America: or, A General Survey of the Political Situation of the Several Powers of the Western Continent . . .* (Philadelphia, 1827), 117.

3. Farrand, *Records,* 2: 667.

4. Cooke, *Federalist,* No. 37: 239. See further Peter B. Knupfer, *The Union as It Is: Constitutional Unionism and Sectional Compromise, 1787–1861* (Chapel Hill, N.C., 1991); William E. Nelson, "Reason and Compromise in the Establishment of the Federal Constitution, 1787–1801," *William and Mary Quarterly* 44 (1987): 458–84.

5. See Wilson's opening address to the Pennsylvania ratifying convention, November 24, 1787, Bailyn, *Debate,* 1: 796–97.

6. See Cooke, *Federalist,* No. 38: 243–46; Elliot, *Debates,* 2: 156 (Ames);

George Washington to Bushrod Washington, November 10, 1787, Bailyn, *Debate,* 1: 306.

7. Samuel Adams to Richard Henry Lee, December 3, 1787, Bailyn, *Debate,* 1: 446.

8. Agrippa IV [James Winthrop], December 4, 1787, Bailyn, *Debate,* 1: 449; see also Centinel [Samuel Bryan] I, ibid., I, 59; Dissent of the Minority of the Pennsylvania Convention, December 18, 1787, ibid., 535.

9. Cooke, *Federalist,* No. 28: 180; ibid., No. 46: 320.

10. Farrand, *Records,* 1: 164–65, 320 (Madison); ibid., 285 (Hamilton); Cooke, *Federalist,* No. 16.

11. Agrippa III, December 4, 1787, Bailyn, *Debate,* 1: 445.

12. See, however, "Letters of the Federal Farmer," Ford, *Pamphlets,* 280: The Farmer (probably Melancton Smith of New York rather than Richard Henry Lee of Virginia) acknowledged "our situation is critical" but went on to argue that "we are in no immediate danger of any commotions" were everybody to "remain cool and temperate." "We are in a state of perfect peace, and in no danger of invasions."

13. See, e.g., Centinel XI, Storing, *Anti-Federalist,* 2: 185–86.

14. *The Government of Nature Delineated; Or an Exact Picture of the New Federal Constitution* (1788), cited in Wood, *Creation,* 489.

15. Charles Warren, *The Making of the Constitution* (Boston, 1928), 755–58, and discussion in Peter S. Onuf, *Origins of the Federal Republic: Jurisdictional Controversies in the United States, 1775–1787* (Philadelphia, 1983), 193. One southern Anti-Federalist, Richard Henry Lee, thought that the "greatness of the powers given & the multitude of Places to be created" had produced "a coalition of Monarchy men, Military Men, Aristocrats, and Drones whose noise, Impudence & zeal exceeds all belief—Whilst the Commercial plunder of the South stimulates the rapacious Trader." Lee to George Mason, October 1, 1787, Bailyn, *Debate,* 1: 45. Cato, a northern Anti-Federalist, noted that there was "a passion for aristocratic distinctions" in the southern states, "where slavery is encouraged, and liberty, of course, less respected, and protected." He doubted that southern representatives would "be as tenacious of the liberties and interests of the more northern states, where freedom, independence, industry, equality, and frugality, are natural to the climate and soil." Cato III, October 25, 1787, *DHRC,* 13: 476. In the convention, as Madison noted, the large states were sometimes "described as the Aristocratic States, ready to oppress the small." At the same time, the small states were sometimes likened to the House of Lords, with need of a veto "to defend them against the more numerous Commons" (Farrand, *Records,* 1: 485). As Wilson remarked, much of this was "a mere illusion of names."

16. Common Sense, "Attack on Paper Money Laws," November 3, 1786, *Paine Writings,* 364–67. On the contract clause, see Steven R. Boyd, "The Contract Clause and the Evolution of American Federalism, 1789–1815," *William and Mary Quarterly* 44 (1987): 529–48. Judicial interpretation of the contract clause was limited and moderate in coming years. The states, as Boyd shows, continued to enjoy substantial power over bankruptcies. So, too, judicial cognizance was often taken of the extreme delicacy and hazard attached to any judicial decree that would overturn the act of a state legislature. (See, e.g., the concurring opinion of Justice Iredell in *Carter v. Bull,* 3 Dallas 386 [1798], *Founders' Constitution,* 3:

407.) The judicial legislation of a century later was a great departure from rather than fulfillment of the original intention in this regard.

The clarity with which the framers treated this issue should not be exaggerated. The framers not only denied the states the right to print money but also refused to the national government the right to incorporate a bank. (They also left untouched the existing state paper emissions; the rule of the Constitution was prospective, not retrospective.) Hamilton's subsequent argument for a bank, with its bold appeal to implied powers, was burdened, but not deterred, by that record. In the early 1790s, Hamilton showed why such an institution was essential for a variety of purposes; that it was not provided would seem significant in assessing the framer's intentions. It must be stressed, however, that the fascinating nexus among debt, taxes, funding, assumption, and a national currency was hardly discussed at all in the convention. Even Hamilton himself had probably not yet grasped the complicated dimensions of this problem, which he would later unfold in successive reports as first secretary of the Treasury.

When the storm did break over the Hamiltonian system, it had little to do with class interests and everything to do with sectional interests. When Jefferson told Washington, in 1792, that the Hamiltonian system was threatening to break the union "into two or more parts," his stress was on the sectional antagonism it aroused (May 23, 1792, Peterson, *Jefferson Writings*, 988). When we review, he said,

> the mass which opposed the original coalescence [the ratification of the Constitution], when we consider that it lay chiefly in the Southern quarter, that the legislature have availed themselves of no occasion of allaying it, but on the contrary whenever Northern & Southern prejudices have come into conflict, the latter have been sacrificed & the former soothed; that the owners of the debt are in the Southern & the holders of it in the Northern division; that the Antifederal champions are now strengthened in argument by the fulfillment of their predictions; that this has been brought about by the Monarchical federalists themselves, who, having been for the new government merely as a stepping stone to monarchy, have themselves adopted the very constructions of the constitution, of which, when advocating its acceptance before the tribunal of the people, they declared it insusceptible; that the republican federalists, who espoused the same government for its intrinsic merits, are disarmed of their weapons, that which they denied as prophecy being now become true history: who can be sure that these things may not proselyte the small number which was wanting to place the majority on the other side?

A good question that, to which the answer was that no one could be sure. Disunion seemed a standing possibility all throughout the 1790s. On fears of disunion during that decade, see particularly James Rogers Sharp, *American Politics in the Early Republic: The New Nation in Crisis* (New Haven, Conn., 1993).

17. *Barron v. The Mayor and City Council of Baltimore*, 7 Pet. 243, 8 L.Ed. 672 (1833).

18. See Eugene W. Hickok Jr., ed., *The Bill of Rights: Original Meaning and Current Understanding* (Charlottesville, Va., 1991); and Peter S. Onuf, *The New Amer-*

ican Nation, 1775–1820, vol. 6, *Ratifying, Amending, and Interpreting the Constitution* (New York, 1991).

CHAPTER 29

1. July 5, Farrand, *Records,* 1: 532 (Gerry).
2. This is well brought out in Murray Forsyth, *Unions of States: The Theory and Practice of Confederation* (New York, 1981).
3. Edmund Randolph, Draft Sketch of Constitution, July 26, 1787, Hutson, *Supplement,* 183.
4. James Brown Scott, *James Madison's Notes . . .* (New York, 1918).
5. Speech of James Wilson, Farrand, *Records,* 1: 405.
6. Cf. the classic formulation, which I have somewhat altered in meaning, of Edward S. Corwin, "The Progress of Constitutional Theory Between the Declaration of Independence and the Meeting of the Philadelphia Convention," *American Historical Review* 30 (1924–25): 511–36. Referring to Madison's proposal of a veto on the legislation of the states, Corwin writes: "Thus was the Balance of Power, which Montesquieu had borrowed from the stock teachings of eighteenth-century diplomacy, to transform it into a maxim of free constitutions, projected into the midway field of federal government" (535).
7. Elliot, *Debates,* 3: 365.
8. The quotation in the preceding paragraph is from Daniel Bell, "The Future World Disorder," *Foreign Policy* 27 (1977): 132. See also David C. Hendrickson, "In Our Own Image: The Sources of American Conduct in World Affairs," *National Interest,* No. 50 (1997/98): 9–21. Analyses of the global political system appearing in the 1990s that explored variations on these themes include Benjamin Barber, *Jihad vs. McWorld* (New York, 1995); Daniel Elazar, *Constitutionalizing Globalization: The Postmodern Revival of Confederal Arrangements* (Lanham, Md., 1998); Daniel Deudney and G. John Ikenberry, "The Logic of the West," *World Policy Journal* 10 (1993–94): 17–25; Thomas Friedman, *The Lexus and the Olive Tree* (New York, 2000); Ian Clark, *Globalization and Fragmentation: International Relations in the Twentieth Century* (New York, 1997); Robert Wright, *Nonzero: The Logic of Human Destiny* (New York, 2000); James Robert Huntley, *Pax Democratica: A Strategy for the Twenty-first Century* (New York, 1998); and G. John Ikenberry, *After Victory: Institutions, Strategic Restraint, and the Rebuilding of Order After Major Wars* (Princeton, N.J., 2001).
9. For my own attempt to "pursue the intimations," see David C. Hendrickson, "Toward Universal Empire: The Dangerous Quest for Absolute Security," *World Policy Journal* 19, no. 3 (2002): 1–11.

APPENDIX

1. For various diagrams and definitions useful in understanding the world of states, see Murray Forsyth, *Unions of States: The Theory and Practice of Confed-*

eration (New York, 1981); Daniel H. Deudney, "The Philadelphian System: Sovereignty, Arms Control, and Balance of Power in the American States-Union, Circa 1787–1861," *International Organization* 49 (1995): 191–228, and other sources at 209 n. 73; Adam Watson, *The Evolution of International Society* (London, 1992), esp. 13–18; Martin Wight, *Systems of States* (Leicester, 1977); J. G. A. Pocock, "States, Republics, and Empires: The American Founding in Early Modern Perspective," in *Conceptual Change and the Constitution*, ed. Terence Ball and J. G. A. Pocock (Lawrence, Kans., 1988), 78–98; Peter Onuf and Nicholas Onuf, *Federal Union, Modern World: The Law of Nations in an Age of Revolutions, 1776–1814* (Madison, Wis., 1993). "Enmity" as a criterion was suggested by Arnold Wolfers, "Amity and Enmity Among Nations," in *Discord and Collaboration: Essays on International Politics* (Baltimore, 1962).

2. See chapter 7.

3. On the "*societas* of sovereign states," see Robert Jackson, *The Global Covenant* (New York, 2000), 97–129, 165–69. Jackson defines it as "the idea and institution that expresses the morality of difference, recognition, respect, regard, dialogue, interaction, exchange, and similar norms that postulate coexistence and reciprocity between independent political communities" (168). On the law of nations more generally, see Wilhelm G. Grewe, *The Epochs of International Law* (Berlin, 2000). On the European concert, see F. H. Hinsley, *Power and the Pursuit of Peace: Theory and Practice in the History of Relations Between States* (Cambridge, 1963); M. S. Anderson, *The Rise of Modern Diplomacy, 1450–1919* (London, 1993); Herbert Butterfield, "Diplomatic Thought 1648–1815: The Quest for Order," *Studies in History and Politics* 2 (1981/82): 9–35; Walter Alison Phillips, *The Confederation of Europe: A Study of the European Alliance, 1813–1823, As an Experiment in the International Organization of Peace* (London, 1920); Carsten Holbraad, *The Concert of Europe: A Study in German and British International Theory* (New York, 1971); and the magisterial study of Paul W. Schroeder, *The Transformation of European Politics, 1763–1848* (Oxford, 1994).

4. Still valuable is Roland N. Stromberg, *Collective Security and American Foreign Policy* (New York, 1963).

5. See, inter alia, G. John Ikenberry, *After Victory: Institutions, Strategic Restraint, and the Rebuilding of Order After Major Wars* (Princeton, N.J., 2001); Helga Haftendorn, Robert O. Keohane, and Celeste A. Wallender, eds., *Imperfect Unions: Security Institutions over Time and Space* (New York, 1999); Emanuel Adler and Michael Barnett, eds., *Security Communities* (Cambridge, 1998); Greg Rasmussen, "Great Power Concerts in Historical Perspective," in *The New Great Power Coalition*, ed. Richard Rosecrance (Lanham, Md., 2001); Robert Jervis, "Security Regimes," in *International Regimes*, ed. Stephen D. Krasner (Ithaca, N.Y., 1983); Forsyth, *Unions of States*; Neta C. Crawford, "A Security Regime Among Democracies: Cooperation Among Iroquois Nations," *International Organization* 48 (1994): 345–85; Thomas Risse-Kappen, *Cooperation Among Democracies: The European Influence on U.S. Foreign Policy* (Princeton, N.J., 1995); and John Gerard Ruggie, *Winning the Peace: America and World Order in the New Era* (New York, 1996).

6. Relevant here are the methodological strictures elaborated by Robert Jackson in *The Global Covenant*, 44–96.

7. See Francis Paul Prucha, *American Indian Treaties: The History of a Political Anomaly* (Berkeley, 1994).

8. Adams to Deonis, March 12, 1818, cited in *The Papers of Henry Clay*, 11 vols. to date, ed. James F. Hopkins et al. (Lexington, Ky., 1959–92), 2: 816 n.

9. "Vision of the Paradise . . . ," *United States Magazine*, March 1779, cited in Peter S. Onuf, *Jefferson's Empire* (Charlottesville, Va., 2000), 58.

10. Samuel P. Huntington, *American Politics: The Promise of Disharmony* (Cambridge, 1980), 5–10; and discussion in the bibliographical essay.

11. On the interplay of state, section, and union (or nation), see D. W. Meinig, *Atlantic America, 1492–1800* (New Haven, Conn., 1986), 439; Lance Banning, "Virginia: Nation, State, and Section," in *Ratifying the Constitution,* ed. Michael Allen Gillespie and Michael Lienesch (Lawrence, Kans., 1989); and Peter S. Onuf, "Constitutional Politics: States, Sections, and the National Interest," in *Toward a More Perfect Union: Six Essays on the Constitution,* ed. Neil L. York (Provo, Utah, 1988), 29–58.

12. The figure is adapted from Robert Jackson and Georg Sørensen, *Introduction to International Relations* (New York, 1999), 146. See also sources and discussion in chapter 3, note 14, and in chapter 21, notes 17 and 18. On the significance of revolution more generally, see Martin Wight, *Power Politics* (New York, 1978), 81–94; David Armstrong, *Revolution and World Order: The Revolutionary State in International Society* (Oxford, 1993); and Stephen M. Walt, *Revolution and War* (Ithaca, N.Y., 1996).

13. Pacificus No. 2, July 3, 1793, *Hamilton Papers,* 15: 59–62; Jefferson to Thomas Mann Randolph, June 24, 1793, quoted in Robert W. Tucker and David C. Hendrickson, *Empire of Liberty* (New York, 1990), 51.

14. The difficulty of proper categorization is a notorious one, and there is an amusing discussion of the point in Martin Wight, *International Theory: The Three Traditions* (New York, 1992), 15. The rationalist tradition, identified with Aquinas, Suarez, Grotius, Hooker, Althusius, Locke, and the American founding fathers, is characterized by Wight as "the broad middle road of European thinking" on international relations. "On one side of it the ground slopes upwards towards the crags and precipices of revolutionism, whether Christian or secular; on the other side it slopes downwards towards the marshes and swamps of realism." Though a *broad* middle road, its edges are difficult to discern, and it seems at times "disconcertingly narrow." "Hamilton, for instance, seems to be on the road, but look again and he is to be found well away from it, on the turf over towards the marshes. Burke is apparently marching sturdily along the road, but his movements are erratic. Kant one would like to think is on it, but he shows a disquieting tendency to dart away, to the other side from Hamilton, towards the crags and precipices. A little later there looms up a pocket of fog, called Hegel, which makes it difficult for some time to know where the road is and who is on it."

For the controversy over whether Kant is on or off the road, see Kai Alderson and Andrew Hurrell, eds., *Hedley Bull on International Society* (New York, 2000), 52 n. 68; Andrew Linklater, "Rationalism," in *Theories of International Relations,* ed. Scott Burchill (New York, 2001), 119–23; Stanley Hoffmann, "International Society," in *Order and Violence: Hedley Bull and International Relations,* ed. J. D. B. Miller and R. J. Vincent (Oxford, 1990), 23–24; F. H. Hinsley, *Power and the Pursuit of States* (Cambridge, 1967), 62–80; Michael Doyle, *Ways of War and Peace* (New York, 1997), 32, 251–311; and the formidable critique of much of the foregoing in Thomas J. Pangle and Peter J. Ahrensdorf, *Justice Among Nations: On the Moral Basis of Power and Peace* (Lawrence, Kans., 1999). See also Pierre Laberge, "Kant on Justice and the Law of Nations," and Fernando R. Tesón, "Kantian International Liberalism," both in *International Society: Diverse Ethical Perspectives*, ed. David R. Mapel and Terry Nardin (Princeton, N.J., 1998). Kant identified closely with the French Revolution, but his denial of a right of revolution made him "anti-revolutionary" in the German political context of the 1790s. The gifted French historian Albert Sorel wrote that Kant "led his disciples up to the giddy heights where his critique held sway, so that they could better admire the scaffolding of balustrades, parapets and guard rails he had so carefully erected to keep them from the abyss." *Europe and the French Revolution* (New York, 1964), 457, and discussion in James J. Sheehan, *German History: 1770–1866* (New York, 1989), 214.

15. *Perpetual Peace: A Philosophical Sketch* (1795), as translated in Pangle and Ahrensdorf, *Justice Among Nations*, 202.

16. *Perpetual Peace, Kant's Political Writings*, ed. Hans Reiss (Cambridge, 1970), 104.

17. As one observer notes, "it is as if Publius and Kant live in different historical periods. For Publius, the fundamental fact is the fragility, rareness and vulnerability of republics. Kant seems to leap over these problems and his argument largely begins with a world where the problems animating Publius have disappeared or been solved. . . . Having posited a state-system populated by democratic republics, Kant is silent on how such polities arise and survive." Daniel Deudney, "Publius Before Kant: Federal Republican Security vs. Democratic Peace," *European Journal of International Relations* (forthcoming). Even matters treated explicitly by Kant, such as the dynamics of the projected movement from the *foedus pacificum* to the *civitas gentium*, leave commentators baffled. "Does the economic evolution of mankind tend to the abolition of war through making warfare so brutal as to be unbearable or through the decay of warfare as contrary to the spirit and interest of the states? If Evil (the conflict of propensities) gives rise to Good (perpetual peace), does it do so through catastrophes brought on by its overwhelming power or through meliorations brought on by its debility?" Pierre Hassner, "Immanuel Kant," in *History of Political Philosophy*, ed. Leo Strauss and Joseph Cropsey (Chicago, 1987).

18. This is obviously the case with respect to Hamilton and Adams, but it is so even for those, like Madison and Jefferson, who shared Kant's conviction that republics based on the representative principle were far less prone to war than the aristocracies and monarchies of Europe. In "Universal Peace," published in 1792, Madison poured scorn on a plan, which he identified with Rousseau, for "a confederation of sovereigns, under a council of deputies, for the double purpose of arbitrating external controversies among nations, and of guarantying their respective governments against internal revolutions." Since the "guarantee clause" would operate to confirm the very governments that were most prone to war, under such a plan "the disease would continue to be *hereditary*, like the government of which it is the offspring." The "first step toward a cure," Madison believed, lay in the in-

stantiation of republican government, but he acknowledged, as Kant did only obliquely, that there would be wars flowing from "the will of the society itself." For these he suggested the expedient, which Kant adopted and which had initially been suggested by Adam Smith, that wars be financed from current revenues rather than debt. "Were a nation to impose such restraints on itself," Madison believed, "avarice would be sure to calculate the expenses of ambition; in the equipoise of these passions, reason would be free to decide for the public good." That equipoise of passions indicates that Madison lived in a Humean rather than Kantian world. Despite real similarities between the two in their respective republican credos, the larger framework of their thought seems distinctly alien. While Kant soared into the stratosphere, Madison never departed too far from terra firma, and he treated the subject hopefully but without illusions: "A universal and perpetual peace, it is to be feared, is in the catalogue of events which will never exist but in the imagination of visionary philosophers, or in the breasts of benevolent enthusiasts. It is still, however, true, that war contains so much folly, as well as wickedness, that much is to be hoped from the progress of reason; and if anything is to be hoped, everything ought to be tried." "Universal Peace," February 2, 1792, in *The Mind of the Founder: Sources of the Political Thought of James Madison,* ed. Marvin Mayers (Hanover, N.H., 1981), 191–94.

19. For "offensive realism," see John J. Mearsheimer, *The Tragedy of Great Power Politics* (New York, 2001); Fareed Zakaria, *From Wealth to Power* (Princeton, N.J., 1998); Stephen M. Walt, "International Relations: One World, Many Theories," *Foreign Policy,* no. 110 (spring 1998): 29–46; and cf. Wight's further breakdown of realism in *International Theory,* 47.

20. The pursuit of particular objectives within the framework of law is well conveyed in Gregg L. Lint, "The American Revolution and the Law of Nations, 1776–1789," *Diplomatic History* 1 (1977): 20–34.

21. See, e.g., Walter LaFeber, *The American Age: United States Foreign Policy at Home and Abroad Since 1750* (New York, 1989); and Walter A. McDougall, *Promised Land, Crusader State: The American Encounter with the World Since 1776* (New York, 1997).

22. Emily S. Rosenberg, "A Call to Revolution: A Roundtable on Early U.S. Foreign Relations," *Diplomatic History* 22 (1998): 63–70. See also Peter S. Onuf, "A Declaration of Independence for Diplomatic Historians," *Diplomatic History* 22 (1998): 71–83.

23. The linkage between constitutional and diplomatic principle is taken up in the important though neglected study of Frank Tannenbaum, *The American Tradition in Foreign Affairs* (Norman, Okla., 1954).

24. See the discussion in Jackson, *Global Covenant,* 162–65.

BIBLIOGRAPHICAL ESSAY

1. Among works focusing on 1787–88, the most important are Max Farrand, *The Framing of the Constitution of the United States* (New Haven, Conn., 1913); Charles Warren, *The Making of the Constitution* (Boston, 1929); and Clinton

Rossiter, *1787: The Grand Convention* (New York, 1966). Two appealing works in a more popular vein are Carl Van Doren, *The Great Rehearsal: The Story of the Making and Ratifying of the Constitution of the United States* (New York, 1948); and Catherine Drinker Bowen, *Miracle at Philadelphia: The Story of the Constitutional Convention, May to September* (Boston, 1966). The best one-volume survey of "The Constitution in History," emphasizing the relation to political history, is Broadus Mitchell and Louise Pearson Mitchell, *A Biography of the Constitution of the United States*, 2d ed. (New York, 1975).

2. House of Representatives, September 3, 1789, *Madison Papers,* 12: 372. Henry Lee to James Madison, ibid., 13: 102–3, 137, cited in Lance Banning, *The Sacred Fire of Liberty: James Madison and the Founding of the Federal Republic* (Ithaca, N.Y., 1995). It is one of the signal accomplishments of Banning's magisterial work to bring clearly into focus the years before and after the writing of the Constitution.

3. Tucker, *View of the Constitution,* 87 (As the prevention of "intestine wars" and "frequent and violent contest with each other . . . was among the most cogent reasons to induce the adoption of the union, so ought it to be among the most powerful, to prevent a dissolution"); William Rawle, *A View of the Constitution of the United States,* 2d ed. (New York, [1829] 1970), 306; Story, *Commentaries,* 3: 758–59 ("Let the history of the Grecian and Italian republics warn us of our dangers. The national constitution is our last, and our only security"). See also James Monroe, *The People, the Sovereigns: Being a Comparison of the Government of the United States with Those of the Republics Which Have Existed Before, with the Causes of Their Decadence and Fall* (Philadelphia, 1867); Henry Baldwin, *A General View of the Origin and Nature of the Constitution and Government of the United States . . .* (Philadelphia, 1837); and George Bancroft, *History of the Formation of the Constitution of the United States of America* (New York, 1882). For a useful secondary study of the early interpreters, see Elizabeth Kelley Bauer, *Commentaries on the Constitution, 1790–1860* (New York, 1952). The prevalence of this theme in congressional orations is well shown in Herman Belz, ed., *The Webster-Hayne Debate on the Nature of the Union: Selected Documents* (Indianapolis, 2000).

4. "The first thing I have at heart is American *liberty,*" said Patrick Henry; "the second thing is American Union." Melancton Smith said the same in the New York ratifying convention: he was ready "to sacrifice every thing for a Union, except the liberties of his country" (both are cited in Storing, *Anti-Federalist,* 24). That, in a nutshell, was Calhoun's whole political creed.

5. Speech on the Revenue Collection [Force] Bill, February 15–16, 1833, in *Union and Liberty: The Political Philosophy of John C. Calhoun,* ed. Ross M. Lence (Indianapolis, 1992), 431.

6. A similar theme is suggested in Kenneth M. Stampp, "The Concept of Perpetual Union," in *The Imperiled Union: Essays on the Background of the Civil War* (New York, 1980), 3–36. See also Alpheus Thomas Mason, "The Federalist— A Split Personality" *American Historical Review* 57 (1952): 627; and idem, "The Nature of Our Federal Union Reconsidered," *Political Science Quarterly* 65 (1950): 502–21. The case for the union is detailed in James G. Randall, *Constitutional Problems Under Lincoln,* rev. ed. (Urbana, Ill., 1951). For the confederacy, see Alexander Hamilton Stephens, *A Constitutional View of the Late War Between the States,* 2 vols. (Philadelphia, 1868–70).

7. Max Farrand, "Compromises of the Constitution," *American Historical Review* 11 (1903–4): 479–89; Richard Hildreth, *The History of the United States of America*, 6 vols., rev. ed. (New York, 1882), 3: 501; George Ticknor Curtis, *History of the Origin, Formation, and Adoption of the Constitution of the United States: With Notices of Its Principal Framers*, 2 vols. (New York, 1854–58). See also Horace Greeley, *The American Conflict: A History of the Great Rebellion in the United States of America, 1860–64: Its Causes, Incidents, and Results: Intended to Exhibit Especially Its Moral and Political Phases, with the Drift and Progress of American Opinion Respecting Human Slavery from 1776 to the Close of the War for the Union* (Chicago, 1864–66); Henry Wilson, *History of the Rise and Fall of the Slave Power in America*, 3 vols. (Boston, 1872–77); and the expert reviews of the nineteenth-century perspective in James H. Hutson, "The Creation of the Constitution: Scholarship at a Standstill," *Reviews in American History* 12 (1984): 463–77; and Staughton Lynd, "The Abolitionist Critique of the Constitution," in *Class Conflict, Slavery, and the United States Constitution* (Indianapolis, 1967), 155–57. As Lynd notes, "Farrand's own magnificent edition of the Convention records amply refutes his contention that the subject of slavery was little discussed" (160).

8. James H. Hutson, "Country, Court, and Constitution: Antifederalism and the Historians," *William and Mary Quarterly* 37 (1981): 340–42. Hutson notes that the post–Civil War historians "declared open season" on the Anti-Federalists and "showered them with contempt," emphasizing this proclivity in von Holst, Edward P. Smith, Orin G. Libby, John Bach McMaster, and John Fiske. The pre–Civil War writers, Hutson notes, were more evenhanded.

9. Hermann Von Holst, *The Constitutional and Political History of the United States*, 8 vols., translated from the German by John J. Lalor et al. (Chicago, 1876–92), 1: 77; Ferdinand Schevill, "Hermann Eduard von Holst," *Dictionary of American Biography*, 5: 177–78.

10. James Truslow Adams, "John Fiske," *Dictionary of American Biography*, 3: 420–23; John Fiske, *The Critical Period of American History, 1783–89* (New York, 1888), vi–vii, 187, 344.

11. James Brown Scott, *James Madison's Notes* . . . (New York, 1918); idem, *The United States of America: A Study in International Organization* (New York, 1920), 467–68. On Scott, see Christopher R. Rossi, *Broken Chain of Being: James Brown Scott and the Origins of Modern International Law* (The Hague, 1998); Frederic L. Kirgis, "The Formative Years of the American Society of International Law," *American Journal of International Law* 90 (1996): 559–89; and George A. Finch, "James Brown Scott, 1866–1943," *American Journal of International Law* 38 (1944): 183–217. Scott's favorite quotation was from the French moralist Joubert: "Might and right control everything in the world; might, until right is ready" (ibid., 184).

12. Warren F. Kuehl, *Hamilton Holt: Journalist, Internationalist, Educator* (Gainesville, Fla., 1960); idem, *Seeking World Order: The United States and International Organization to 1920* (Nashville, Tenn., 1969); Merle E. Curti, *Peace or War: The American Struggle, 1636–1936* (New York, [1936] 1972); Harley A. Notter, *The Origins of the Foreign Policy of Woodrow Wilson* (New York, 1937); Thomas J. Knock, *To End All Wars: Woodrow Wilson and the Quest for a New World Order* (New York, 1992); Ruhl J. Bartlett, *The League to Enforce Peace*

(Chapel Hill, N.C., 1944); William Howard Taft, George W. Wichersham, and A. Lawrence Lowell, *The Covenantor: Letters on the Covenant of the League of Nations* (Boston, 1919); James Brown Scott, ed., *President Wilson's Foreign Policy: Messages, Addresses, Papers* (New York, 1918); and Theodore Roosevelt, "International Peace," Address Before the Nobel Prize Committee Delivered at Christiania, Norway, May 5, 1910, *The Outlook,* May 10, 1910. In this address, Roosevelt noted "that the Constitution of the United States, notably in the establishment of the Supreme Court and in the methods adopted for securing peace and good relations among and between the different States, offers certain valuable analogies to what should be striven for in order to secure, through the Hague courts and conferences, a species of world federation for international peace and justice." Roosevelt acknowledged that there were "fundamental differences between what the United States Constitution does and what we should even attempt at this time to secure at The Hague" but still insisted on the utility of the comparison: "[T]he methods adopted in the American Constitution to prevent hostilities between the States, and to secure the supremacy of the Federal Court in certain classes of cases, are well worth the study of those who seek at The Hague to obtain the same results on a world scale" (p. 20).

13. Editorial Notes, *The New Republic,* February 3, 1917, p. 2.

14. The means by which this restatement of the unionist paradigm took place is a complicated subject, and one hesitates to broach in a few paragraphs a problem that can only be well unfolded in a book. (A "fascinating subject," to paraphrase John Adams, "and if I were not too lazy I would undertake it.") Briefly, however, it may be said that the pattern of ideological antagonism laid bare by Michael J. Hogan for the period after 1945 was nearly all anticipated in the period from 1914 to 1920 (*A Cross of Iron: Harry S. Truman and the Origins of the National Security State* [Cambridge, 1998]). It was in that earlier era that the great restatement took place in thought. In addition to the works cited in note 12, see Robert David Johnson, *The Peace Progressives and American Foreign Policy* (Cambridge, 1995); Roland N. Stromberg, *Collective Security and American Foreign Policy: From the League of Nations to NATO* (New York, 1963); William C. Widenor, *Henry Cabot Lodge and the Search for an American Foreign Policy* (Berkeley, 1980); Frank Ninkovich, *Modernity and Power: A History of the Domino Theory in the Twentieth Century* (Chicago, 1994); and Warren F. Kuehl and Lynne K. Dunn, *Keeping the Covenant: American Internationalists and the League of Nations, 1919–1939* (Kent, Ohio, 1997).

15. John Fiske, *American Political Ideas Viewed from the Standpoint of Universal History* (New York, 1885); Frederick Merk, with Lois Bannister Merk, *Manifest Destiny and Mission in American History: A Reinterpretation* (New York, 1966).

16. Frederick Jackson Turner, "The Significance of the Section in American History," in *The Significance of Sections in American History* (New York, 1932), 40, 26. The themes of this essay are partly anticipated in a letter sent by Turner to Woodrow Wilson on the eve of the latter's embarkation to the Paris Peace Conference, reprinted in Frederick Jackson Turner, "American Sectionalism and World Organization," William Diamond, ed., *American Historical Review* 47 (1942): 545–51, and with further editorial commentary in Arthur S. Link, ed., *The Papers of Woodrow Wilson,* 68

vols. (Princeton, N.J., 1966–), 53: 264–70. See also Richard Hofstadter, *The Progressive Historians: Turner, Beard, Parrington* (New York, 1968); Ray Allen Billington, *Frederick Jackson Turner: Historian, Scholar, Teacher* (New York, 1973). On the frontier thesis, see idem, *The American Frontier Thesis: Attack and Defense* (Washington, D.C., 1971); George Rogers Taylor, ed., *The Turner Thesis Concerning the Role of the Frontier in American History*, 3d ed. (Lexington, Mass., 1976); and the engaging reconsideration in Patricia Nelson Limerick, "Turnerians All: The Dream of a Helpful History in an Intelligible World," *American Historical Review* 100 (1995): 697–716. For complaints among Turnerians over the unbalanced character of the criticism directed against Turner, much of which ignored the sectional theme of Turner's maturity, see Michael C. Steiner, "The Significance of Turner's Sectional Thesis," *Western Historical Quarterly* 10 (1979): 437–66. On Turner's assimilation of southern plantation economy to agrarian frontier, see Staughton Lynd, "On Turner, Beard, and Slavery," *Class Conflict*, 135–52; and Avery Craven, "The 'Turner Theories' and the South," *Journal of Southern History* 5 (1939): 291–314.

17. Parrington quoted in Samuel P. Huntington, *American Politics: The Promise of Disharmony* (Cambridge, Mass., 1981), 5–6. This passage, which Huntington calls "the essence of the Progressive paradigm," was written for but not used in Vernon Louis Parrington, *Main Currents in American Thought: An Interpretation of American Literature from the Beginnings to 1920* (New York, 1927–30). The passage was discovered and cited by Hofstadter, *Progressive Historians*, 438. See further Arthur A. Ekirch Jr., "Parrington and the Decline of American Liberalism," *American Quarterly* 3 (1951): 295–308.

18. Clarence Streit, *Union Now: A Proposal for a Federal Union of the Democracies of the North Atlantic* (New York, 1939); Merrill Jensen, *The New Nation: A History of the United States During the Confederation, 1781–1789* (Boston, [1950] 1981), xiv–xviii, 422–28. Van Doren, *Great Rehearsal*, vii–x, also put the founding in the context of the problem of international peace but stressed the need for a universal form of security organization. Streit's emphasis was on federal union among the democracies of the North Atlantic. See the luminous survey in Wesley T. Wooley, *Alternatives to Anarchy: American Supranationalism Since World War II* (Bloomington, Ind., 1988). Though Jensen invoked Andrew C. McLaughlin against Fiske, the tenor of McLaughlin's argument in *The Confederation and the Constitution, 1783–1789* (New York, 1905) was much closer to Fiske's *Critical Period* than to Jensen's *New Nation*. For the denial of the critical period thesis, see also Charles A. Beard, *An Economic Interpretation of the Constitution of the United States* (New York, 1913), 48; and E. James Ferguson, *The Power of the Purse: A History of American Public Finance, 1776–1790* (Chapel Hill, N.C., 1961). See further Thomas P. Slaughter, "Merrill Jensen and the Revolution of 1787," *Reviews in American History* 15 (1987): 691–701.

19. Huntington, *American Politics*, 5–10, calls the three interpretations "the one, the two, and the many." Representative works in the "consensus" tradition, though ranging beyond the constitutional era, include Richard Hofstadter, *The American Political Tradition and the Men Who Made It* (New York, 1948); Daniel J. Boorstin, *The Genius of American Politics* (Chicago, 1953); David Potter, *People of Plenty: Economic Abundance and the American Character* (Chicago, 1954); Louis Hartz, *The Liberal Tradition in America: An Interpretation of American Po-*

litical Thought Since the Revolution (New York, 1955); Daniel Bell, *The End of Ideology: On the Exhaustion of Political Ideas in the Fifties* (Glencoe, Ill., 1960); and Seymour Martin Lipset, *The First New Nation: The United States in Historical and Comparative Perspective* (New York, 1963). For the pluralists, see Arthur F. Bentley, *The Process of Government: A Study of Social Pressures* (Chicago, 1908); Robert A. Dahl, *A Preface to Democratic Theory* (Chicago, 1956); Theodore J. Lowi, *The End of Liberalism: Ideology, Policy, and the Crisis of Public Authority* (New York, 1969); and William A. Schambra, ed., *As Far as Republican Principles Will Admit: Essays by Martin Diamond* (Washington, D.C., 1992). Though the "consensus school" is often represented to have taken a sunny and optimistic view of American life, that is misleading. While the consensus historians had little use for the class analysis that had preoccupied the Progressives, they found much fault with the consensus they described. Hartz described a pervasive Lockean consensus that contributed to McCarthyism and that made America ill fitted to understand its role in the world, the latter theme also being broached in Boorstin and Potter. The pluralist paradigm, as Huntington notes, was "the dominant interpretation of American politics among political scientists after World War II" and is "quite compatible with the consensus paradigm, since the conflicts among interest groups over particular issues can be conceived of as occurring within the framework of a broad agreement on basic political values. In fact, one paradigm almost implies the existence of the other: they differ in that one stresses the basic agreement and the other the specific issues that are fought over within the context of this agreement." Huntington, *American Politics,* 8. My use of the term "liberal-pluralism" later in this chapter reflects the overall compatibility of the "two schools." Contemporary exemplification of its outlook and premises may be found in Alan Brinkley, Nelson W. Polsby, and Kathleen M. Sullivan, *New Federalist Papers: Essays in Defense of the Constitution* (New York, 1997); and Samuel H. Beer, *To Make a Nation: The Rediscovery of American Federalism* (Cambridge, 1993).

20. Robert E. Brown, *Charles Beard and the Constitution: A Critical Analysis of "An Economic Interpretation of the Constitution"* (Princeton, N.J., 1956); Forrest McDonald, *We the People: The Economic Origins of the Constitution* (Chicago, 1958); and the assessments of the voluminous controversy in Stanley M. Elkins and Eric McKitrick, *The Founding Fathers: Young Men of the Revolution* (Washington, D.C., 1962); Jack P. Greene, ed., *The Reinterpretation of the American Revolution: 1763–1789* (New York, 1968); and Hutson, "Creation of the Constitution." For Beard's own questioning of the primacy of material factors during World War II, see Donald W. White, *The American Century: The Rise and Decline of the United States as a World Power* (New Haven, Conn., 1996). For the renewed interest in ideas, the work of Douglas Adair was pivotal. See *Fame and the Founding Fathers: Essays by Douglas Adair,* ed. Trevor Colbourn (Indianapolis, n.d. [1974]). Bailyn's long prolegomenon to his *Pamphlets of the American Revolution,* of which only the first volume out of a projected four was published, later appeared as *The Ideological Origins of the American Revolution* (Cambridge, Mass., 1967). The enlarged edition published in 1992 has a "Commentary on the Constitution" as a postscript. J. G. A. Pocock's early essays were gathered in *Politics, Language, and Time: Essays on Political Thought and History* (New York, 1971). For McDonald's own retrospective on *We the People* and *E Pluribus Unum: The Formation of the American*

Republic, 1776–1790 (Boston, 1965), see Forrest McDonald, *Novus Ordo Seclorum: The Intellectual Origins of the Constitution* (Lawrence, Kans., 1985), vii–ix.

21. Gordon S. Wood, *The Creation of the American Republic: 1776–1787* (Chapel Hill, N.C., 1969), 626; "Forum: *The Creation of the American Republic, 1776–1787:* A Symposium of Views and Reviews," *William and Mary Quarterly* 44 (1987): 549–640; and the curious reconsideration in Gordon Wood, ed., *The Confederation and the Constitution* (Boston, 1973), xiv. Wood entered into a sharp dispute with Jackson Turner Main in the 1970s, but this was primarily over the metahistorical issue of the relative significance of ideas and interests in historical causation. Their frameworks of interpretation, laying stresses on political division within the states and slighting continental politics, were otherwise quite close. See particularly by Main, *Political Parties Before the Constitution* (Chapel Hill, N.C., 1973). Main unfolded the politico-economic infrastructure, and Wood the ideological superstructure, of a common interpretation stressing the Constitution as "an aristocratic document designed to curb the democratic excesses of the Revolution."

22. For review of the bicentennial contributions, see Peter S. Onuf, "Reflections on the Founding: Constitutional Historiography in Bicentennial Perspective," *William and Mary Quarterly* 46 (1989): 341–75, emphasizing at 356–64 ("Toward Federalism") the growing interest in federal questions and sectional controversies among historians. Though, as Onuf remarks, much of the bicentennial contributions did not reflect any startling new perspectives, the range of excellent work produced in the context of that event is remarkable. It was anything but an "intellectual bust," as one journalist characterized it. Valuable works produced with the occasion in mind include Leonard W. Levy and Dennis J. Mahoney, eds., *The Framing and Ratification of the Constitution* (New York, 1987); Terence Ball and J. G. A. Pocock, eds., *Conceptual Change and the Constitution* (Lawrence, Kans., 1988); Richard Beeman, Stephen Botein, and Edward C. Carter II, ed., *Beyond Confederation: Origins of the Constitution and American National Identity* (Chapel Hill, N.C., 1987); David E. Narrett and Joyce S. Goldberg, eds., *Essays on Liberty and Federalism: The Shaping of the U.S. Constitution* (College Station, Tex., 1988); Neil L. York, *Toward a More Perfect Union: Six Essays on the Constitution* (Provo, Utah, 1988); Raoul Berger, *Federalism: The Founders' Design* (Norman, Okla., 1987); Michael Lienesch, *New Order of the Ages: Time, the Constitution and the Making of Modern Political Thought* (Princeton, N.J., 1988); Donald S. Lutz, *The Origins of American Constitutionalism* (Baton Rouge, La., 1988); Philip B. Kurland and Ralph Lerner, *The Founders' Constitution,* 5 vols. (Chicago, 1987); McDonald, *Novus Ordo Seclorum;* Richard B. Morris, *The Forging of the Union, 1781–1789* (New York, 1987); Edmund S. Morgan, *Inventing the People: The Rise of Popular Sovereignty in England and America* (New York, 1988); Thomas L. Pangle, *The Spirit of Modern Republicanism: The Moral Vision of the American Founders and the Philosophy of Locke* (Chicago, 1988); Michael G. Kammen, *A Machine That Would Go of Itself: The Constitution in American Culture* (New York, 1986); Irving Kristol and Nathan Glazer, eds., "The Constitutional Order, 1787–1987," *The Public Interest* 86 (winter 1987): 1–140; Jack N. Rakove, "The Great Compromise: Ideas, Interests, and the Politics of Constitution-Making," *William and Mary Quarterly* 44 (1987):

424–57; and idem, "The Madisonian Moment," *University of Chicago Law Review* 55 (1988): 473–505. Rakove's work later culminated in *Original Meanings: Politics and Ideas in the Making of the Constitution* (New York, 1996). He also edited *Interpreting the Constitution: The Debate over Original Intent* (Boston, 1990), which gathered the most important essays of the bicentennial period on that jurisprudential question. Peter S. Onuf, ed., *New American Nation: 1775–1820*, Vol. 5, *The Federal Constitution* (New York, 1991), contains many of the most important essays by historians and political scientists produced on the occasion of the bicentennial, including particularly contributions from Michael P. Zuckert, Cathy Matson, Jack Rakove, Isaac Kramnick, Shlomo Slonim, Daniel W. Howe, and Stephen A. Conrad.

23. David Hackett Fischer, *Albion's Seed: Four British Folkways in America* (New York, 1989); D. W. Meinig, *The Shaping of America: A Geographical Perspective on 500 Years of History*, 3 vols. to date (New Haven, Conn., 1986–); John Murrin, "The Great Inversion, or Court Versus Country: A Comparison of the Revolution Settlements in England (1688–1721) and America (1776–1816)," in *Three British Revolutions: 1641, 1688, 1776*, ed. J. G. A. Pocock (Princeton, N.J., 1980); idem, "A Roof Without Walls: The Dilemma of American National Identity," in Beeman, *Beyond Confederation*, 333–48; idem, "1787: The Invention of American Federalism," Narrett and Goldberg, *Essays on Liberty and Federalism.*
Meinig and Fischer differ from one another and from Turner in several respects:

1. Whereas Fischer presents a "modified germ theory" to account for the persistence through time of America's regional societies, distinguishing himself from Turner's environmentalism, Meinig's profession of historical geography makes him a natural-born environmentalist, as was Turner.
2. Meinig's geographic orientation has the signal advantage of bringing into the American story the perspectives of "core" and "periphery," whereas Fischer's thesis obliges him to trace the fortunes of the core and to neglect those on the other side of the "encounter."
3. Though both Meinig and Fischer are fairly styled as neo-Turnerian with respect to the sectional thesis, both are emphatically anti-Turnerian with respect to the frontier thesis—Fischer because he presents a "modified germ theory," and Meinig, inter alia, because of his emphasis on both sides of the Indian-white encounter. See particularly the sharp criticism of Turner in D. W. Meinig, *Continental America, 1800–1967* (New Haven, Conn., 1993), 258–64, and the rancorous exchange in "Forum: *Albion's Seed: Four British Folkways in America*—A Symposium," *William and Mary Quarterly* 48 (1991): 223–308.
4. The four regional societies identified by Meinig and Fischer are not quite the same regional societies. Both, of course, see a distinct New England, but whereas Meinig bifurcates the South into distinct Virginian and Carolinian societies, Fischer bifurcates the middle colonies, seeing there two streams to Meinig's one. Turner had great difficulty in characterizing the western streams, and this played an important role in delaying publication of *The United States, 1830–1850: The Nation and Its Sections* (New York, 1935), which was edited by M. H. Crissey, Max Farrand, and Avery Craven and published after Turner's death in 1932.

5. Whereas Meinig emphasizes (correctly, in my view) the transformative effect of the Civil War, both Turner and Fischer minimize that event in tracing the significance of the section in American history.

24. Peter S. Onuf, *The Origins of the Federal Republic: Jurisdictional Controversies in the United States* (Philadelphia, 1983), 209; Bernard Bailyn, *The Ideological Origins of the American Revolution* (Cambridge, 1967); Storing, *Anti-Federalist*. See also by Onuf the works cited in chapter 3, note 2. Something of Onuf's line of inquiry was suggested in the works of Jack P. Greene and J. G. A. Pocock. Greene, in *Peripheries and Center: Constitutional Development in the Extended Polities of the British Empire and the United States* (Athens, Ga., 1986), treated both Britain's "extensive and detached empire" and America's post-1776 extended polity as associations distinguished by an acknowledged right of autonomy at the periphery and hence subject to powerful centrifugal forces. That framework, which also recognized the potency of the centripetal forces, suggested a political setting in which the questions taken up in the unionist paradigm were quite relevant. Pocock stressed in various bicentennial contributions the importance of placing America's federal discourse in the context of speculation over the character of the European state system and its web of treaties and alliances, a system that was also sometimes described as a "federal republic." Pocock, "States, Republics, and Empires: The American Founding in Early Modern Perspective," in Ball and Pocock, *Conceptual Change*, 55–77; idem, *The Politics of Extent and the Problems of Freedom* (Colorado Springs, Colo., 1988). In his *Barbarism and Religion* (Cambridge, 1999), the first two volumes in a projected series on the intellectual world that Gibbon inhabited, the historiographical background to these themes in a variety of European enlightenments is brilliantly developed. Pocock identifies as "the Enlightened narrative" an account recording "the descent from classical antiquity into the darkness of 'barbarism and religion,' and the emergence from the latter set of conditions of a 'Europe' in which civil society could defend itself against disruption by either. This history had two themes: the emergence of a system of sovereign states—multiple monarchies, confederacies, and republics—in which the ruling authority was competent to maintain civil government and conduct an independent *Aussenpolitik;* and the emergence of a shared civilization of manners and commerce, through which, in addition to treaties and statecraft, the independent states could be thought to constitute a confederation or republic" (ibid., 2: 20). Put in Pocockian terms, what I have been calling the unionist paradigm is "the Enlightened narrative" problematized; it represents the working out, under American conditions, of the basic hopes and fears identified in that discourse. In the course of moving from "balance of power" to "federal union," the American version of modernity and progress both repudiates and imbibes various aspects of the tale told by the principal thinkers—Giannone, Voltaire, Hume, Robertson, Smith, Ferguson, and Gibbon—whom Pocock explores in his second volume, *Narratives of Civil Government*. Since it was the crisis of the confederation that above all made problematic the American version of the Enlightened narrative, the formation of the federal constitution may be seen as a striking manifestation—perhaps the most striking manifestation—of the American Enlightenment. American thought simultaneously incorporates and sharply qualifies

this discourse of state system, commerce, treaties, balance of power, standing armies, and universal monarchy.

25. Probably a more accurate translation of Onuf's "new world order" is "new order for the new world" rather than "new order for the whole world." On the ideological origins of the Bush administration's "new world order," which was universalist in announced design, see Robert W. Tucker and David C. Hendrickson, *The Imperial Temptation: The New World Order and America's Purpose* (New York, 1992).

26. Daniel H. Deudney, "The Philadelphian System: Sovereignty, Arms Control, and Balance of Power in the American States-Union, Circa 1787–1861," *International Organization* 49 (1995): 191–228. For two distinguished exceptions to this general neglect, see Gottfried Dietze, *The Federalist: A Classic on Federalism and Free Government* (Baltimore, 1960), pt. 2; and Gerald Stourzh, *Alexander Hamilton and the Idea of Republican Government* (Stanford, Calif., 1970). Both Dietze and Stourzh, however, wrote outside the main currents of thought in political science and history. In *Politics Among Nations: The Struggle for Power and Peace,* 4th ed. (New York, [1948] 1967), Hans J. Morgenthau cited John Jay in *Federalist* No. 2: "Providence has been pleased to give this one connected country to one united people; a people descended from the same ancestors, speaking the same language, professing the same religion, attached to the same principles of government, [and] very similar in their manners and customs." Morgenthau went on to argue that the Philadelphia convention had simply replaced "one constitution, one sovereignty, one state with another one, both resting upon the same preexisting community." The United States, he concluded, "was founded upon a moral and political community the Constitution did not create but found already in existence." Kenneth N. Waltz, *Man, the State, and War: A Theoretical Analysis* (New York, 1959), used Hamilton's early contributions to the *Federalist* to drive home the point that a world of difference existed between the state and the state system, the one a domain of rightful authority and possessing a monopoly of the legitimate means of violence, the other subject to powerful systemic pressure leading to rivalry and war. Waltz did not allow for the possibility (as Hamilton had done) that a choice falling between these abstract poles, made necessary by the actual distribution of power among the confederating units, was a historical possibility. A framework too rigidly Hobbesian induced within the American science of international politics after 1945 a binary framework opposing "state" and "state system" that discouraged recognition of the diversity of forms and power relationships characteristic of the world of states. That science might have started with Althusius rather than Hobbes; alas, it did not. Had it done so, it would have more easily accommodated in its theoretical framework federative systems that were units made up of many units and systems of states within a larger system of states. As Rufus Davis notes, "the matter of international relations and federal theory is not so easily disentangled in the noncompartmentalized world of medieval and early modern thought, especially not to the scholars who first tried to explain the nature of these alliances." S. Rufus Davis, *The Federal Principle: A Journey Through Time in Quest of a Meaning* (Berkeley, 1978), 38. See also Onuf and Onuf, *Federal Union,* pt. 1. Whether Deudney's contribution will be registered by the various fields to which it is relevant remains to be seen. Inauspicious on this score is the absence of "The Philadelphian System"

from the long references section of *International Organization* at Fifty: Exploration and Contestation in the Study of World Politics, ed. Peter J. Katzenstein, Robert O. Keohane, and Stephen D. Krasner, 52 (1998): 1013–61.

27. Beard, *Economic Interpretation;* Parrington, "Addenda," in *Main Currents,* 410; Alexander M. Bickel, *The Least Dangerous Branch: The Supreme Court at the Bar of Politics* (Indianapolis, 1962); Alexander M. Bickel and Benno C. Schmidt, *The Judiciary and Responsible Government, 1910–1921* (New York, 1984).

28. Raymond Aron, *Progress and Disillusion: The Dialectics of Modern Society* (New York, 1968); idem, *An Essay on Freedom,* trans. Helen Weaver (New York, 1970). See also Martin Diamond, "The Federalist," in *History of Political Philosophy,* ed. Leo Strauss and Joseph Cropsey (Chicago, 1953); Robert A. Dahl, *A Preface to Democratic Theory* (Chicago, 1956); idem, *After the Revolution: Authority in a Good Society* (New Haven, Conn., 1970).

29. William P. Murphy, *The Triumph of Nationalism: State Sovereignty, the Founding Fathers, and the Making of the Constitution* (Chicago, 1967). See also Michael Lind, "The Confederate Theory of the Constitution," in *Up From Conservatism: Why the Right Is Wrong for America* (New York, 1996).

30. William Winslow Crosskey, *Politics and the Constitution in the History of the United States,* 3 vols. (vol. 3 with William Jeffrey) (Chicago, 1953–80); Richard B. Morris, *Government and Labor in Early America* (New York, 1946); Richard B. Morris and the Editors of *Life, The Making of a Nation, 1775–1789* (New York, 1963); William Letwin, *Economic Policy of the Constitution: The Original Intent* (Colorado Springs, Colo., 1988).

31. Parrington, *Main Currents;* Harry V. Jaffa, *Crisis of the House Divided: An Interpretation of the Issues in the Lincoln-Douglas Debates* (New York, 1959); Robert A. Goldwin, *Why Blacks, Women, and Jews Are Not Mentioned in the Constitution, and Other Unorthodox Views* (Washington, D.C., 1990).

32. An exception among consensus historians is Robert E. Brown, *Reinterpretation of the Formation of the American Constitution* (Boston, 1963), 48.

33. Lynd, *Class Conflict,* 153–83; Wood, *Creation,* 626; William M Wiecek, "The Witch at the Christening: Slavery and the Constitution's Origins," Levy and Mahoney, *Framing and Ratification,* 167–84; idem, *The Sources of Antislavery Constitutionalism in America, 1760–1848* (Ithaca, N.Y., 1979); Paul Finkelman, "Slavery and the Constitutional Convention: Making a Covenant with Death," in Beeman, *Beyond Confederation,* 188–225; idem, *An Imperfect Union: Slavery, Federalism, and Comity* (Chapel Hill, N.C., 1981); idem, *Slavery and the Founders: Race and Liberty in the Age of Jefferson* (Armonk, N.Y., 1996); and Leonard L. Richards, *The Slave Power: The Free North and Southern Domination, 1780–1860* (Baton Rouge, La., 2000). Representative of the characteristic view of twentieth-century historiography that there was no important three-fifths compromise at the convention is Howard A. Ohline, "Republicanism and Slavery: Origins of the Three-Fifths Clause in the United States Constitution," *William and Mary Quarterly* 28 (1971): 563–84.

The most apt summation of the framers' larger outlook on slavery is Don Fehrenbacher's. The Constitution, he suggests, was "bifocal" on the subject, with the framers recognizing slavery's existence and giving it protection while also subjecting it to restrictions that they hoped would doom it over time. "It is as though the framers were half-consciously trying to frame two constitutions, one for their own time and the other for the ages, with slavery viewed bifocally—that is, plainly visible at their feet, but disappearing when they lifted their eyes." Don E. Fehrenbacher, *The Dred Scott Case: Its Significance in American Law and Politics* (New York, 1978), 27; and, to similar effect, William W. Freehling, "The Founding Fathers and Slavery," *American Historical Review* 77 (1972): 81–93.

INDEX